Thank you for taking volume 31 home with you!
Back when chapter 1 was still only a twinkle
in my eye, I daydreamed about the sort of
content I'd want in this series if it happened to
find success and go on long enough. That's the
content we're finally getting to now. Amazing,
huh? So thank you so much for reading. I really
mean it.

KOHEI HORIKOSHI

MY HERO ACADEMIA

31

SHONEN JUMP Edition

STORY & ART KOHEI HORIKOSHI

TRANSLATION & ENGLISH ADAPTATION **Caleb Cook**
TOUCH-UP ART & LETTERING **John Hunt**
DESIGNER **Julian [JR] Robinson**
SHONEN JUMP SERIES EDITOR **John Bae**
GRAPHIC NOVEL EDITOR **Mike Montesa**

Printed in the U.S.A.

Published by VIZ Media, LLC
P.O. Box 77010
San Francisco, CA 94107

10 9 8 7 6 5 4 3 2 1
First printing, July 2022

PARENTAL ADVISORY
MY HERO ACADEMIA is rated T for Teen
and is recommended for ages 13 and up.
This volume contains fantasy violence.

MY HERO ACADEMIA vol.31

Izuku Midoriya and Toshinori Yagi

KOHEI HORIKOSHI

One day, people began manifesting special abilities that came to be known as "Quirks," and before long, the world was full of superpowered humans. But with the advent of these exceptional individuals came an increase in crime, and governments alone were unable to deal with the situation. At the same time, others emerged to oppose the spread of evil! As if straight from the comic books, these heroes keep the peace and are even officially authorized to fight crime. Our story begins when a certain Quirkless boy and lifelong hero fan meets the world's number one hero, starting him on his path to becoming the greatest hero ever!

ALL MIGHT

IZUKU MIDORIYA

HAWKS

SHOTA AIZAWA

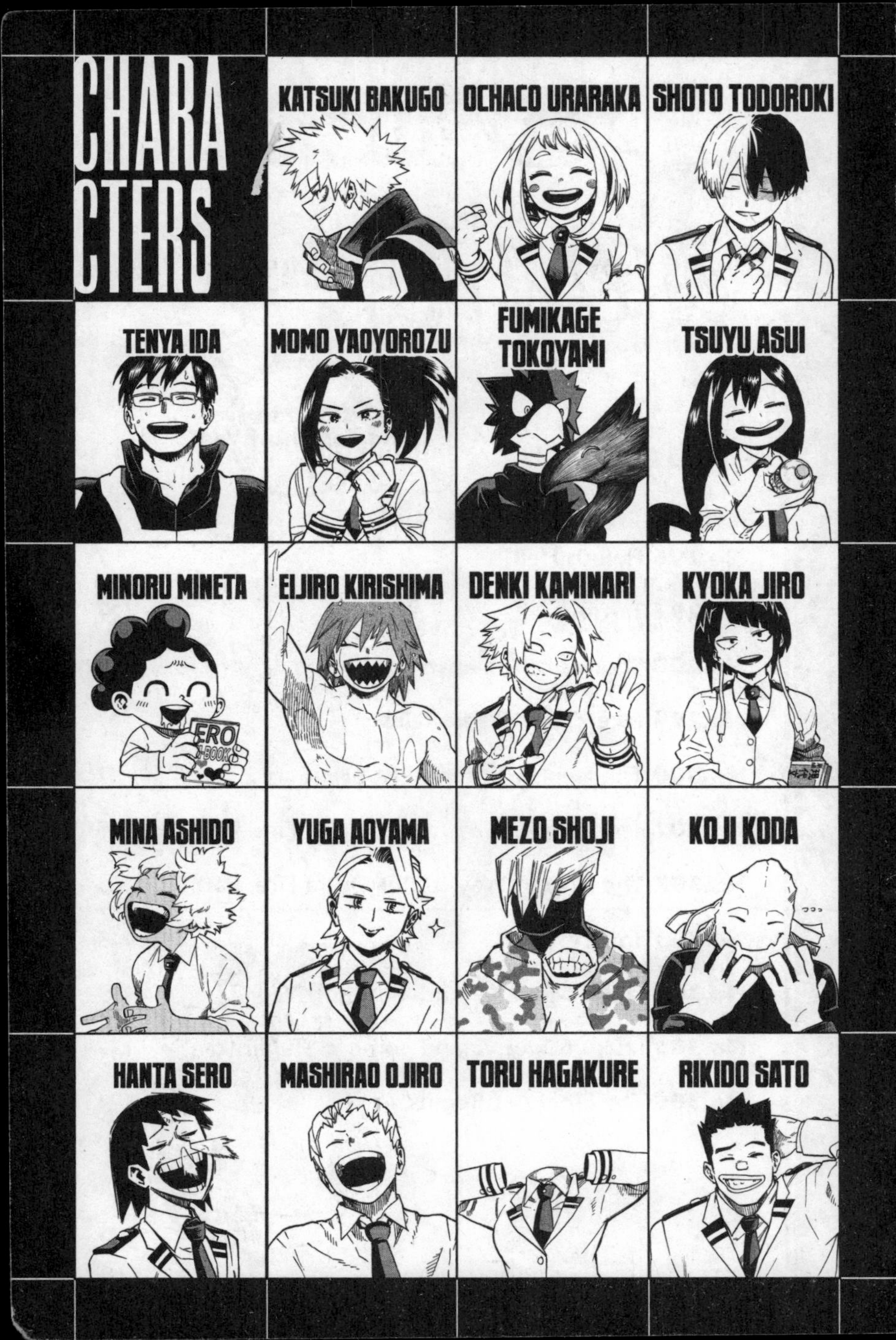
CHARACTERS
KATSUKI BAKUGO
OCHACO URARAKA
SHOTO TODOROKI
TENYA IDA
MOMO YAOYOROZU
FUMIKAGE TOKOYAMI
TSUYU ASUI
MINORU MINETA
ERO H-BOOK
EIJIRO KIRISHIMA
DENKI KAMINARI
KYOKA JIRO
MINA ASHIDO
YUGA AOYAMA
MEZO SHOJI
KOJI KODA
HANTA SERO
MASHIRAO OJIRO
TORU HAGAKURE
RIKIDO SATO

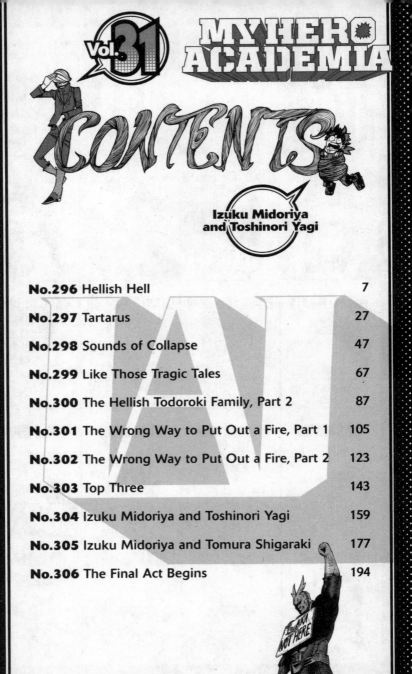

Vol.31 MY HERO ACADEMIA

CONTENTS

Izuku Midoriya and Toshinori Yagi

I AM
NOT HERE

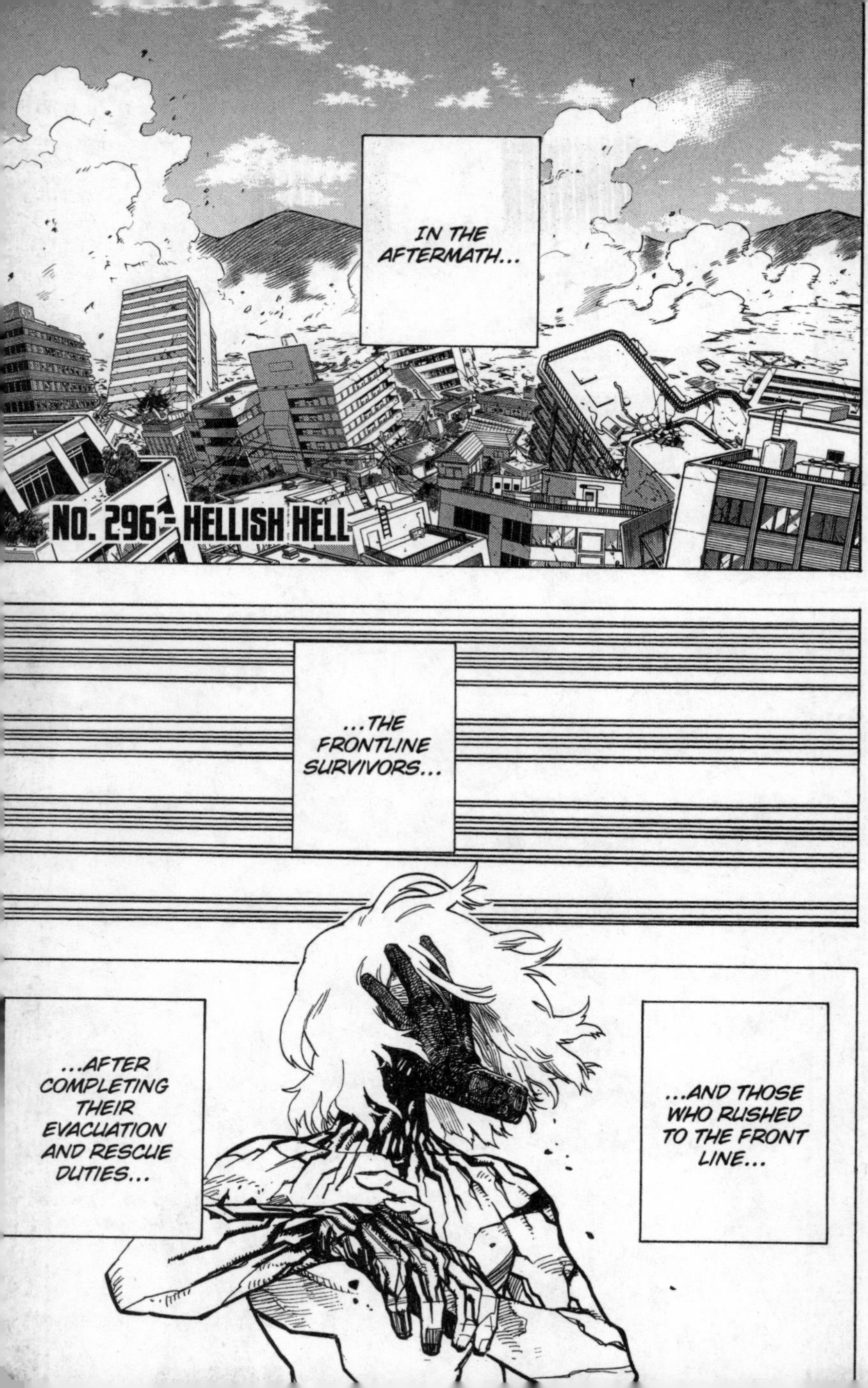
IN THE AFTERMATH...
No. 296 - HELLISH HELL
...THE FRONTLINE SURVIVORS...
...AND THOSE WHO RUSHED TO THE FRONT LINE...
...AFTER COMPLETING THEIR EVACUATION AND RESCUE DUTIES...

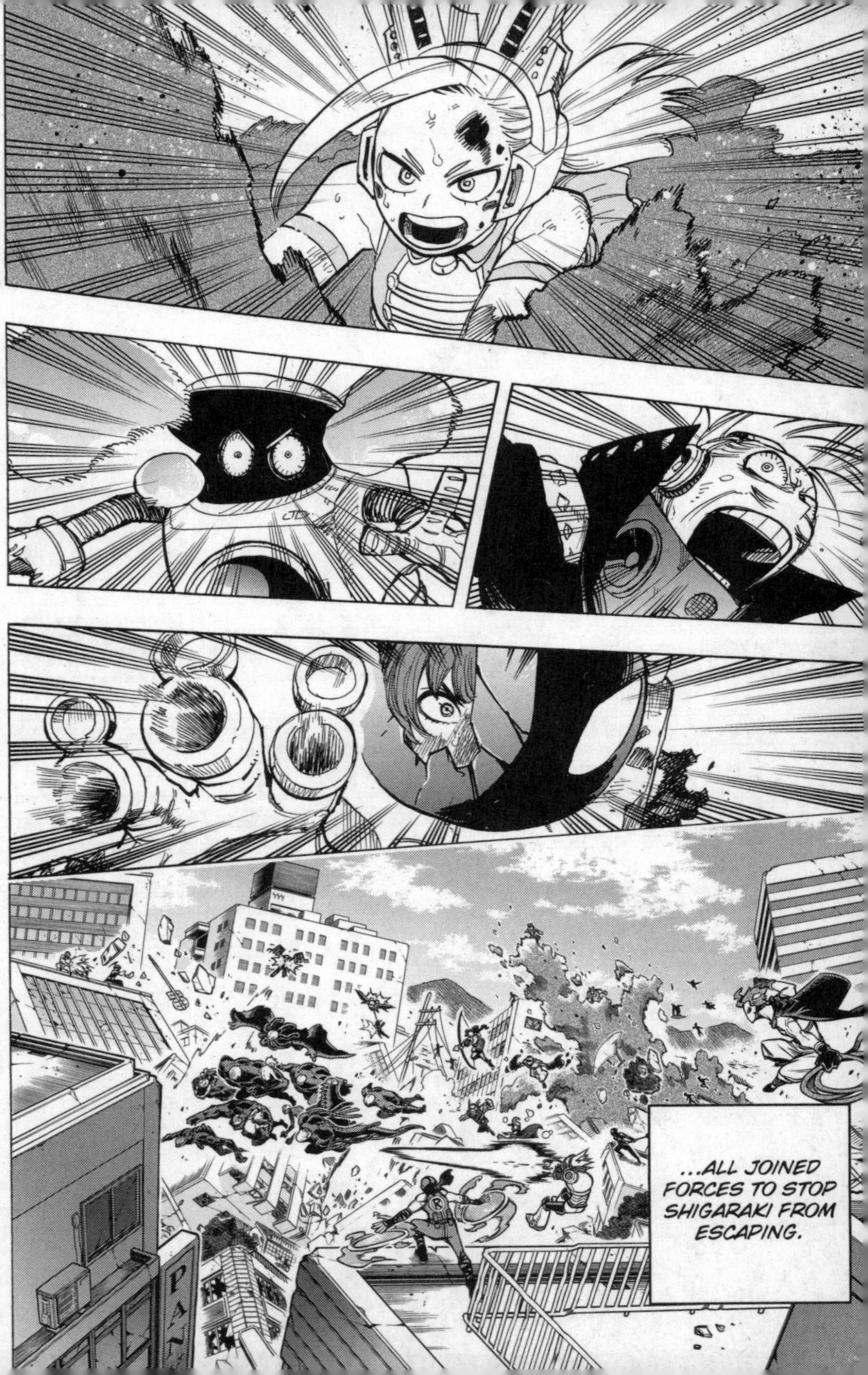
...ALL JOINED FORCES TO STOP SHIGARAKI FROM ESCAPING.

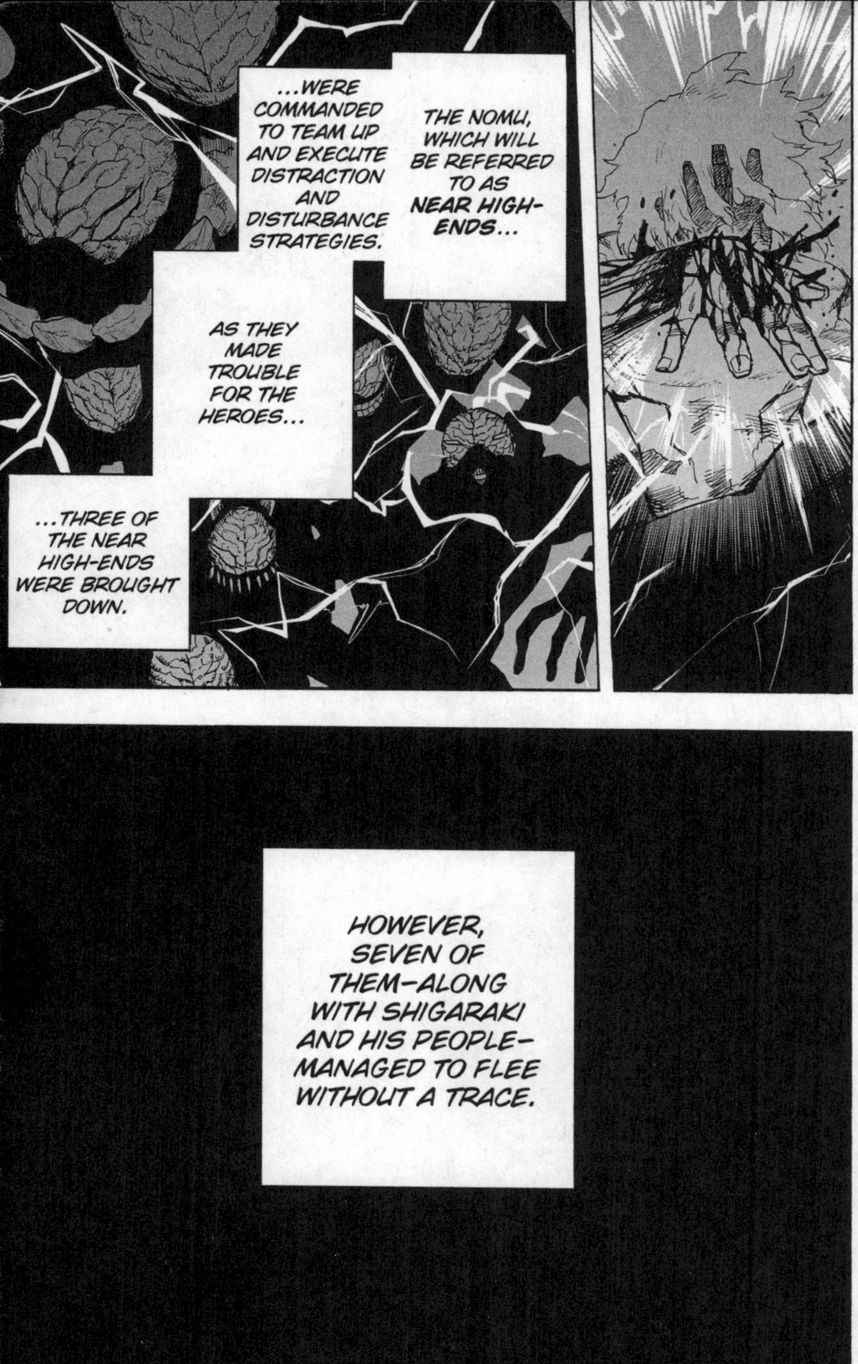
THE NOMU, WHICH WILL BE REFERRED TO AS NEAR HIGH-ENDS...
...WERE COMMANDED TO TEAM UP AND EXECUTE DISTRACTION AND DISTURBANCE STRATEGIES.
AS THEY MADE TROUBLE FOR THE HEROES...
...THREE OF THE NEAR HIGH-ENDS WERE BROUGHT DOWN.
HOWEVER, SEVEN OF THEM—ALONG WITH SHIGARAKI AND HIS PEOPLE—MANAGED TO FLEE WITHOUT A TRACE.

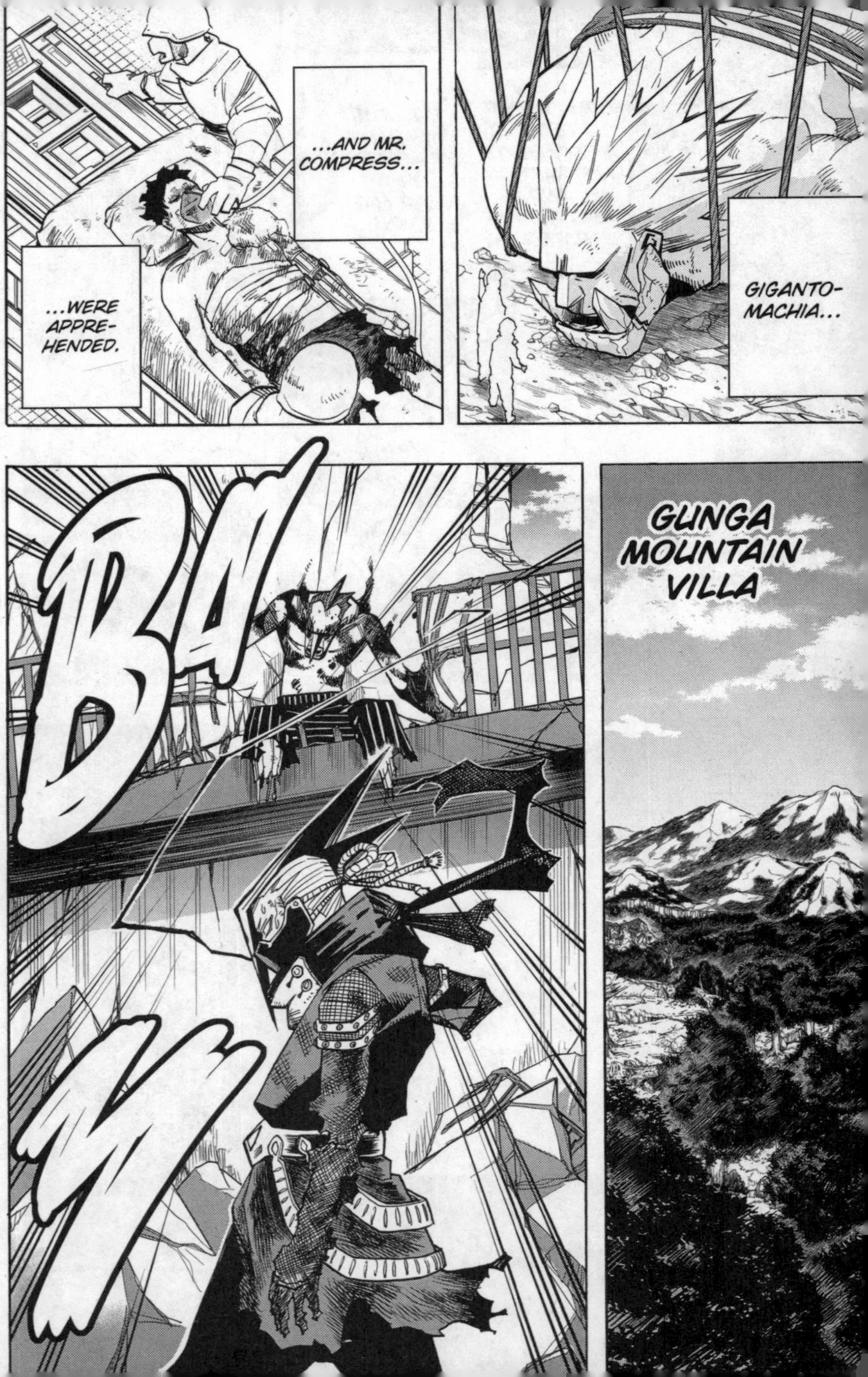
GIGANTO-MACHIA...
...AND MR. COMPRESS...
...WERE APPRE-HENDED.
GUNGA MOUNTAIN VILLA
BAM

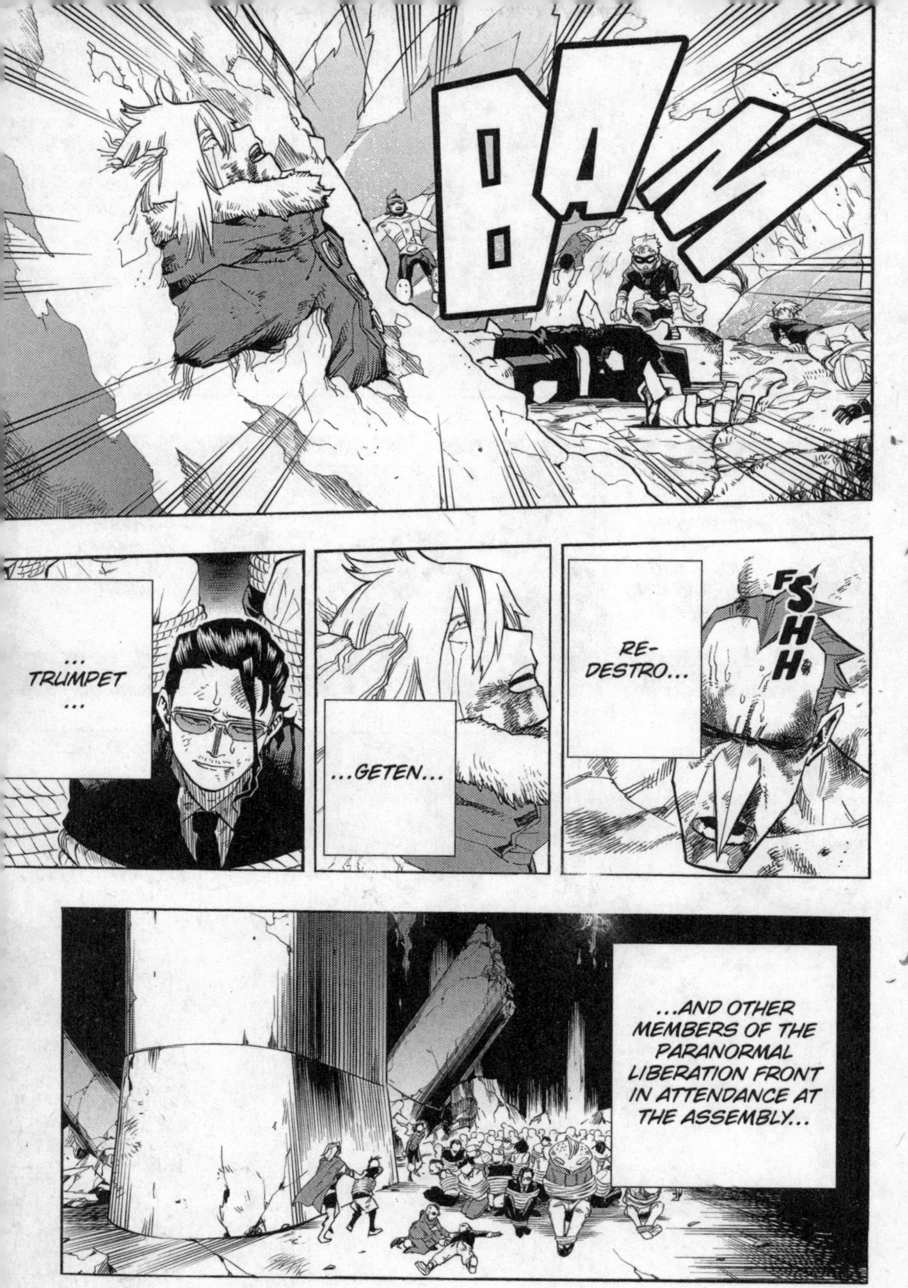
BAM
RE-DESTRO...
FSHH
...GETEN...
... TRUMPET ...
...AND OTHER MEMBERS OF THE PARANORMAL LIBERATION FRONT IN ATTENDANCE AT THE ASSEMBLY...

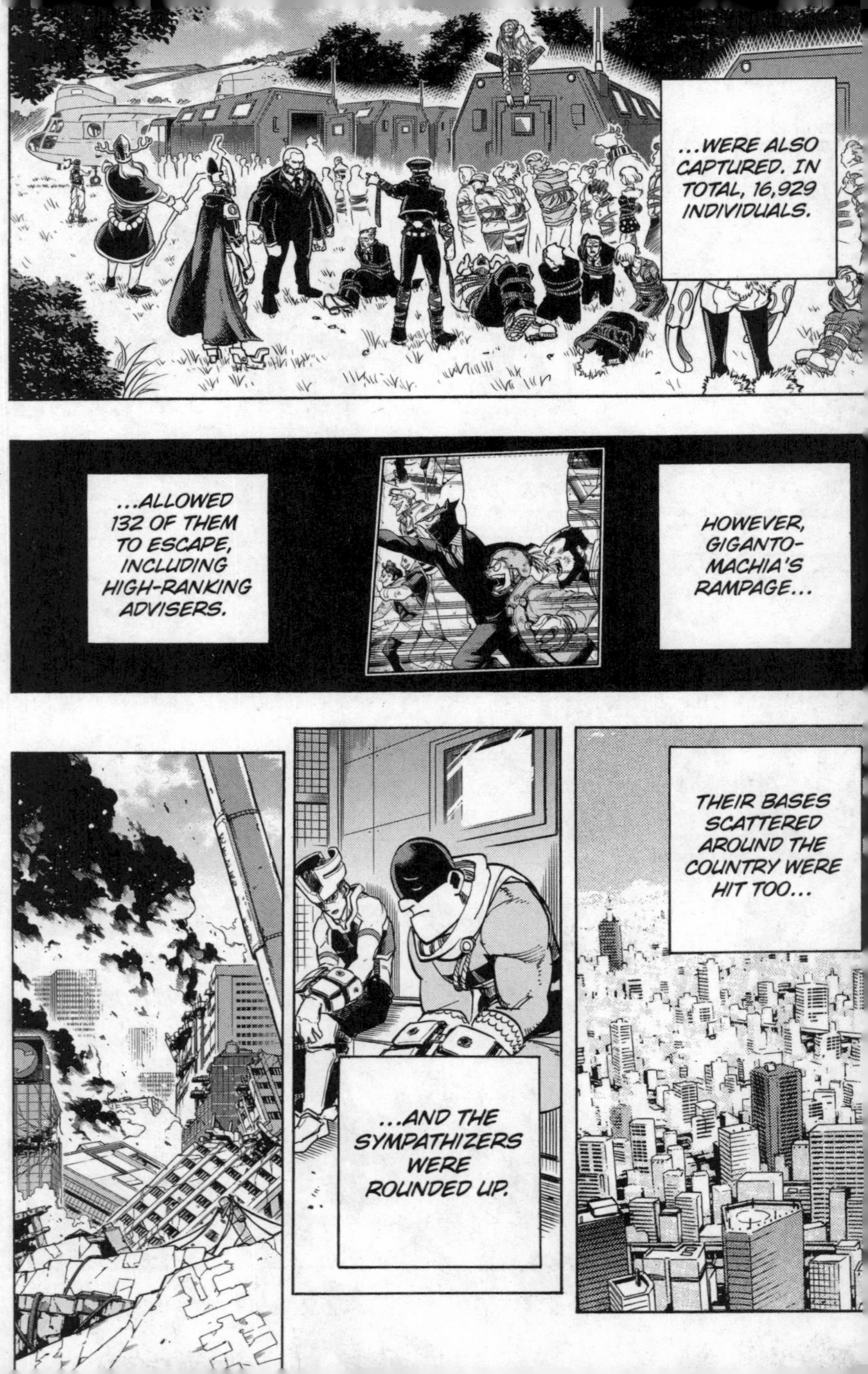
...WERE ALSO CAPTURED. IN TOTAL, 16,929 INDIVIDUALS.
HOWEVER, GIGANTO-MACHIA'S RAMPAGE...
...ALLOWED 132 OF THEM TO ESCAPE, INCLUDING HIGH-RANKING ADVISERS.
THEIR BASES SCATTERED AROUND THE COUNTRY WERE HIT TOO...
...AND THE SYMPATHIZERS WERE ROUNDED UP.

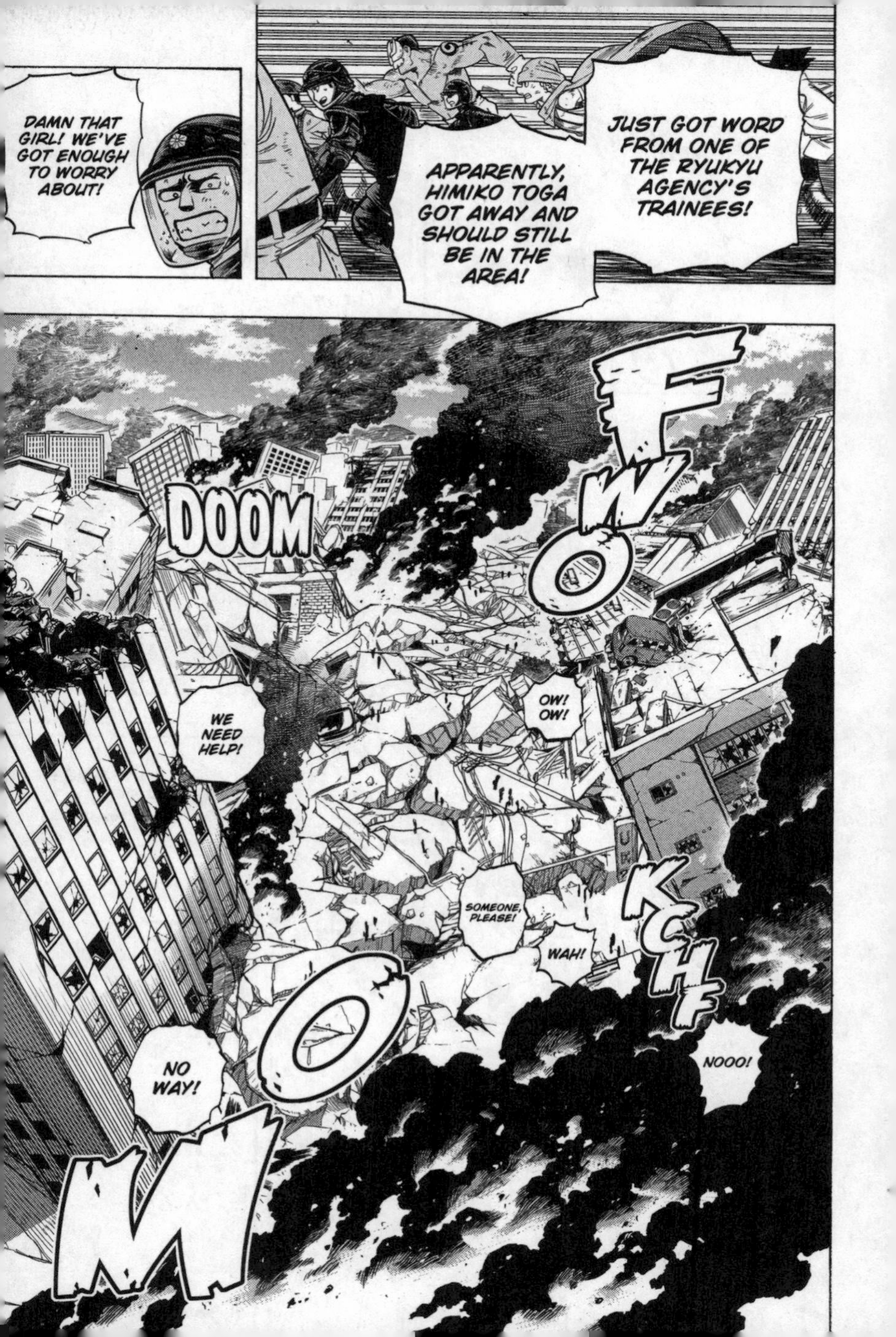
JUST GOT WORD FROM ONE OF THE RYUKYU AGENCY'S TRAINEES!
APPARENTLY, HIMIKO TOGA GOT AWAY AND SHOULD STILL BE IN THE AREA!
DAMN THAT GIRL! WE'VE GOT ENOUGH TO WORRY ABOUT!
FWOOM
DOOM
OW! OW!
WE NEED HELP!
KCHF
SOMEONE, PLEASE!
WAH!
NOOO!
NO WAY!

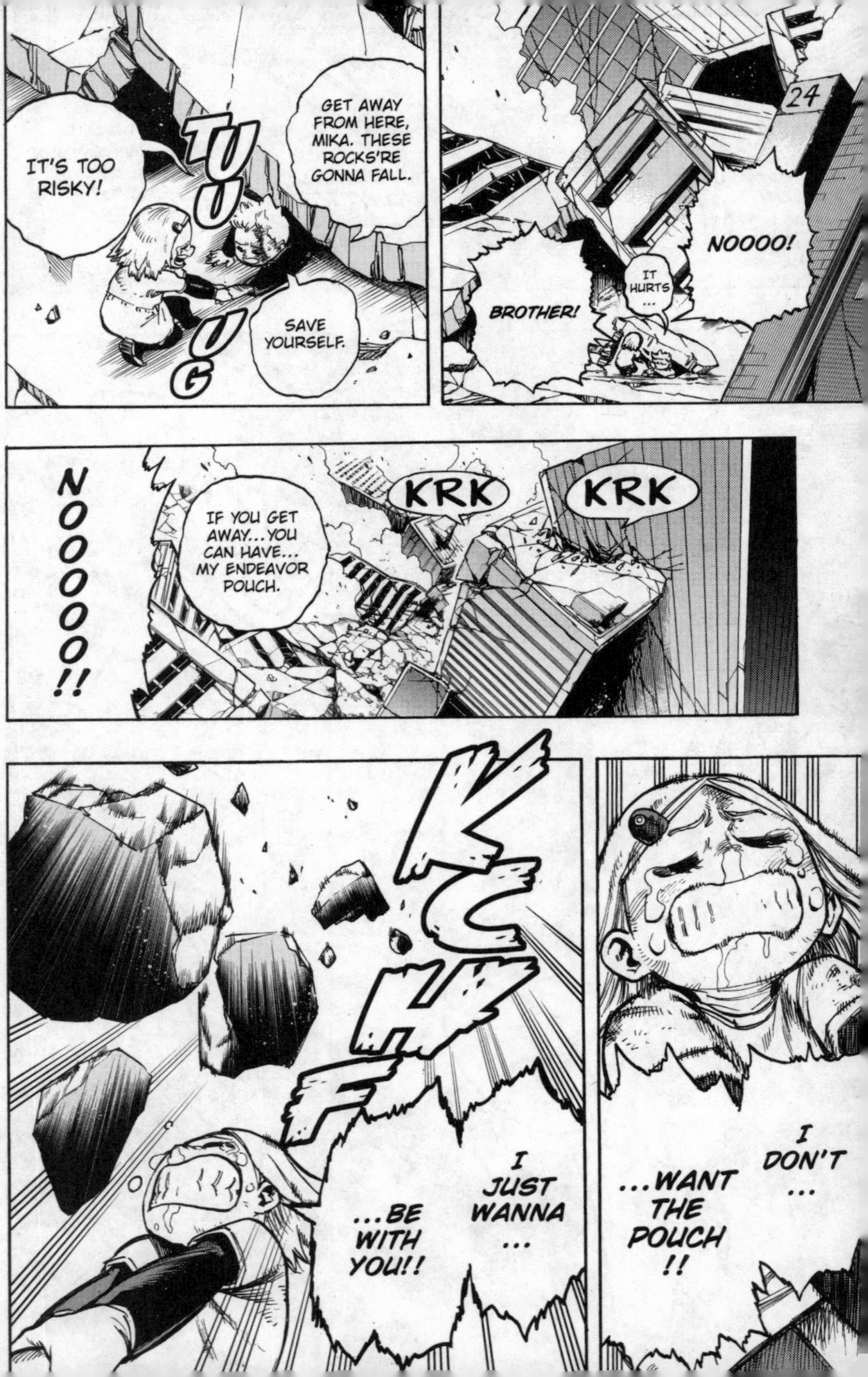
NOOOO!
IT HURTS ...
BROTHER!
GET AWAY FROM HERE, MIKA. THESE ROCKS'RE GONNA FALL.
TUUUG
IT'S TOO RISKY!
SAVE YOURSELF.
KRK
KRK
IF YOU GET AWAY...YOU CAN HAVE... MY ENDEAVOR POUCH.
NOOOOOOO!!
I DON'T ...
...WANT THE POUCH!!
KCHF
I JUST WANNA ...
...BE WITH YOU!!

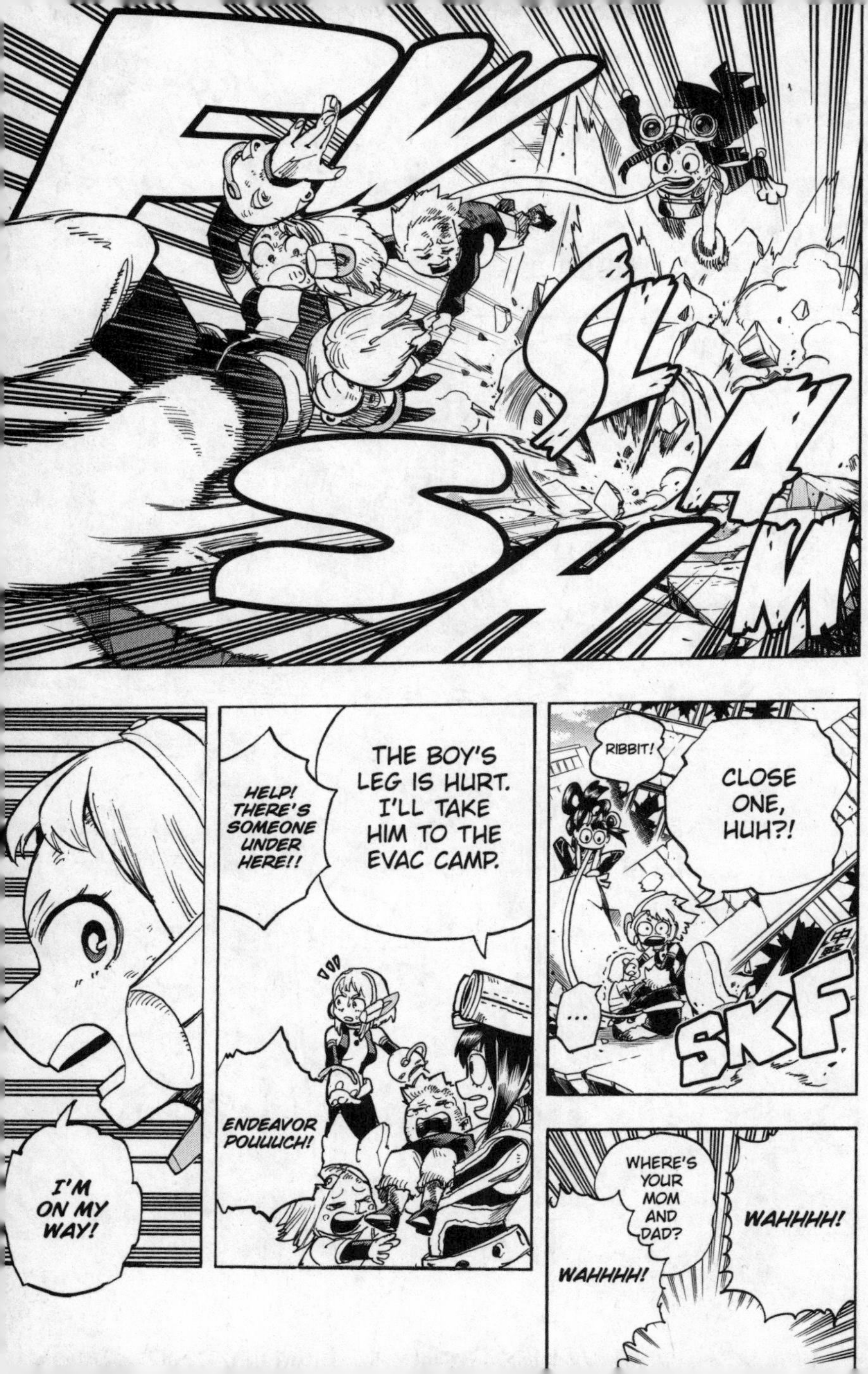
SLAM
RIBBIT!
CLOSE ONE, HUH?!
...
SKF
WHERE'S YOUR MOM AND DAD?
WAHHHH!
WAHHHH!
THE BOY'S LEG IS HURT. I'LL TAKE HIM TO THE EVAC CAMP.
HELP! THERE'S SOMEONE UNDER HERE!!
ENDEAVOR POUUUCH!
I'M ON MY WAY!

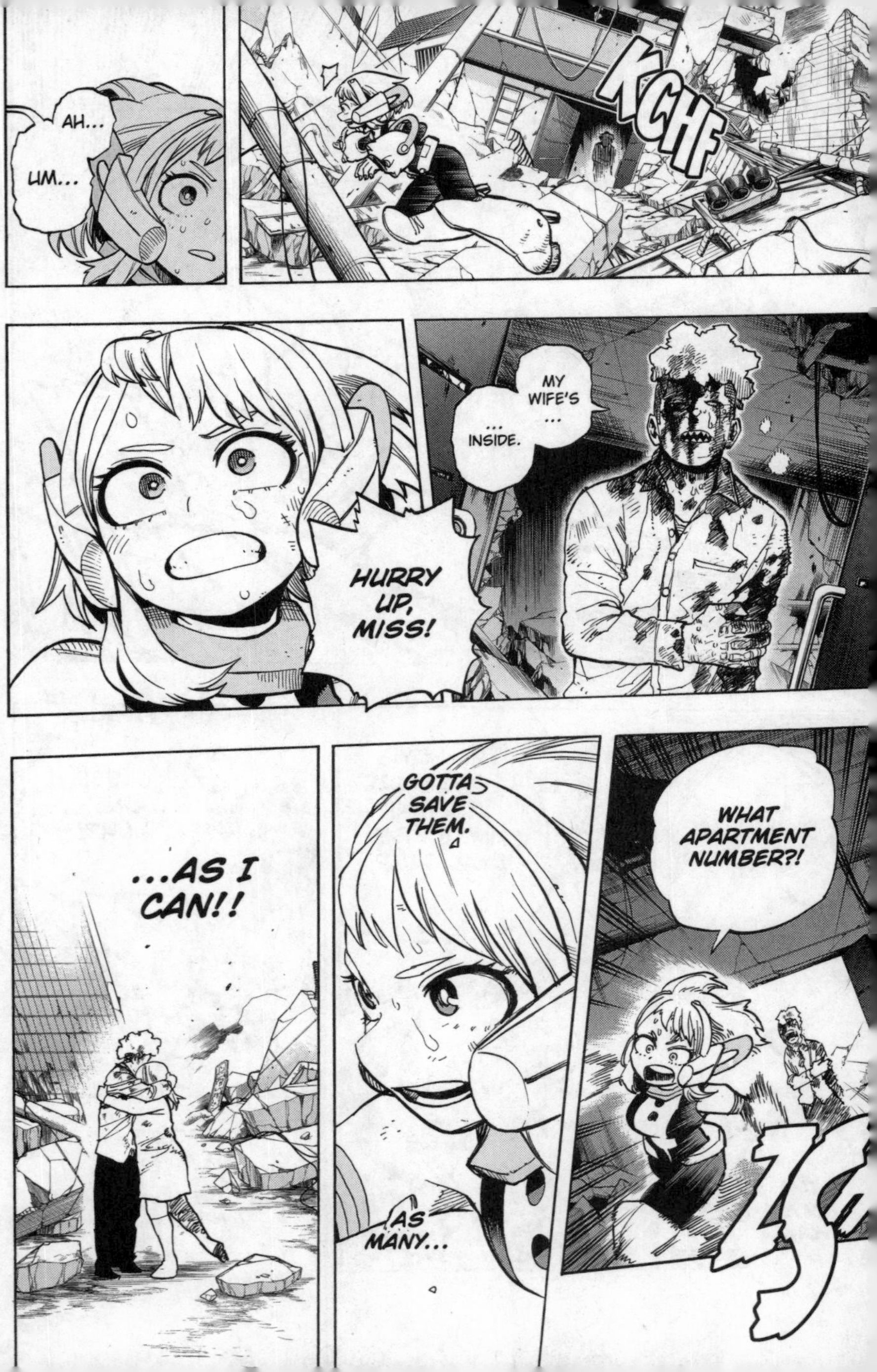
KCHF
AH...
UM...
MY WIFE'S ...
... INSIDE.
HURRY UP, MISS!
WHAT APARTMENT NUMBER?!
GOTTA SAVE THEM.
AS MANY...
...AS I CAN!!

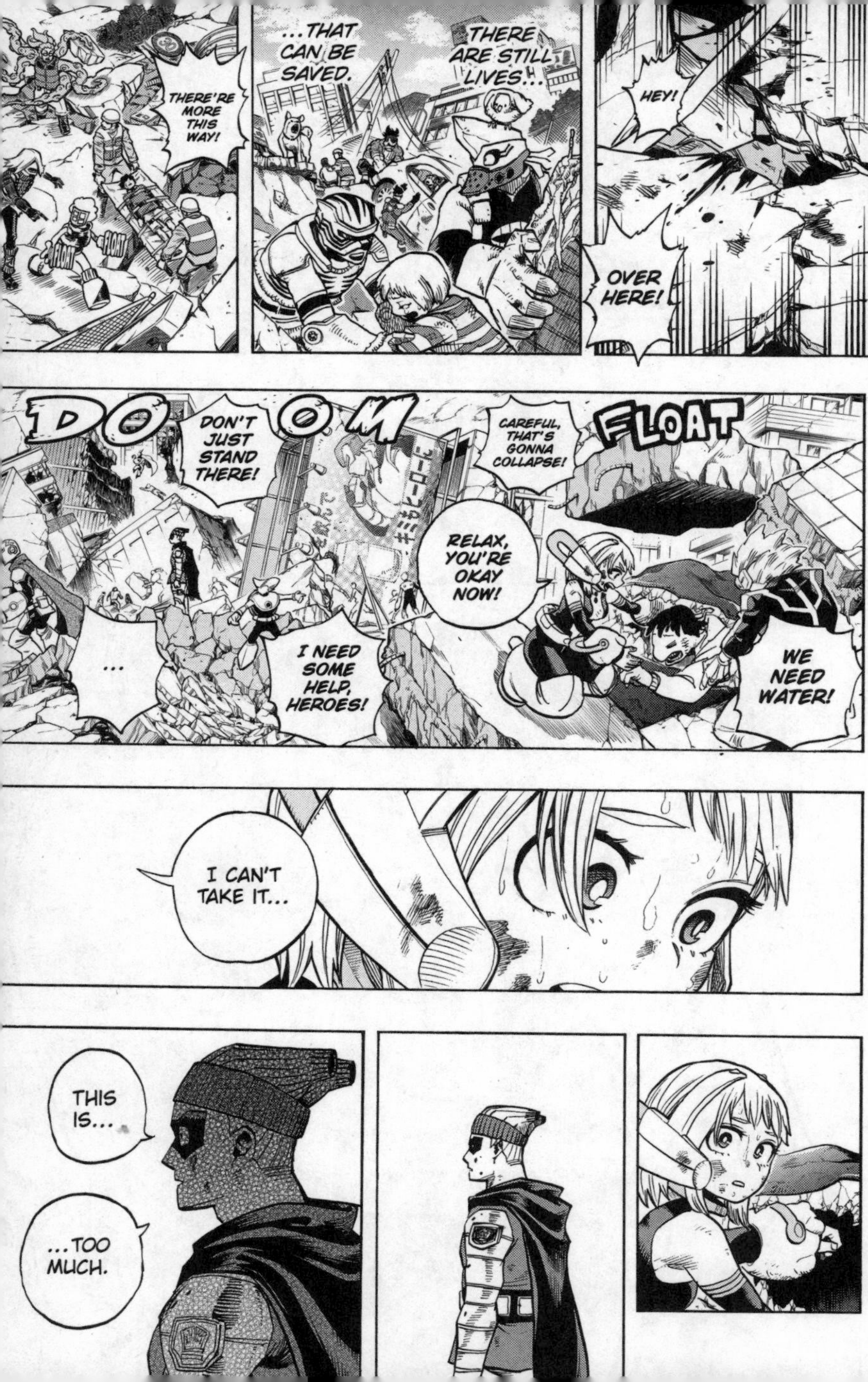
HEY!
OVER HERE!
THERE ARE STILL LIVES...
...THAT CAN BE SAVED.
THERE'RE MORE THIS WAY!
FLOAT
FLOAT
FLOAT
CAREFUL, THAT'S GONNA COLLAPSE!
WE NEED WATER!
RELAX, YOU'RE OKAY NOW!
DO OM
DON'T JUST STAND THERE!
I NEED SOME HELP, HEROES!
...
I CAN'T TAKE IT...
THIS IS...
...TOO MUCH.

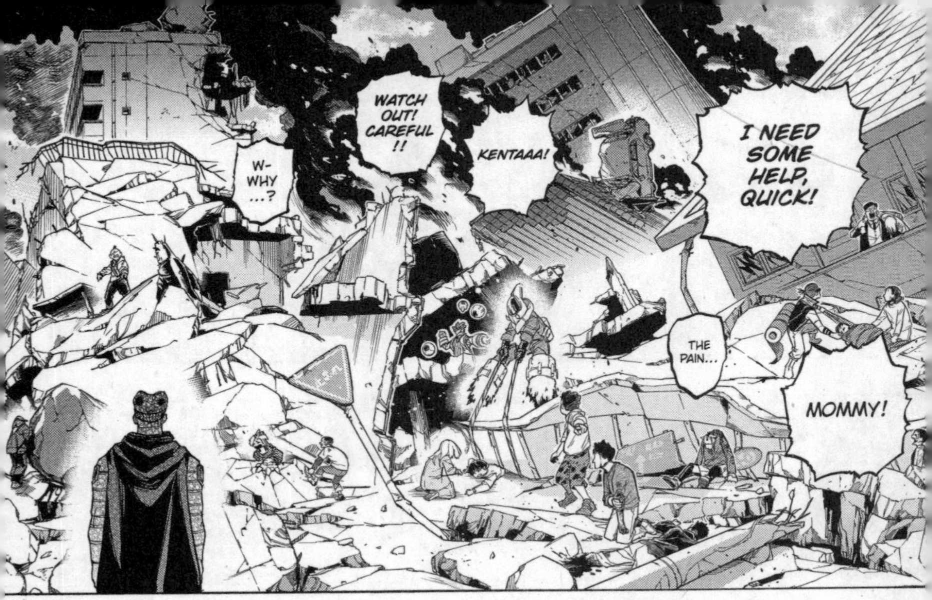
I NEED SOME HELP, QUICK!
KENTAAA!
WATCH OUT! CAREFUL!!
W-WHY...?
MOMMY!
THE PAIN...

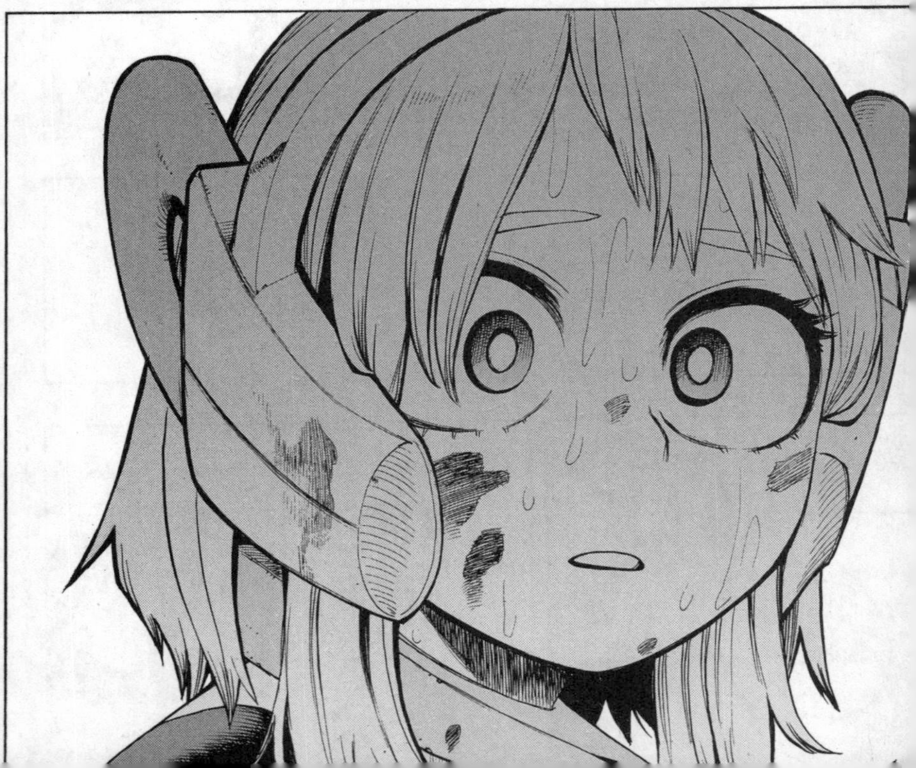

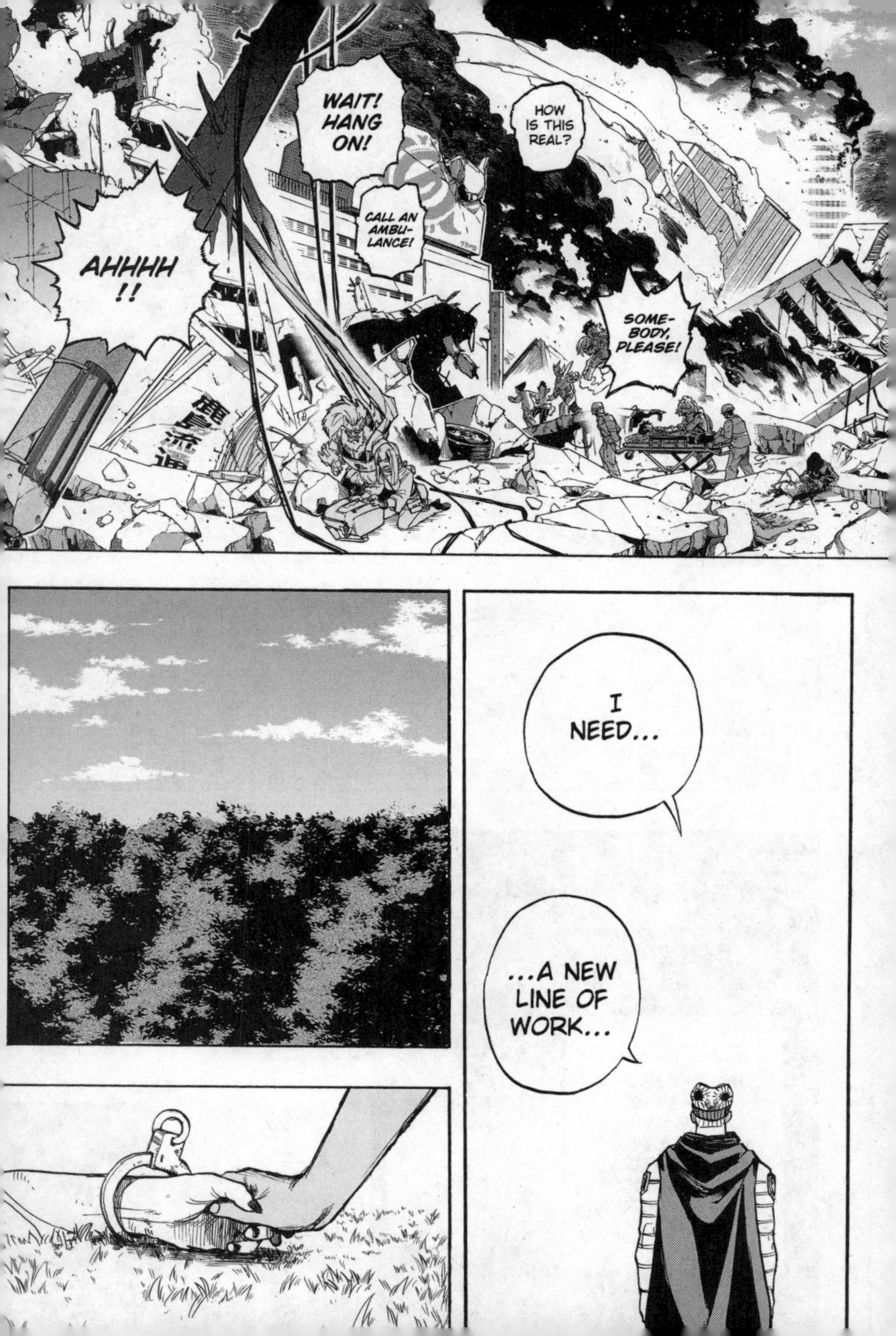
HOW IS THIS REAL?
WAIT! HANG ON!
CALL AN AMBULANCE!
SOME-BODY, PLEASE!
AHHHH!!
I NEED...
...A NEW LINE OF WORK...

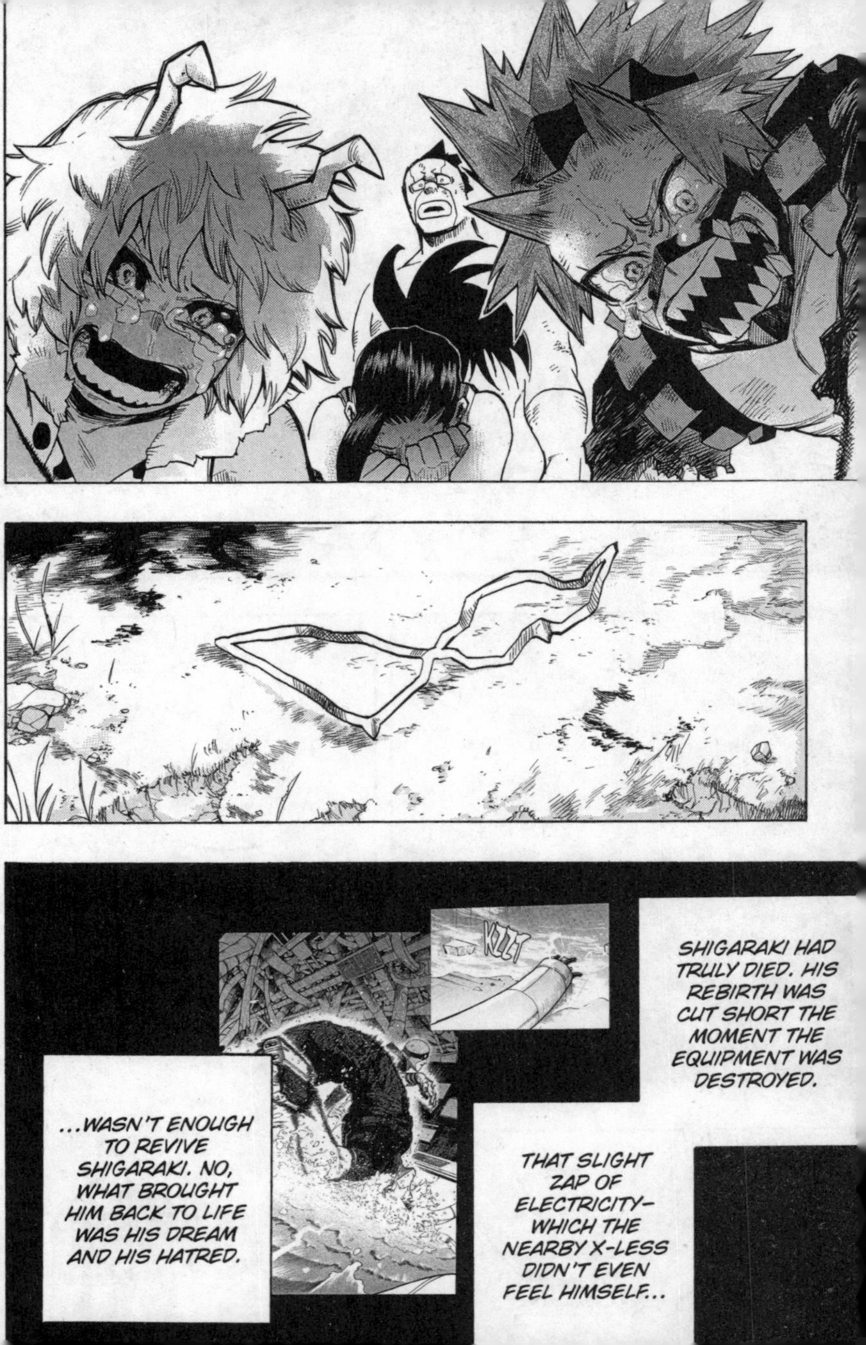
SHIGARAKI HAD TRULY DIED. HIS REBIRTH WAS CUT SHORT THE MOMENT THE EQUIPMENT WAS DESTROYED.
KZZT
THAT SLIGHT ZAP OF ELECTRICITY—WHICH THE NEARBY X-LESS DIDN'T EVEN FEEL HIMSELF...
...WASN'T ENOUGH TO REVIVE SHIGARAKI. NO, WHAT BROUGHT HIM BACK TO LIFE WAS HIS DREAM AND HIS HATRED.

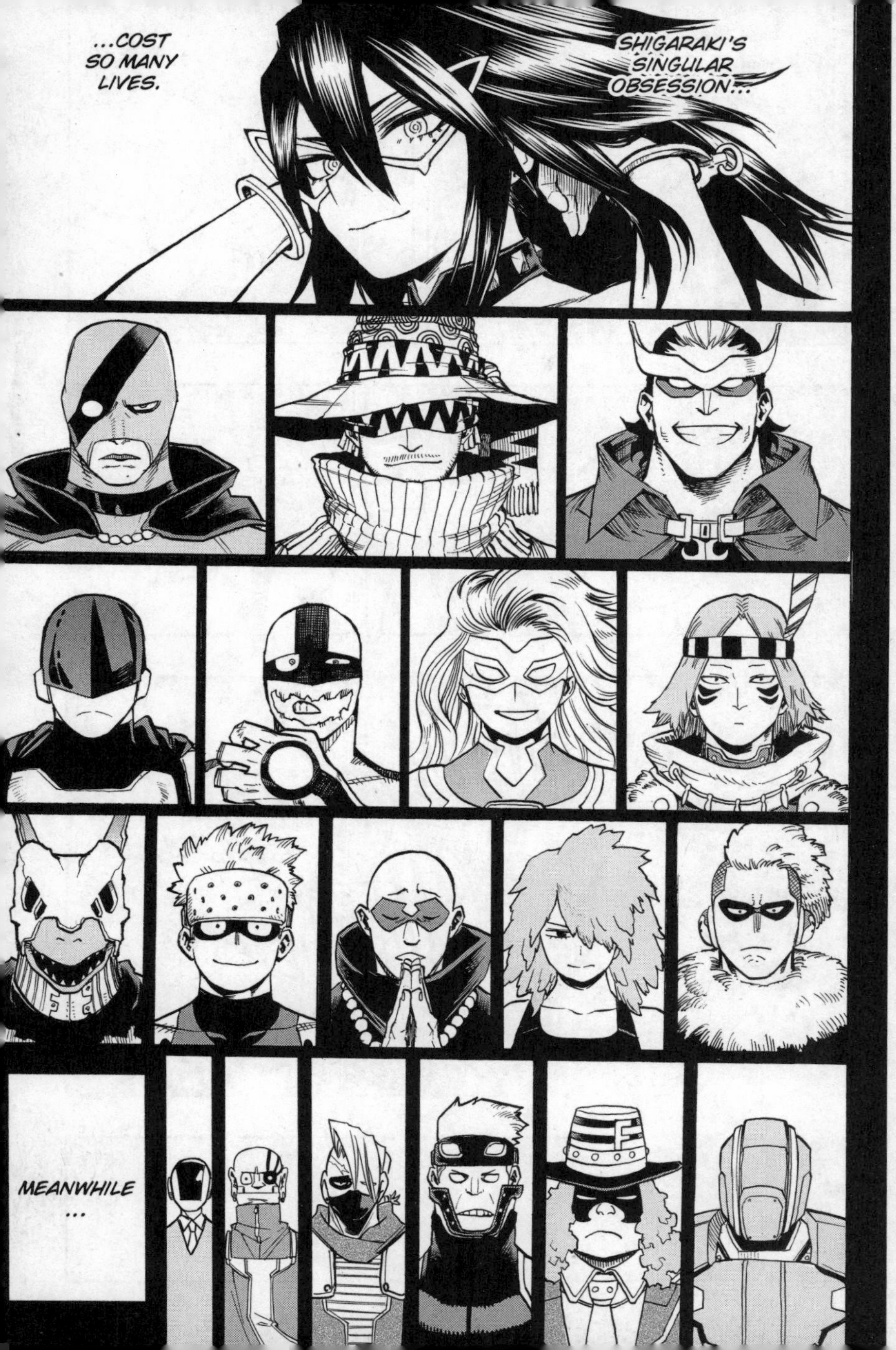
SHIGARAKI'S SINGULAR OBSESSION...
...COST SO MANY LIVES.
MEANWHILE ...

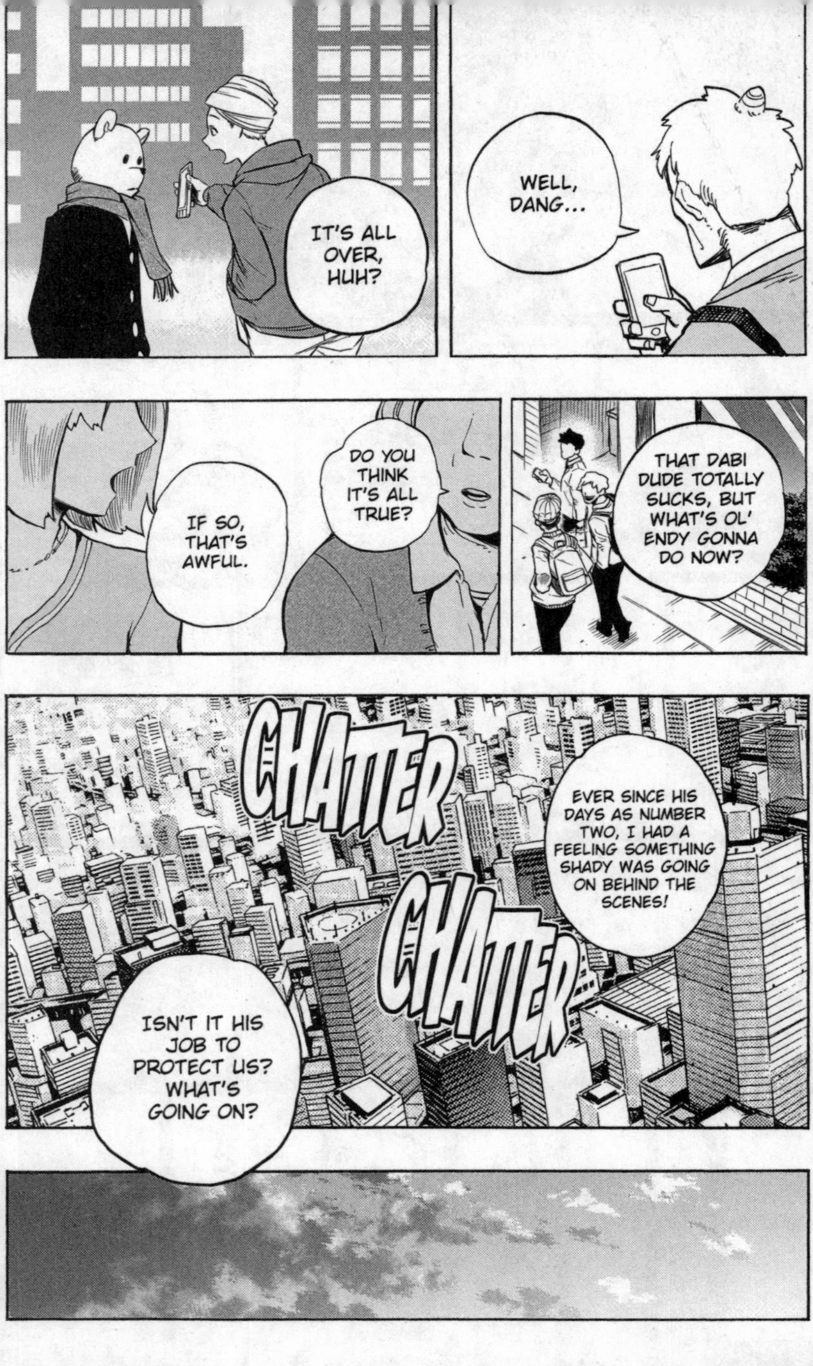
WELL, DANG...
IT'S ALL OVER, HUH?
THAT DABI DUDE TOTALLY SUCKS, BUT WHAT'S OL' ENDY GONNA DO NOW?
DO YOU THINK IT'S ALL TRUE?
IF SO, THAT'S AWFUL.
CHATTER
CHATTER
EVER SINCE HIS DAYS AS NUMBER TWO, I HAD A FEELING SOMETHING SHADY WAS GOING ON BEHIND THE SCENES!
ISN'T IT HIS JOB TO PROTECT US? WHAT'S GOING ON?

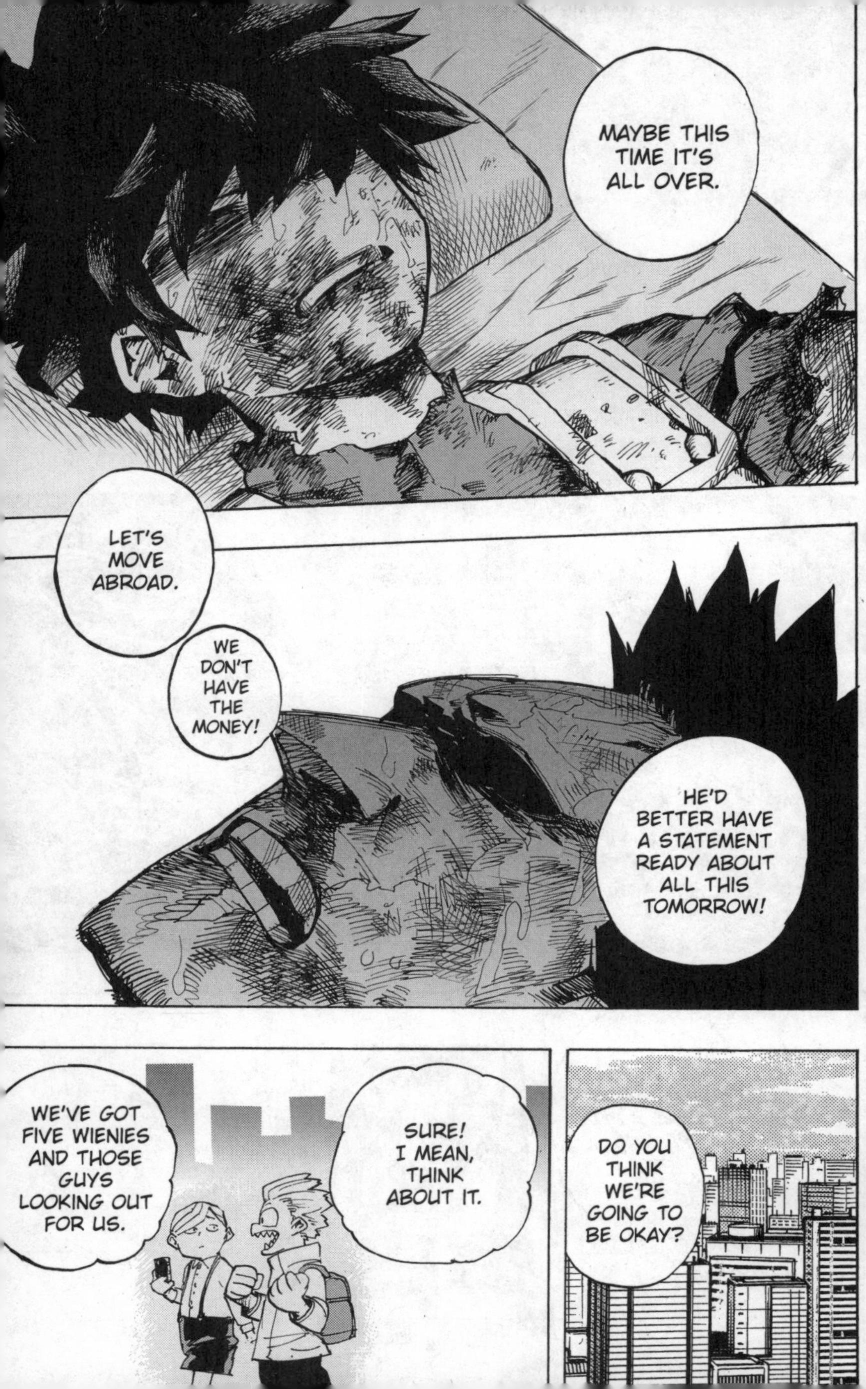
MAYBE THIS TIME IT'S ALL OVER.
HE'D BETTER HAVE A STATEMENT READY ABOUT ALL THIS TOMORROW!
WE DON'T HAVE THE MONEY!
LET'S MOVE ABROAD.
DO YOU THINK WE'RE GOING TO BE OKAY?
SURE! I MEAN, THINK ABOUT IT.
WE'VE GOT FIVE WIENIES AND THOSE GUYS LOOKING OUT FOR US.

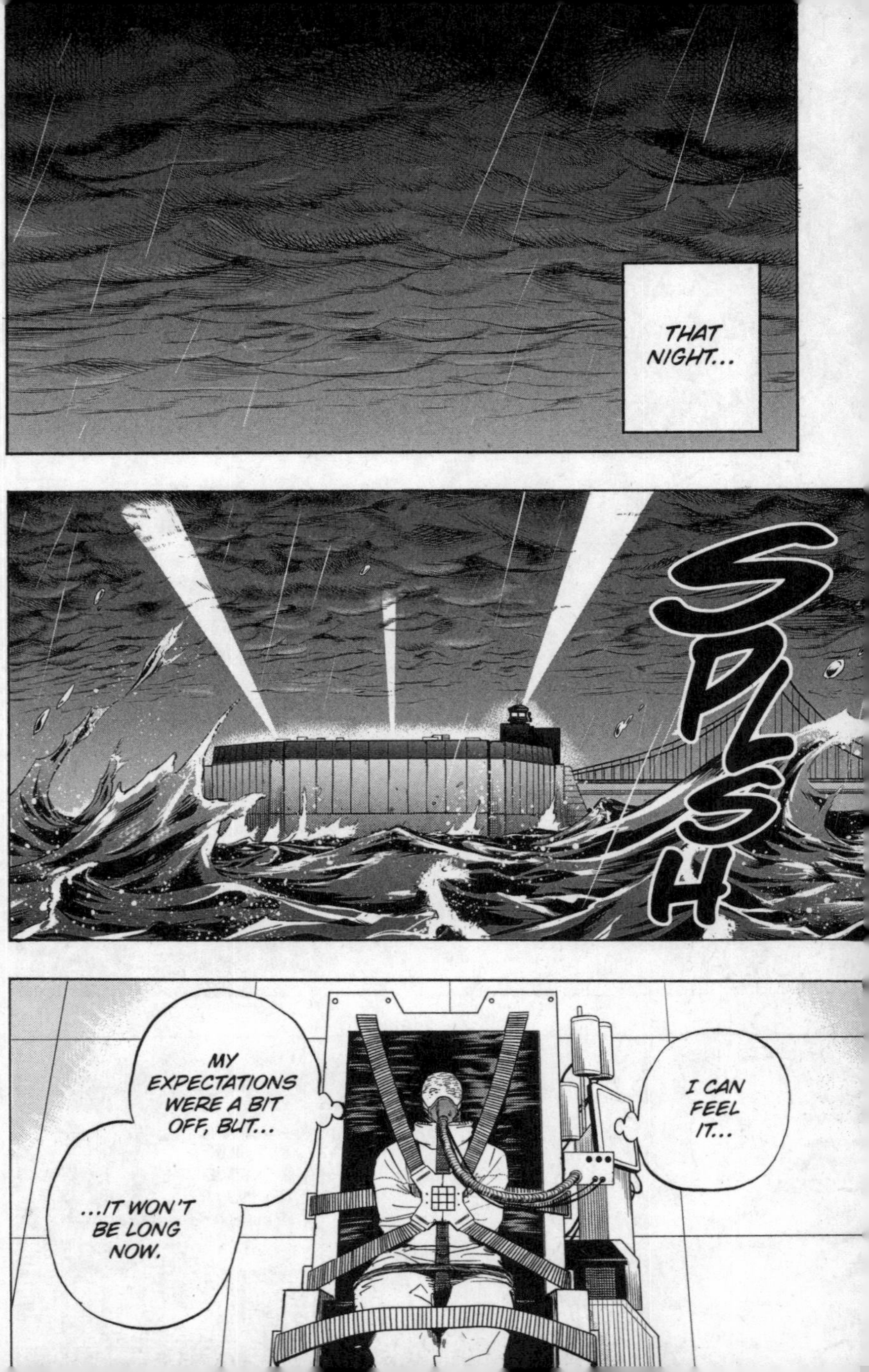
THAT NIGHT...
SPLSH
I CAN FEEL IT...
MY EXPECTATIONS WERE A BIT OFF, BUT...
...IT WON'T BE LONG NOW.

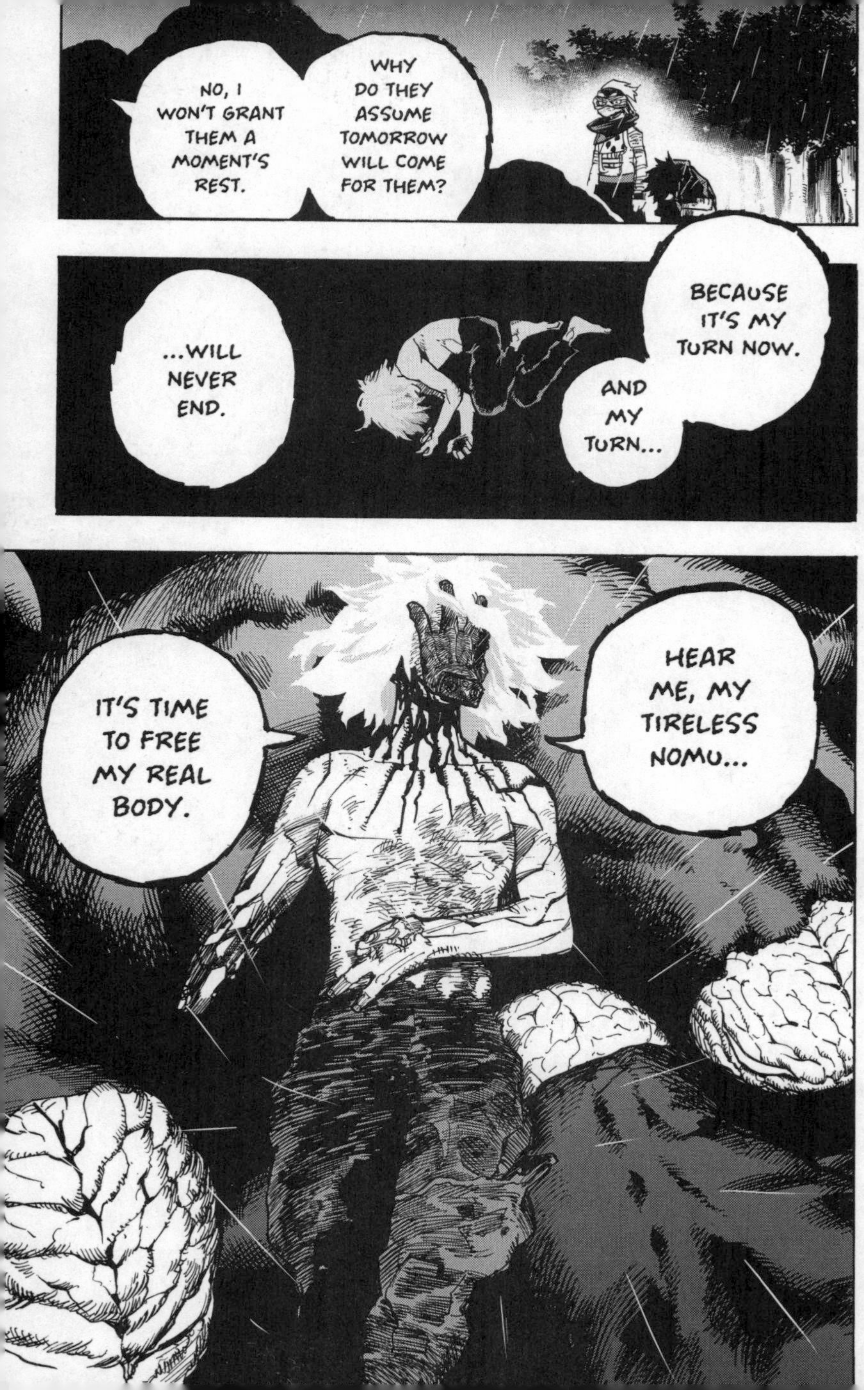
WHY DO THEY ASSUME TOMORROW WILL COME FOR THEM?
NO, I WON'T GRANT THEM A MOMENT'S REST.
BECAUSE IT'S MY TURN NOW.
AND MY TURN...
...WILL NEVER END.
HEAR ME, MY TIRELESS NOMU...
IT'S TIME TO FREE MY REAL BODY.

MIDNIGHT

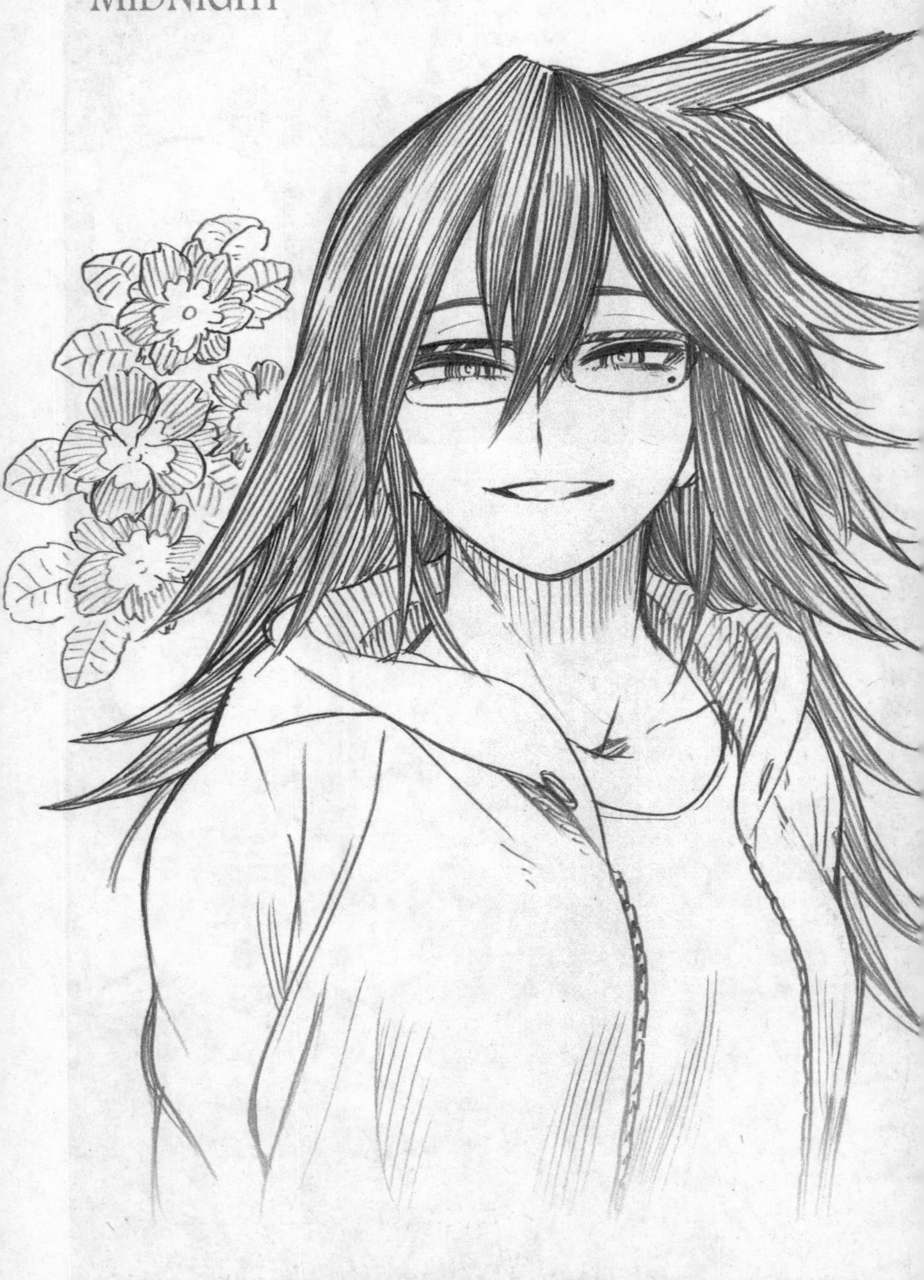

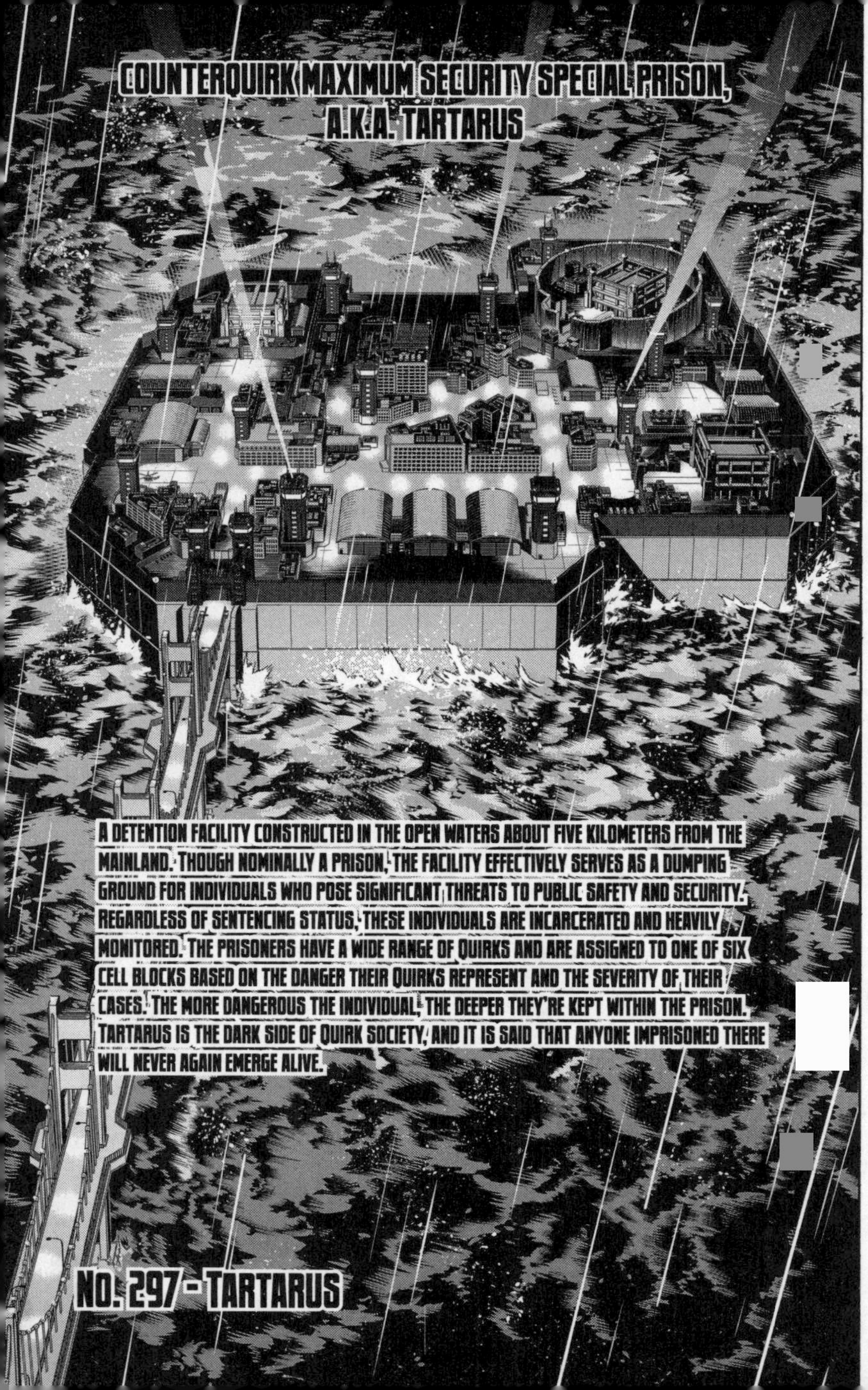
COUNTERQUIRK MAXIMUM SECURITY SPECIAL PRISON, A.K.A. TARTARUS
A DETENTION FACILITY CONSTRUCTED IN THE OPEN WATERS ABOUT FIVE KILOMETERS FROM THE MAINLAND. THOUGH NOMINALLY A PRISON, THE FACILITY EFFECTIVELY SERVES AS A DUMPING GROUND FOR INDIVIDUALS WHO POSE SIGNIFICANT THREATS TO PUBLIC SAFETY AND SECURITY. REGARDLESS OF SENTENCING STATUS, THESE INDIVIDUALS ARE INCARCERATED AND HEAVILY MONITORED. THE PRISONERS HAVE A WIDE RANGE OF QUIRKS AND ARE ASSIGNED TO ONE OF SIX CELL BLOCKS BASED ON THE DANGER THEIR QUIRKS REPRESENT AND THE SEVERITY OF THEIR CASES. THE MORE DANGEROUS THE INDIVIDUAL, THE DEEPER THEY'RE KEPT WITHIN THE PRISON. TARTARUS IS THE DARK SIDE OF QUIRK SOCIETY, AND IT IS SAID THAT ANYONE IMPRISONED THERE WILL NEVER AGAIN EMERGE ALIVE.
NO. 297 - TARTARUS

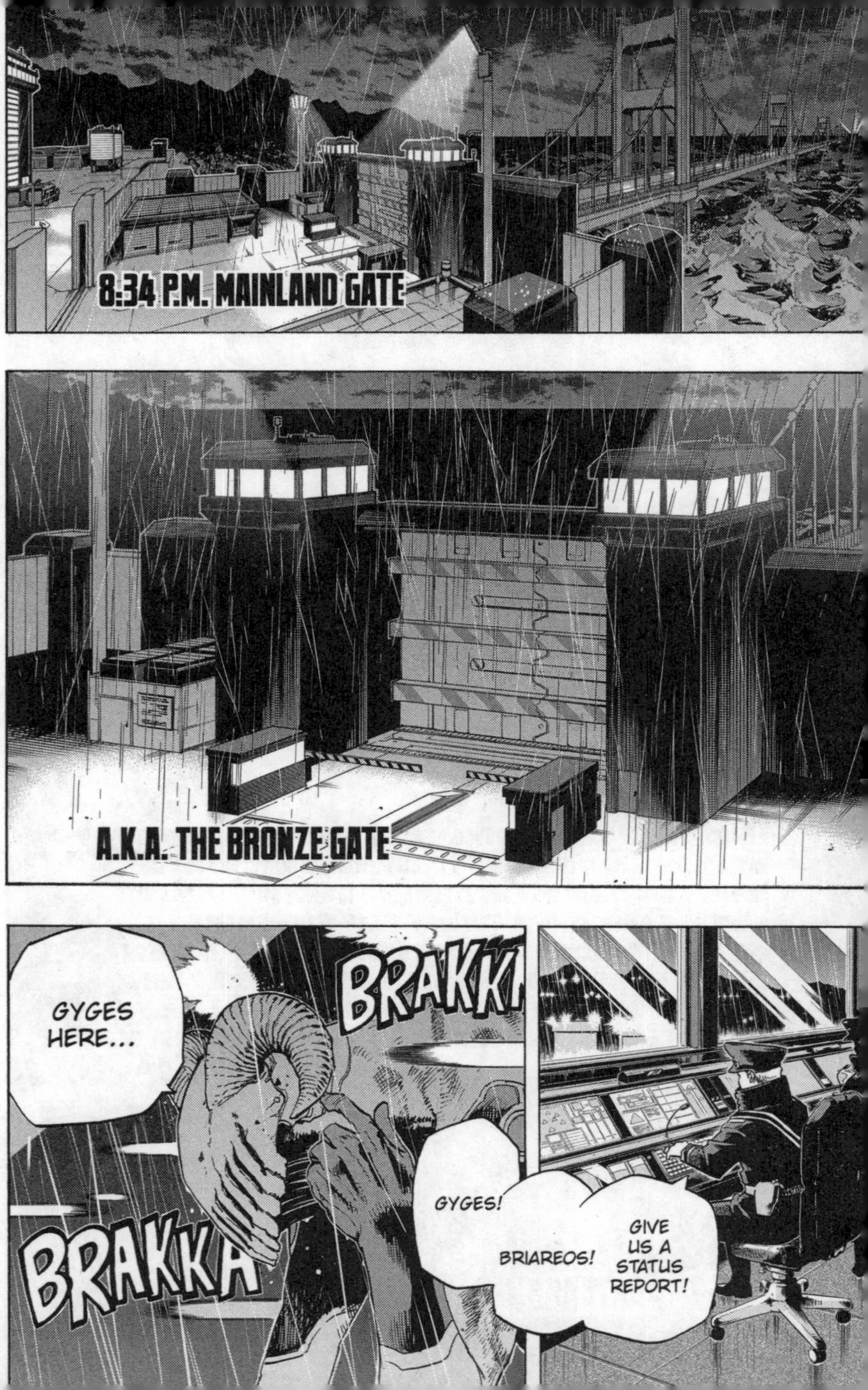
8:34 P.M. MAINLAND GATE
A.K.A. THE BRONZE GATE
GYGES!
BRIAREOS!
GIVE US A STATUS REPORT!
BRAKKI
GYGES HERE...
BRAKKA

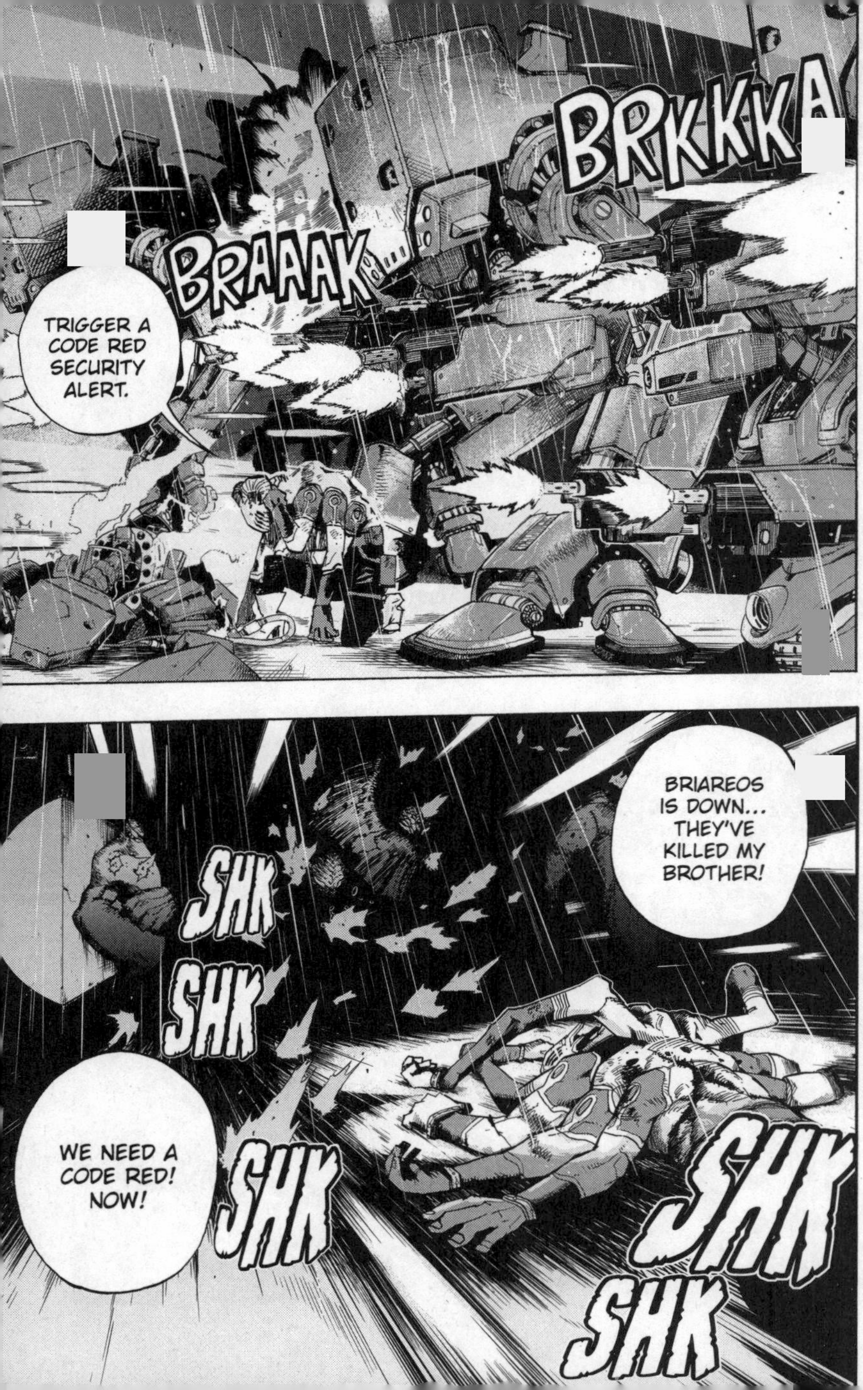
BRKKKA
BRAAAK
TRIGGER A CODE RED SECURITY ALERT.
BRIAREOS IS DOWN... THEY'VE KILLED MY BROTHER!
SHK
SHK
SHK
WE NEED A CODE RED! NOW!
SHK
SHK

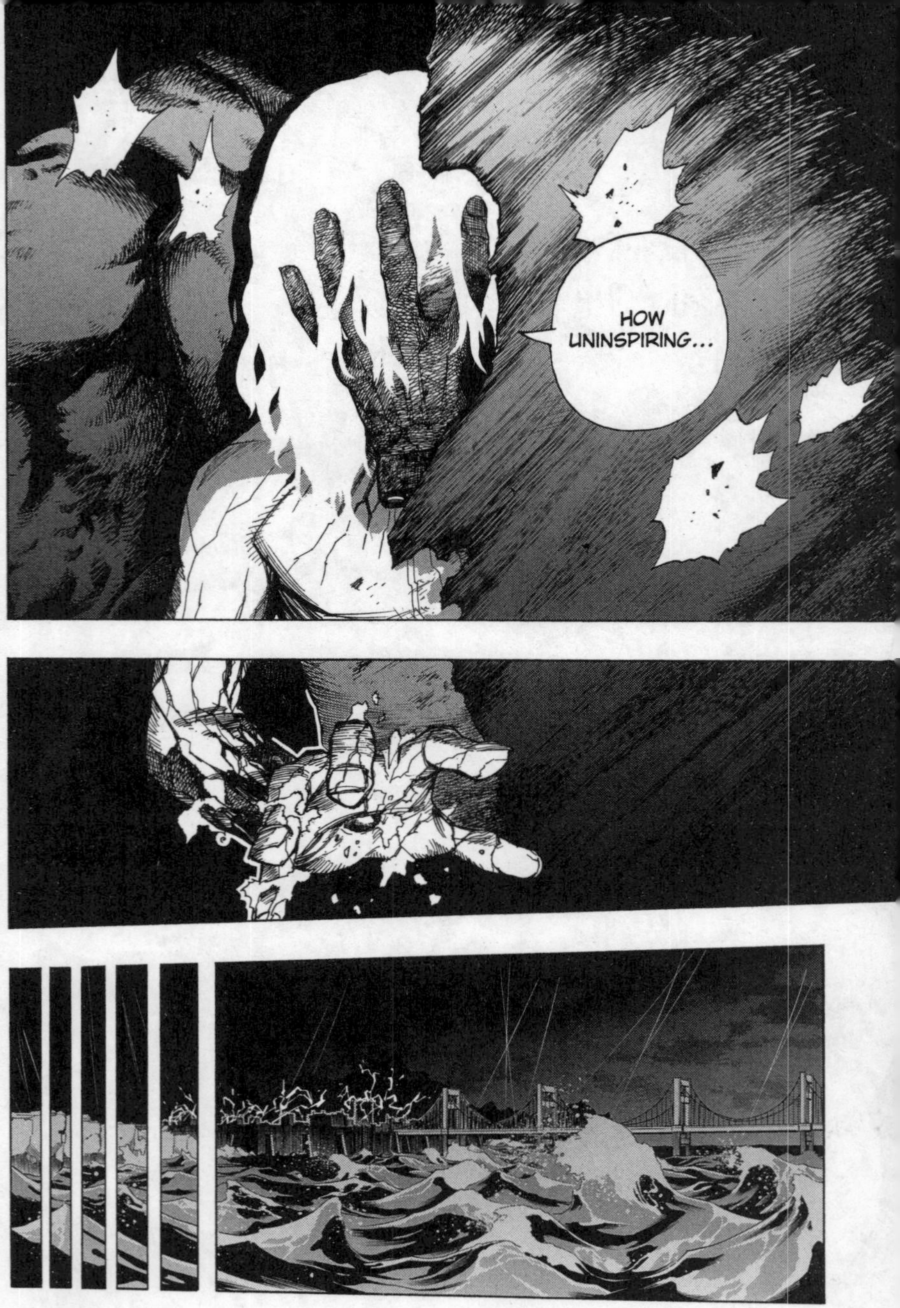
HOW UNINSPIRING...

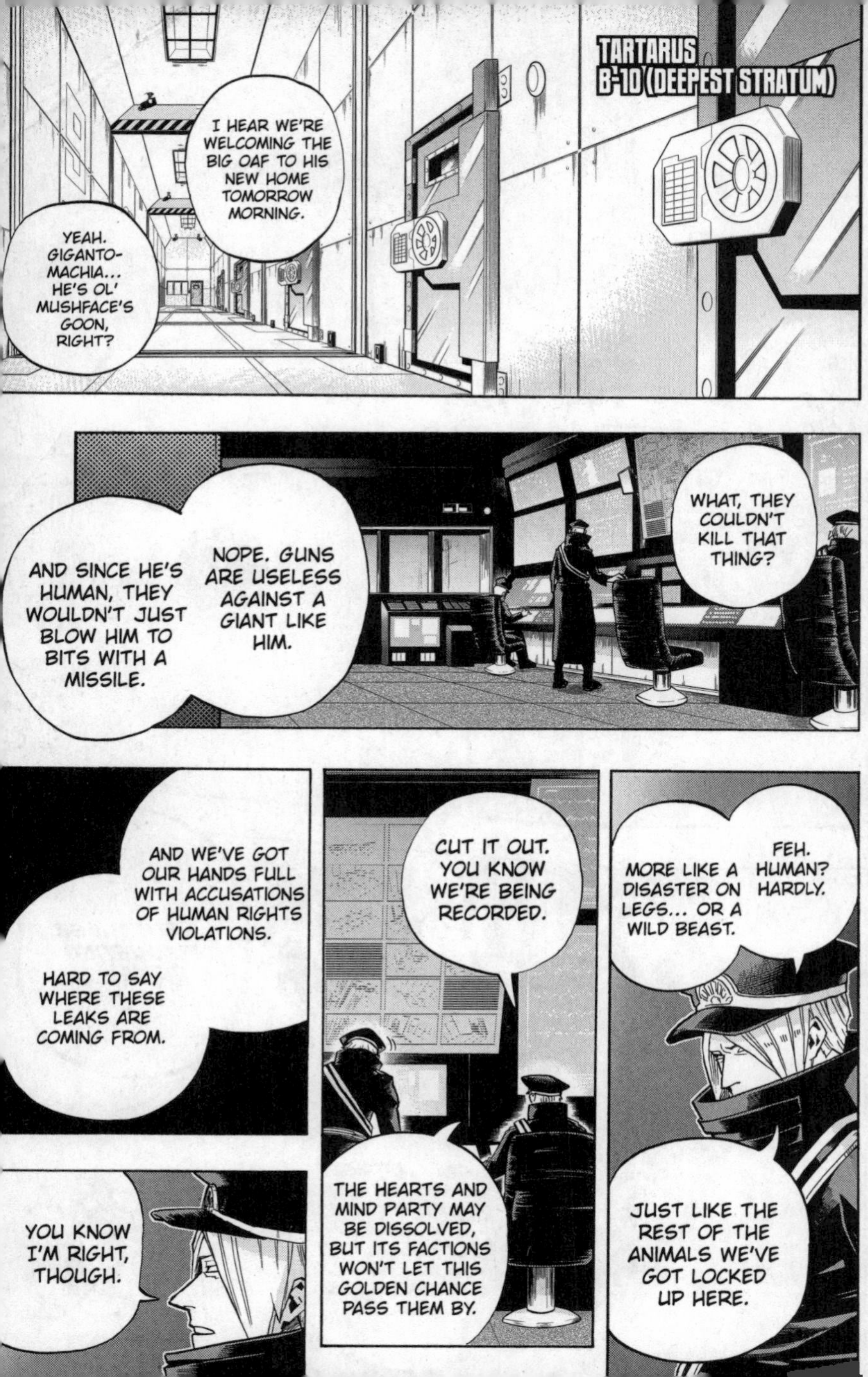
TARTARUS B-10 (DEEPEST STRATUM)
I HEAR WE'RE WELCOMING THE BIG OAF TO HIS NEW HOME TOMORROW MORNING.
YEAH. GIGANTO-MACHIA... HE'S OL' MUSHFACE'S GOON, RIGHT?
WHAT, THEY COULDN'T KILL THAT THING?
NOPE. GUNS ARE USELESS AGAINST A GIANT LIKE HIM.
AND SINCE HE'S HUMAN, THEY WOULDN'T JUST BLOW HIM TO BITS WITH A MISSILE.
FEH. HUMAN? HARDLY.
MORE LIKE A DISASTER ON LEGS... OR A WILD BEAST.
JUST LIKE THE REST OF THE ANIMALS WE'VE GOT LOCKED UP HERE.
CUT IT OUT. YOU KNOW WE'RE BEING RECORDED.
THE HEARTS AND MIND PARTY MAY BE DISSOLVED, BUT ITS FACTIONS WON'T LET THIS GOLDEN CHANCE PASS THEM BY.
AND WE'VE GOT OUR HANDS FULL WITH ACCUSATIONS OF HUMAN RIGHTS VIOLATIONS.
HARD TO SAY WHERE THESE LEAKS ARE COMING FROM.
YOU KNOW I'M RIGHT, THOUGH.

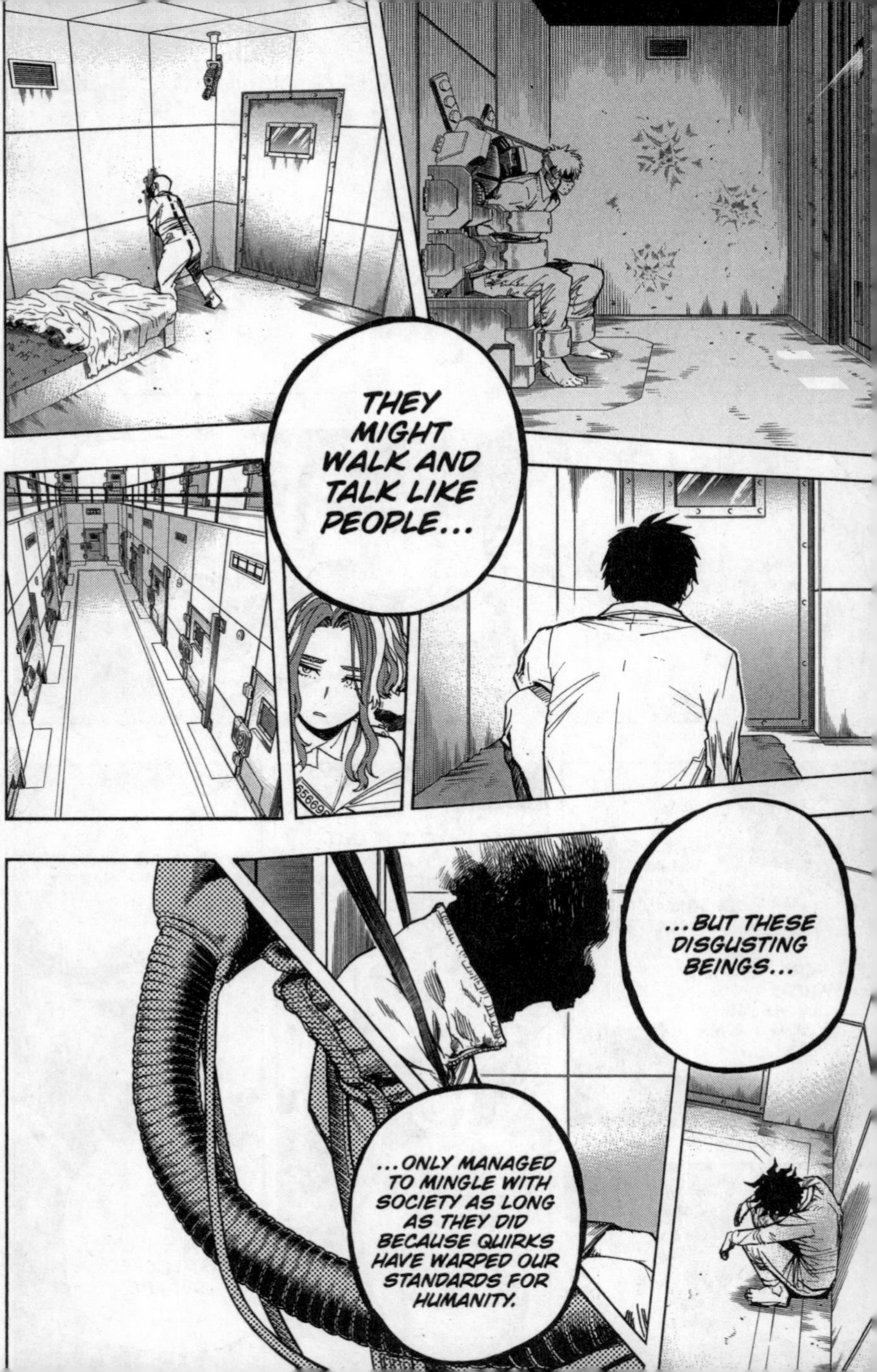
THEY MIGHT WALK AND TALK LIKE PEOPLE...
...BUT THESE DISGUSTING BEINGS...
...ONLY MANAGED TO MINGLE WITH SOCIETY AS LONG AS THEY DID BECAUSE QUIRKS HAVE WARPED OUR STANDARDS FOR HUMANITY.

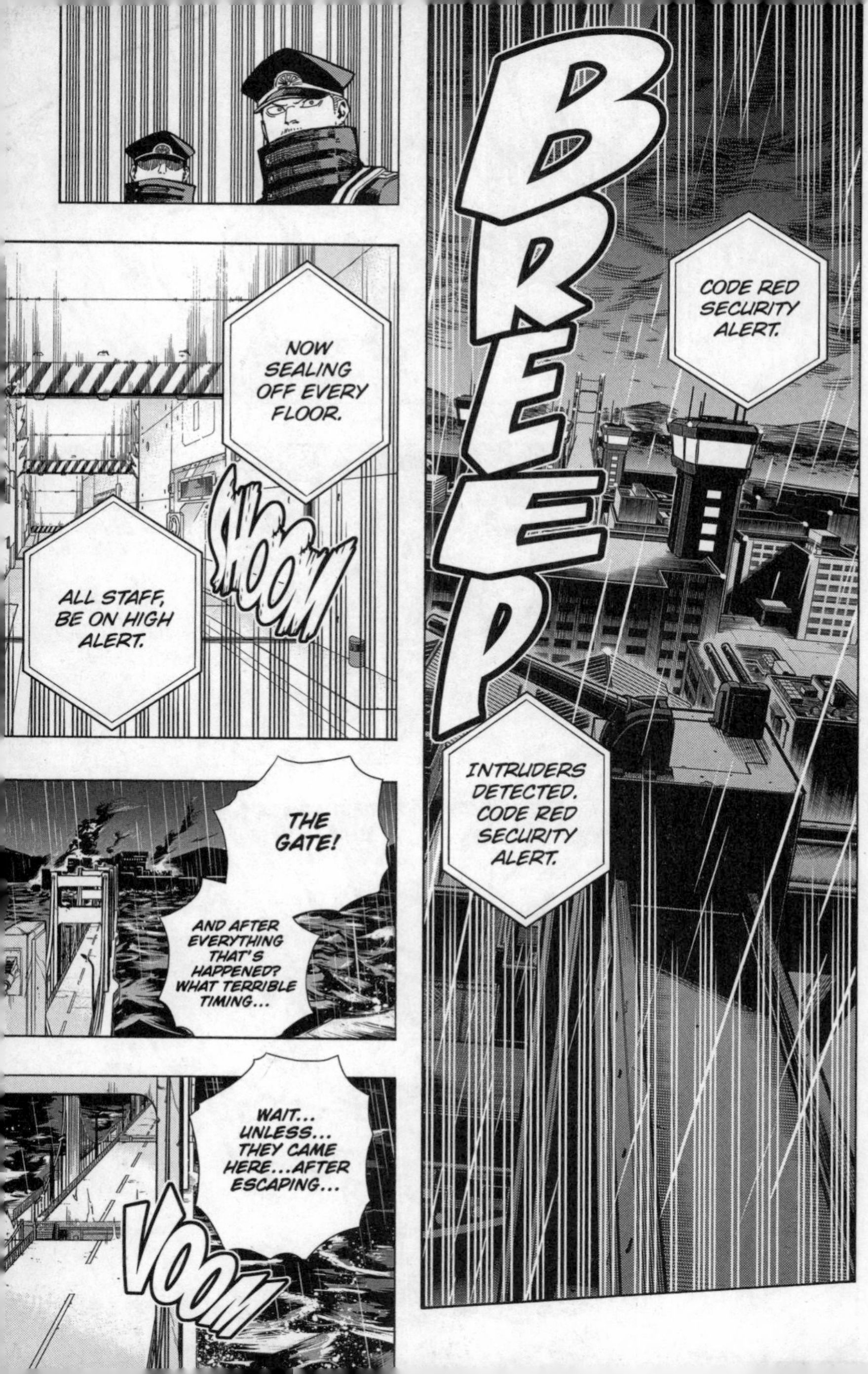
BREEP
CODE RED SECURITY ALERT.
INTRUDERS DETECTED. CODE RED SECURITY ALERT.
NOW SEALING OFF EVERY FLOOR.
SHOOM
ALL STAFF, BE ON HIGH ALERT.
THE GATE!
AND AFTER EVERYTHING THAT'S HAPPENED? WHAT TERRIBLE TIMING...
WAIT... UNLESS... THEY CAME HERE...AFTER ESCAPING...
VOOM

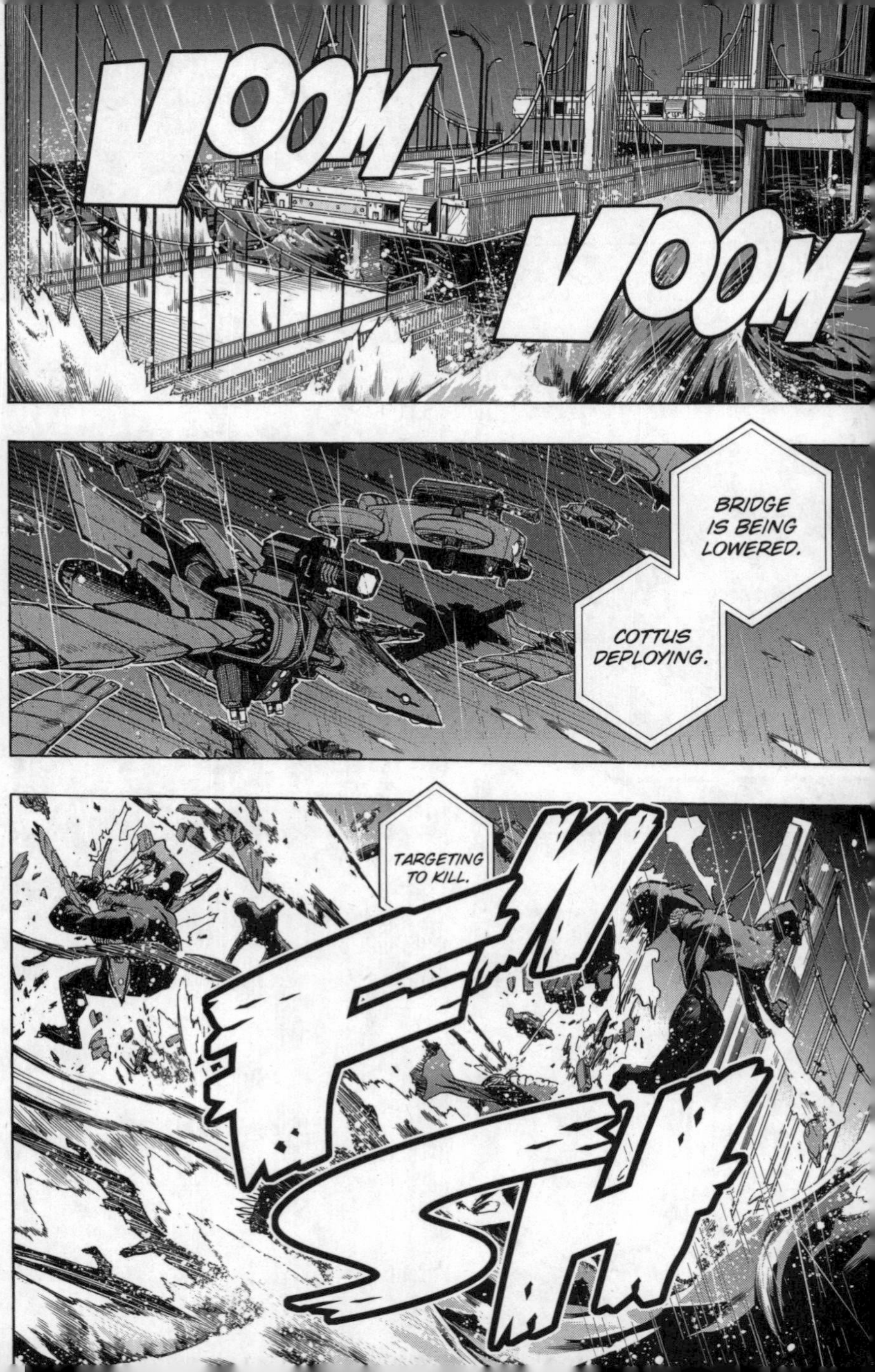
VOOM
VOOM
BRIDGE IS BEING LOWERED.
COTTUS DEPLOYING.
TARGETING TO KILL.
FWSH

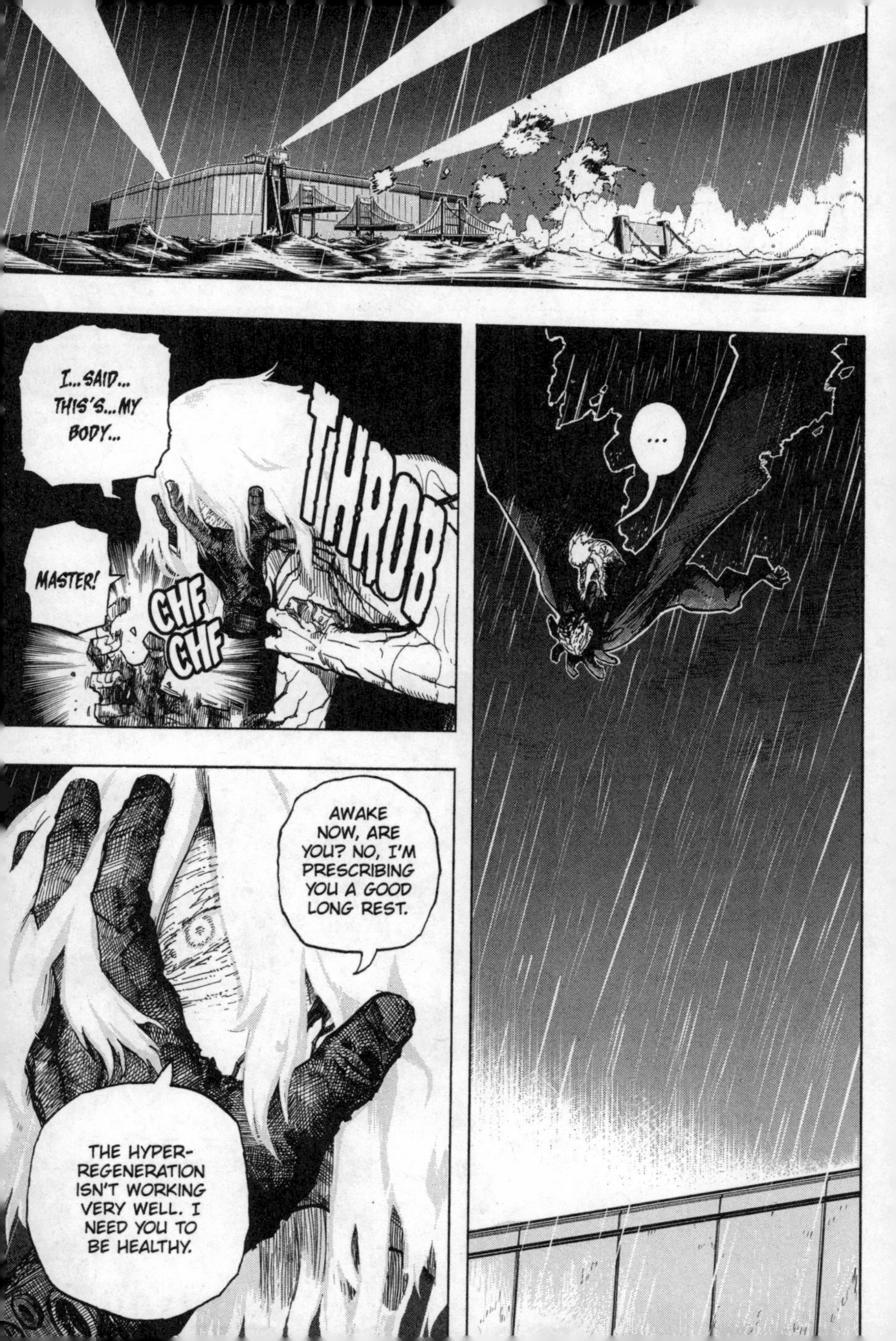
...
I... SAID... THIS'S... MY BODY...
THROB
MASTER!
CHF CHF
AWAKE NOW, ARE YOU? NO, I'M PRESCRIBING YOU A GOOD LONG REST.
THE HYPER-REGENERATION ISN'T WORKING VERY WELL. I NEED YOU TO BE HEALTHY.

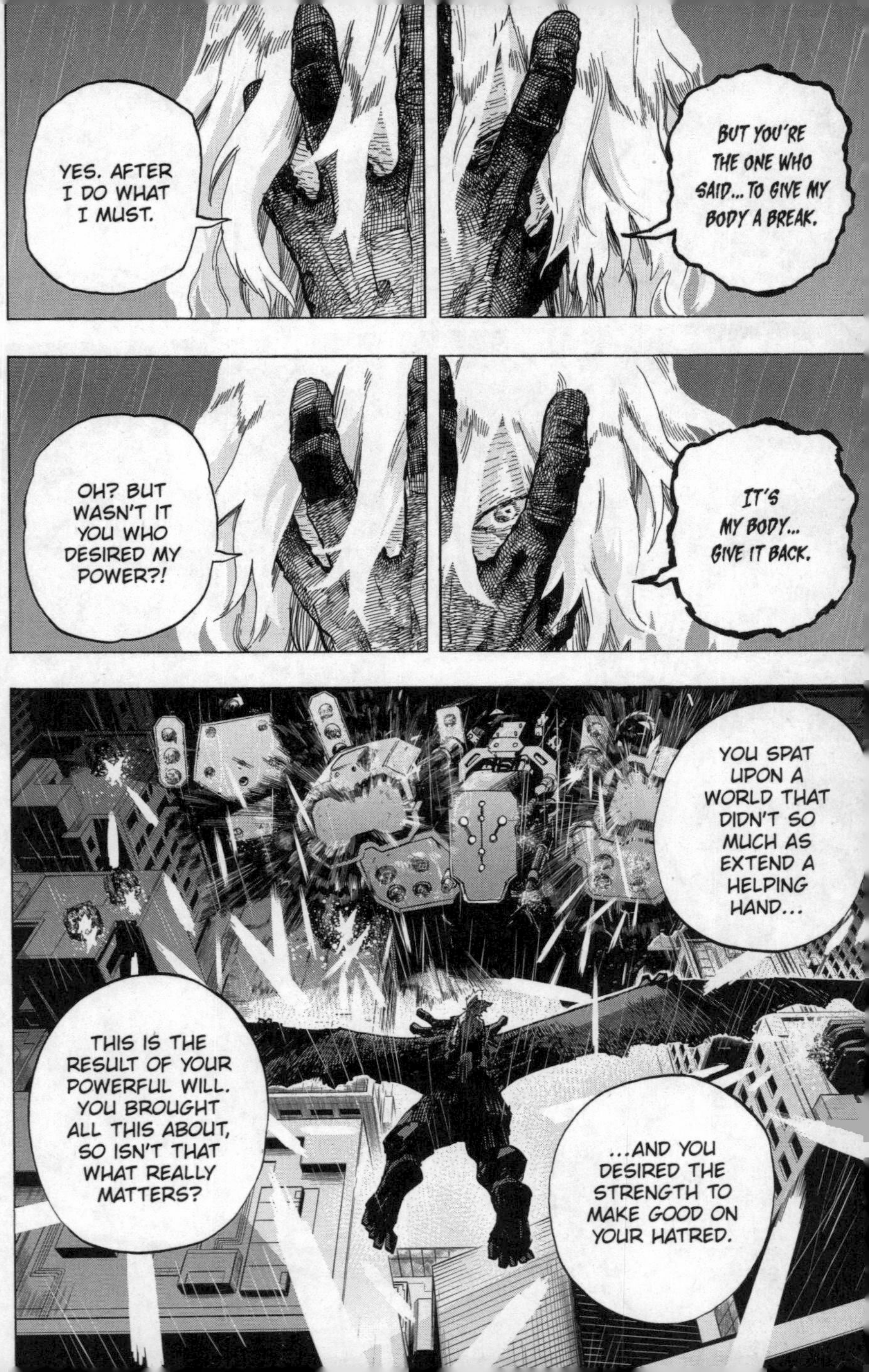

BUT YOU'RE THE ONE WHO SAID... TO GIVE MY BODY A BREAK.
YES. AFTER I DO WHAT I MUST.
IT'S MY BODY... GIVE IT BACK.
OH? BUT WASN'T IT YOU WHO DESIRED MY POWER?!
YOU SPAT UPON A WORLD THAT DIDN'T SO MUCH AS EXTEND A HELPING HAND...
...AND YOU DESIRED THE STRENGTH TO MAKE GOOD ON YOUR HATRED.
THIS IS THE RESULT OF YOUR POWERFUL WILL. YOU BROUGHT ALL THIS ABOUT, SO ISN'T THAT WHAT REALLY MATTERS?

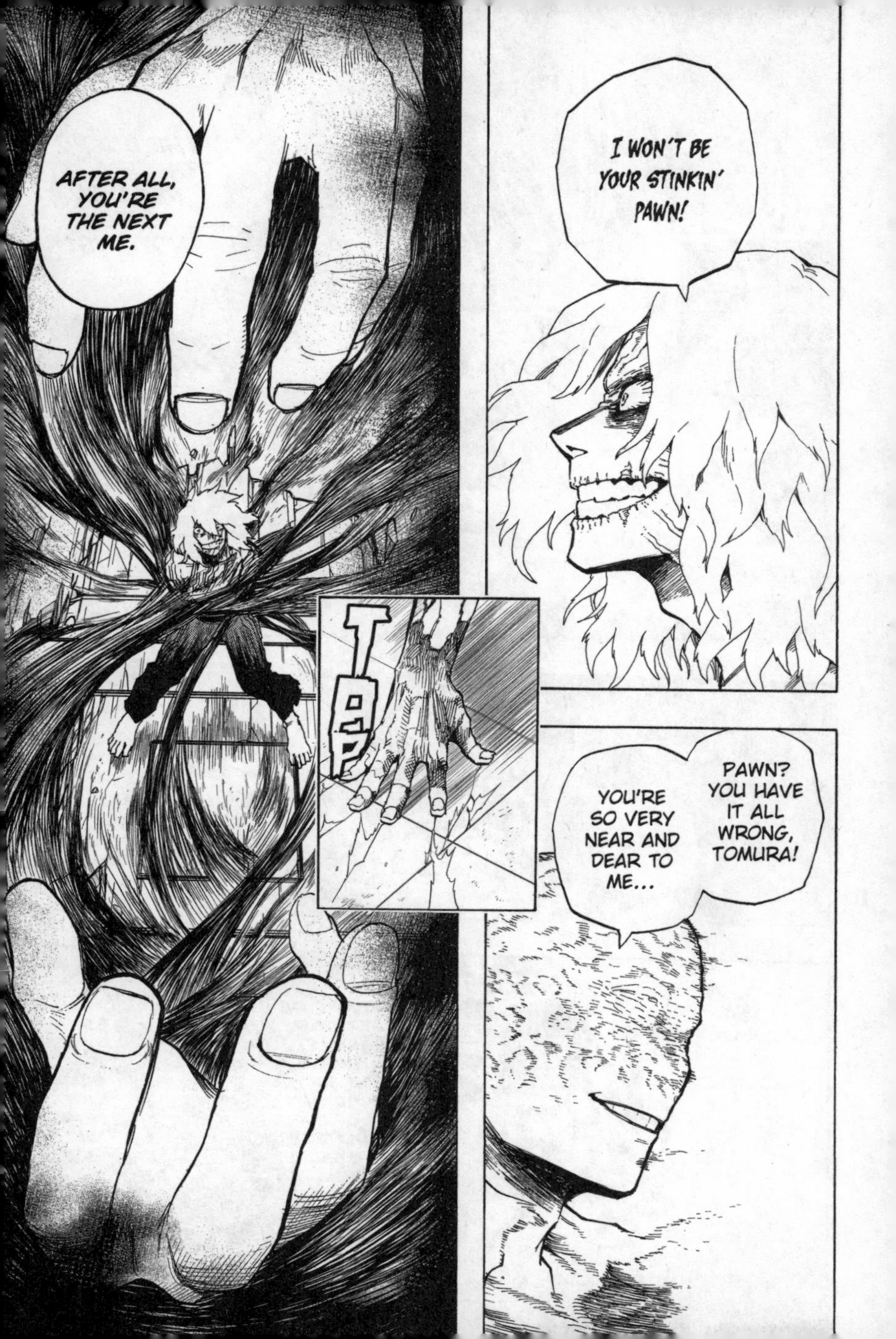
I WON'T BE YOUR STINKIN' PAWN!
PAWN? YOU HAVE IT ALL WRONG, TOMURA!
YOU'RE SO VERY NEAR AND DEAR TO ME...
TAP
AFTER ALL, YOU'RE THE NEXT ME.

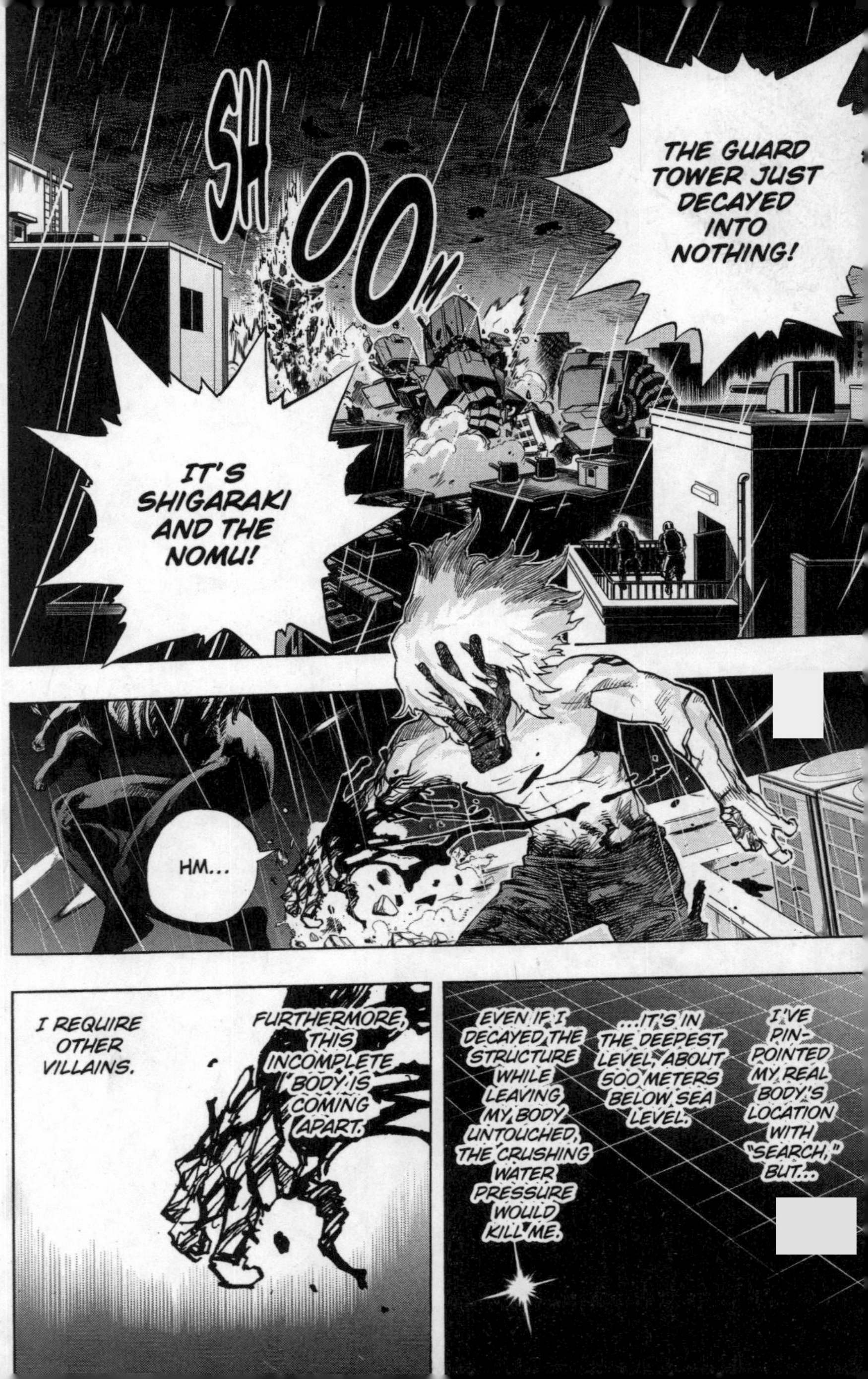
THE GUARD TOWER JUST DECAYED INTO NOTHING!
SHOOM
IT'S SHIGARAKI AND THE NOMU!
HM...
I'VE PIN-POINTED MY REAL BODY'S LOCATION WITH "SEARCH," BUT...
...IT'S IN THE DEEPEST LEVEL, ABOUT 500 METERS BELOW SEA LEVEL.
EVEN IF I DECAYED THE STRUCTURE WHILE LEAVING MY BODY UNTOUCHED, THE CRUSHING WATER PRESSURE WOULD KILL ME.
FURTHERMORE, THIS INCOMPLETE BODY IS COMING APART.
I REQUIRE OTHER VILLAINS.

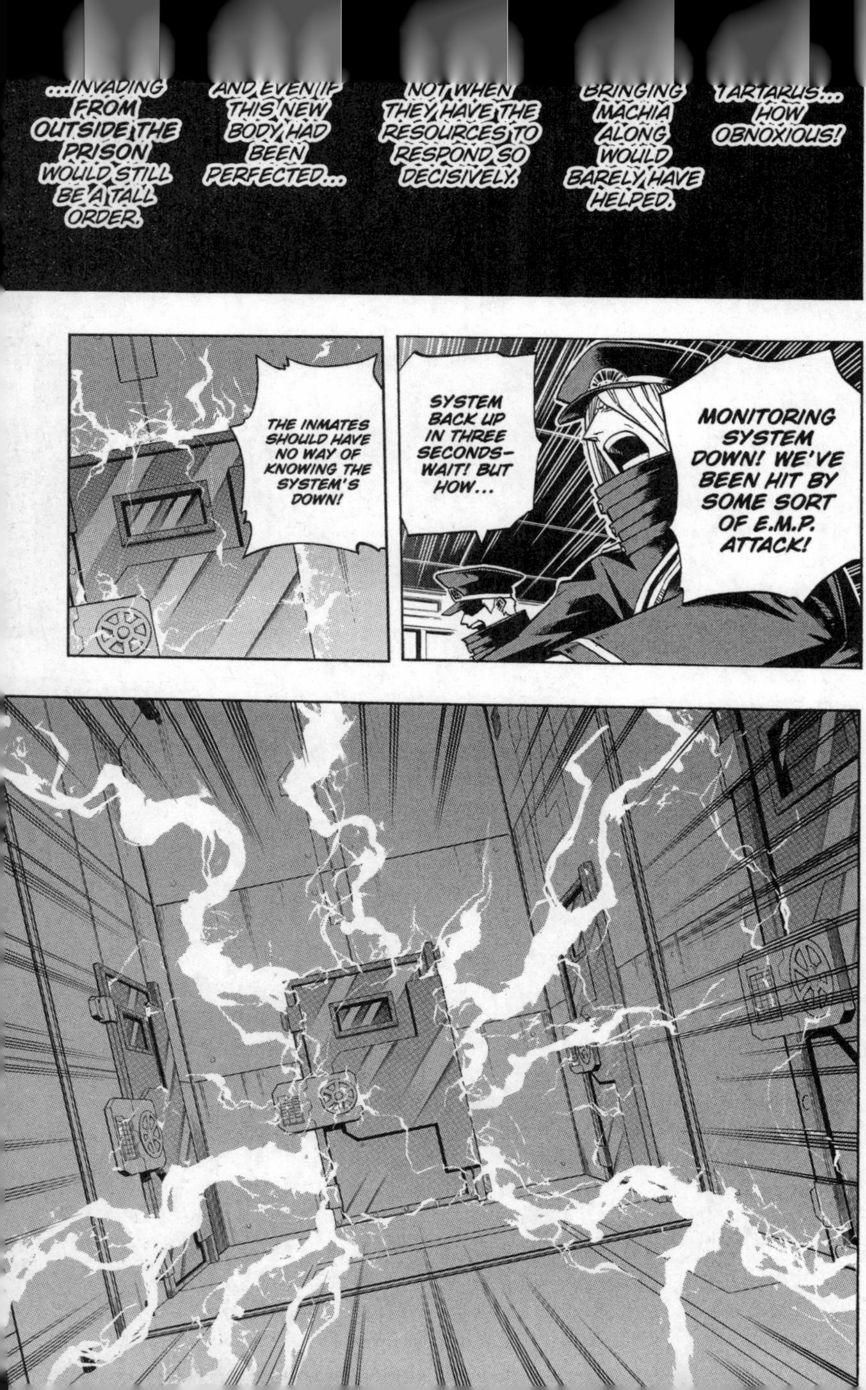
TARTARUS... HOW OBNOXIOUS!
BRINGING MACHIA ALONG WOULD BARELY HAVE HELPED.
NOT WHEN THEY HAVE THE RESOURCES TO RESPOND SO DECISIVELY.
AND EVEN IF THIS NEW BODY HAD BEEN PERFECTED...
...INVADING FROM OUTSIDE THE PRISON WOULD STILL BE A TALL ORDER.
MONITORING SYSTEM DOWN! WE'VE BEEN HIT BY SOME SORT OF E.M.P. ATTACK!
SYSTEM BACK UP IN THREE SECONDS- WAIT! BUT HOW...
THE INMATES SHOULD HAVE NO WAY OF KNOWING THE SYSTEM'S DOWN!

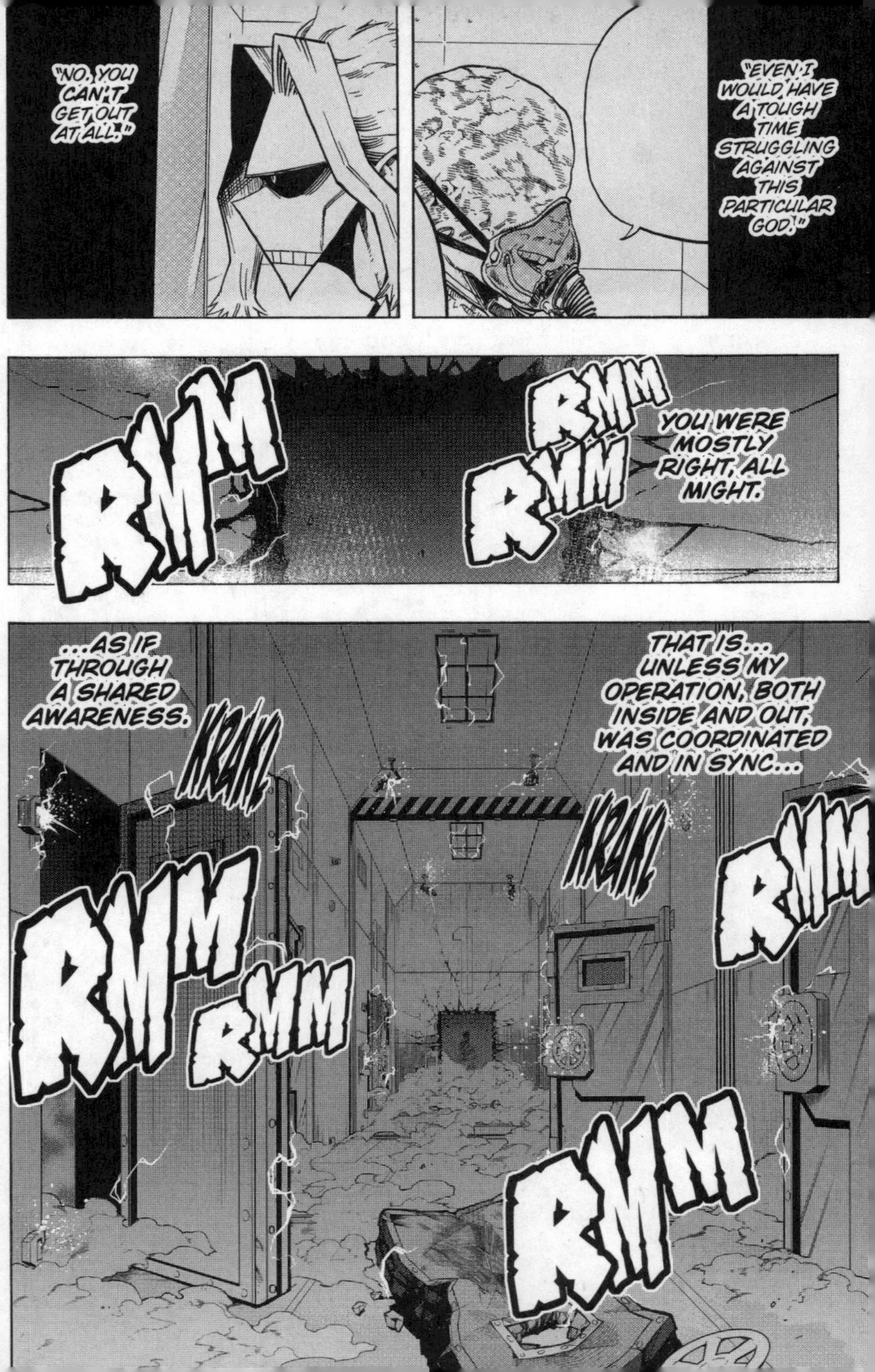
"EVEN I WOULD HAVE A TOUGH TIME STRUGGLING AGAINST THIS PARTICULAR GOD."
"NO, YOU CAN'T GET OUT AT ALL."
YOU WERE MOSTLY RIGHT, ALL MIGHT.
RMM RMM
RMM
THAT IS... UNLESS MY OPERATION, BOTH INSIDE AND OUT, WAS COORDINATED AND IN SYNC...
...AS IF THROUGH A SHARED AWARENESS.
RMM
KRAK!
KRAK!
RMM RMM
RMM

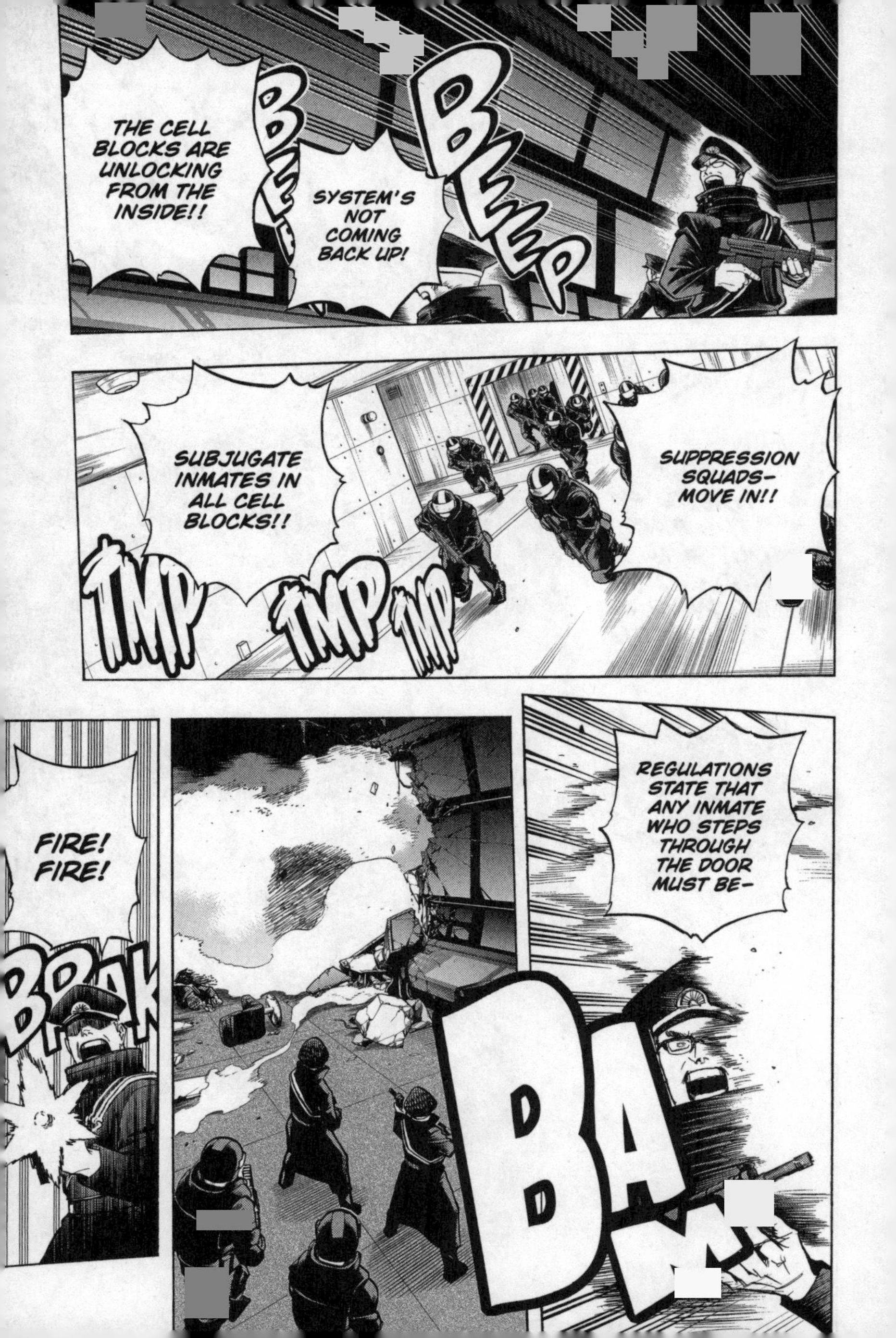
BLEEP
SYSTEM'S NOT COMING BACK UP!
THE CELL BLOCKS ARE UNLOCKING FROM THE INSIDE!!
SUPPRESSION SQUADS-MOVE IN!!
SUBJUGATE INMATES IN ALL CELL BLOCKS!!
TMP TMP TMP
REGULATIONS STATE THAT ANY INMATE WHO STEPS THROUGH THE DOOR MUST BE-
BA
FIRE! FIRE!
BRAK

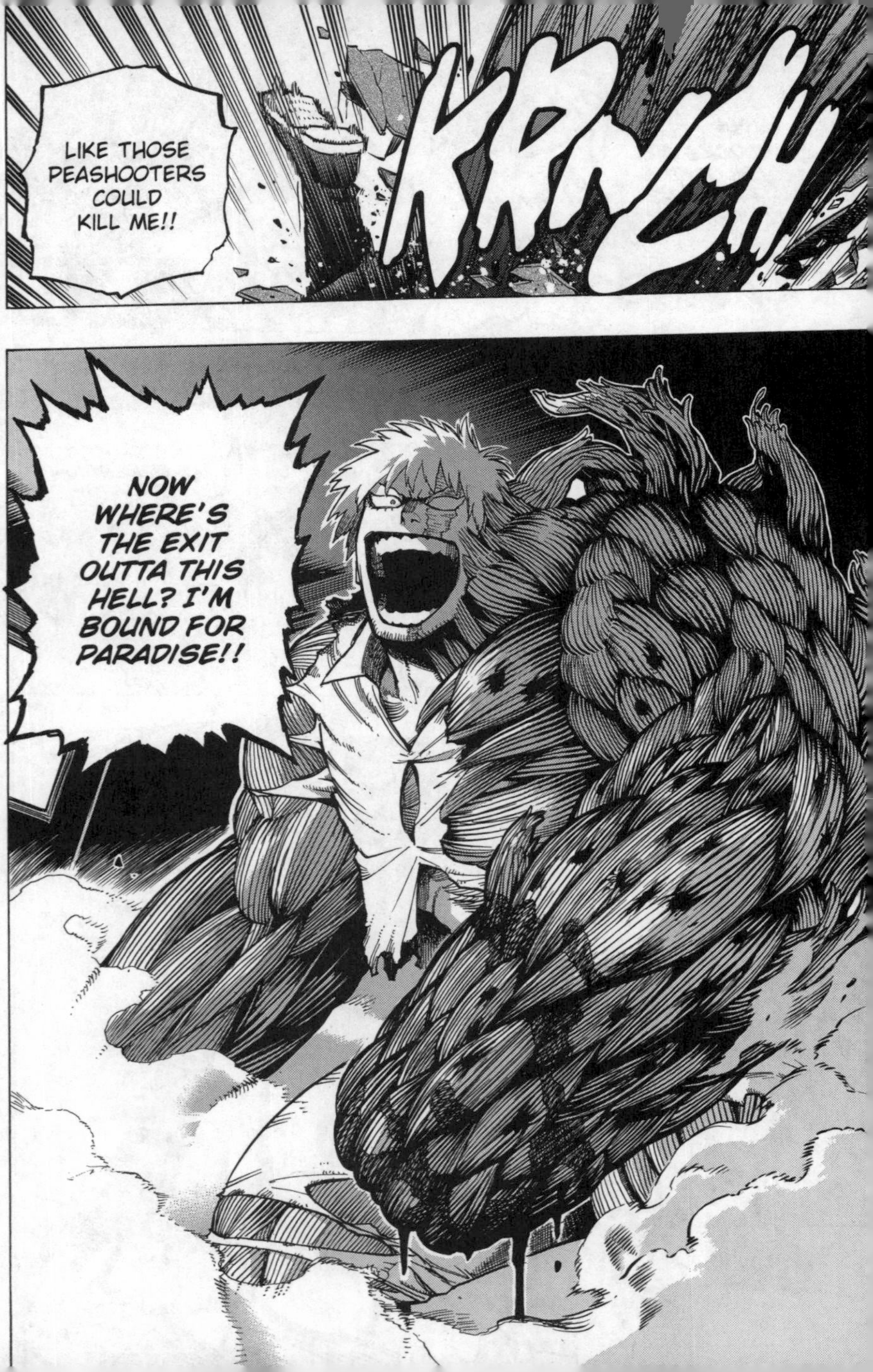
KRNCH
LIKE THOSE PEASHOOTERS COULD KILL ME!!
NOW WHERE'S THE EXIT OUTTA THIS HELL? I'M BOUND FOR PARADISE!!

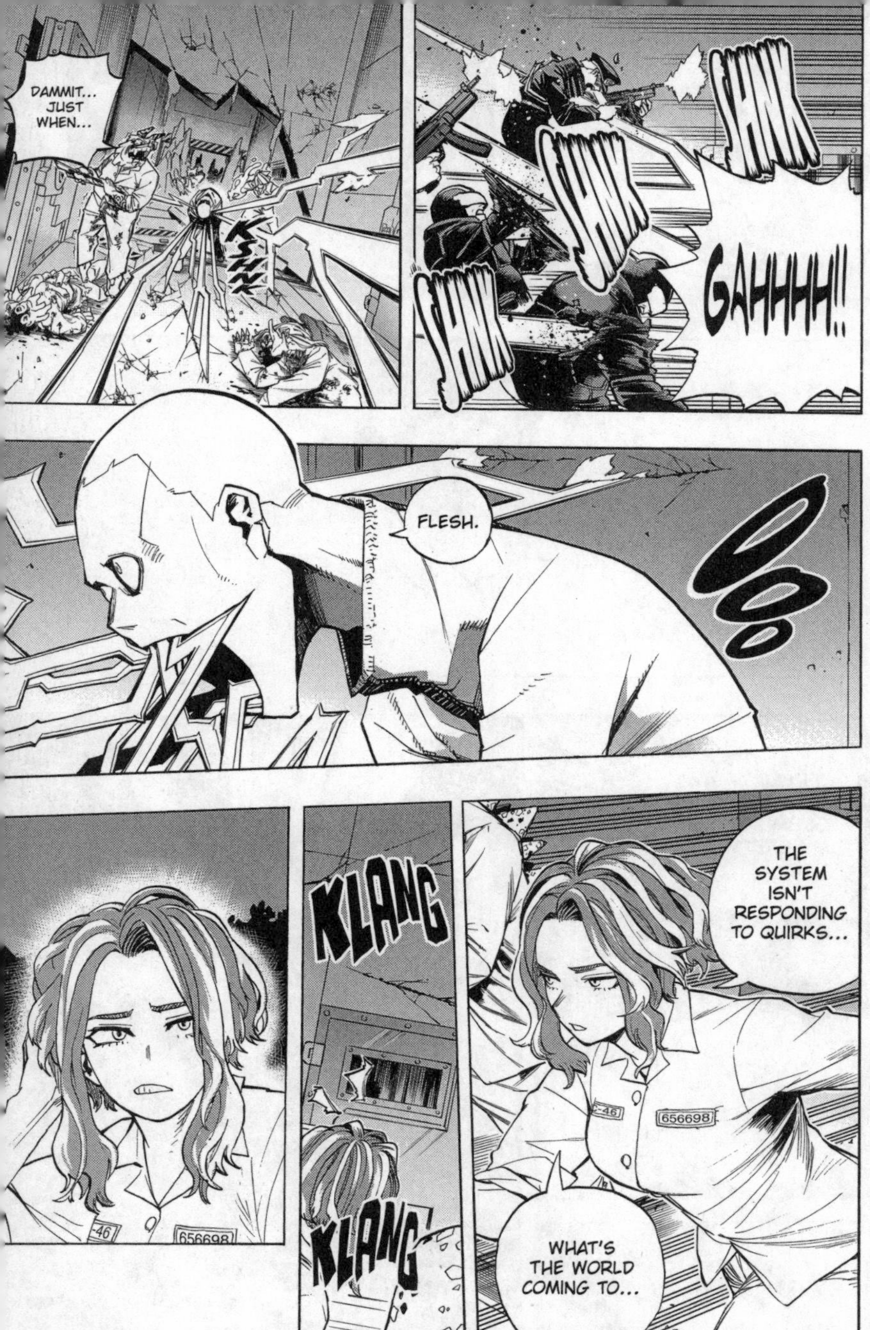
SHANK
SHANK
SHANK
GAHHHH!!
DAMMIT... JUST WHEN...
KSHNK
FLESH.
OOO
THE SYSTEM ISN'T RESPONDING TO QUIRKS...
656698
WHAT'S THE WORLD COMING TO...
KLANG
KLANG
656698

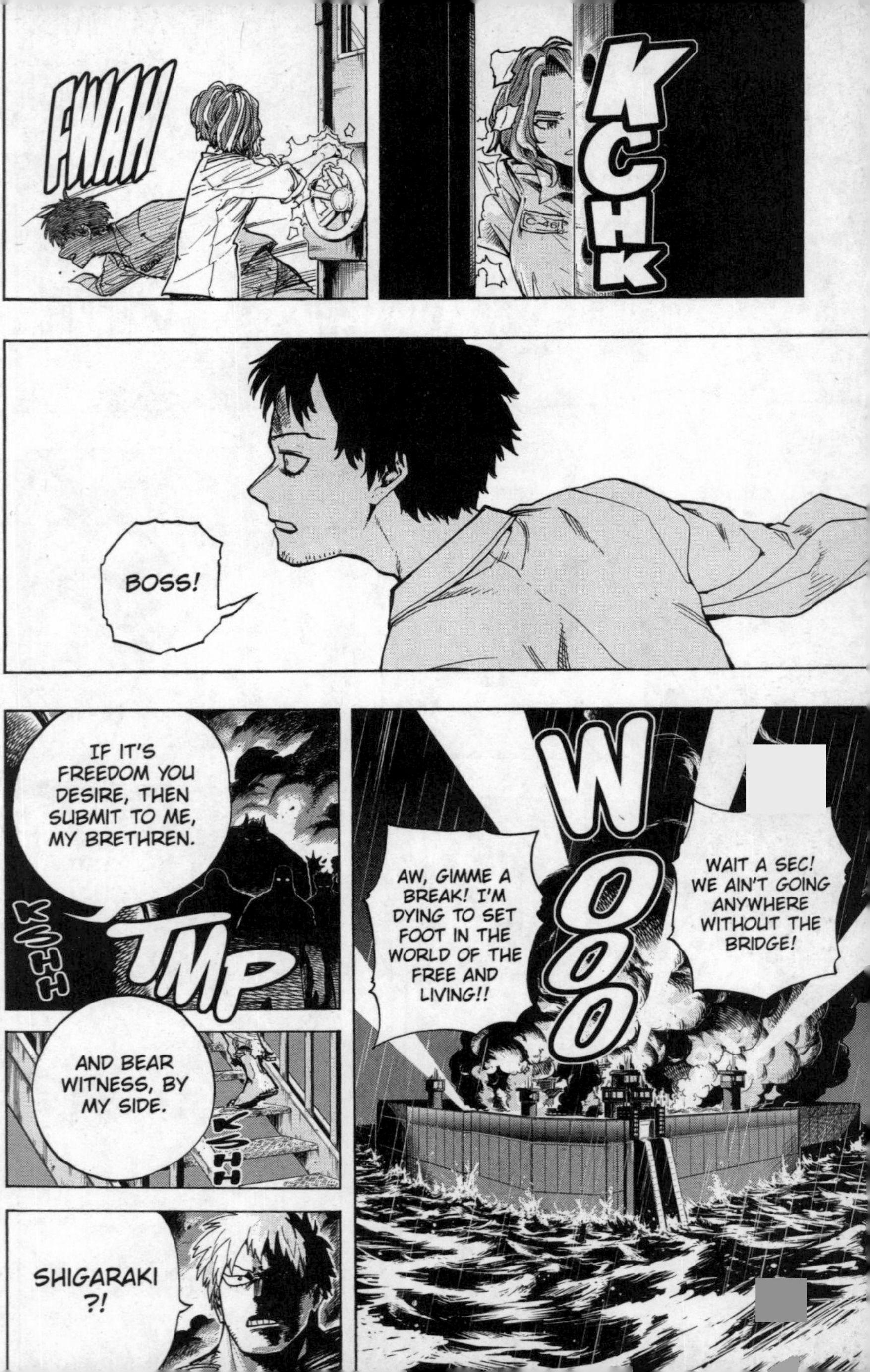
KCHK
FWAH
BOSS!
WOOO
WAIT A SEC! WE AIN'T GOING ANYWHERE WITHOUT THE BRIDGE!
AW, GIMME A BREAK! I'M DYING TO SET FOOT IN THE WORLD OF THE FREE AND LIVING!!
IF IT'S FREEDOM YOU DESIRE, THEN SUBMIT TO ME, MY BRETHREN.
KSHH
TMP
AND BEAR WITNESS, BY MY SIDE.
KSHH
SHIGARAKI ?!

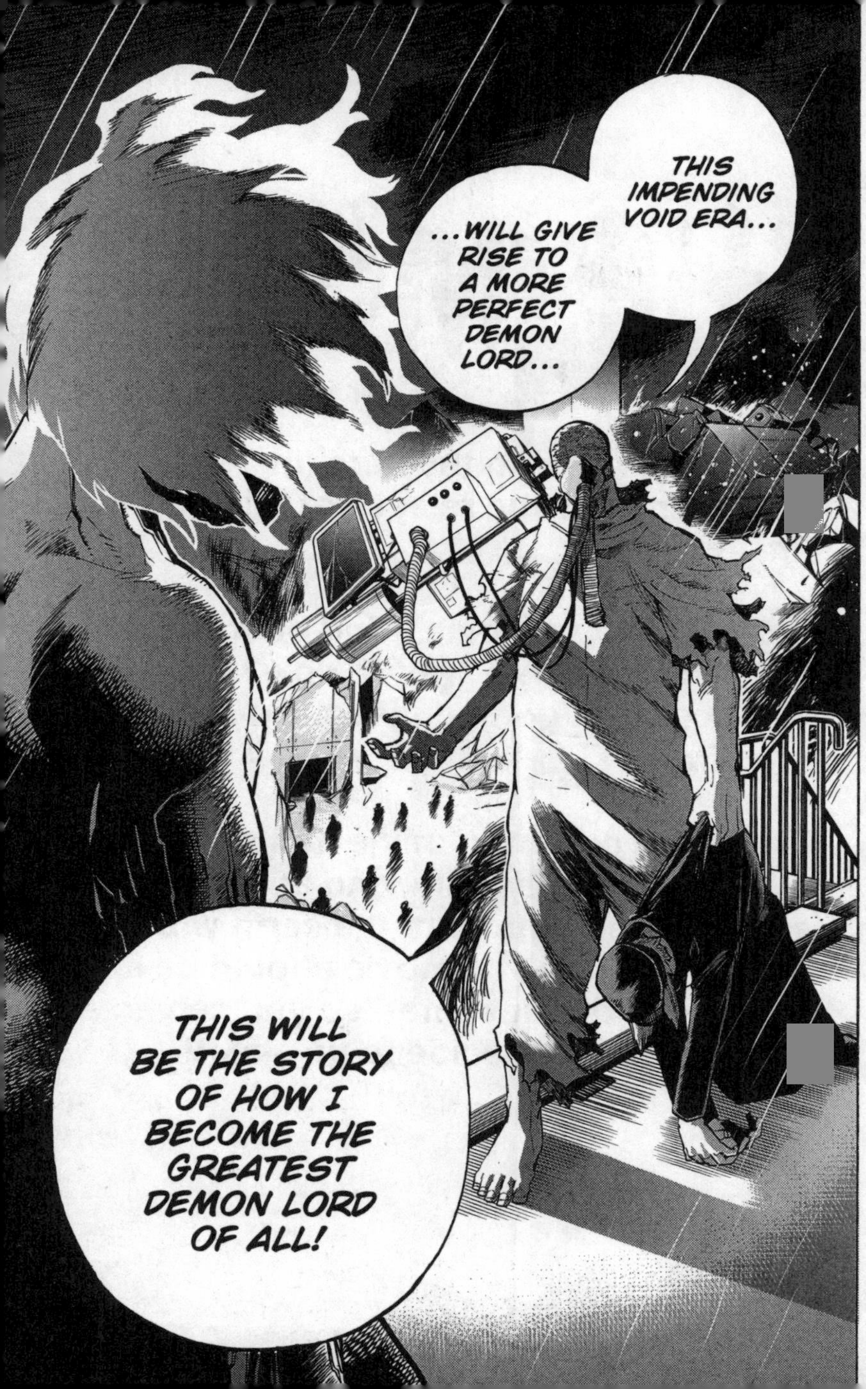
THIS IMPENDING VOID ERA...
...WILL GIVE RISE TO A MORE PERFECT DEMON LORD...
THIS WILL BE THE STORY OF HOW I BECOME THE GREATEST DEMON LORD OF ALL!

THE MOVIE

Movie #3 will be in theaters (in Japan) just in time for the release of this book (in Japan)!

Wow. The third movie. Kind of crazy, no? I keep asking, "How? How??" And yet there it is, getting made. I'm so grateful.

Unlike the current plotline in the manga (which is brutally grim, and as dark as a cave at the bottom of the earth with no light bulbs), this movie should be a cheery ray of sunshine—so you can rest easy if you decide to go see it!

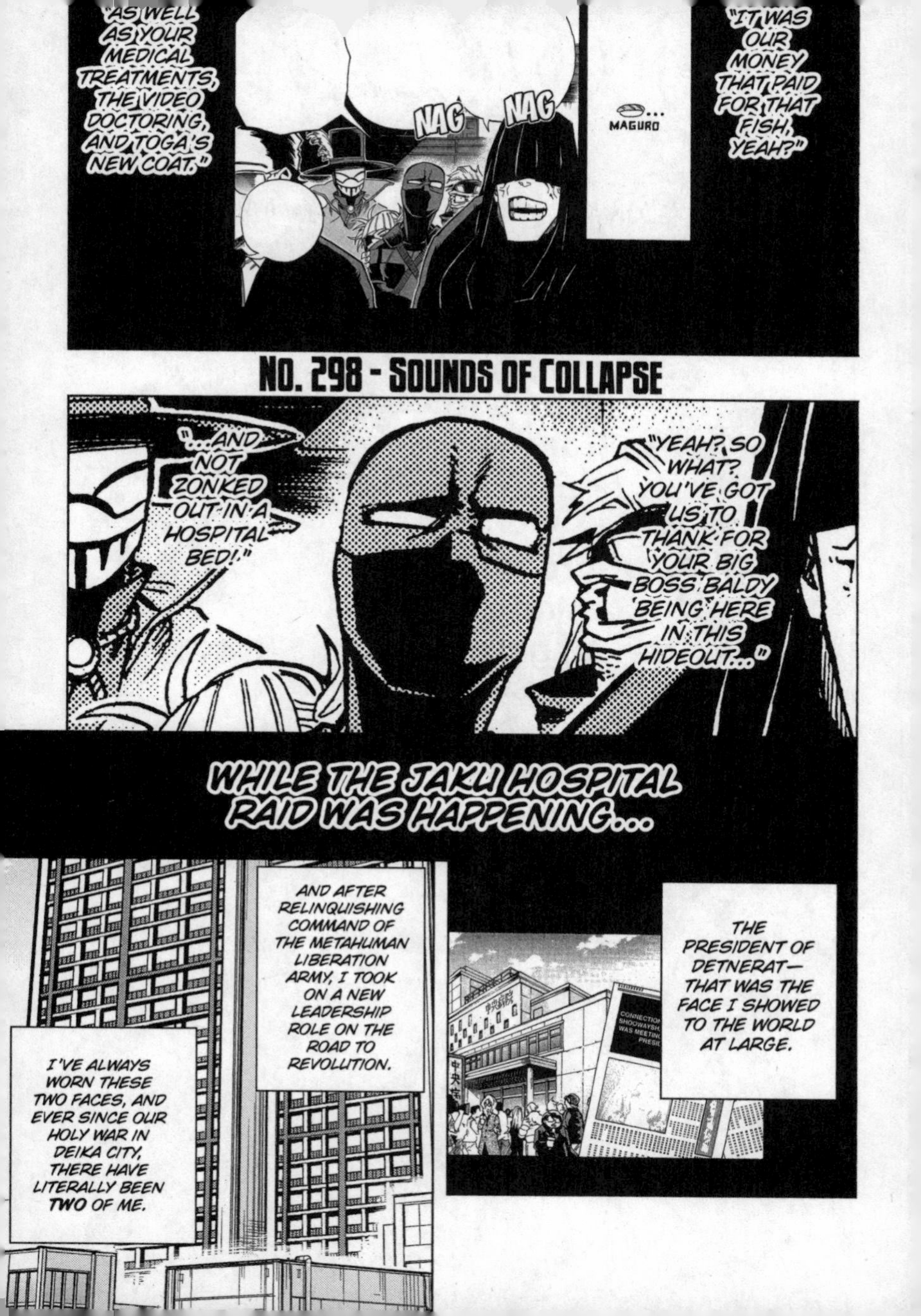
"IT WAS OUR MONEY THAT PAID FOR THAT FISH, YEAH?"
...
MAGURO
NAG NAG
"AS WELL AS YOUR MEDICAL TREATMENTS, THE VIDEO DOCTORING, AND TOGA'S NEW COAT."
No. 298 - Sounds of Collapse
"YEAH? SO WHAT? YOU'VE GOT US TO THANK FOR YOUR BIG BOSS BALDY BEING HERE IN THIS HIDEOUT..."
"...AND NOT ZONKED OUT IN A HOSPITAL BED!"
WHILE THE JAKU HOSPITAL RAID WAS HAPPENING...
THE PRESIDENT OF DETNERAT—THAT WAS THE FACE I SHOWED TO THE WORLD AT LARGE.
AND AFTER RELINQUISHING COMMAND OF THE METAHUMAN LIBERATION ARMY, I TOOK ON A NEW LEADERSHIP ROLE ON THE ROAD TO REVOLUTION.
I'VE ALWAYS WORN THESE TWO FACES, AND EVER SINCE OUR HOLY WAR IN DEIKA CITY, THERE HAVE LITERALLY BEEN TWO OF ME.

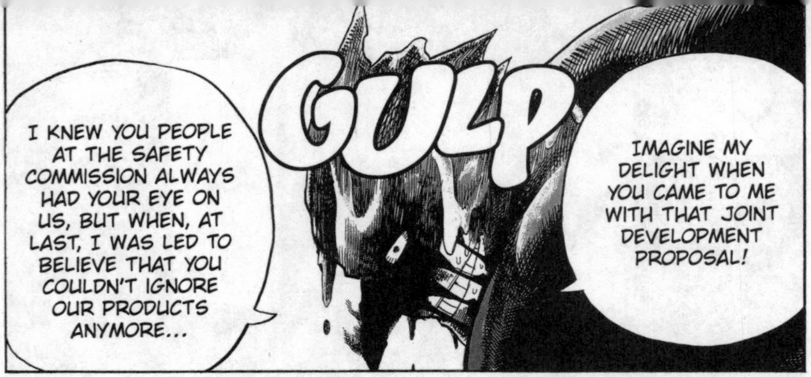
GULP
IMAGINE MY DELIGHT WHEN YOU CAME TO ME WITH THAT JOINT DEVELOPMENT PROPOSAL!
I KNEW YOU PEOPLE AT THE SAFETY COMMISSION ALWAYS HAD YOUR EYE ON US, BUT WHEN, AT LAST, I WAS LED TO BELIEVE THAT YOU COULDN'T IGNORE OUR PRODUCTS ANYMORE...

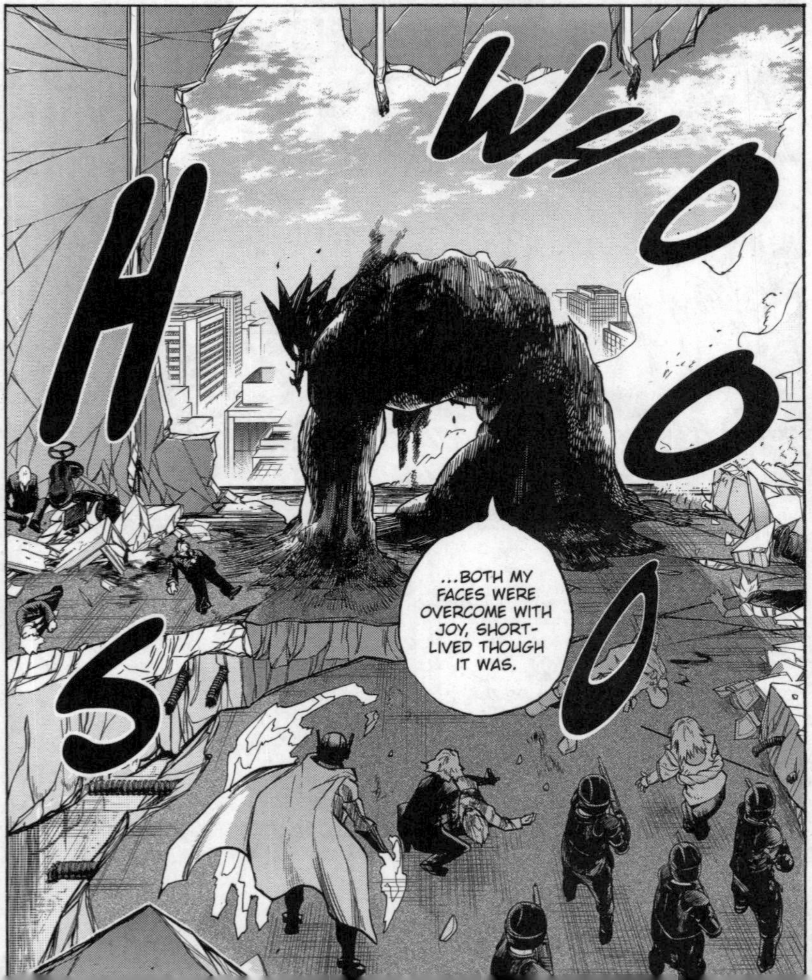
WHOOOO
HS
...BOTH MY FACES WERE OVERCOME WITH JOY, SHORT-LIVED THOUGH IT WAS.

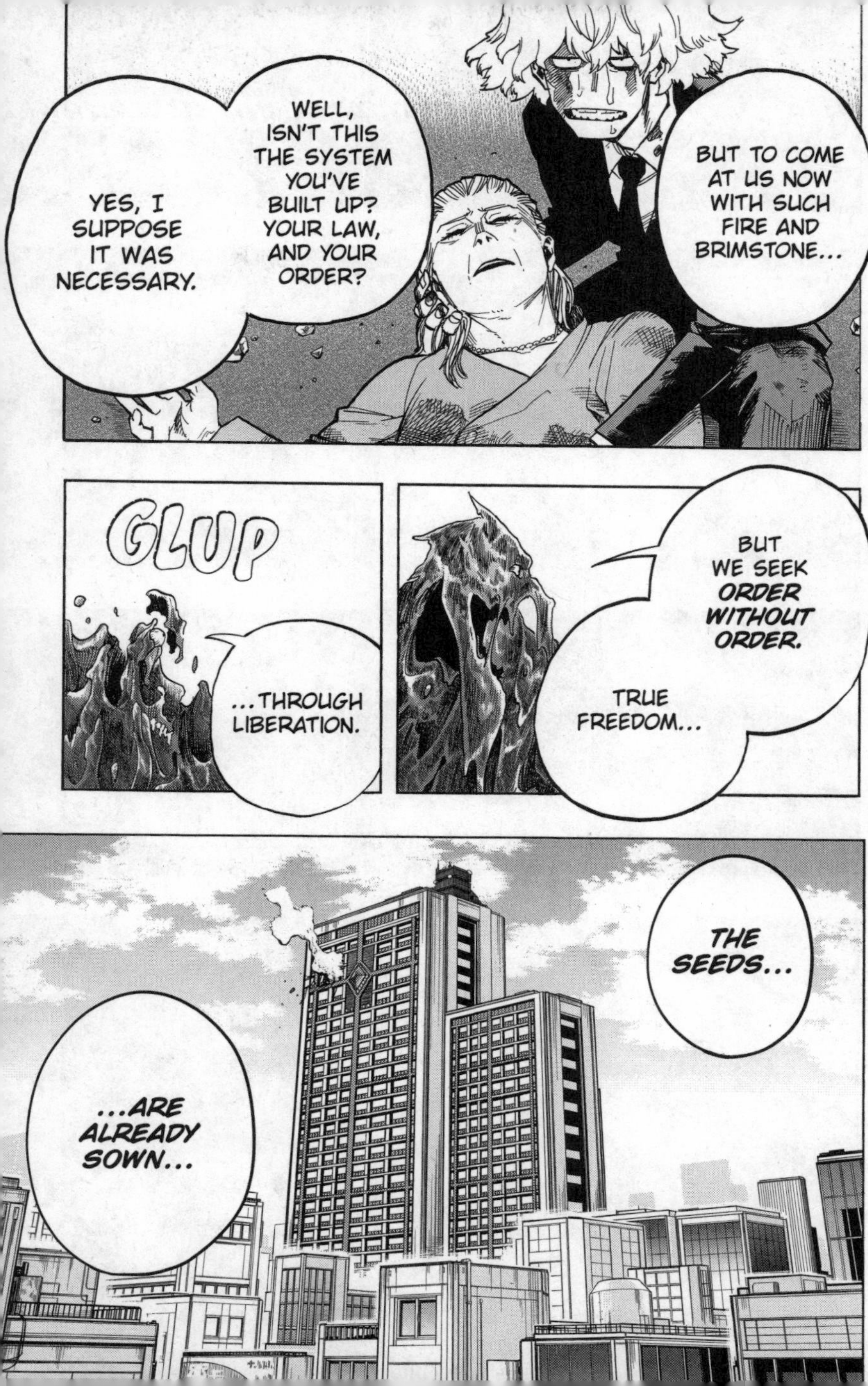
BUT TO COME AT US NOW WITH SUCH FIRE AND BRIMSTONE...
WELL, ISN'T THIS THE SYSTEM YOU'VE BUILT UP? YOUR LAW, AND YOUR ORDER?
YES, I SUPPOSE IT WAS NECESSARY.
BUT WE SEEK ORDER WITHOUT ORDER.
TRUE FREEDOM...
GLUP
...THROUGH LIBERATION.
THE SEEDS...
...ARE ALREADY SOWN...

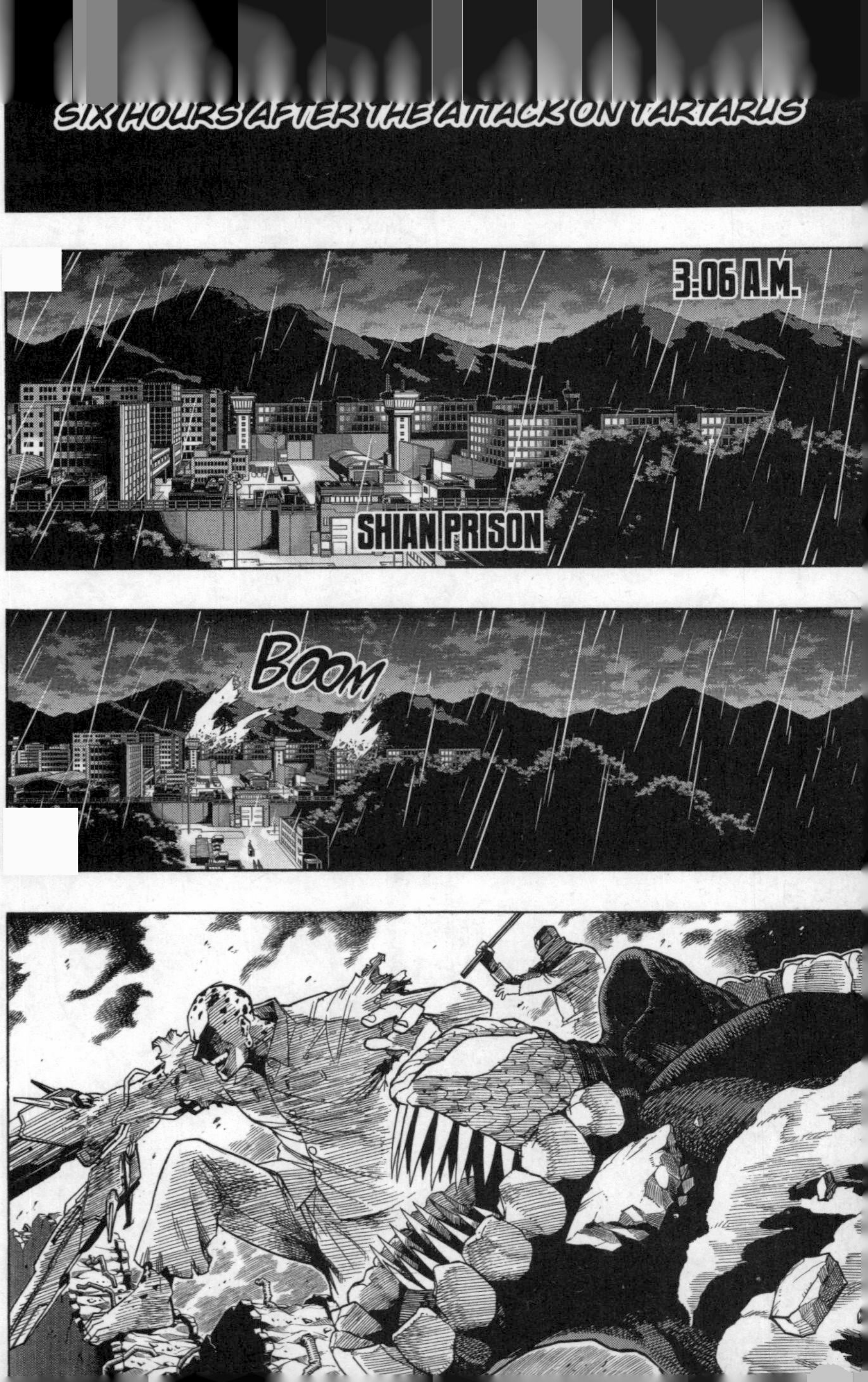
SIX HOURS AFTER THE ATTACK ON TARTARUS
3:06 A.M.
SHIAN PRISON
BOOM

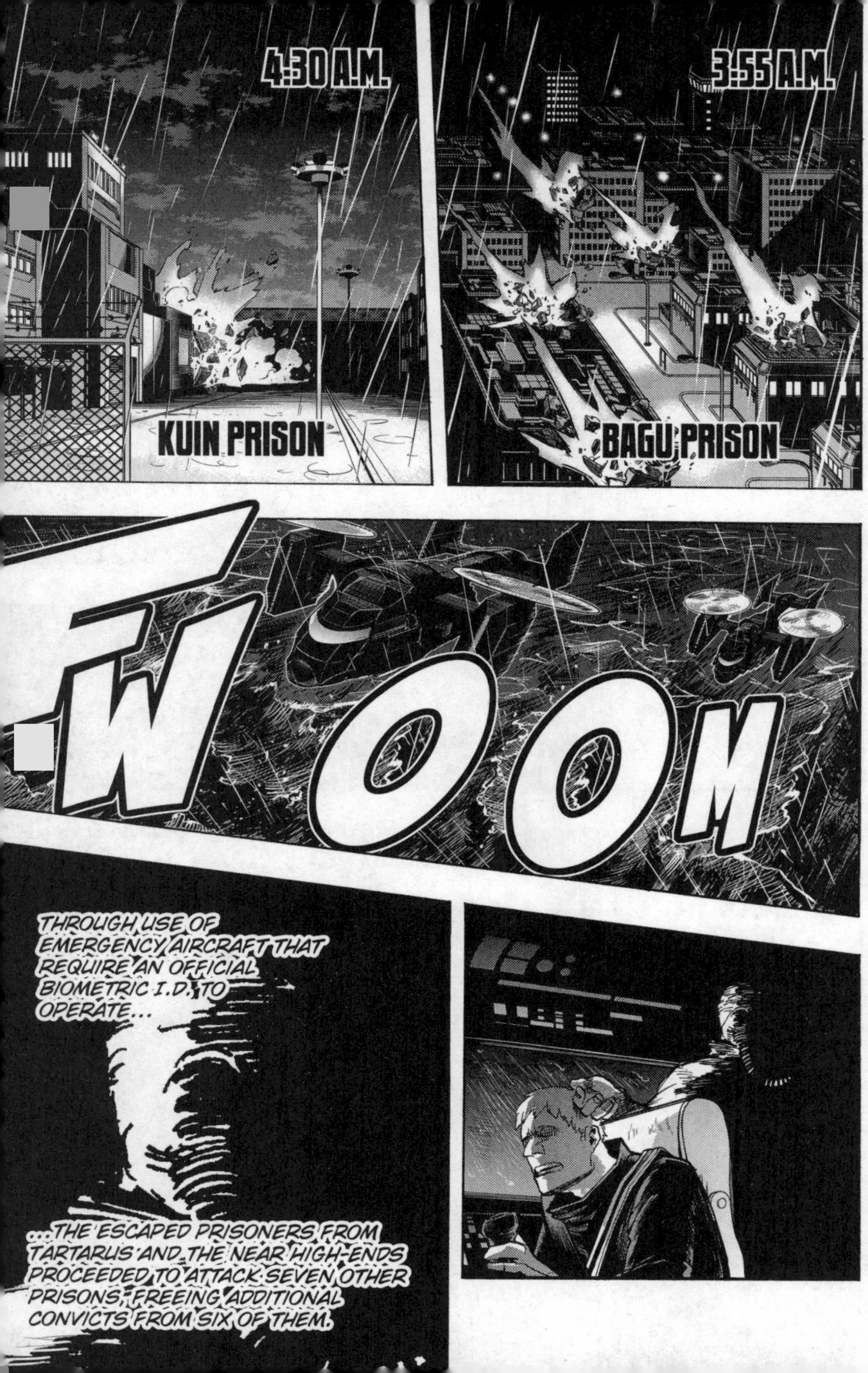
3:55 A.M.
BAGU PRISON
4:30 A.M.
KUIN PRISON
WOOM
THROUGH USE OF EMERGENCY AIRCRAFT THAT REQUIRE AN OFFICIAL BIOMETRIC I.D. TO OPERATE...
...THE ESCAPED PRISONERS FROM TARTARUS AND THE NEAR HIGH-ENDS PROCEEDED TO ATTACK SEVEN OTHER PRISONS, FREEING ADDITIONAL CONVICTS FROM SIX OF THEM.

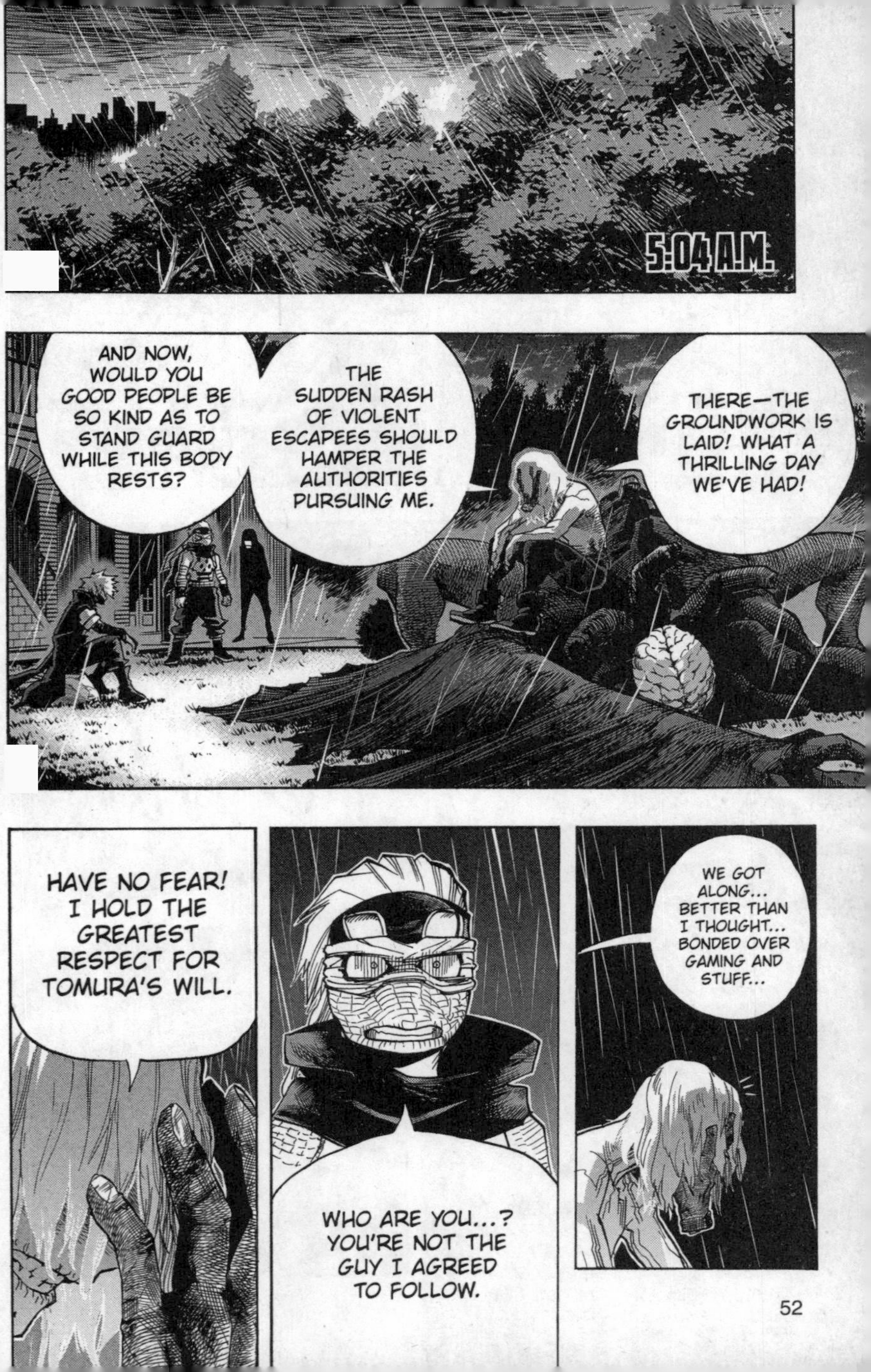
5:04 A.M.
THERE—THE GROUNDWORK IS LAID! WHAT A THRILLING DAY WE'VE HAD!
THE SUDDEN RASH OF VIOLENT ESCAPEES SHOULD HAMPER THE AUTHORITIES PURSUING ME.
AND NOW, WOULD YOU GOOD PEOPLE BE SO KIND AS TO STAND GUARD WHILE THIS BODY RESTS?
WE GOT ALONG... BETTER THAN I THOUGHT... BONDED OVER GAMING AND STUFF...
WHO ARE YOU...? YOU'RE NOT THE GUY I AGREED TO FOLLOW.
HAVE NO FEAR! I HOLD THE GREATEST RESPECT FOR TOMURA'S WILL.

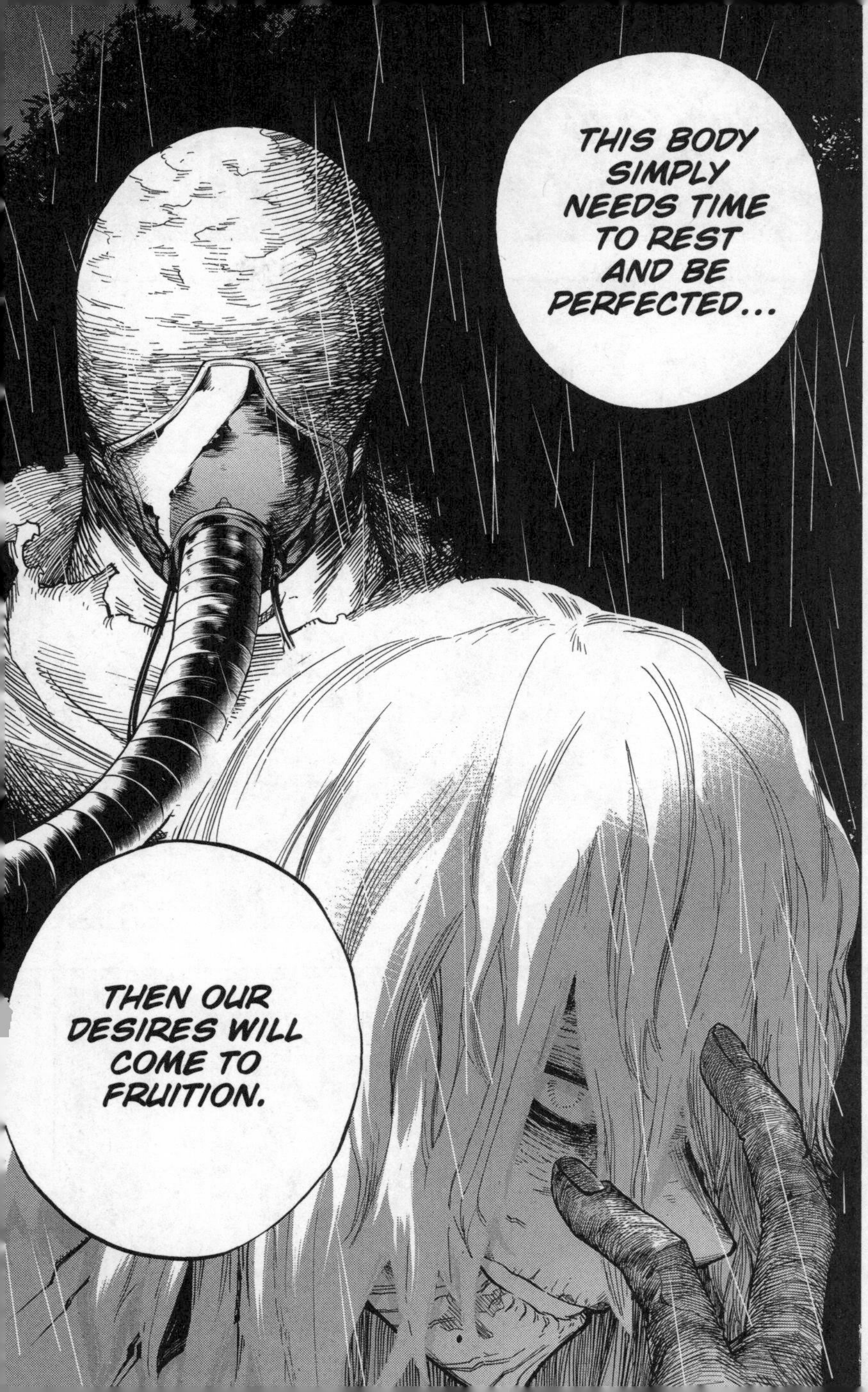
THIS BODY SIMPLY NEEDS TIME TO REST AND BE PERFECTED...
THEN OUR DESIRES WILL COME TO FRUITION.

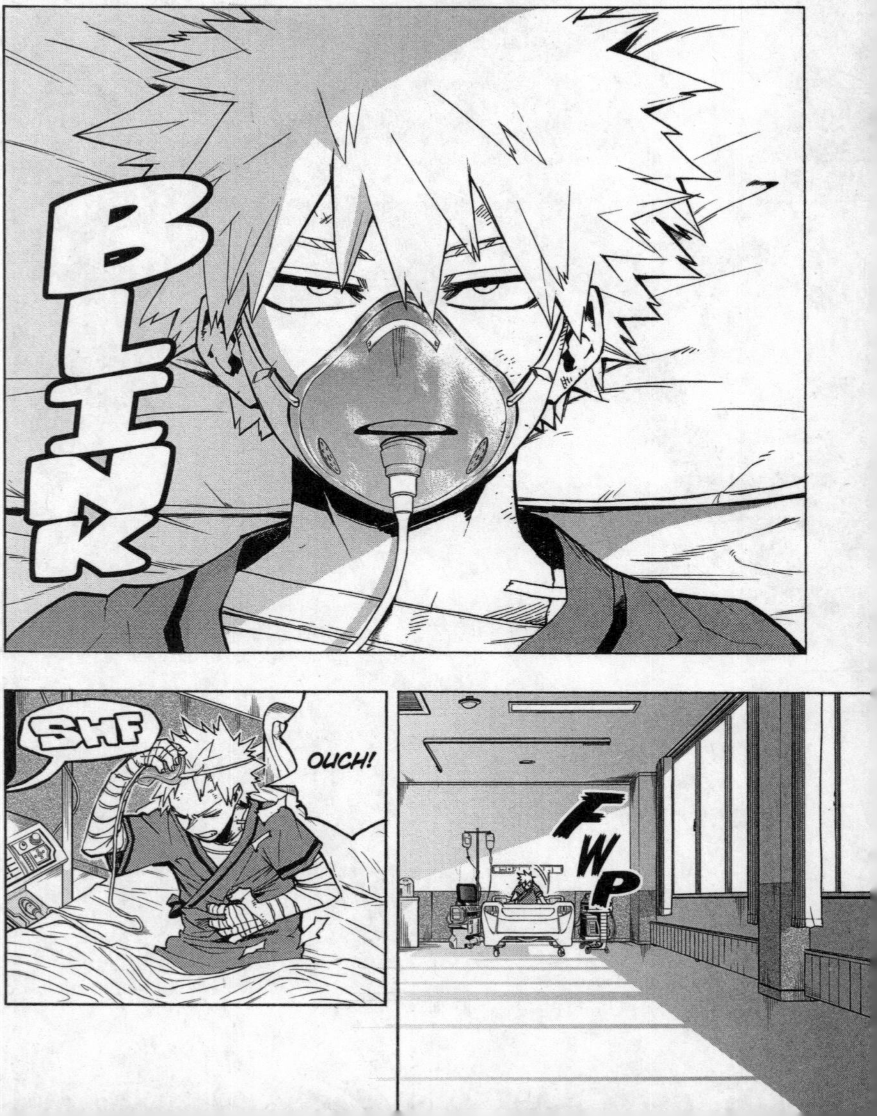
BLINK
FWP
SHF
OUCH!

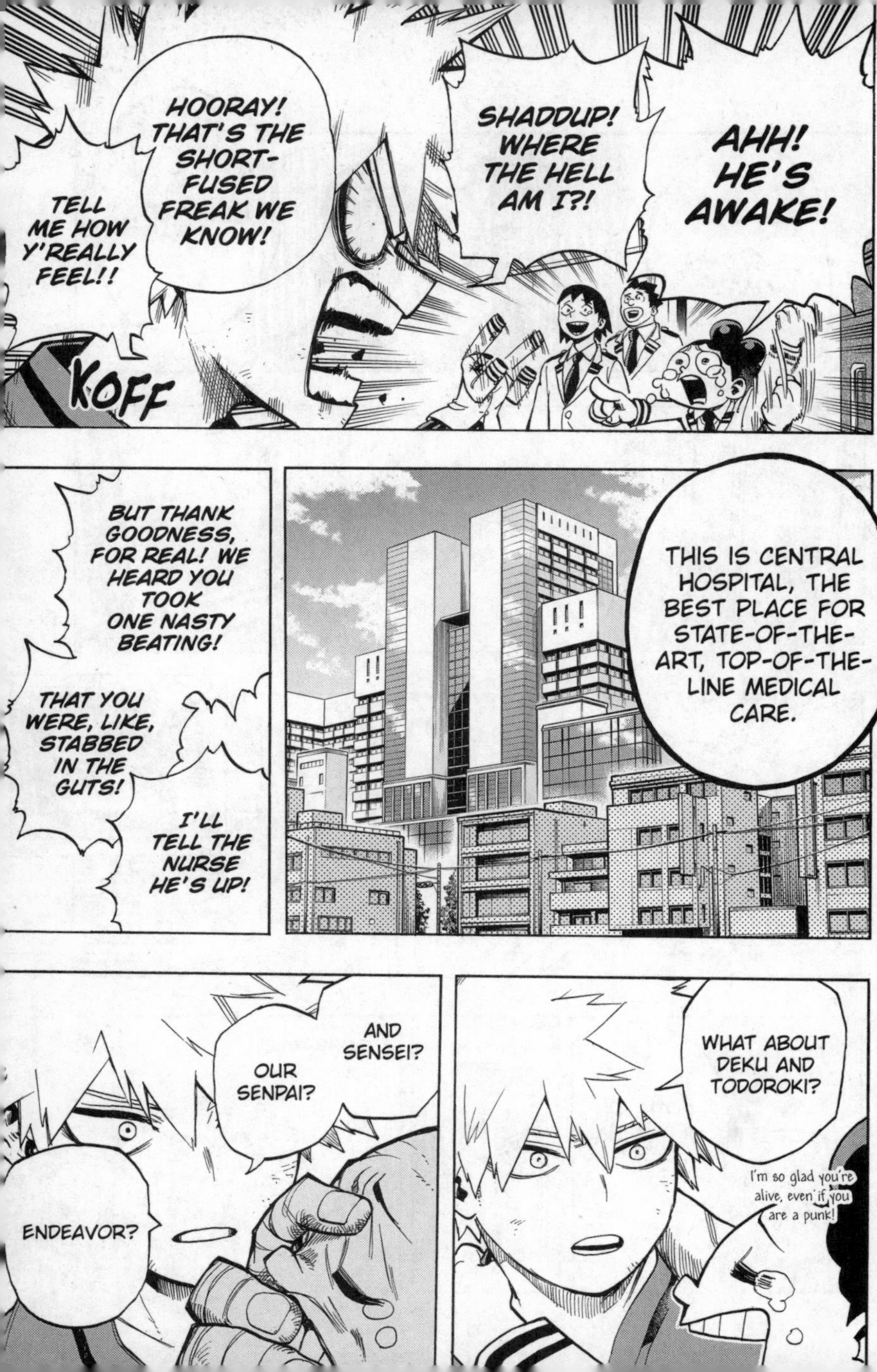
AHH! HE'S AWAKE!
SHADDUP! WHERE THE HELL AM I?!
HOORAY! THAT'S THE SHORT-FUSED FREAK WE KNOW!
TELL ME HOW Y'REALLY FEEL!!
KOFF
THIS IS CENTRAL HOSPITAL, THE BEST PLACE FOR STATE-OF-THE-ART, TOP-OF-THE-LINE MEDICAL CARE.
BUT THANK GOODNESS, FOR REAL! WE HEARD YOU TOOK ONE NASTY BEATING!
THAT YOU WERE, LIKE, STABBED IN THE GUTS!
I'LL TELL THE NURSE HE'S UP!
WHAT ABOUT DEKU AND TODOROKI?
I'm so glad you're alive, even if you are a punk!
AND SENSEI?
OUR SENPAI?
ENDEAVOR?

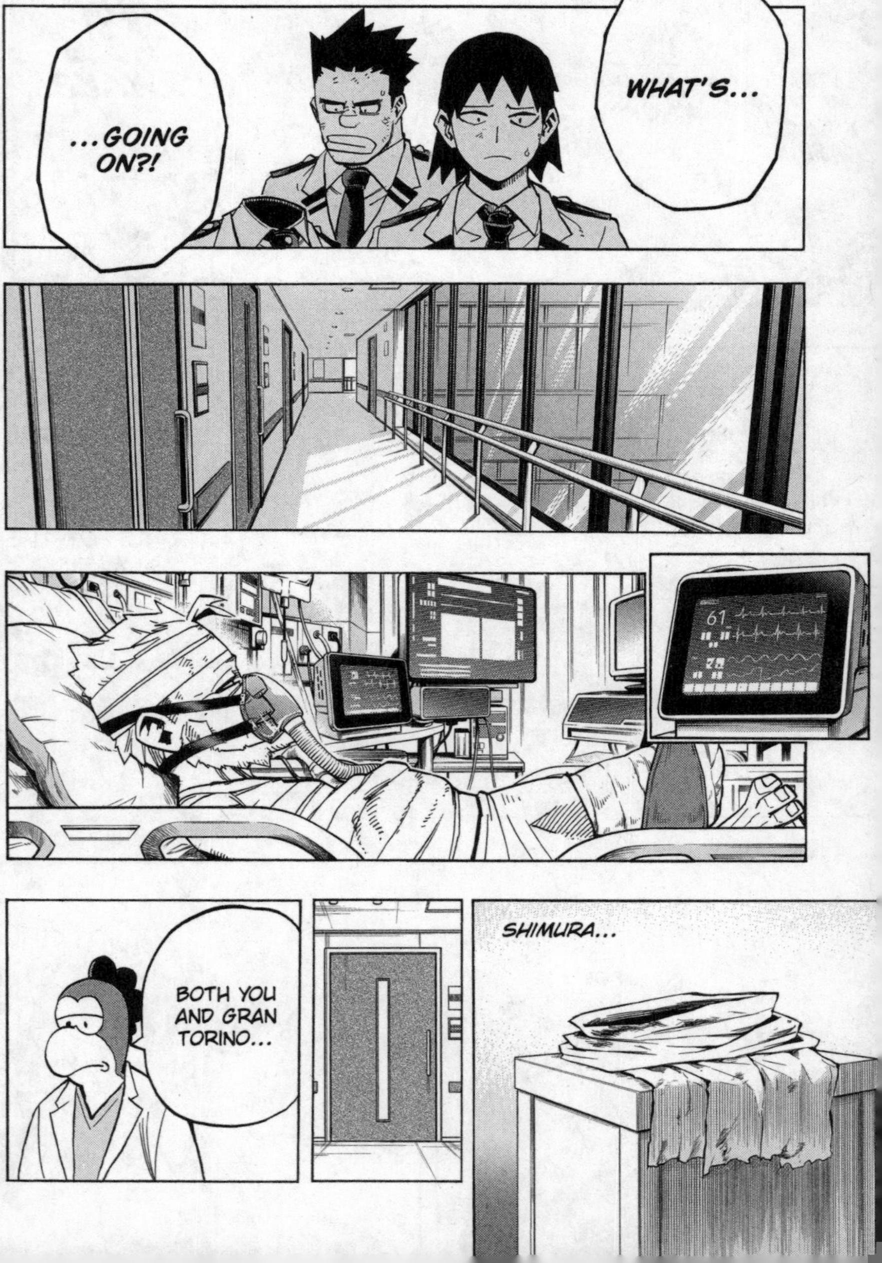
WHAT'S...
...GOING ON?!
SHIMURA...
BOTH YOU AND GRAN TORINO...

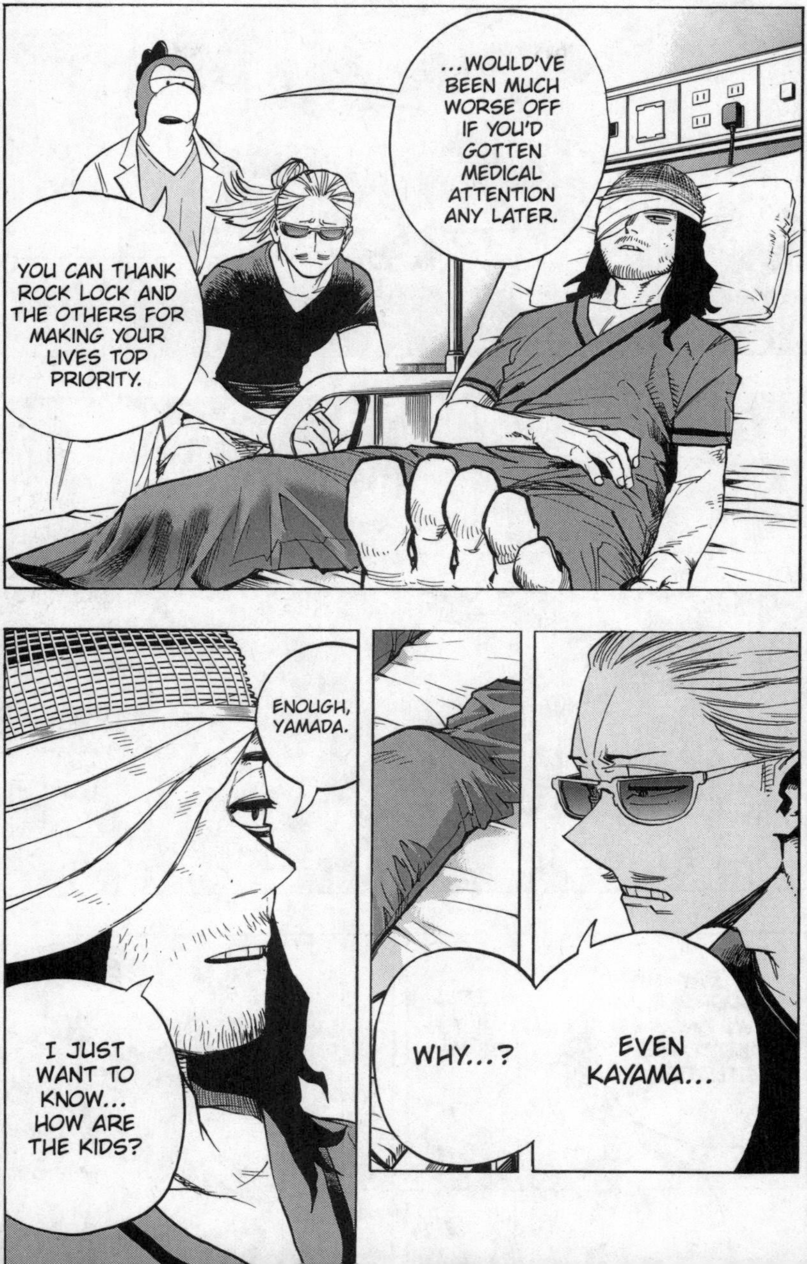
...WOULD'VE BEEN MUCH WORSE OFF IF YOU'D GOTTEN MEDICAL ATTENTION ANY LATER.
YOU CAN THANK ROCK LOCK AND THE OTHERS FOR MAKING YOUR LIVES TOP PRIORITY.
EVEN KAYAMA...
WHY...?
ENOUGH, YAMADA.
I JUST WANT TO KNOW... HOW ARE THE KIDS?

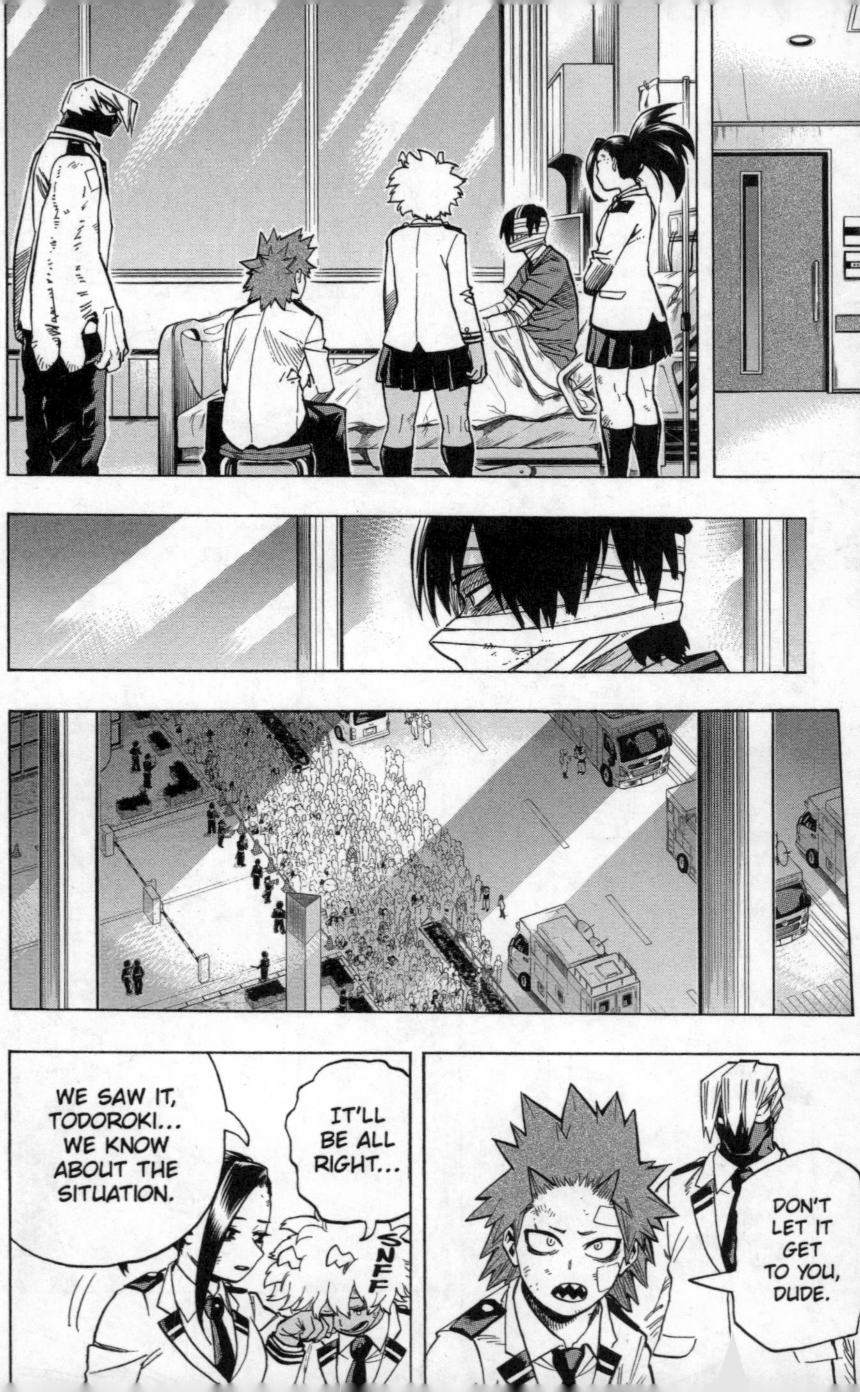
DON'T LET IT GET TO YOU, DUDE.
IT'LL BE ALL RIGHT...
SNFF
WE SAW IT, TODOROKI... WE KNOW ABOUT THE SITUATION.

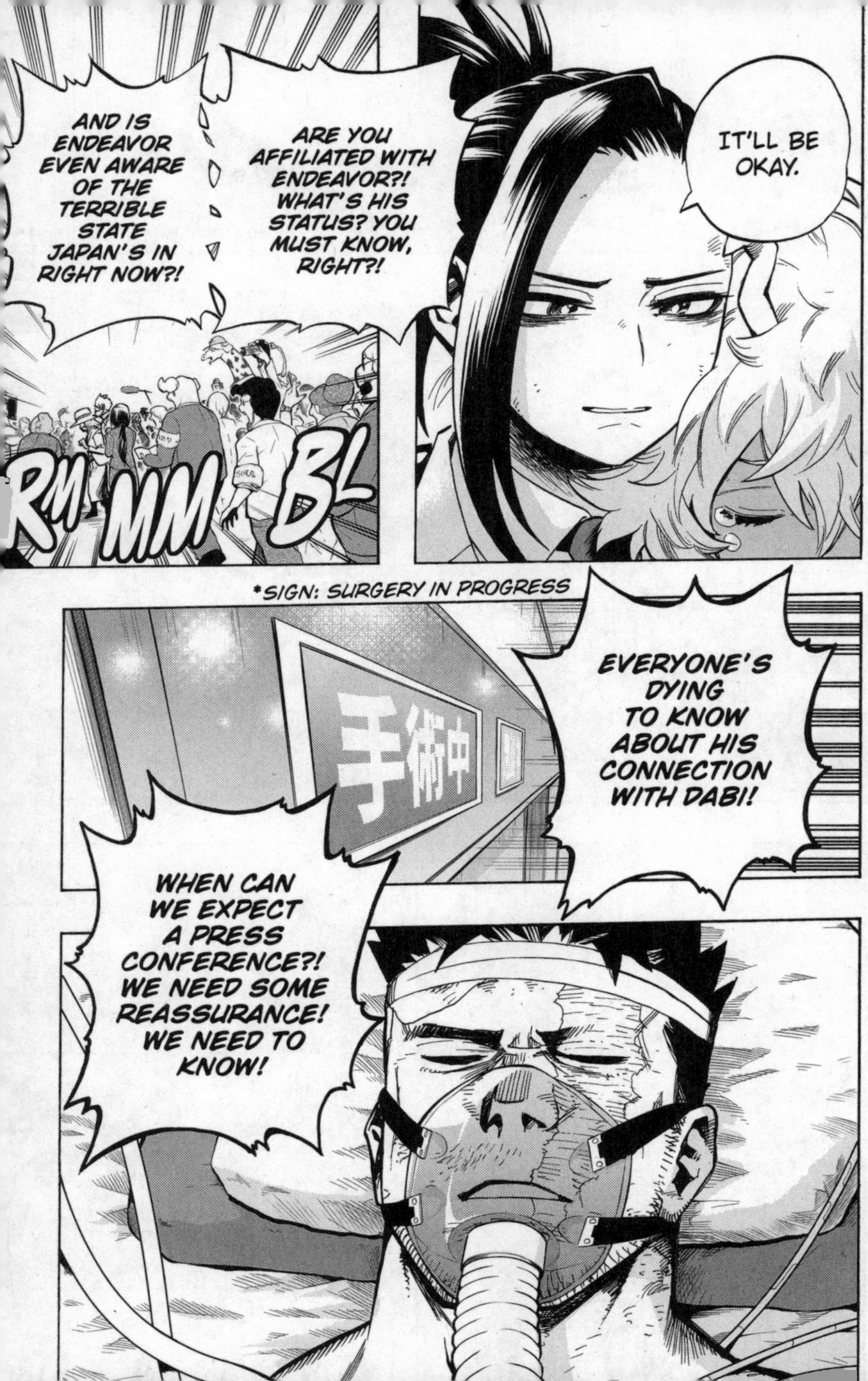
IT'LL BE OKAY.
ARE YOU AFFILIATED WITH ENDEAVOR?! WHAT'S HIS STATUS? YOU MUST KNOW, RIGHT?!
AND IS ENDEAVOR EVEN AWARE OF THE TERRIBLE STATE JAPAN'S IN RIGHT NOW?!
RMMMBL
*SIGN: SURGERY IN PROGRESS
EVERYONE'S DYING TO KNOW ABOUT HIS CONNECTION WITH DABI!
手術中
WHEN CAN WE EXPECT A PRESS CONFERENCE?! WE NEED SOME REASSURANCE! WE NEED TO KNOW!

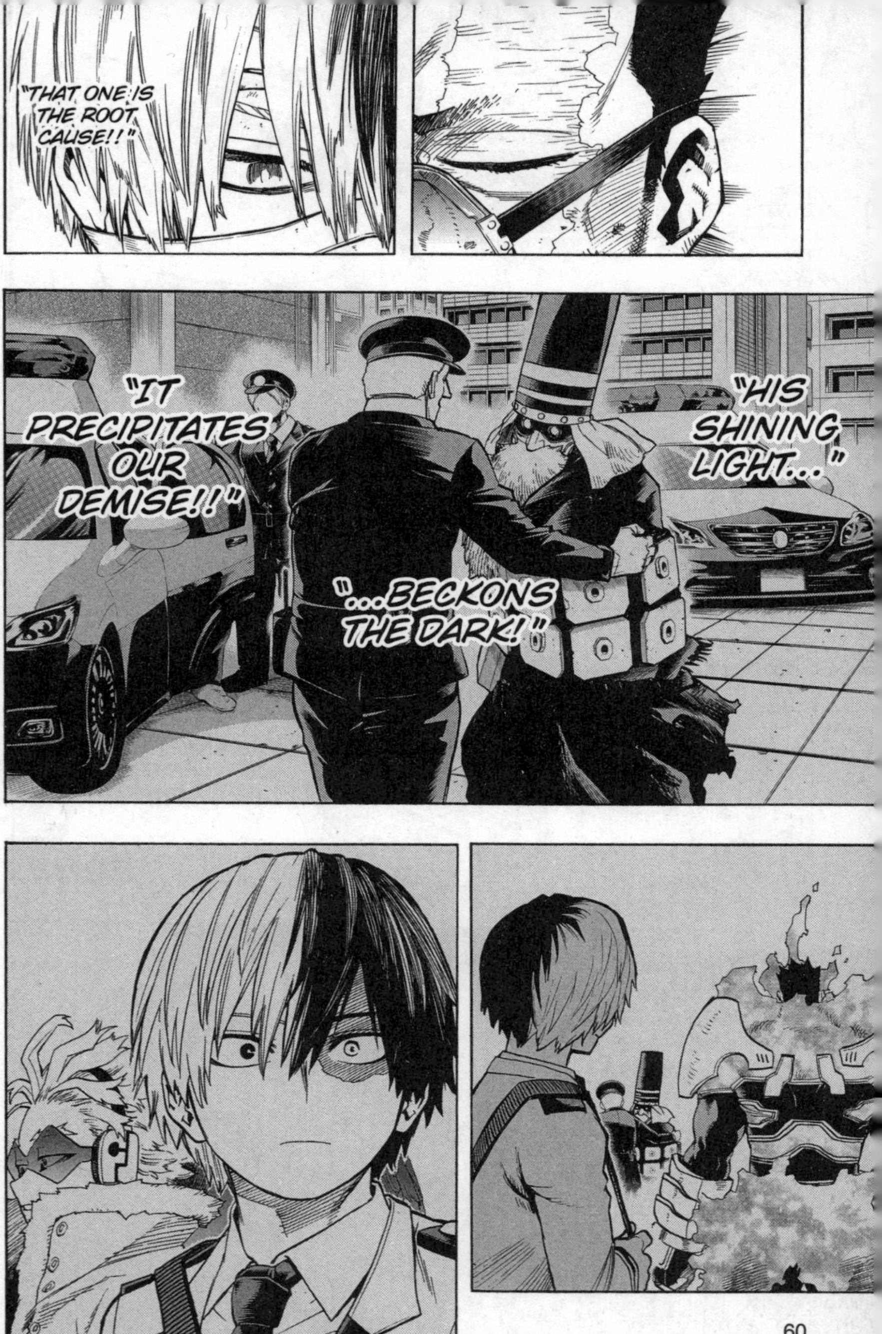
"THAT ONE IS THE ROOT CAUSE!!"
"HIS SHINING LIGHT..."
"...BECKONS THE DARK!"
"IT PRECIPITATES OUR DEMISE!!"

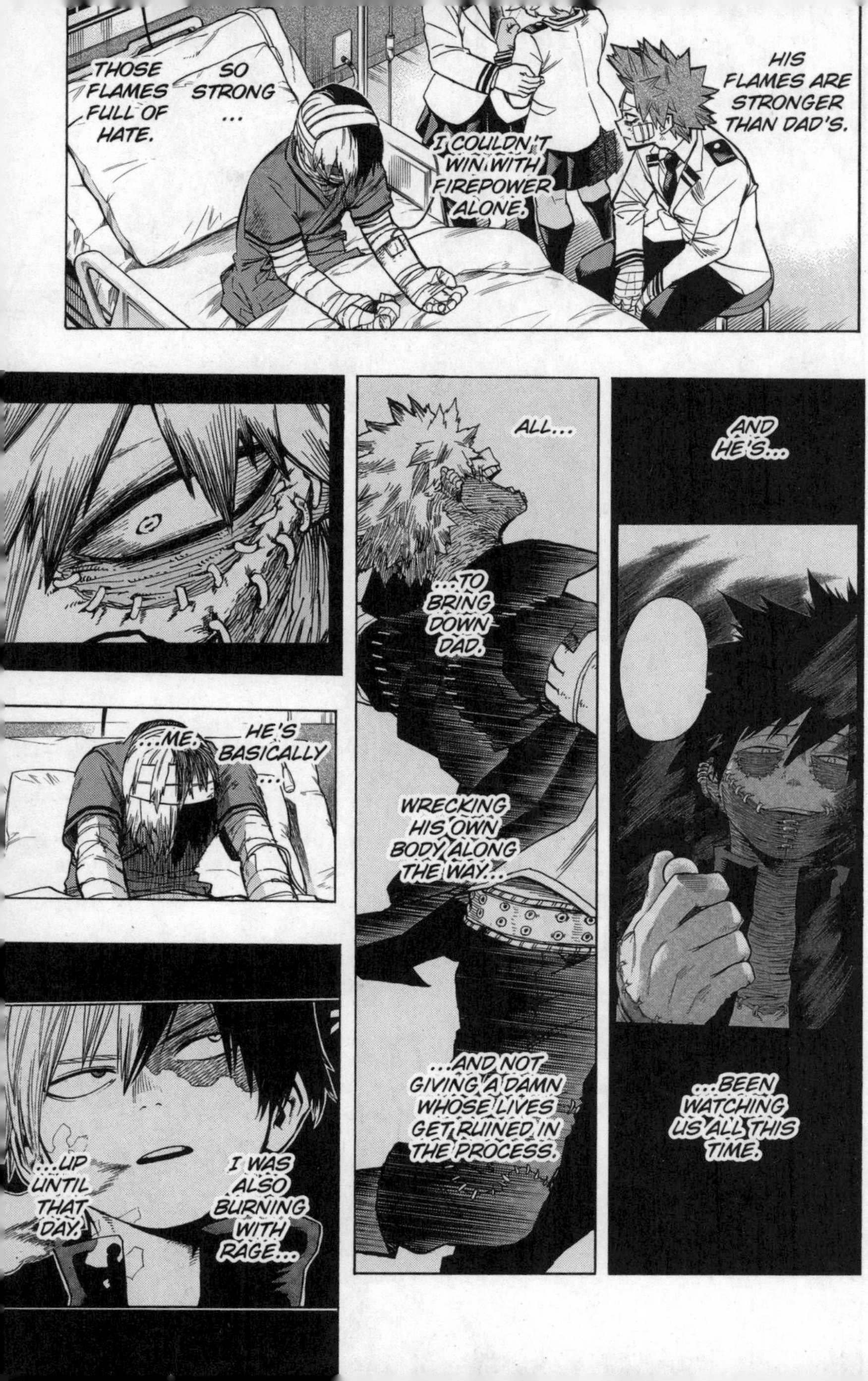
HIS FLAMES ARE STRONGER THAN DAD'S.
I COULDN'T WIN WITH FIREPOWER ALONE.
SO STRONG ...
THOSE FLAMES FULL OF HATE.
HE'S BASICALLY ...
...ME.
I WAS ALSO BURNING WITH RAGE...
...UP UNTIL THAT DAY.
ALL...
...TO BRING DOWN DAD.
WRECKING HIS OWN BODY ALONG THE WAY...
...AND NOT GIVING A DAMN WHOSE LIVES GET RUINED IN THE PROCESS.
...AND HE'S...
...BEEN WATCHING US ALL THIS TIME.

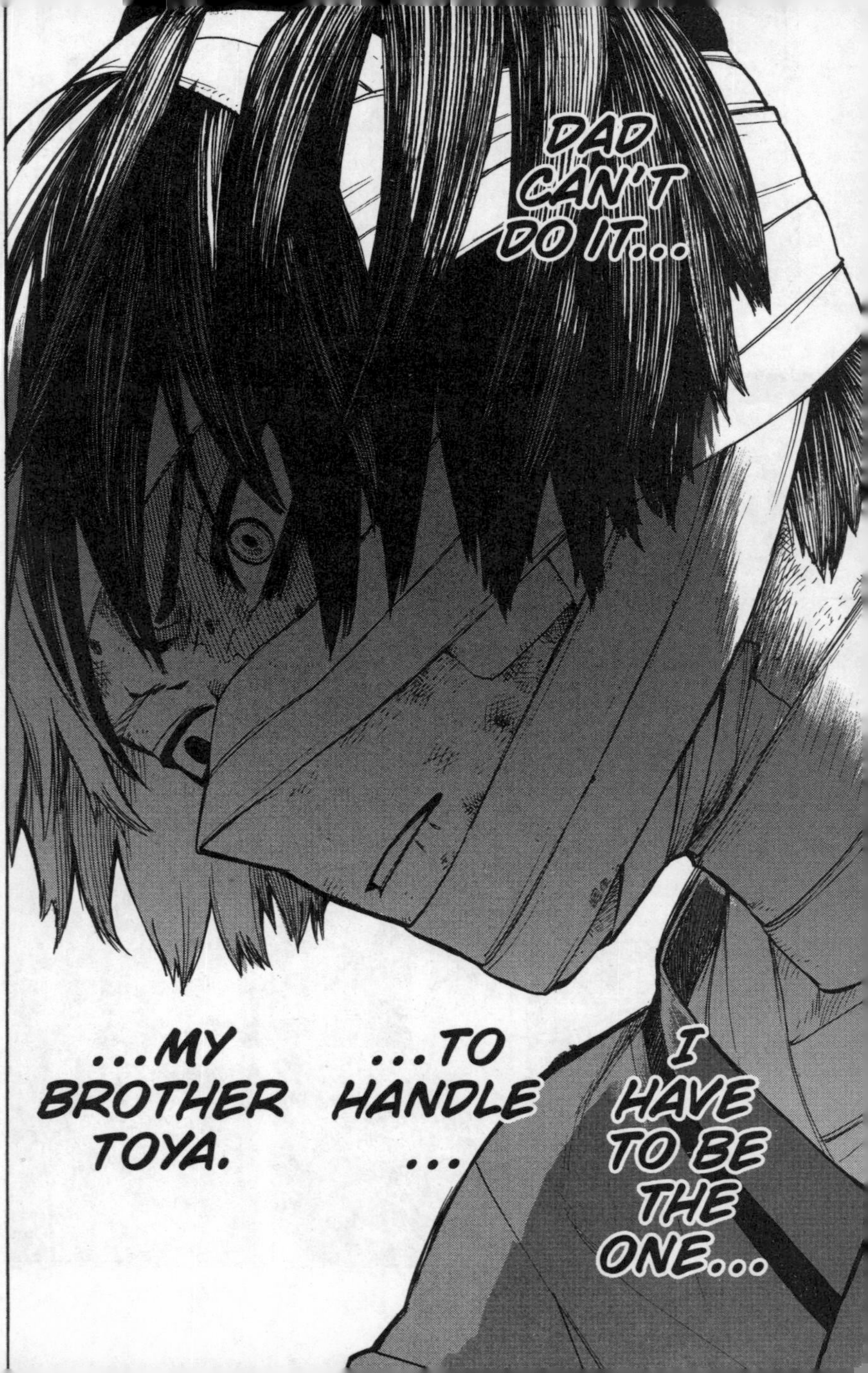
DAD CAN'T DO IT...
I HAVE TO BE THE ONE...
...TO HANDLE ...
...MY BROTHER TOYA.

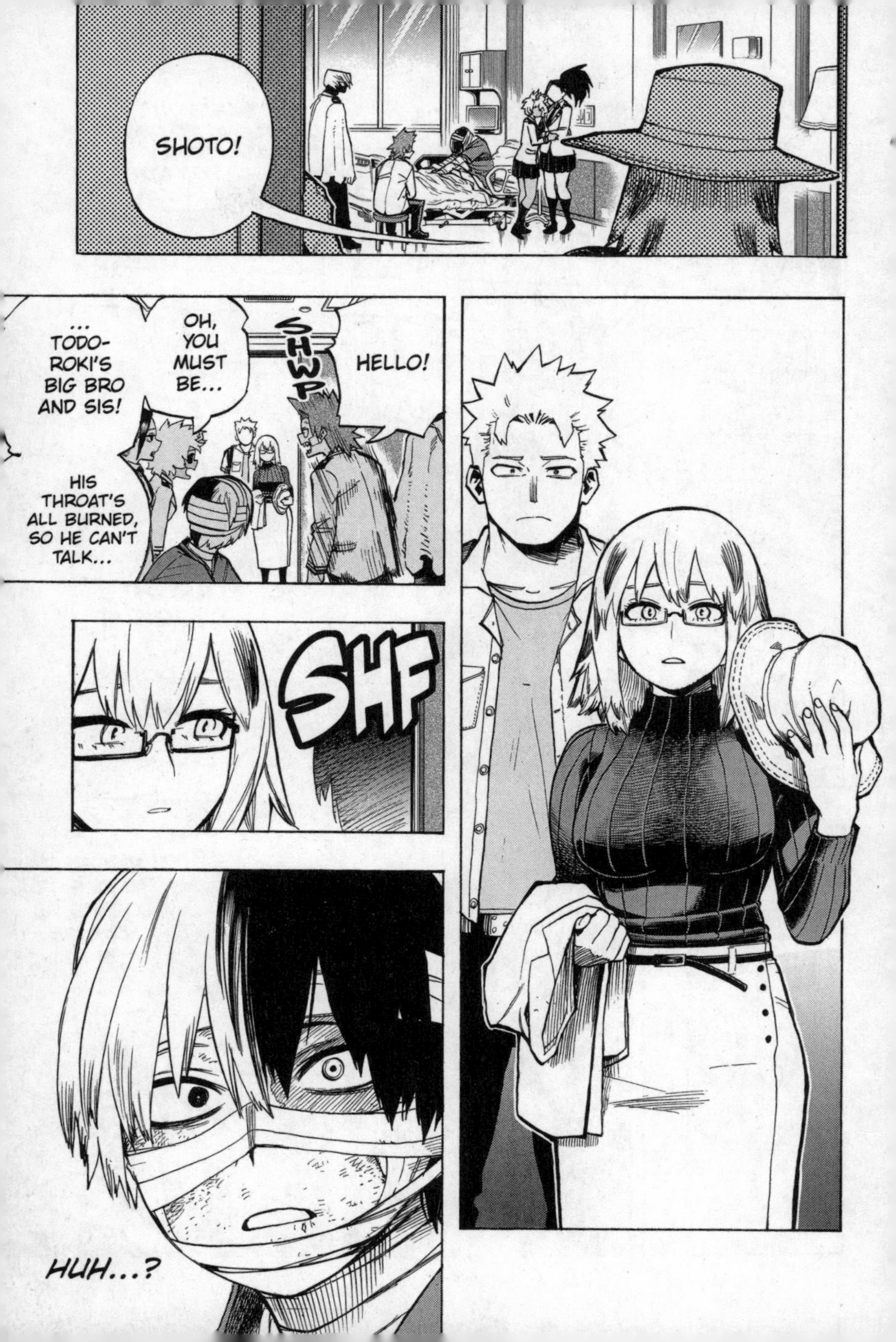
SHOTO!
HELLO!
SHWP
OH, YOU MUST BE...
... TODO-ROKI'S BIG BRO AND SIS!
HIS THROAT'S ALL BURNED, SO HE CAN'T TALK...
SHF
HUH...?

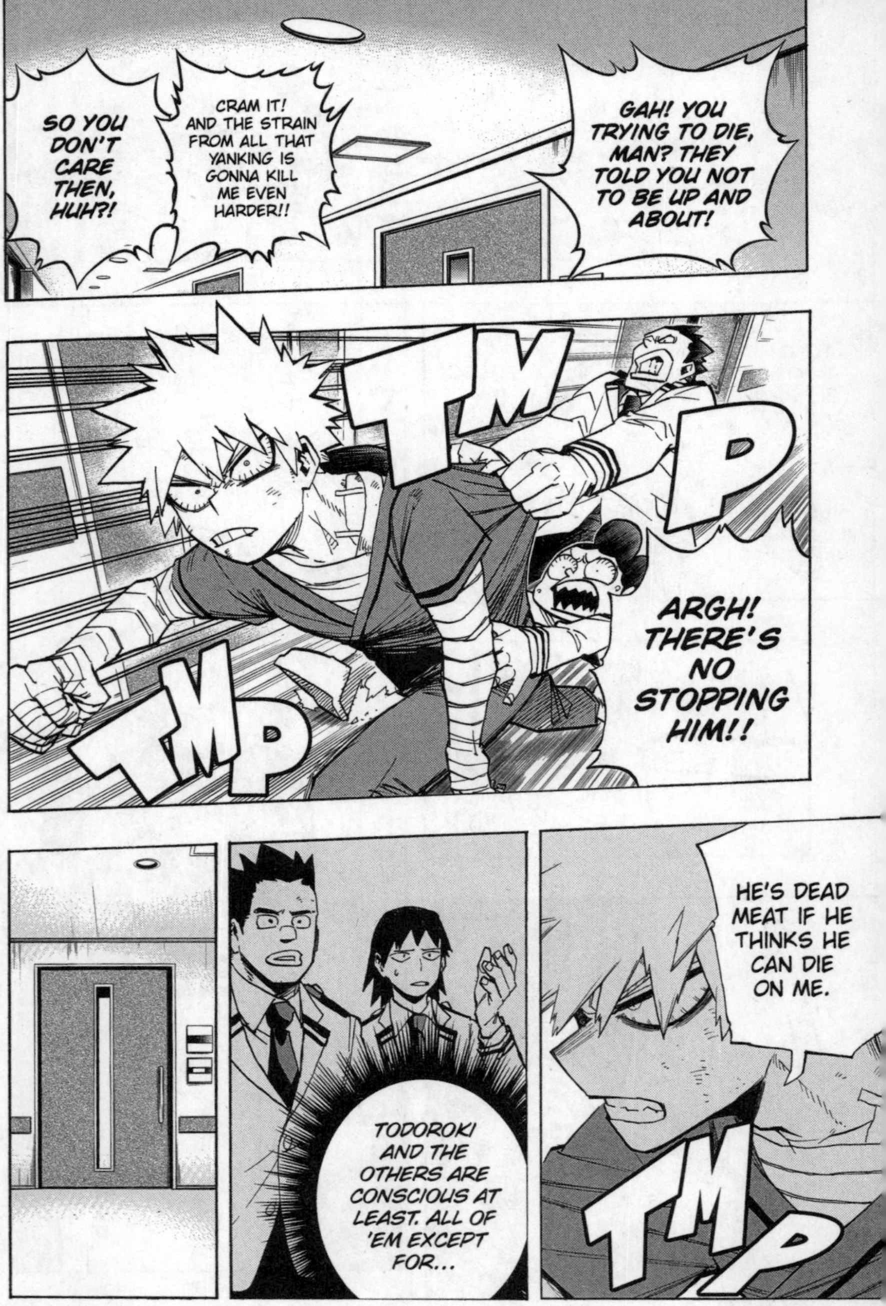
GAH! YOU TRYING TO DIE, MAN? THEY TOLD YOU NOT TO BE UP AND ABOUT!
CRAM IT! AND THE STRAIN FROM ALL THAT YANKING IS GONNA KILL ME EVEN HARDER!!
SO YOU DON'T CARE THEN, HUH?!
TMP
ARGH! THERE'S NO STOPPING HIM!!
TMP
HE'S DEAD MEAT IF HE THINKS HE CAN DIE ON ME.
TMP
TODOROKI AND THE OTHERS ARE CONSCIOUS AT LEAST. ALL OF 'EM EXCEPT FOR...

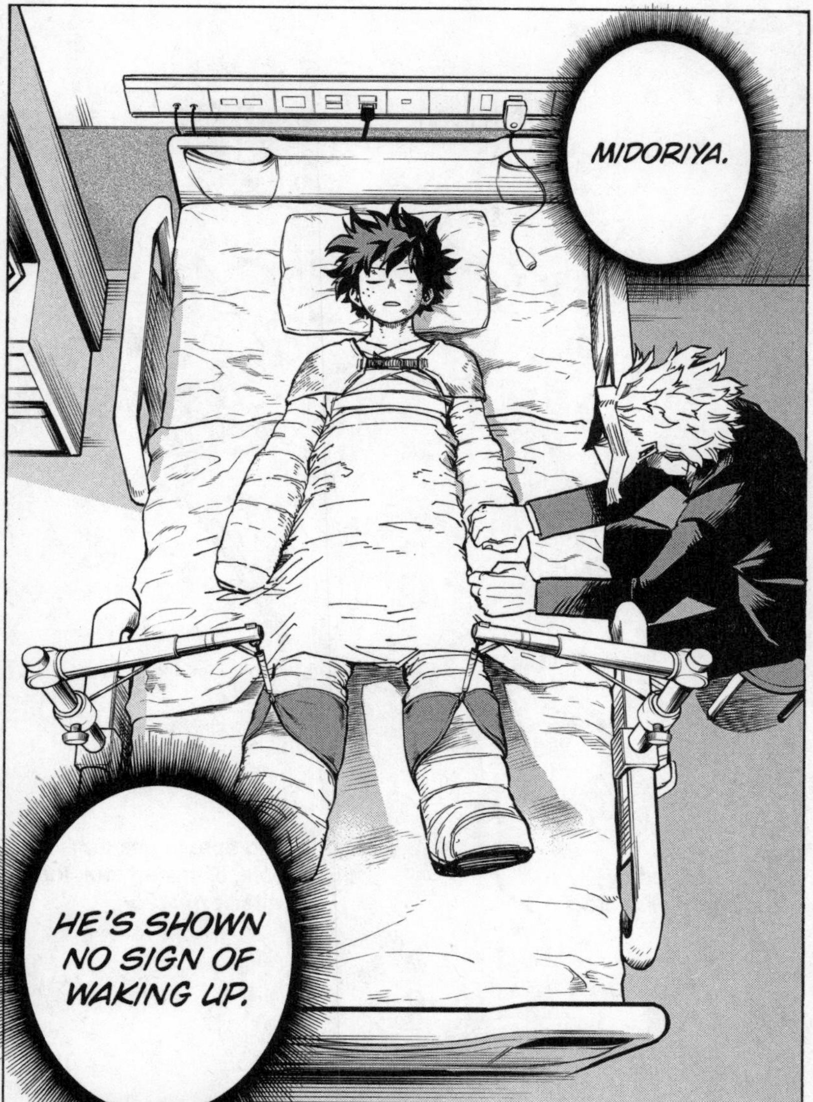
MIDORIYA.
HE'S SHOWN NO SIGN OF WAKING UP.

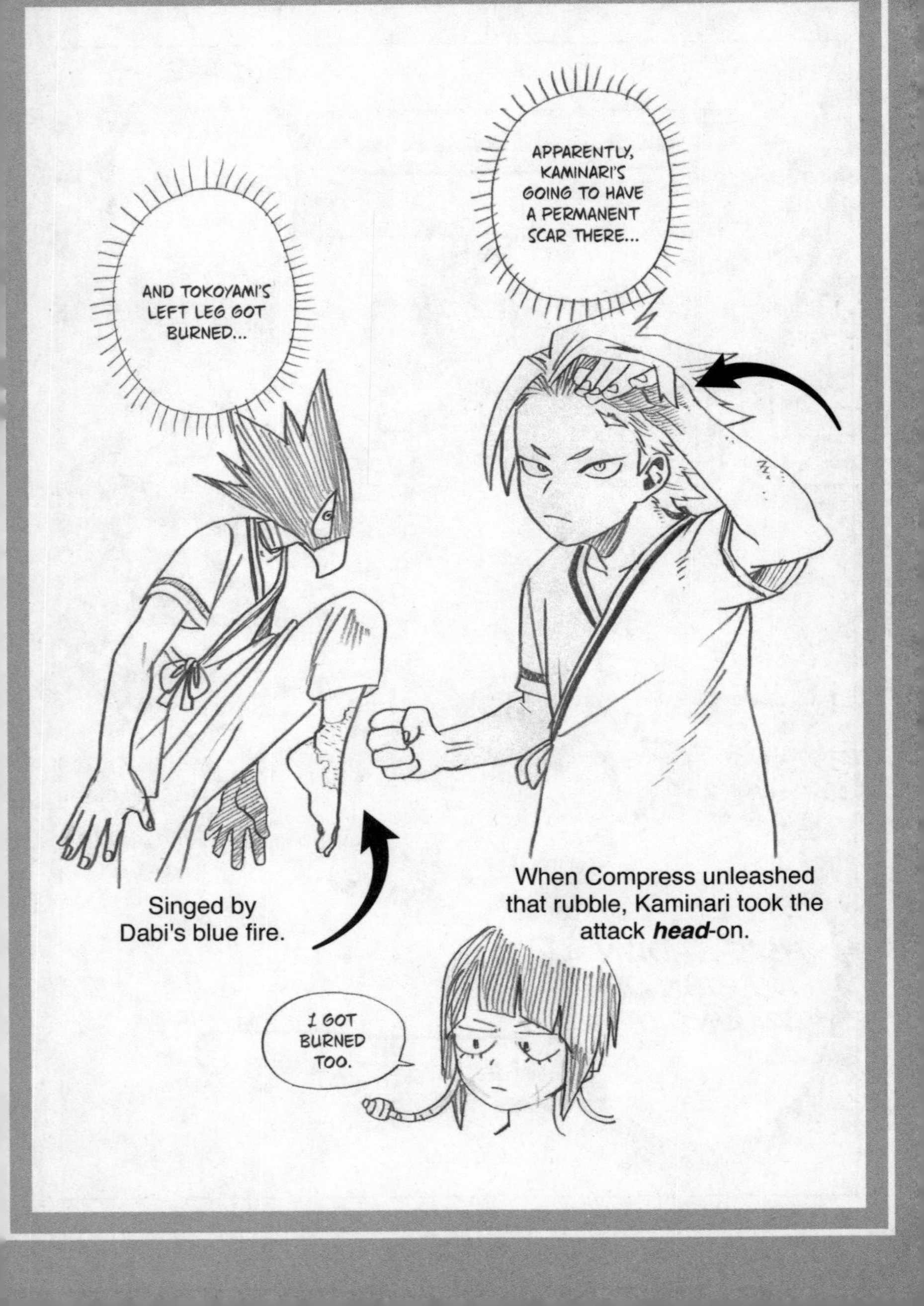
APPARENTLY, KAMINARI'S GOING TO HAVE A PERMANENT SCAR THERE...
AND TOKOYAMI'S LEFT LEG GOT BURNED...
When Compress unleashed that rubble, Kaminari took the attack ***head***-on.
Singed by Dabi's blue fire.
I GOT BURNED TOO.

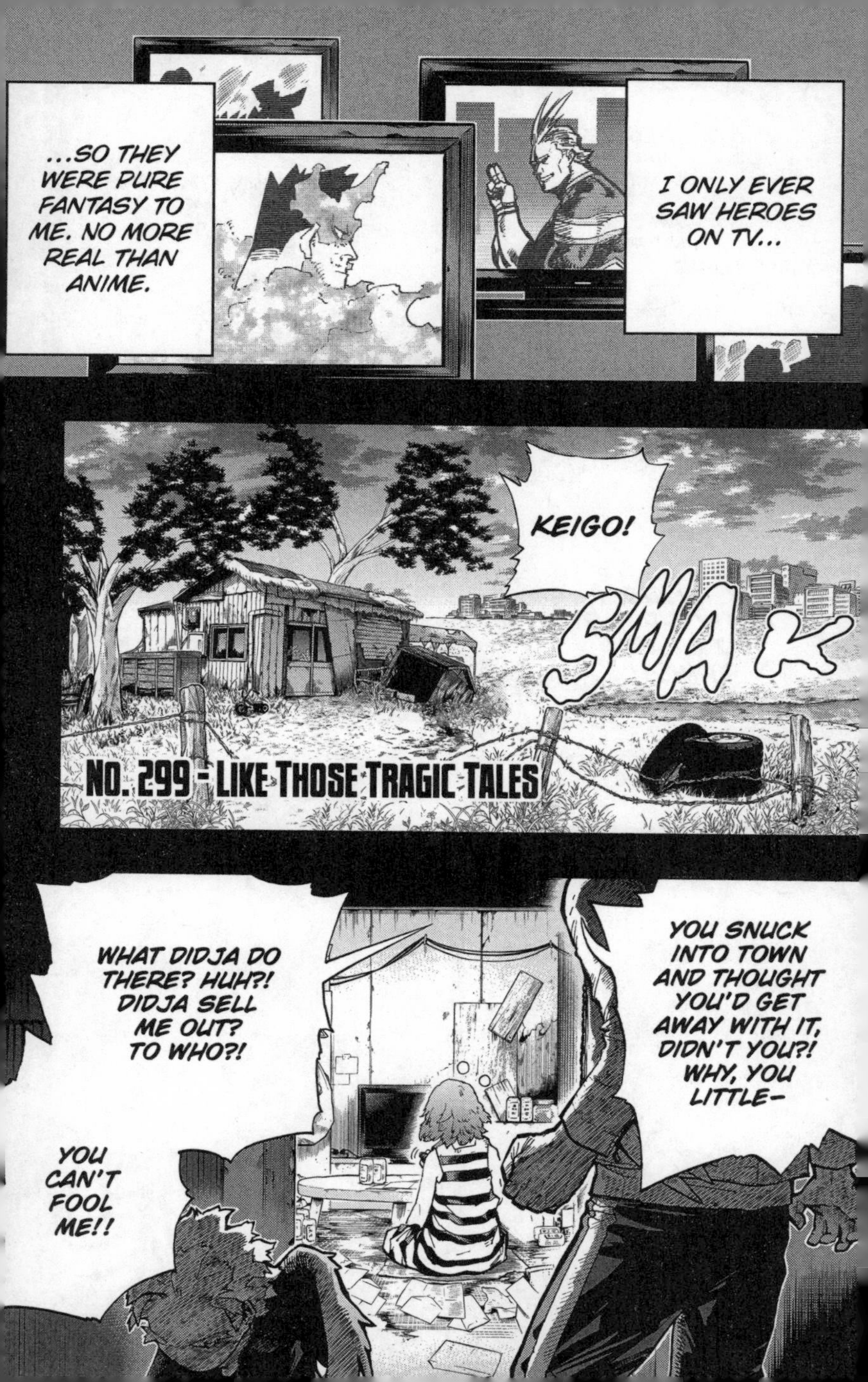
I ONLY EVER SAW HEROES ON TV...
...SO THEY WERE PURE FANTASY TO ME. NO MORE REAL THAN ANIME.
KEIGO!
SMAK
NO. 299 - LIKE THOSE TRAGIC TALES
YOU SNUCK INTO TOWN AND THOUGHT YOU'D GET AWAY WITH IT, DIDN'T YOU?! WHY, YOU LITTLE-
WHAT DIDJA DO THERE? HUH?! DIDJA SELL ME OUT? TO WHO?!
YOU CAN'T FOOL ME!!

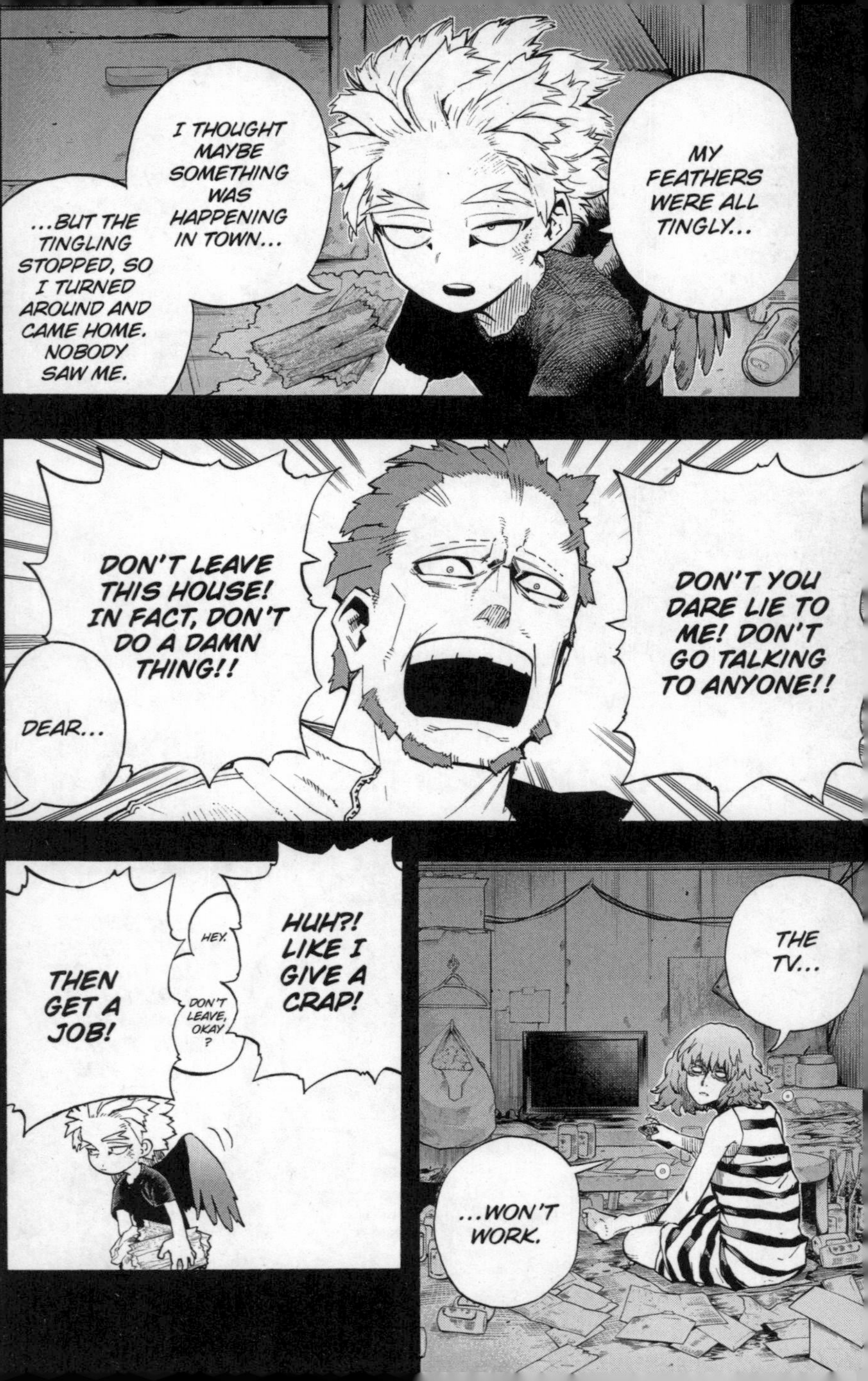
MY FEATHERS WERE ALL TINGLY...
I THOUGHT MAYBE SOMETHING WAS HAPPENING IN TOWN...
...BUT THE TINGLING STOPPED, SO I TURNED AROUND AND CAME HOME. NOBODY SAW ME.
DON'T YOU DARE LIE TO ME! DON'T GO TALKING TO ANYONE!!
DON'T LEAVE THIS HOUSE! IN FACT, DON'T DO A DAMN THING!!
DEAR...
THE TV...
...WON'T WORK.
HUH?! LIKE I GIVE A CRAP!
HEY.
DON'T LEAVE, OKAY?
THEN GET A JOB!

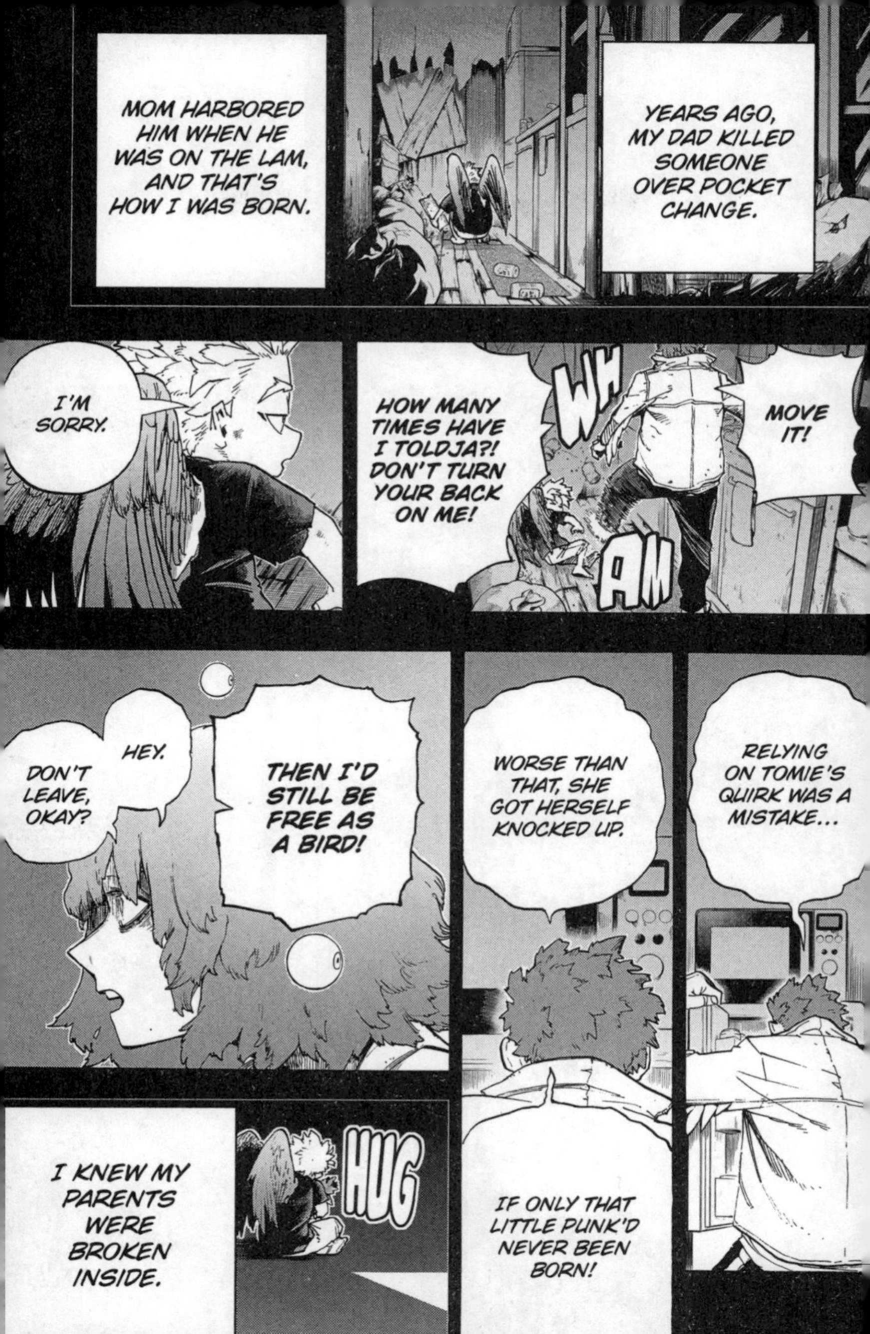
YEARS AGO, MY DAD KILLED SOMEONE OVER POCKET CHANGE.
MOM HARBORED HIM WHEN HE WAS ON THE LAM, AND THAT'S HOW I WAS BORN.
MOVE IT!
WHAM
HOW MANY TIMES HAVE I TOLDJA?! DON'T TURN YOUR BACK ON ME!
I'M SORRY.
RELYING ON TOMIE'S QUIRK WAS A MISTAKE...
WORSE THAN THAT, SHE GOT HERSELF KNOCKED UP.
IF ONLY THAT LITTLE PUNK'D NEVER BEEN BORN!
THEN I'D STILL BE FREE AS A BIRD!
HEY.
DON'T LEAVE, OKAY?
HUG
I KNEW MY PARENTS WERE BROKEN INSIDE.

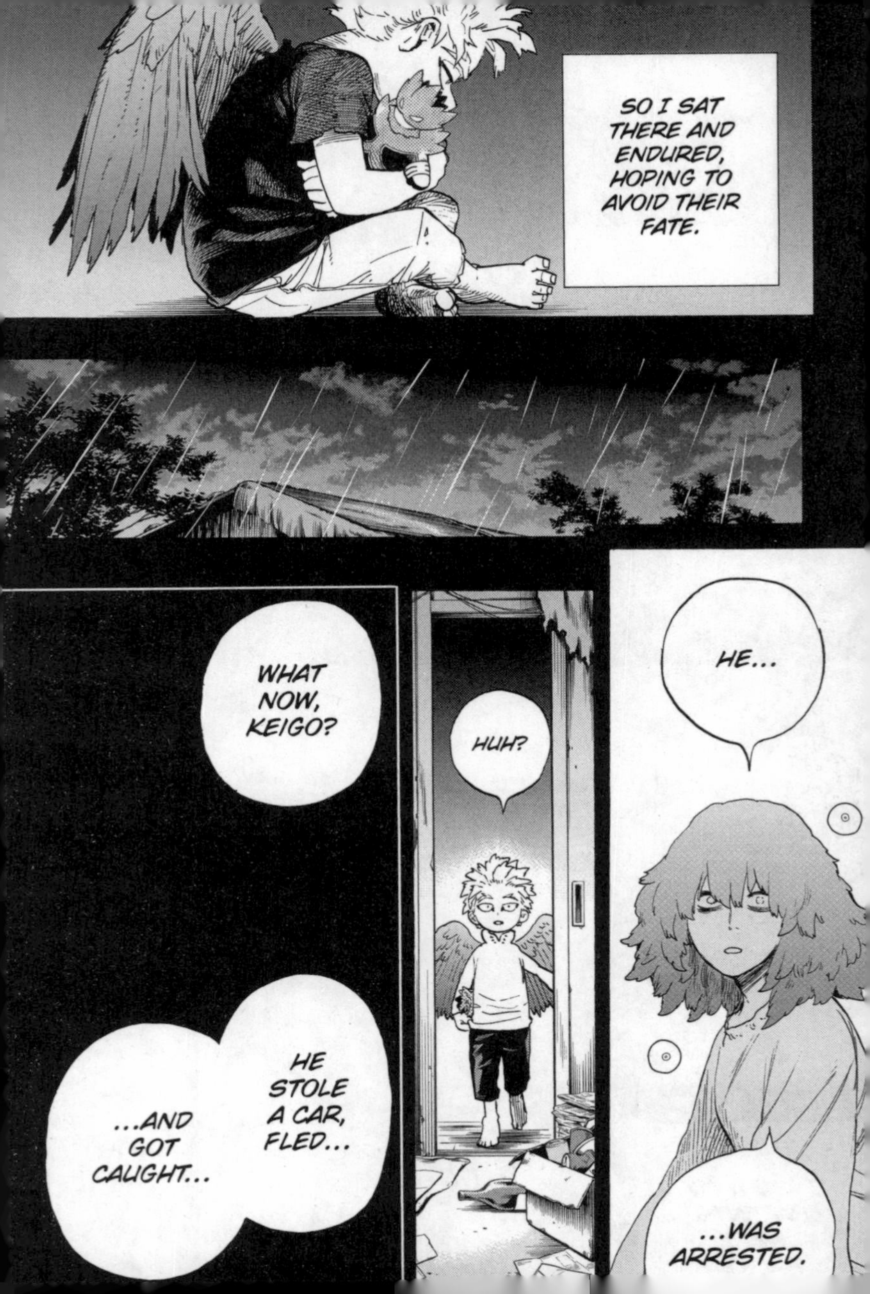
SO I SAT THERE AND ENDURED, HOPING TO AVOID THEIR FATE.
HE...
...WAS ARRESTED.
HUH?
WHAT NOW, KEIGO?
HE STOLE A CAR, FLED...
...AND GOT CAUGHT...

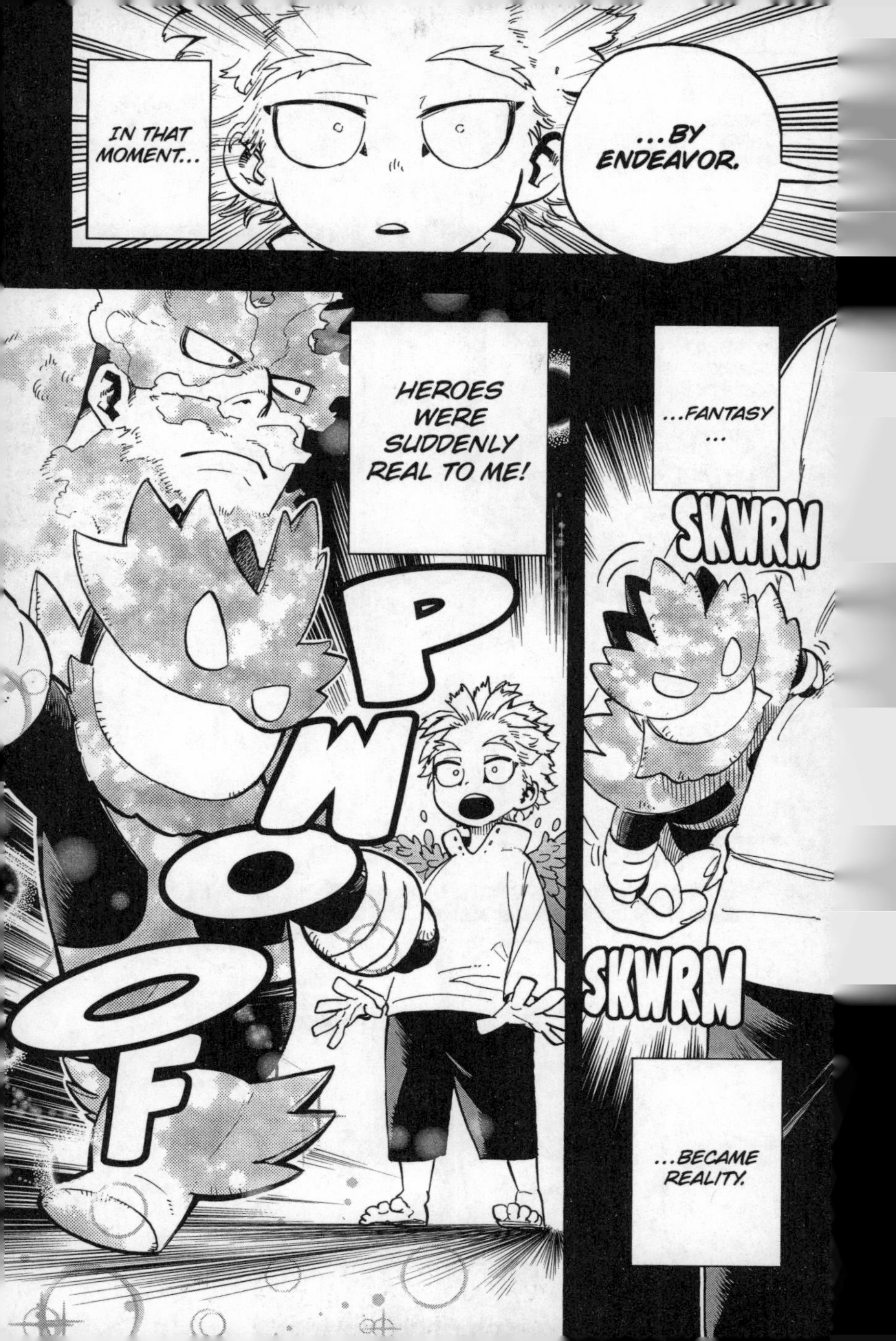
...BY ENDEAVOR.
IN THAT MOMENT...
...FANTASY ...
SKWRM
SKWRM
...BECAME REALITY.
HEROES WERE SUDDENLY REAL TO ME!
PWOOF

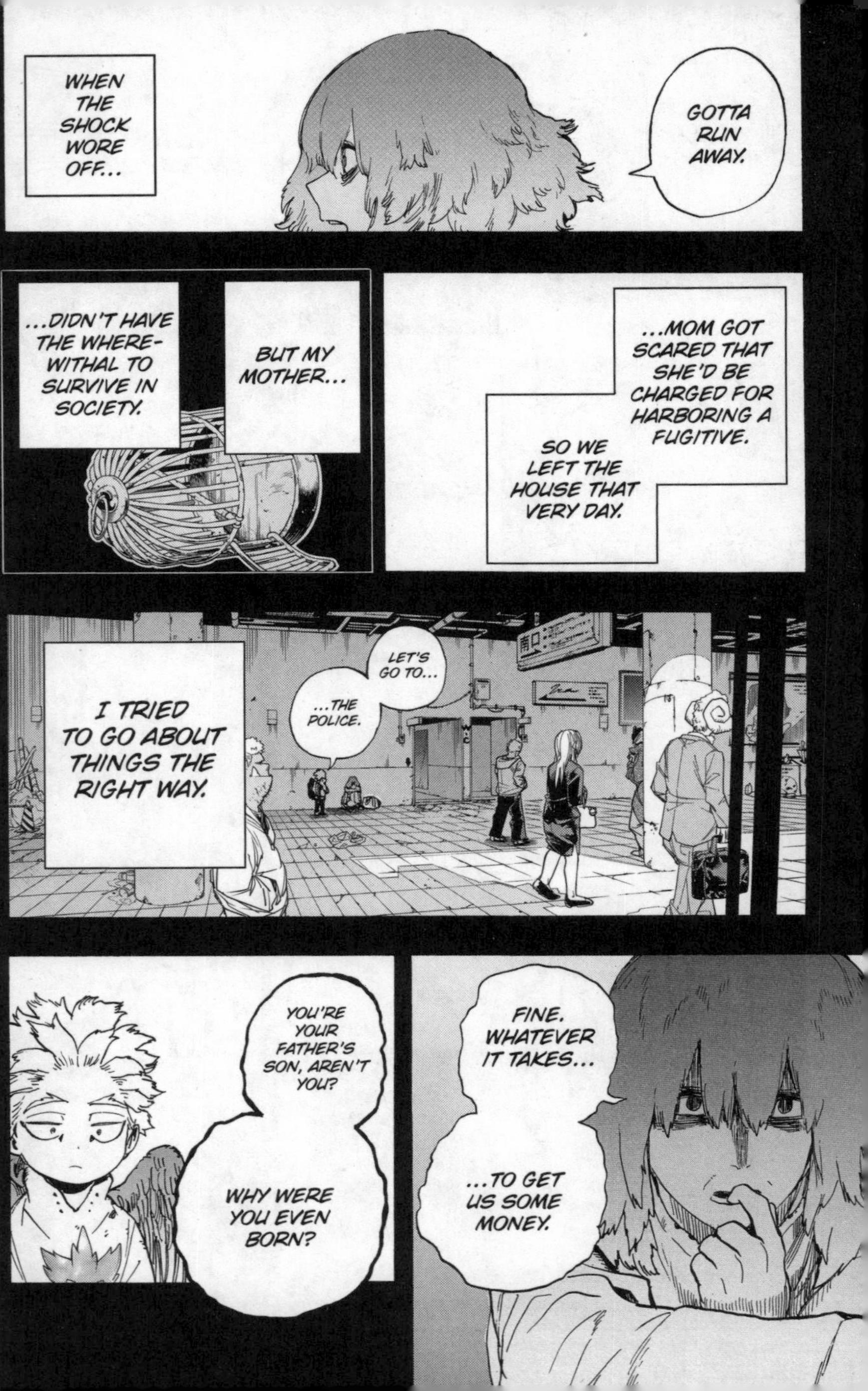
GOTTA RUN AWAY.
WHEN THE SHOCK WORE OFF...
...MOM GOT SCARED THAT SHE'D BE CHARGED FOR HARBORING A FUGITIVE.
SO WE LEFT THE HOUSE THAT VERY DAY.
BUT MY MOTHER...
...DIDN'T HAVE THE WHERE-WITHAL TO SURVIVE IN SOCIETY.
LET'S GO TO...
...THE POLICE.
I TRIED TO GO ABOUT THINGS THE RIGHT WAY.
FINE. WHATEVER IT TAKES...
...TO GET US SOME MONEY.
YOU'RE YOUR FATHER'S SON, AREN'T YOU?
WHY WERE YOU EVEN BORN?

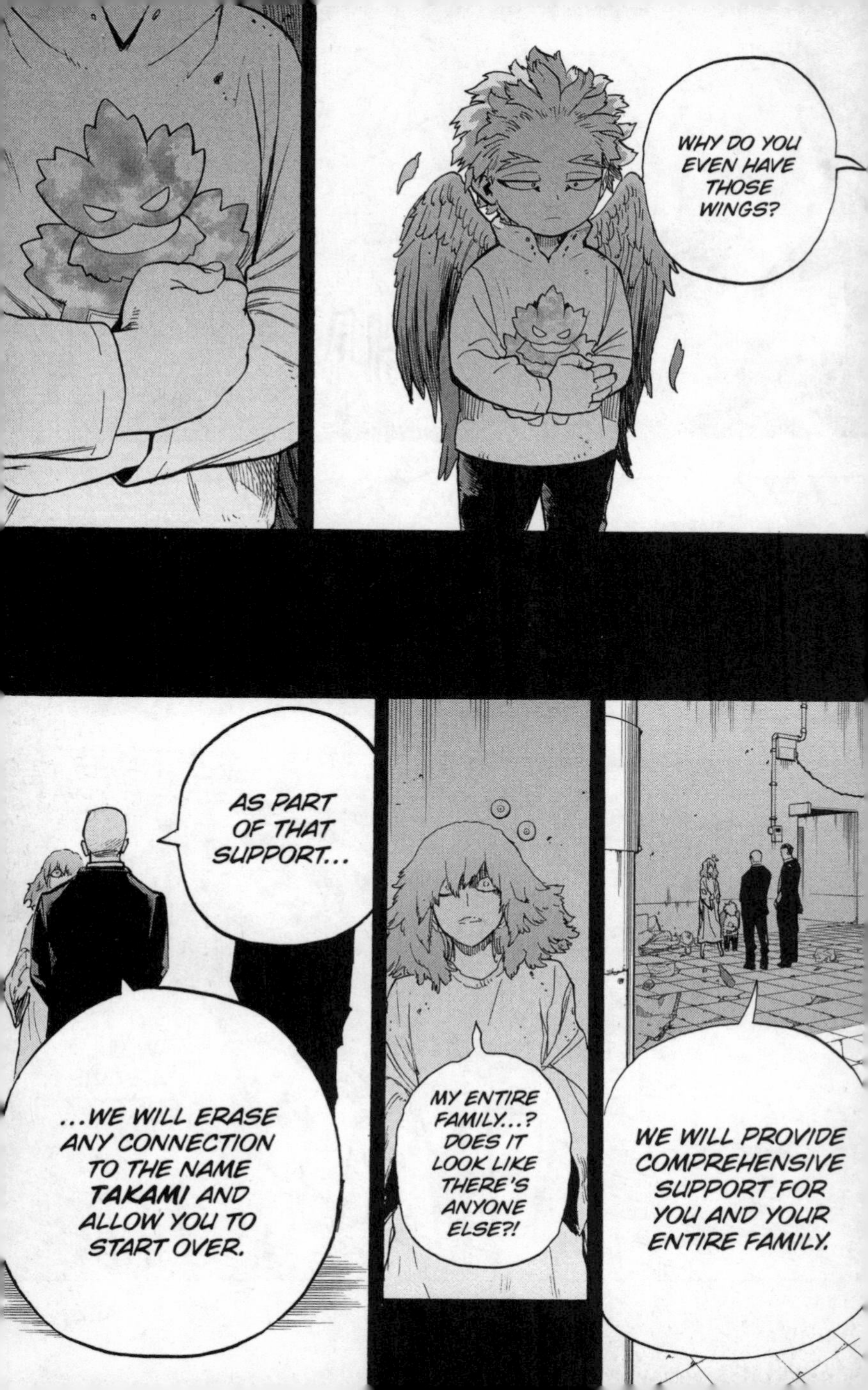
WHY DO YOU EVEN HAVE THOSE WINGS?
WE WILL PROVIDE COMPREHENSIVE SUPPORT FOR YOU AND YOUR ENTIRE FAMILY.
MY ENTIRE FAMILY...? DOES IT LOOK LIKE THERE'S ANYONE ELSE?!
AS PART OF THAT SUPPORT...
...WE WILL ERASE ANY CONNECTION TO THE NAME TAKAMI AND ALLOW YOU TO START OVER.

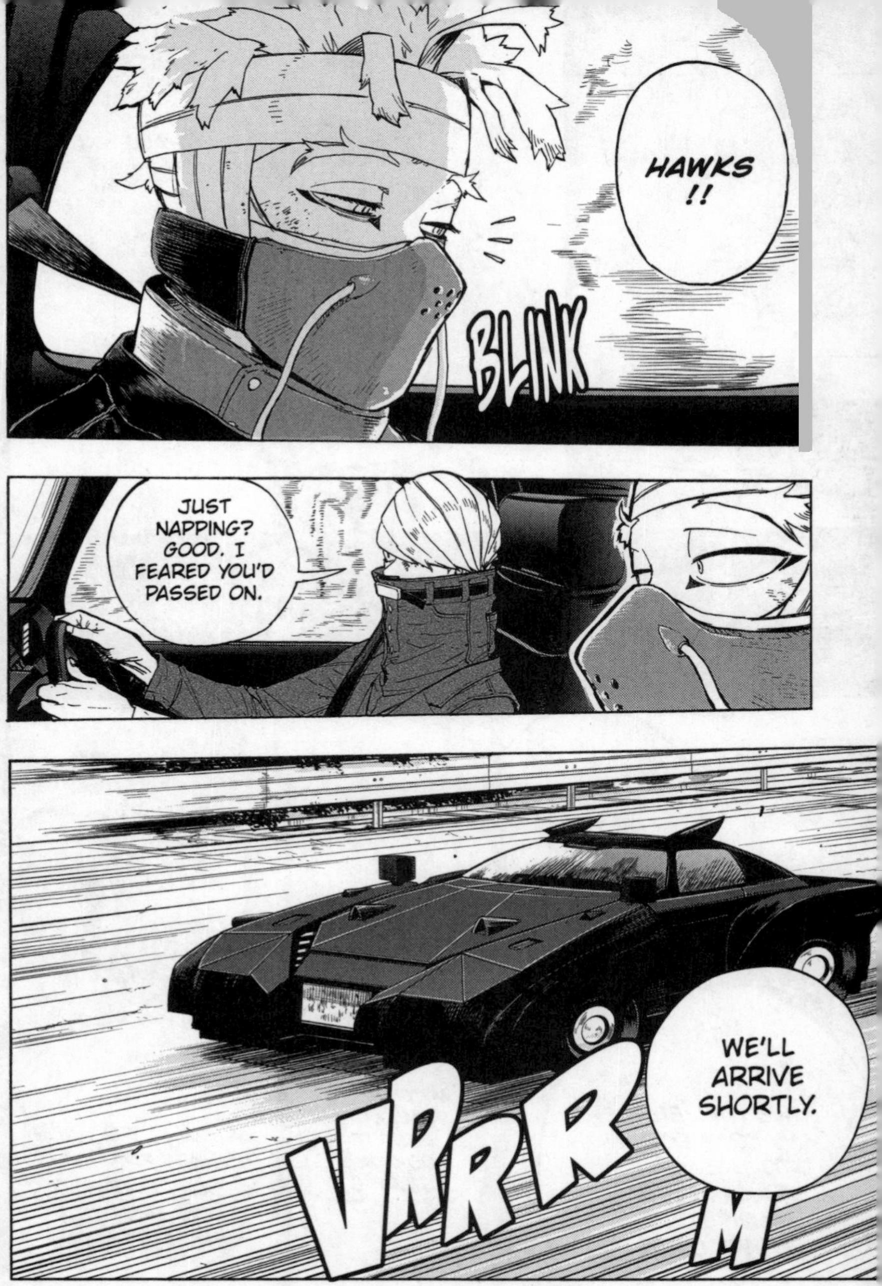
HAWKS !!
BLINK
JUST NAPPING? GOOD. I FEARED YOU'D PASSED ON.
WE'LL ARRIVE SHORTLY.
VRRRM

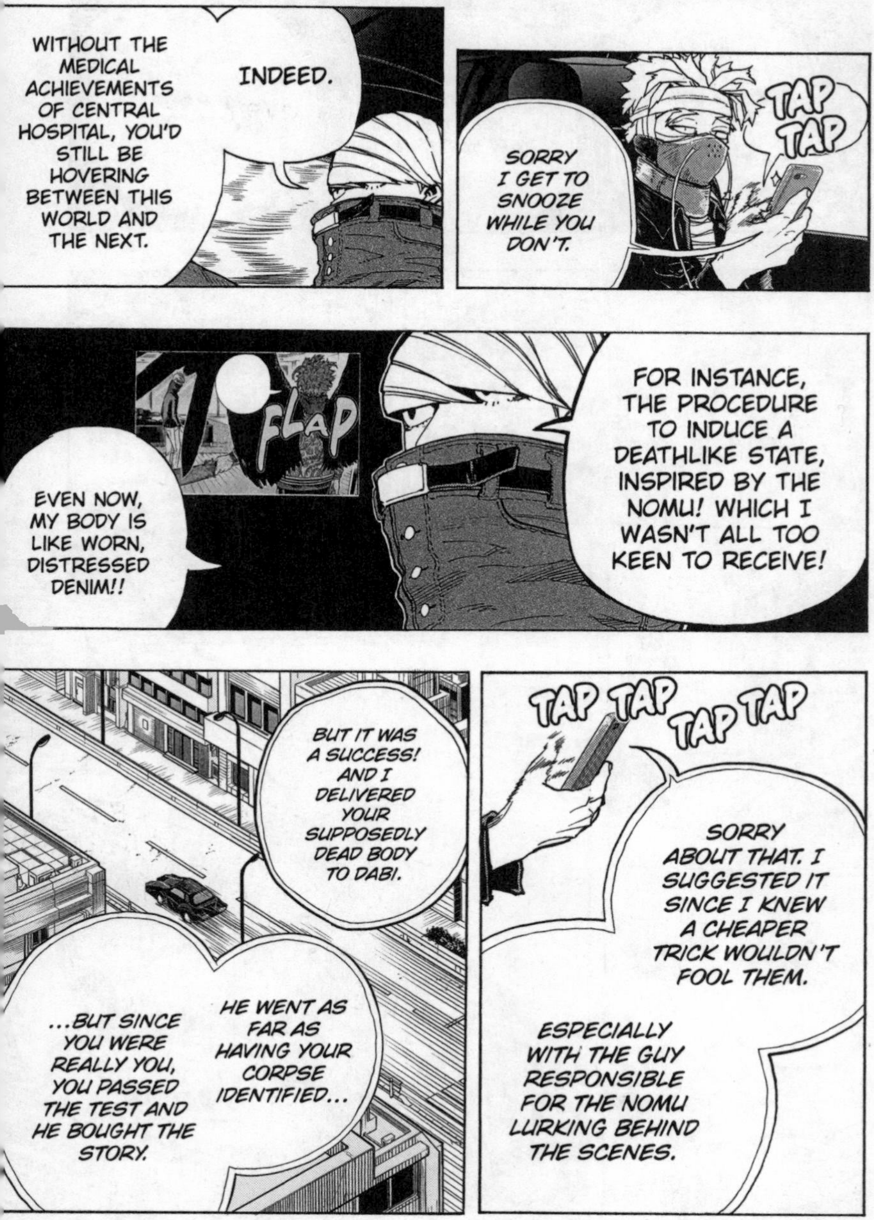
SORRY I GET TO SNOOZE WHILE YOU DON'T.
TAP TAP
INDEED.
WITHOUT THE MEDICAL ACHIEVEMENTS OF CENTRAL HOSPITAL, YOU'D STILL BE HOVERING BETWEEN THIS WORLD AND THE NEXT.
FOR INSTANCE, THE PROCEDURE TO INDUCE A DEATHLIKE STATE, INSPIRED BY THE NOMU! WHICH I WASN'T ALL TOO KEEN TO RECEIVE!
FLAP
EVEN NOW, MY BODY IS LIKE WORN, DISTRESSED DENIM!!
TAP TAP TAP TAP
SORRY ABOUT THAT. I SUGGESTED IT SINCE I KNEW A CHEAPER TRICK WOULDN'T FOOL THEM.
ESPECIALLY WITH THE GUY RESPONSIBLE FOR THE NOMU LURKING BEHIND THE SCENES.
BUT IT WAS A SUCCESS! AND I DELIVERED YOUR SUPPOSEDLY DEAD BODY TO DABI.
HE WENT AS FAR AS HAVING YOUR CORPSE IDENTIFIED...
...BUT SINCE YOU WERE REALLY YOU, YOU PASSED THE TEST AND HE BOUGHT THE STORY.

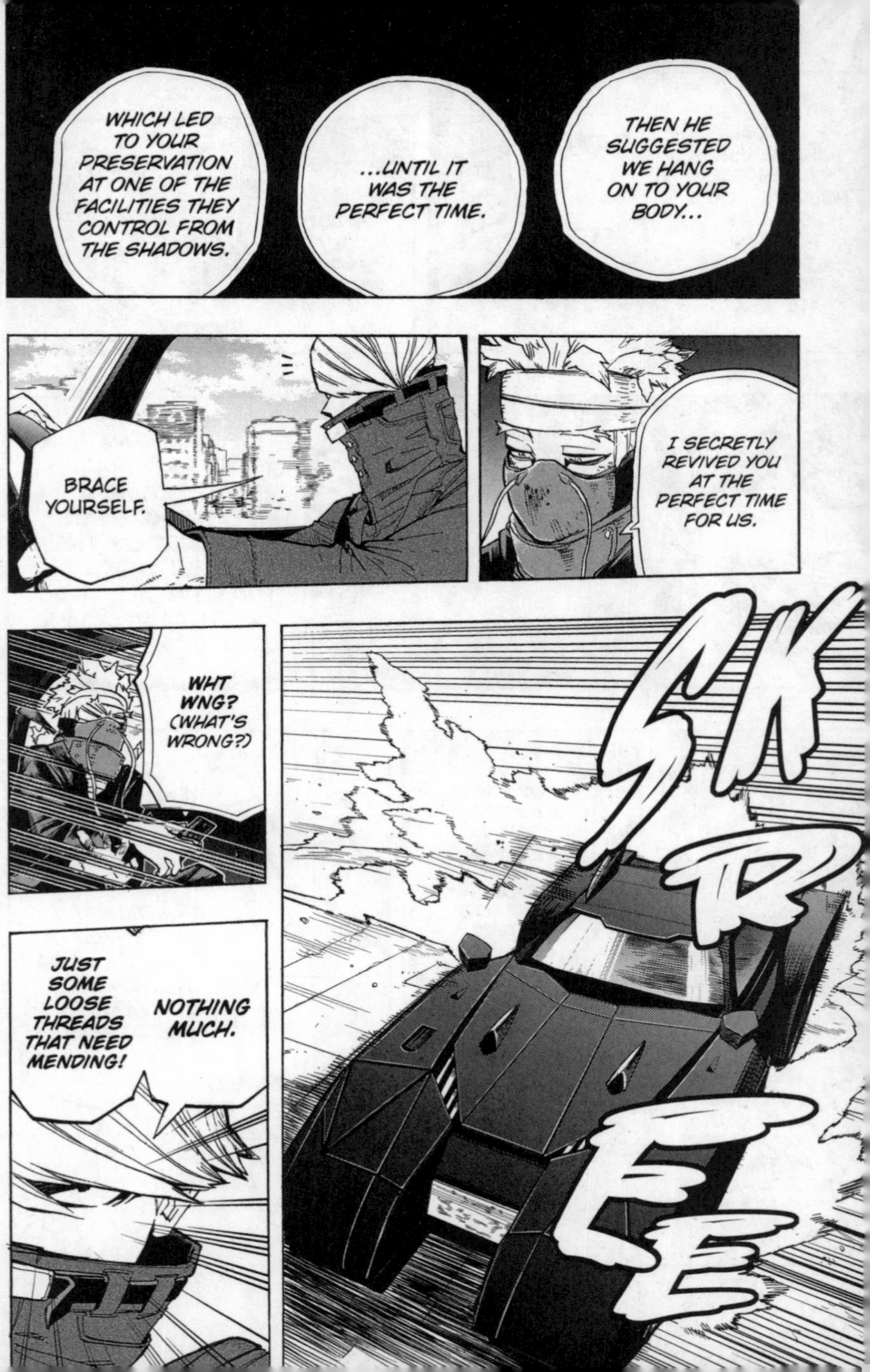
THEN HE SUGGESTED WE HANG ON TO YOUR BODY...
...UNTIL IT WAS THE PERFECT TIME.
WHICH LED TO YOUR PRESERVATION AT ONE OF THE FACILITIES THEY CONTROL FROM THE SHADOWS.
I SECRETLY REVIVED YOU AT THE PERFECT TIME FOR US.
BRACE YOURSELF.
SKREE
WHT WNG? (WHAT'S WRONG?)
NOTHING MUCH.
JUST SOME LOOSE THREADS THAT NEED MENDING!

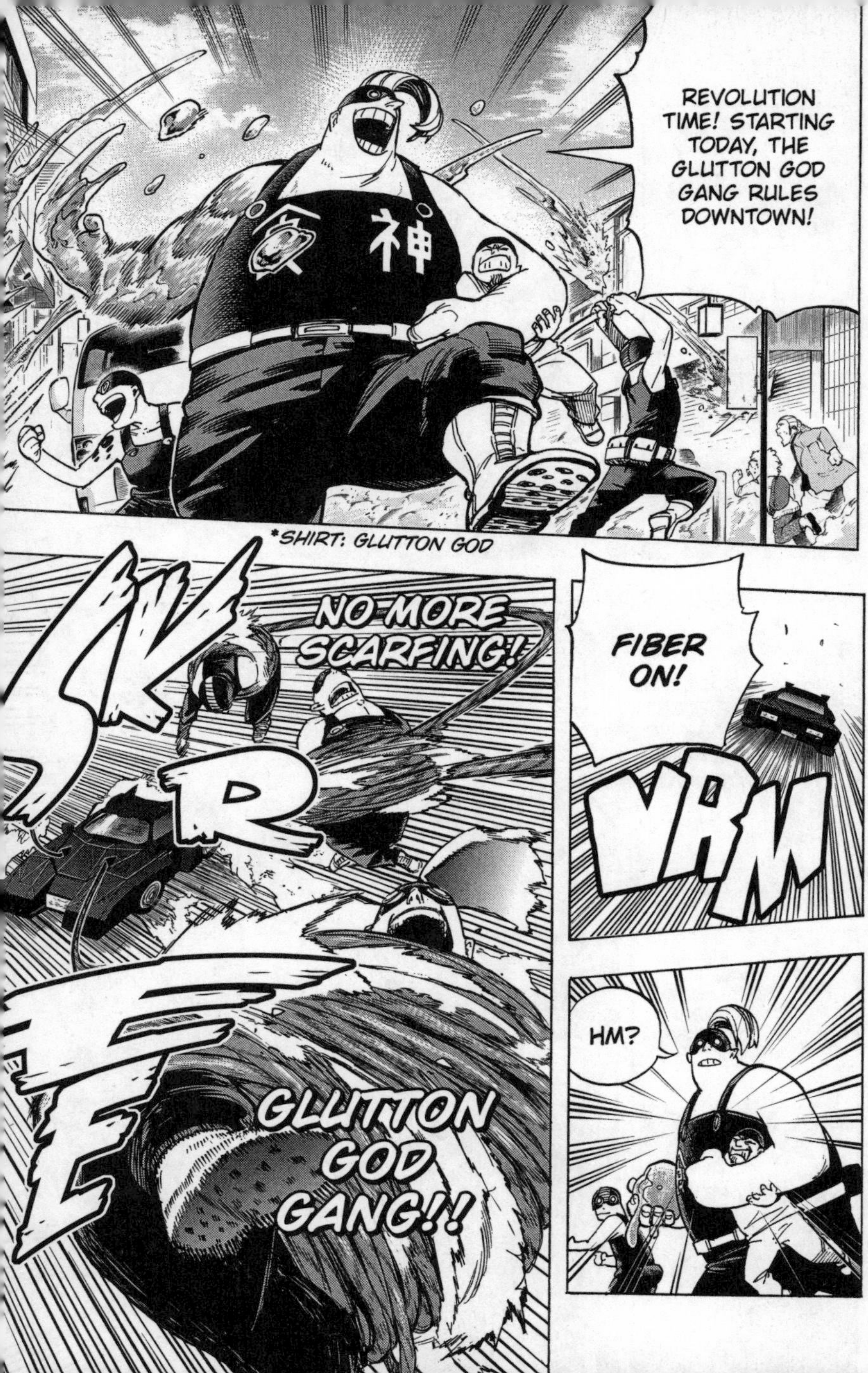
REVOLUTION TIME! STARTING TODAY, THE GLUTTON GOD GANG RULES DOWNTOWN!
*SHIRT: GLUTTON GOD
FIBER ON!
VRM
HM?
SKRF
NO MORE SCARFING!
GLUTTON GOD GANG!!

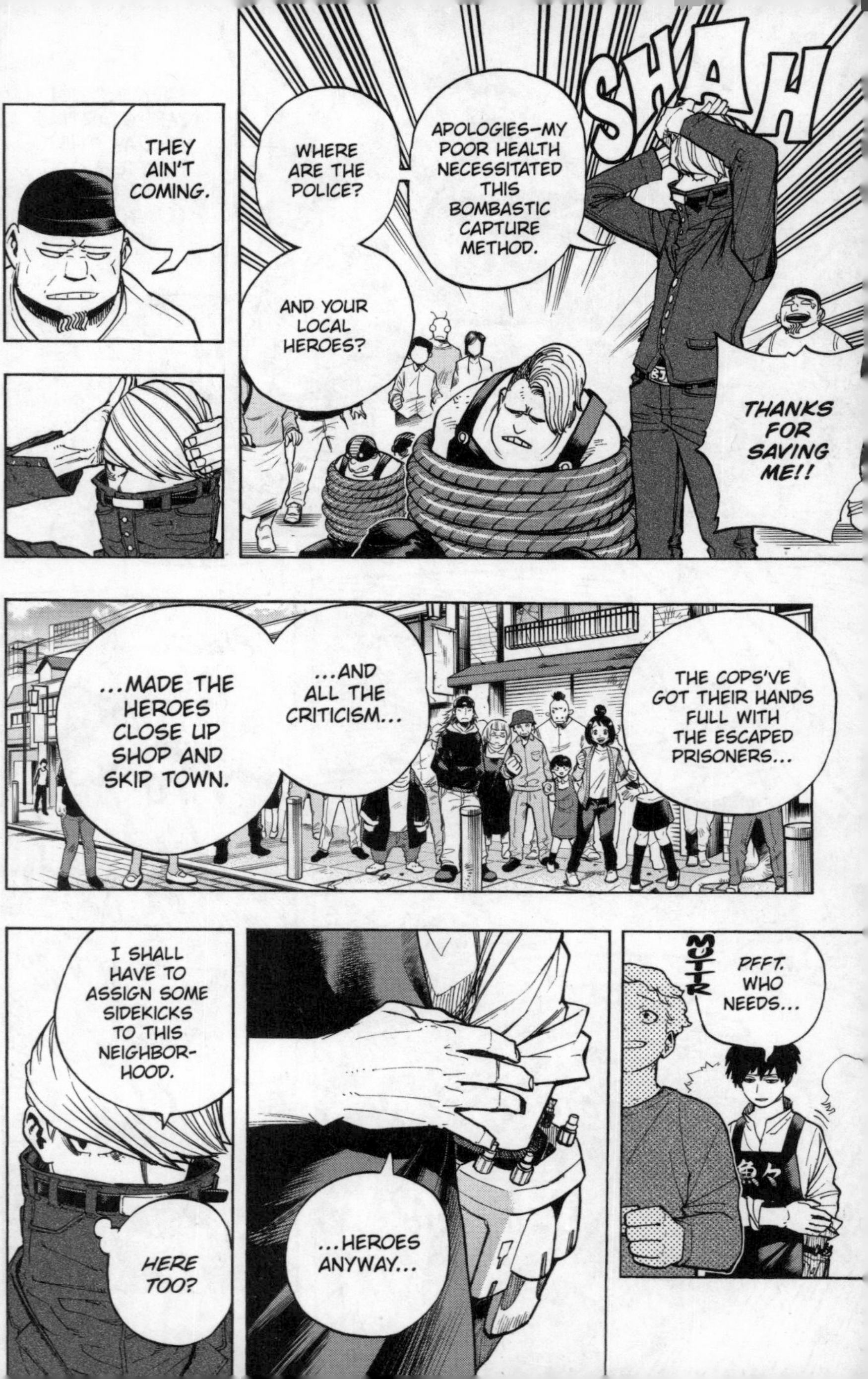
SHAH
THANKS FOR SAVING ME!!
APOLOGIES—MY POOR HEALTH NECESSITATED THIS BOMBASTIC CAPTURE METHOD.
WHERE ARE THE POLICE?
AND YOUR LOCAL HEROES?
THEY AIN'T COMING.
THE COPS'VE GOT THEIR HANDS FULL WITH THE ESCAPED PRISONERS...
...AND ALL THE CRITICISM...
...MADE THE HEROES CLOSE UP SHOP AND SKIP TOWN.
MUTTR
PFFT. WHO NEEDS...
...HEROES ANYWAY...
I SHALL HAVE TO ASSIGN SOME SIDEKICKS TO THIS NEIGHBOR-HOOD.
HERE TOO?

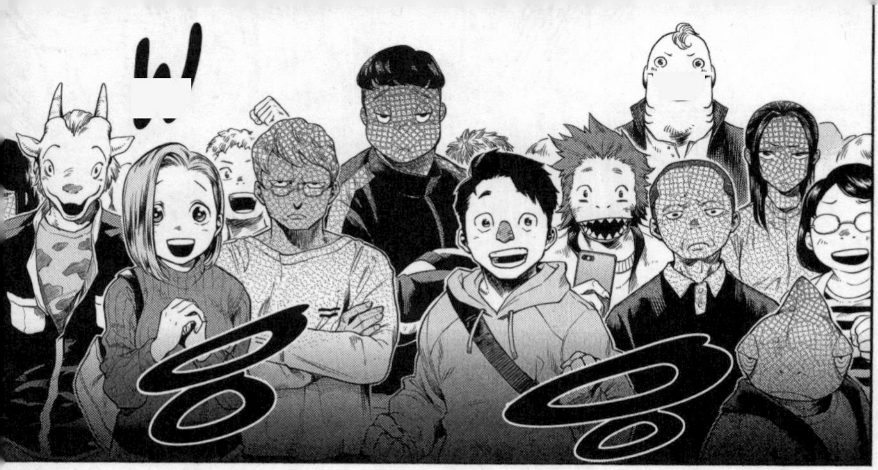

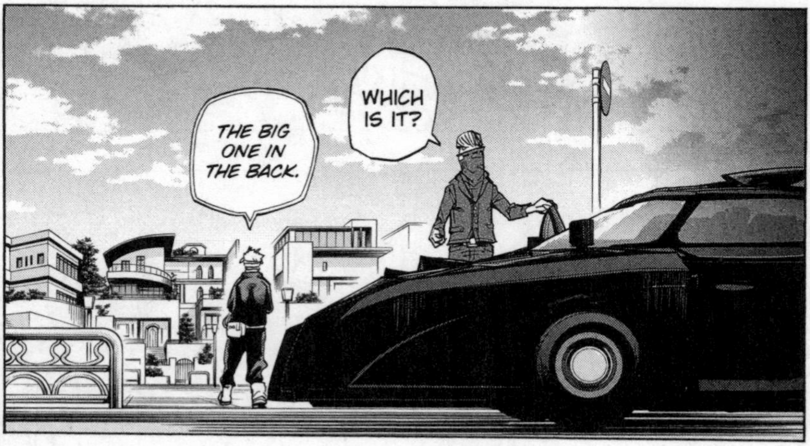
WHICH IS IT?
THE BIG ONE IN THE BACK.

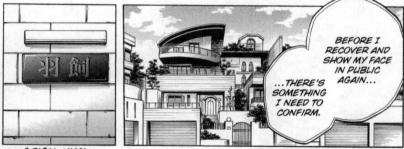

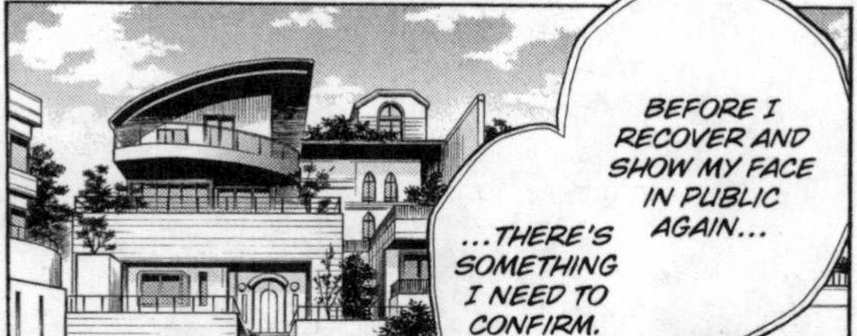
BEFORE I RECOVER AND SHOW MY FACE IN PUBLIC AGAIN...
...THERE'S SOMETHING I NEED TO CONFIRM.

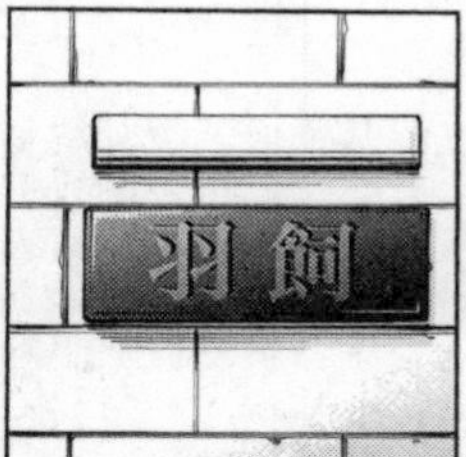
羽飼

*SIGN: UKAI

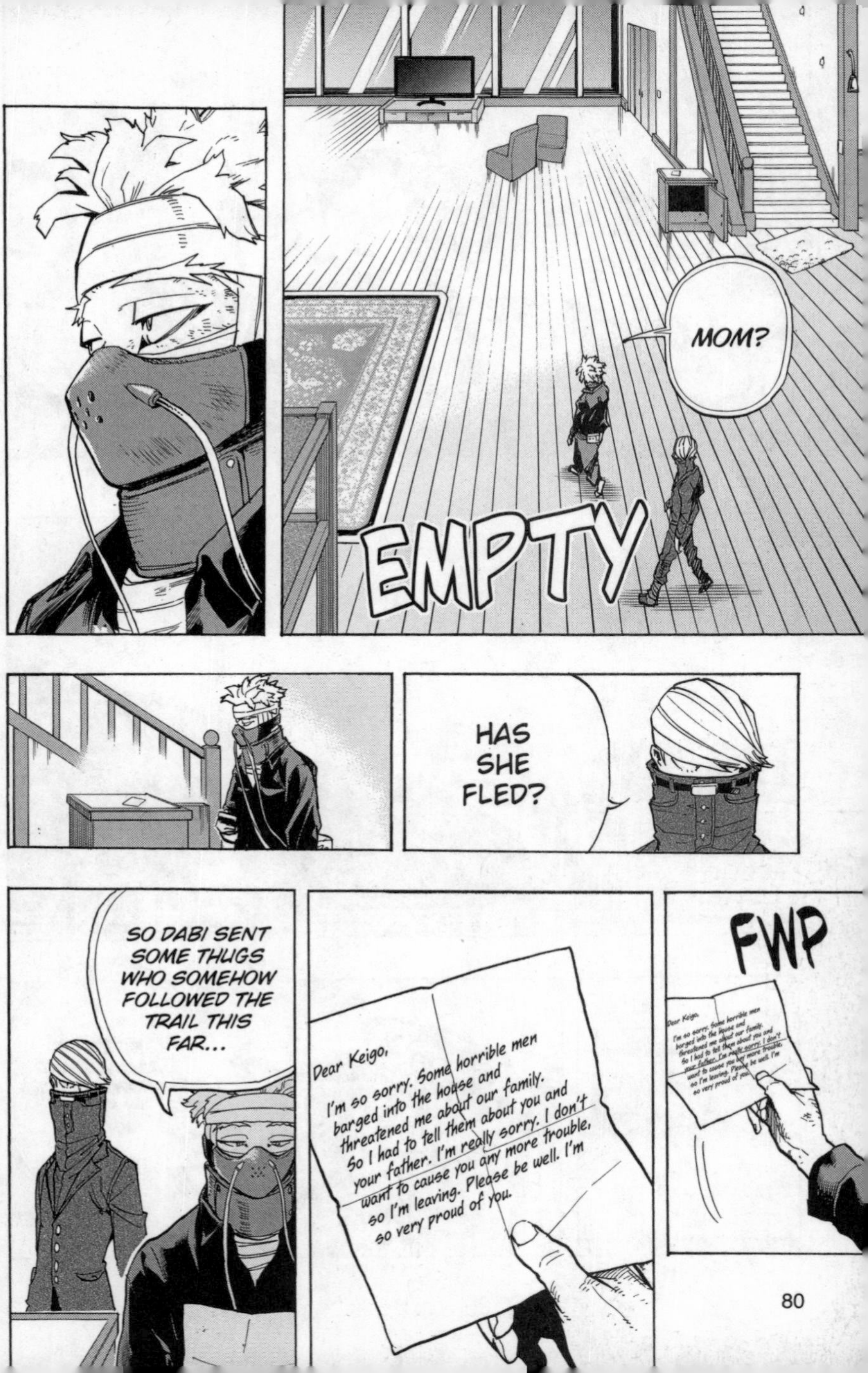
MOM?
EMPTY
HAS SHE FLED?
SO DABI SENT SOME THUGS WHO SOMEHOW FOLLOWED THE TRAIL THIS FAR...
Dear Keigo,
I'm so sorry. Some horrible men barged into the house and threatened me about our family. So I had to tell them about you and your father. I'm really sorry. I don't want to cause you any more trouble, so I'm leaving. Please be well. I'm so very proud of you.
FWP

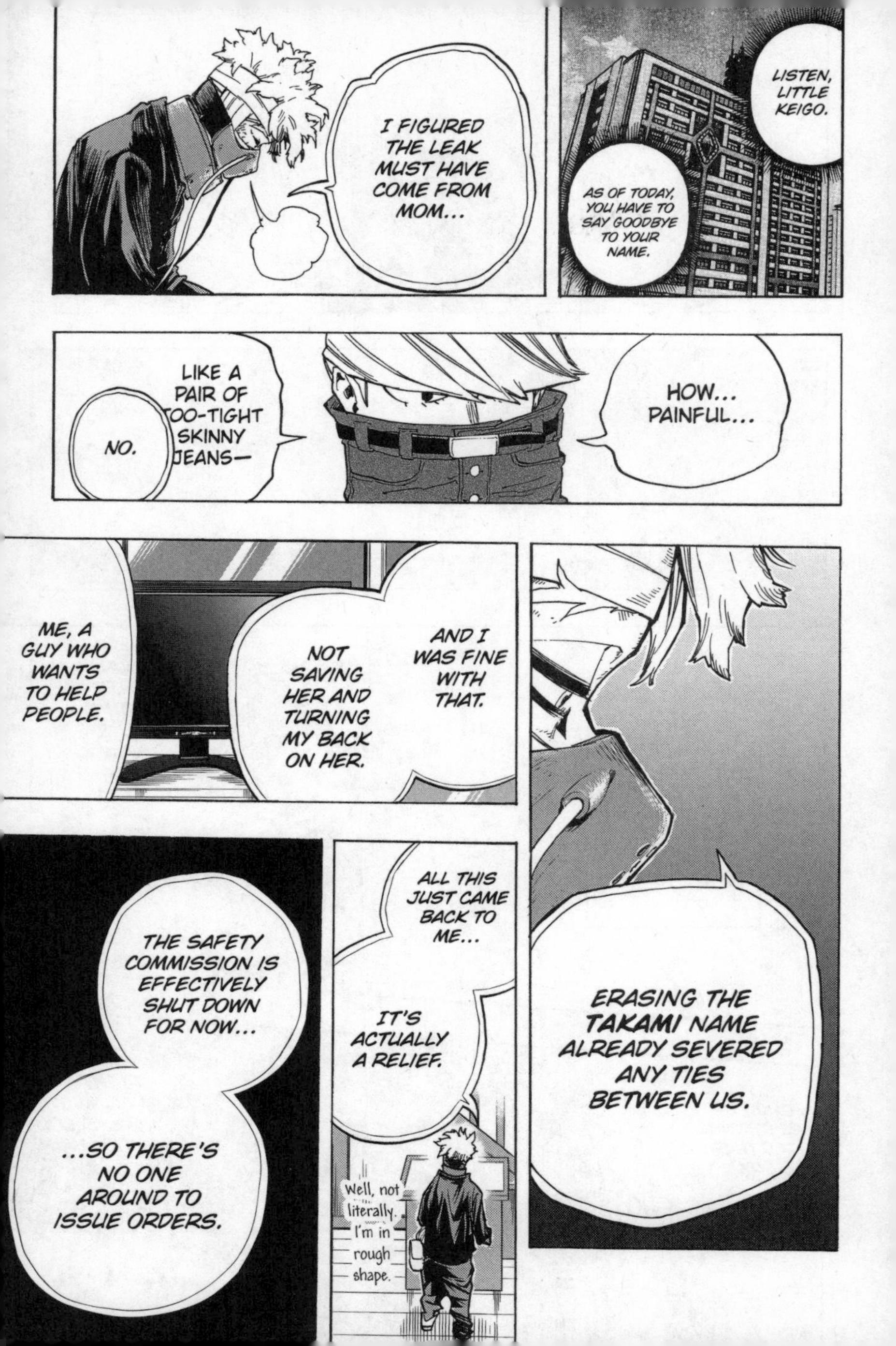
LISTEN, LITTLE KEIGO.
AS OF TODAY, YOU HAVE TO SAY GOODBYE TO YOUR NAME.
I FIGURED THE LEAK MUST HAVE COME FROM MOM...
HOW... PAINFUL...
LIKE A PAIR OF TOO-TIGHT SKINNY JEANS—
NO.
ERASING THE TAKAMI NAME ALREADY SEVERED ANY TIES BETWEEN US.
AND I WAS FINE WITH THAT.
NOT SAVING HER AND TURNING MY BACK ON HER.
ME, A GUY WHO WANTS TO HELP PEOPLE.
ALL THIS JUST CAME BACK TO ME...
IT'S ACTUALLY A RELIEF.
Well, not literally. I'm in rough shape.
THE SAFETY COMMISSION IS EFFECTIVELY SHUT DOWN FOR NOW...
...SO THERE'S NO ONE AROUND TO ISSUE ORDERS.

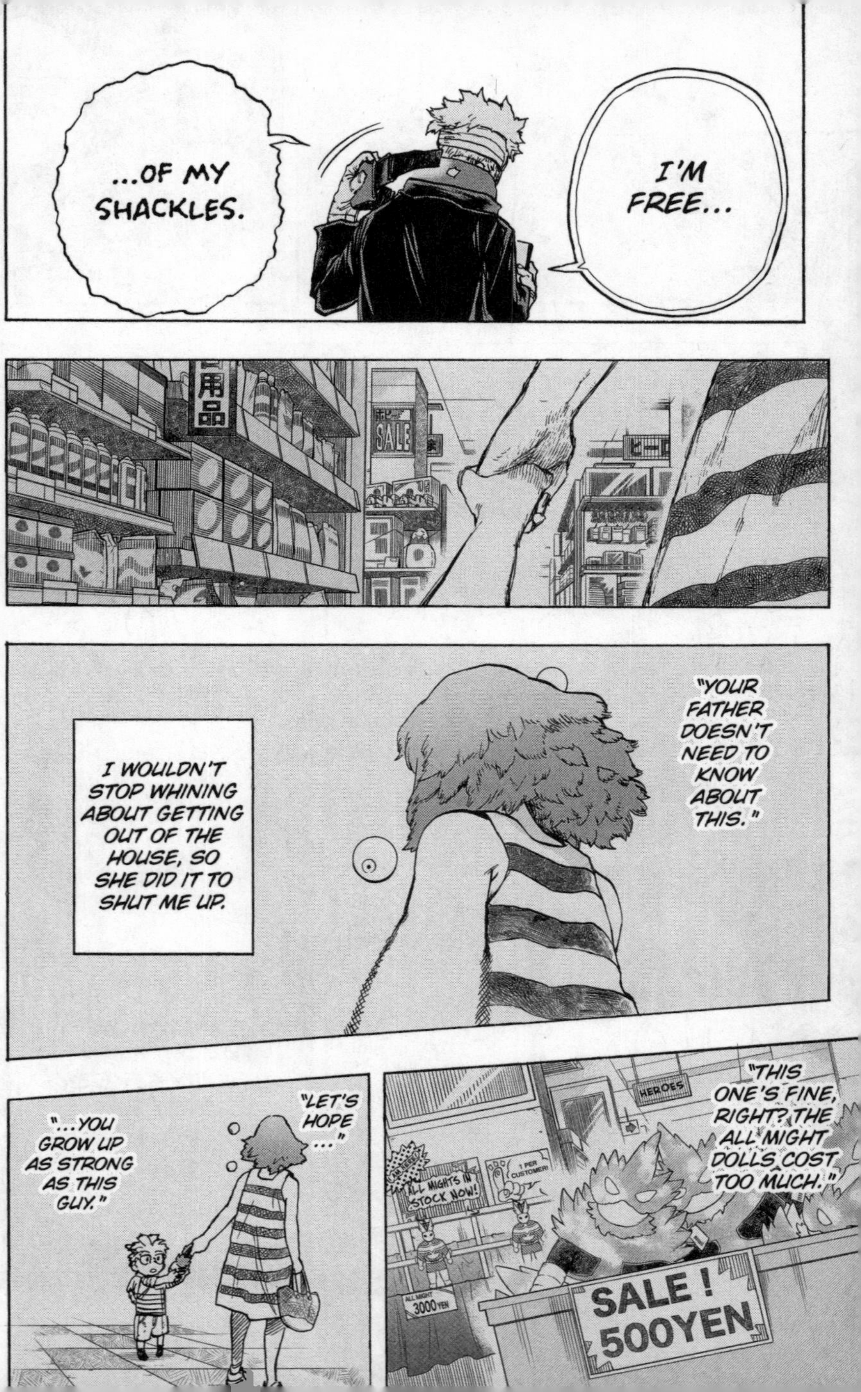
I'M FREE...
...OF MY SHACKLES.
SALE
"YOUR FATHER DOESN'T NEED TO KNOW ABOUT THIS."
I WOULDN'T STOP WHINING ABOUT GETTING OUT OF THE HOUSE, SO SHE DID IT TO SHUT ME UP.
"THIS ONE'S FINE, RIGHT? THE ALL MIGHT DOLLS COST TOO MUCH."
HEROES
1 PER CUSTOMER!
ALL MIGHTS IN STOCK NOW!
ALL MIGHT 3000 YEN
SALE ! 500YEN
"LET'S HOPE ..."
"...YOU GROW UP AS STRONG AS THIS GUY."

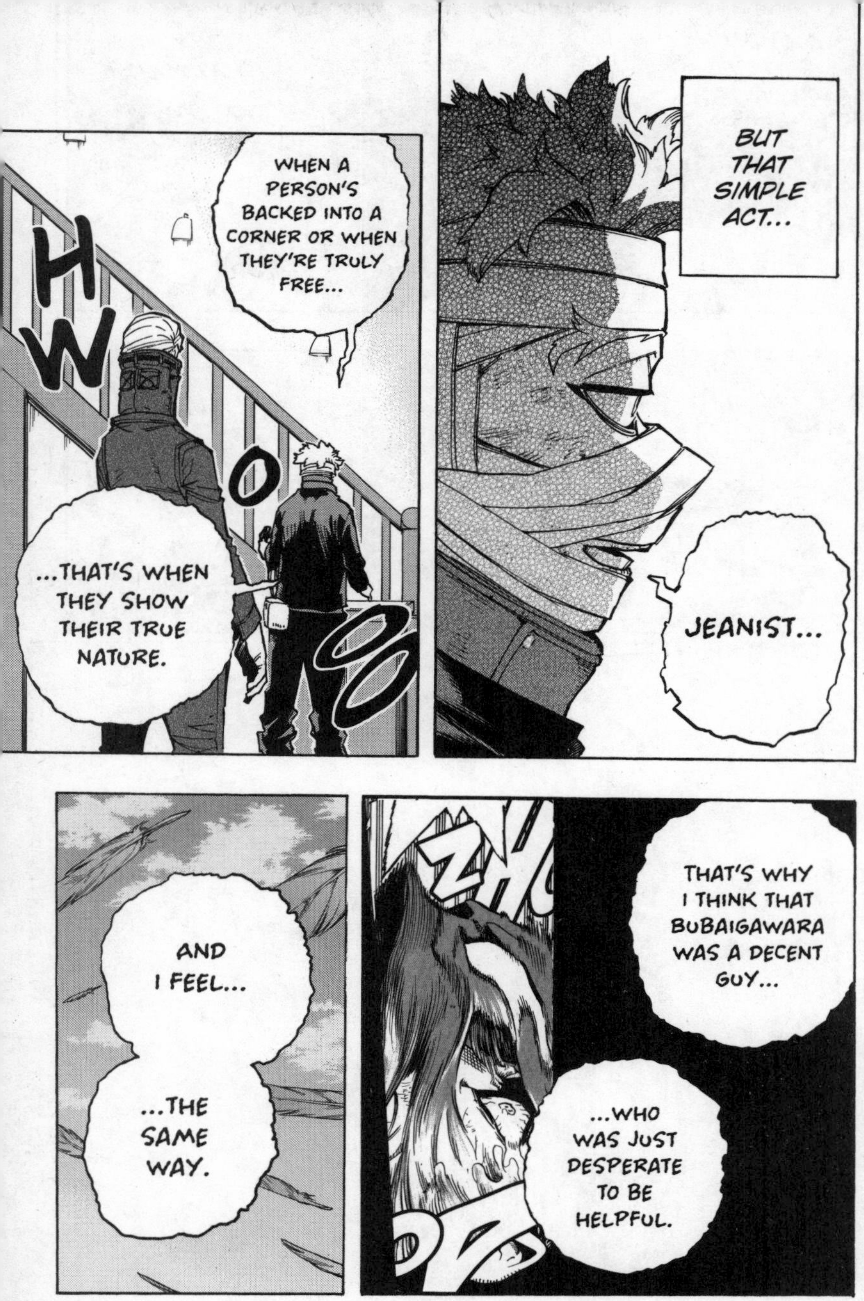
BUT THAT SIMPLE ACT...
JEANIST...
WHEN A PERSON'S BACKED INTO A CORNER OR WHEN THEY'RE TRULY FREE...
HWOOO
...THAT'S WHEN THEY SHOW THEIR TRUE NATURE.
ZHO
THAT'S WHY I THINK THAT BUBAIGAWARA WAS A DECENT GUY...
...WHO WAS JUST DESPERATE TO BE HELPFUL.
AND I FEEL...
...THE SAME WAY.

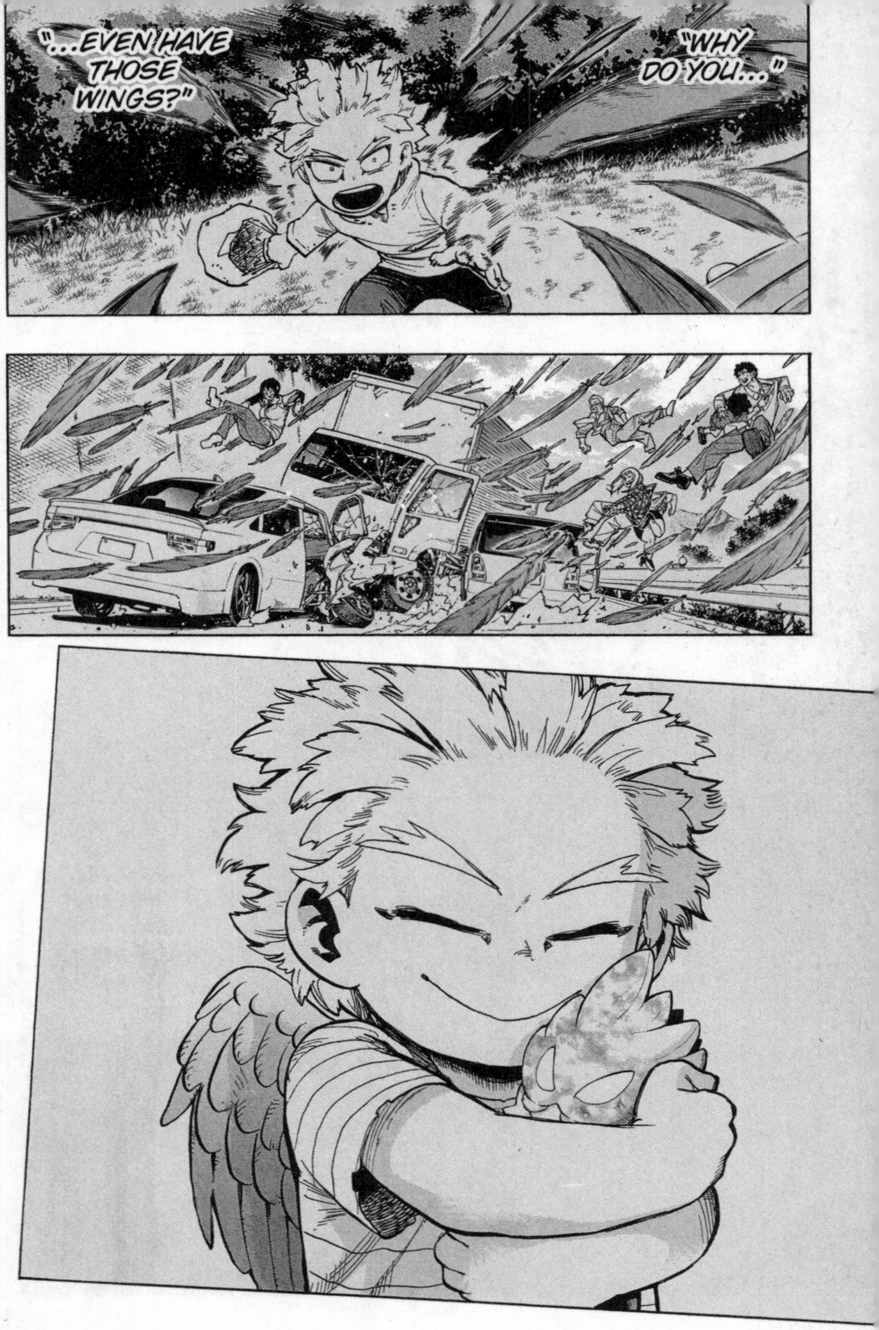
"WHY DO YOU..."
"...EVEN HAVE THOSE WINGS?"

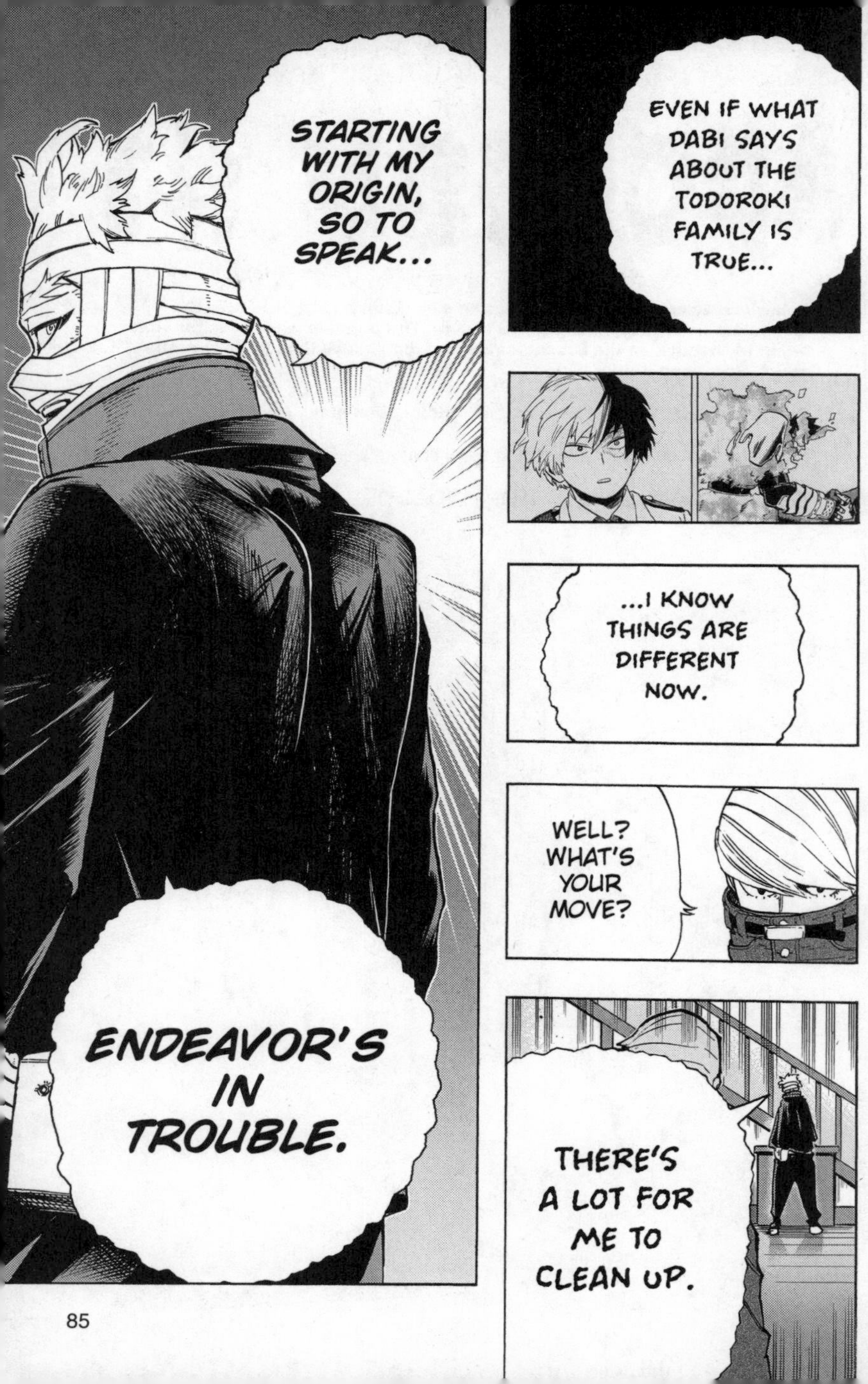

EVEN IF WHAT DABI SAYS ABOUT THE TODOROKI FAMILY IS TRUE...
...I KNOW THINGS ARE DIFFERENT NOW.
WELL? WHAT'S YOUR MOVE?
THERE'S A LOT FOR ME TO CLEAN UP.
STARTING WITH MY ORIGIN, SO TO SPEAK...
ENDEAVOR'S IN TROUBLE.

APOLOGY #1

In the weekly chapter release of Hawks's backstory, I forgot to give the characters an appropriate regional accent. The problem was, I was running behind schedule, so the accent consultant didn't have time to go over the script. Sorry about that.

By the way, that accent consultant is Yoritomi, one of my former editors.

Recently, Yoritomi got promoted to team leader.

Treat me to a meal or two, Mr. Fancypants Boss Man!

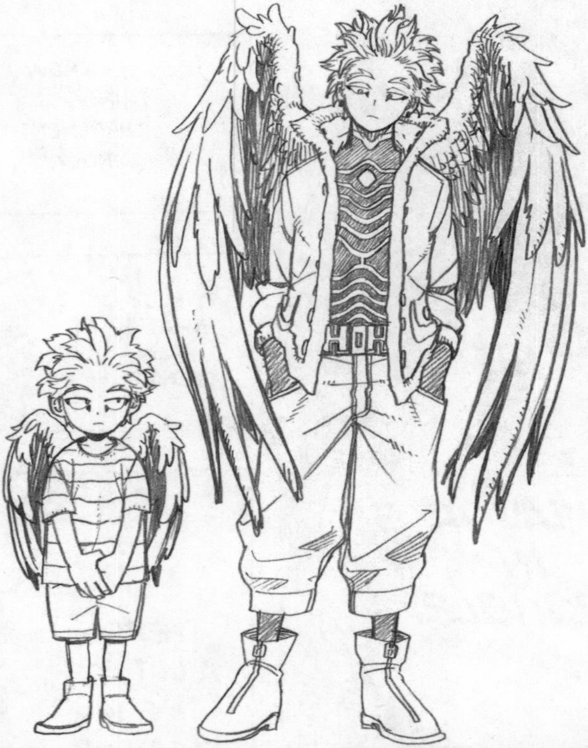
HOK

No. 300 - The Hellish Todoroki Family, Part 2

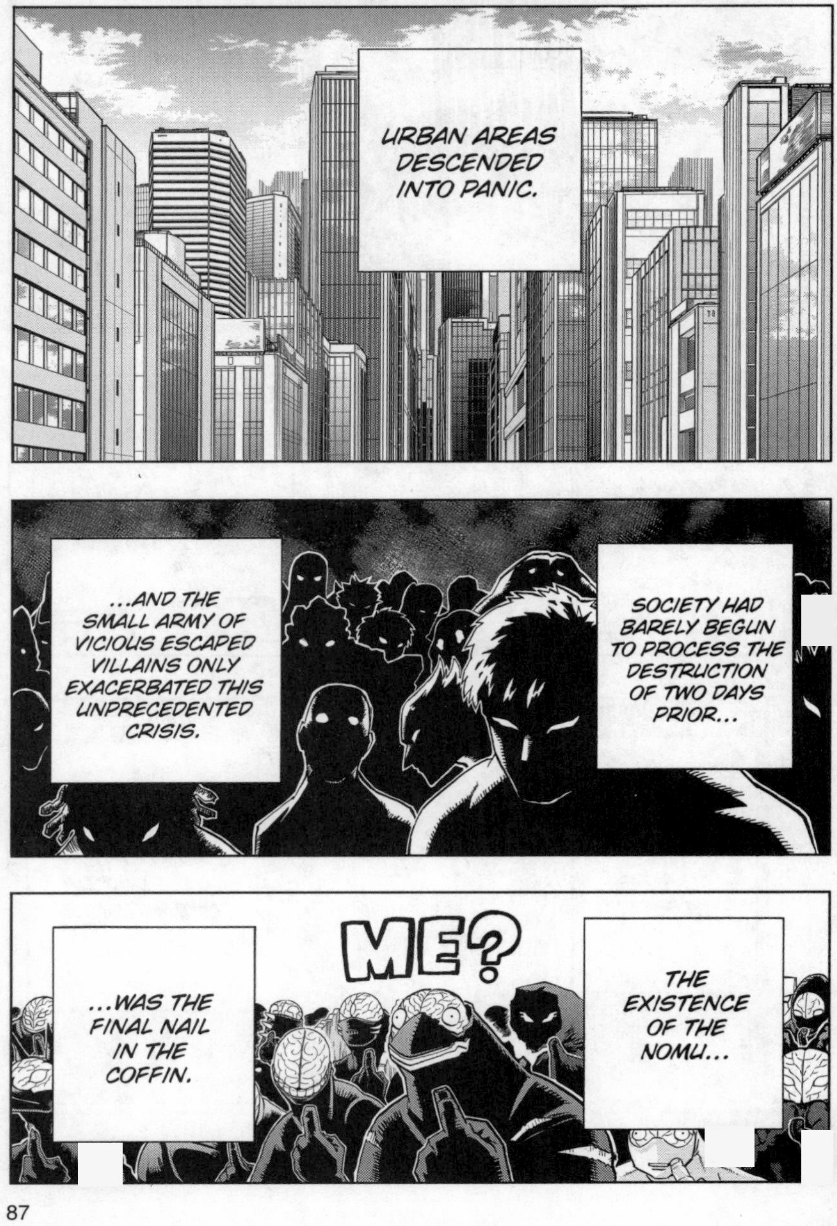
URBAN AREAS DESCENDED INTO PANIC.
SOCIETY HAD BARELY BEGUN TO PROCESS THE DESTRUCTION OF TWO DAYS PRIOR...
...AND THE SMALL ARMY OF VICIOUS ESCAPED VILLAINS ONLY EXACERBATED THIS UNPRECEDENTED CRISIS.
THE EXISTENCE OF THE NOMU...
ME?
...WAS THE FINAL NAIL IN THE COFFIN.

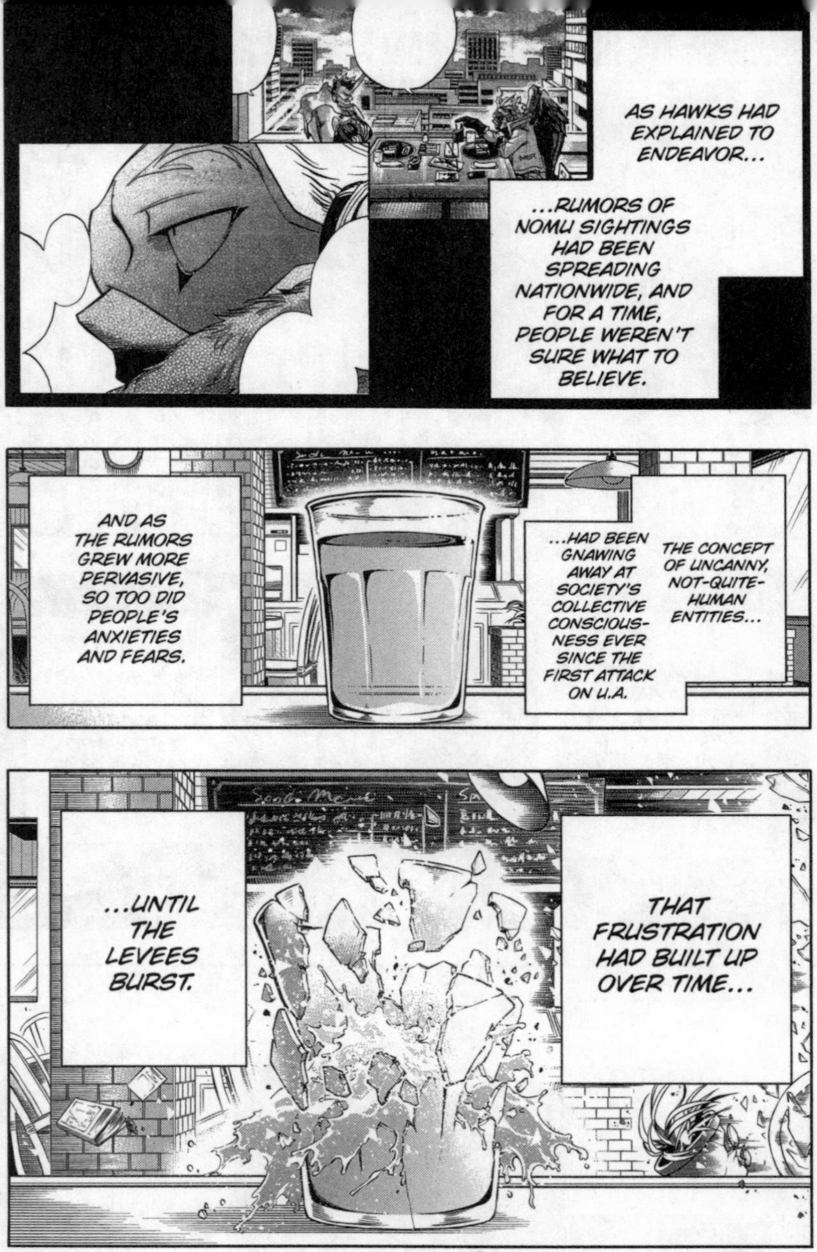
AS HAWKS HAD EXPLAINED TO ENDEAVOR...
...RUMORS OF NOMU SIGHTINGS HAD BEEN SPREADING NATIONWIDE, AND FOR A TIME, PEOPLE WEREN'T SURE WHAT TO BELIEVE.
THE CONCEPT OF UNCANNY, NOT-QUITE-HUMAN ENTITIES...
...HAD BEEN GNAWING AWAY AT SOCIETY'S COLLECTIVE CONSCIOUSNESS EVER SINCE THE FIRST ATTACK ON U.A.
AND AS THE RUMORS GREW MORE PERVASIVE, SO TOO DID PEOPLE'S ANXIETIES AND FEARS.
THAT FRUSTRATION HAD BUILT UP OVER TIME...
...UNTIL THE LEVEES BURST.

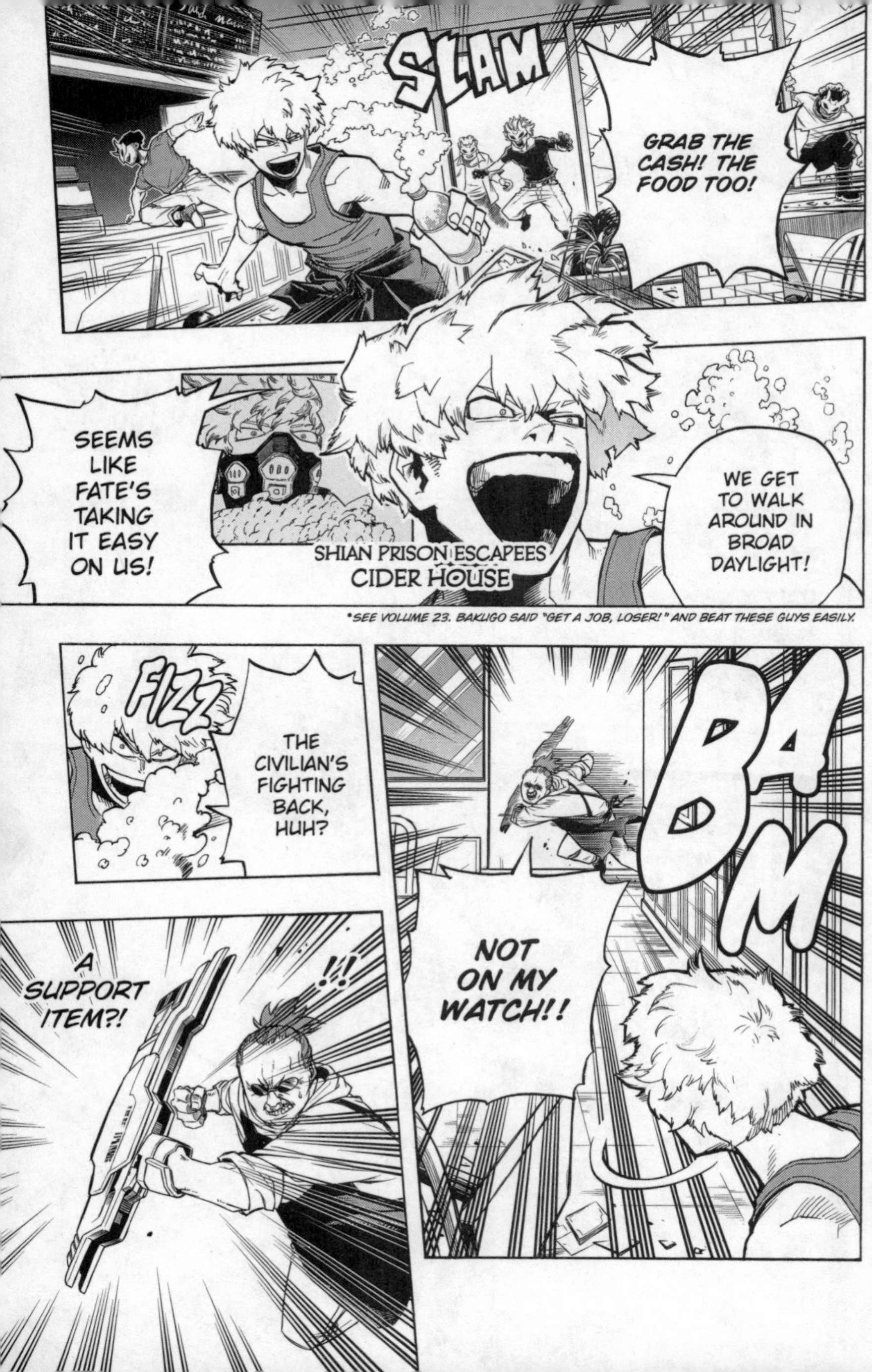
SLAM
GRAB THE CASH! THE FOOD TOO!
WE GET TO WALK AROUND IN BROAD DAYLIGHT!
SEEMS LIKE FATE'S TAKING IT EASY ON US!
SHIAN PRISON ESCAPEES
CIDER HOUSE
*SEE VOLUME 23. BAKUGO SAID "GET A JOB, LOSER!" AND BEAT THESE GUYS EASILY.
BAM
NOT ON MY WATCH!!
FIZZ
THE CIVILIAN'S FIGHTING BACK, HUH?
!!
A SUPPORT ITEM?!

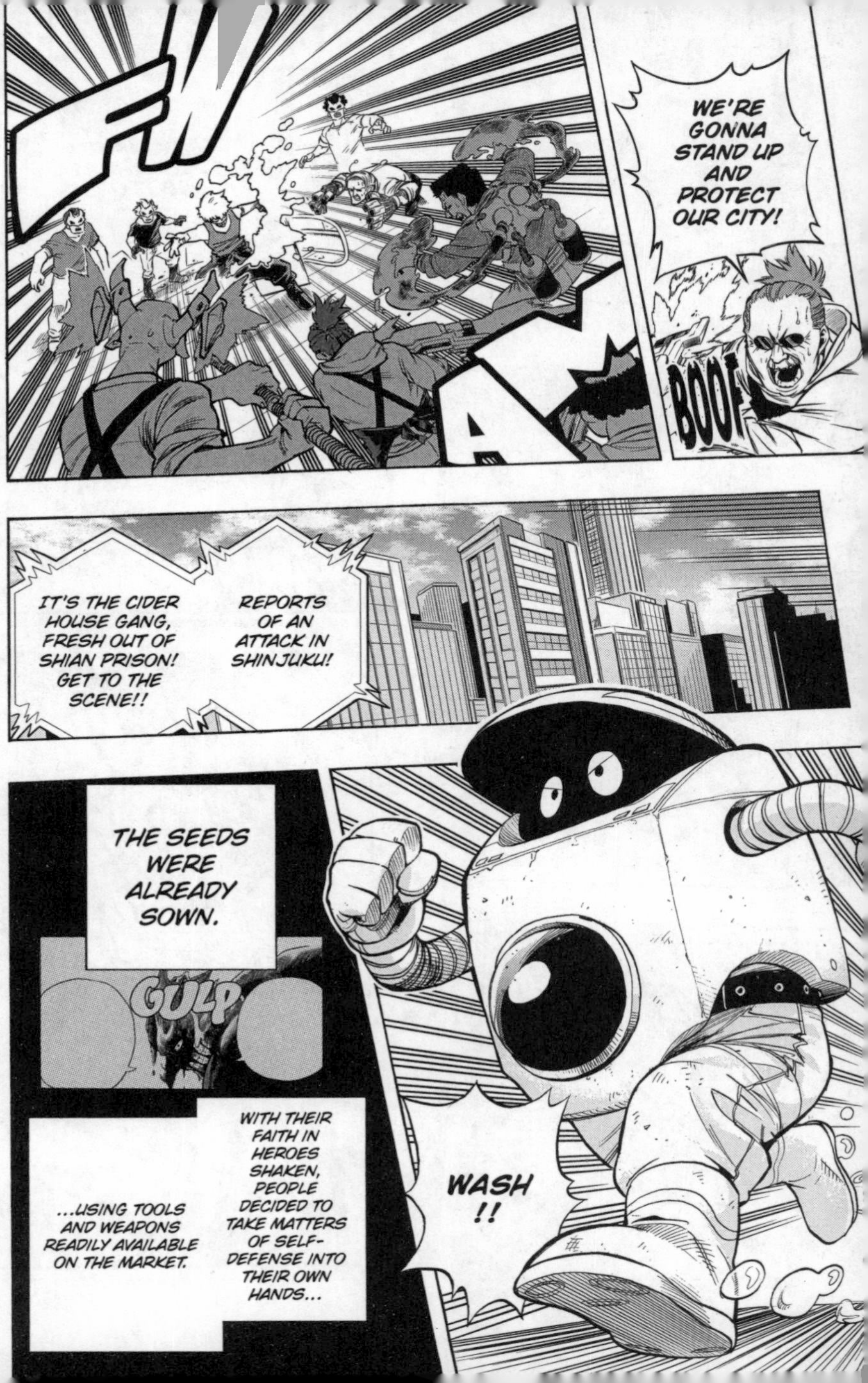
WE'RE GONNA STAND UP AND PROTECT OUR CITY!
BOOF
FW
REPORTS OF AN ATTACK IN SHINJUKU!
IT'S THE CIDER HOUSE GANG, FRESH OUT OF SHIAN PRISON! GET TO THE SCENE!!
WASH!!
THE SEEDS WERE ALREADY SOWN.
GULP
WITH THEIR FAITH IN HEROES SHAKEN, PEOPLE DECIDED TO TAKE MATTERS OF SELF-DEFENSE INTO THEIR OWN HANDS...
...USING TOOLS AND WEAPONS READILY AVAILABLE ON THE MARKET.

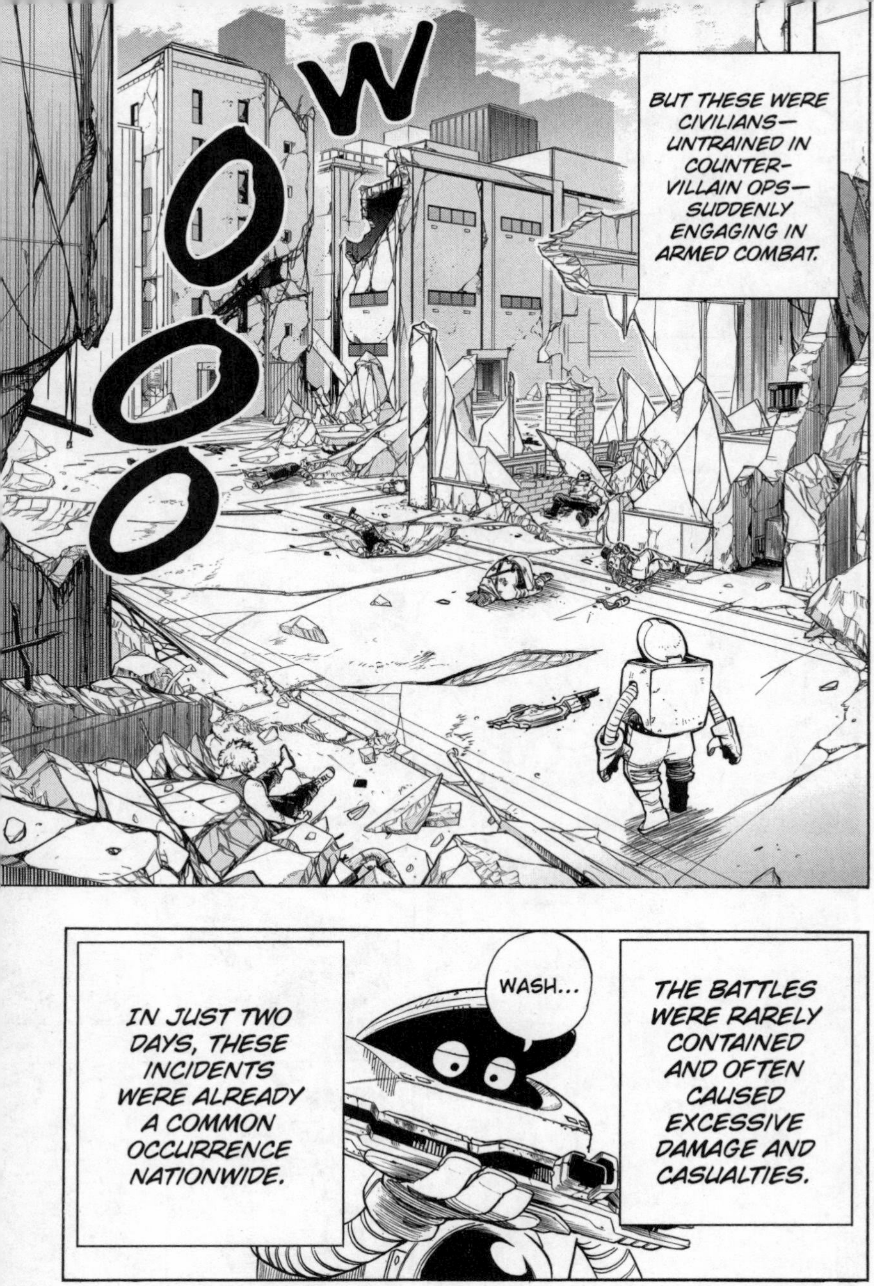
BUT THESE WERE CIVILIANS— UNTRAINED IN COUNTER-VILLAIN OPS— SUDDENLY ENGAGING IN ARMED COMBAT.
WOOO
THE BATTLES WERE RARELY CONTAINED AND OFTEN CAUSED EXCESSIVE DAMAGE AND CASUALTIES.
WASH...
IN JUST TWO DAYS, THESE INCIDENTS WERE ALREADY A COMMON OCCURRENCE NATIONWIDE.

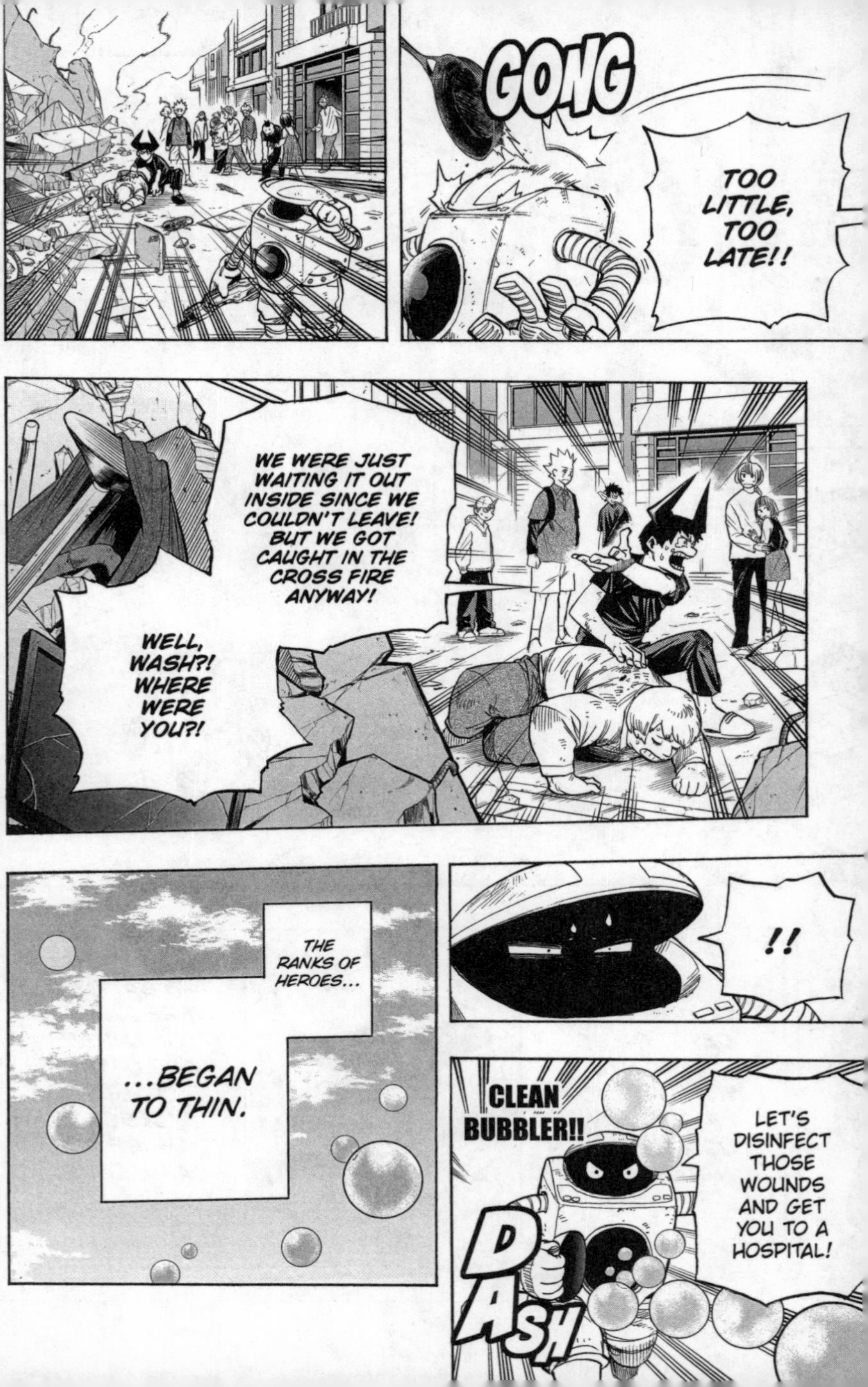
GONG
TOO LITTLE, TOO LATE!!
WE WERE JUST WAITING IT OUT INSIDE SINCE WE COULDN'T LEAVE! BUT WE GOT CAUGHT IN THE CROSS FIRE ANYWAY!
WELL, WASH?! WHERE WERE YOU?!
!!
LET'S DISINFECT THOSE WOUNDS AND GET YOU TO A HOSPITAL!
CLEAN BUBBLER!!
DASH
THE RANKS OF HEROES...
...BEGAN TO THIN.

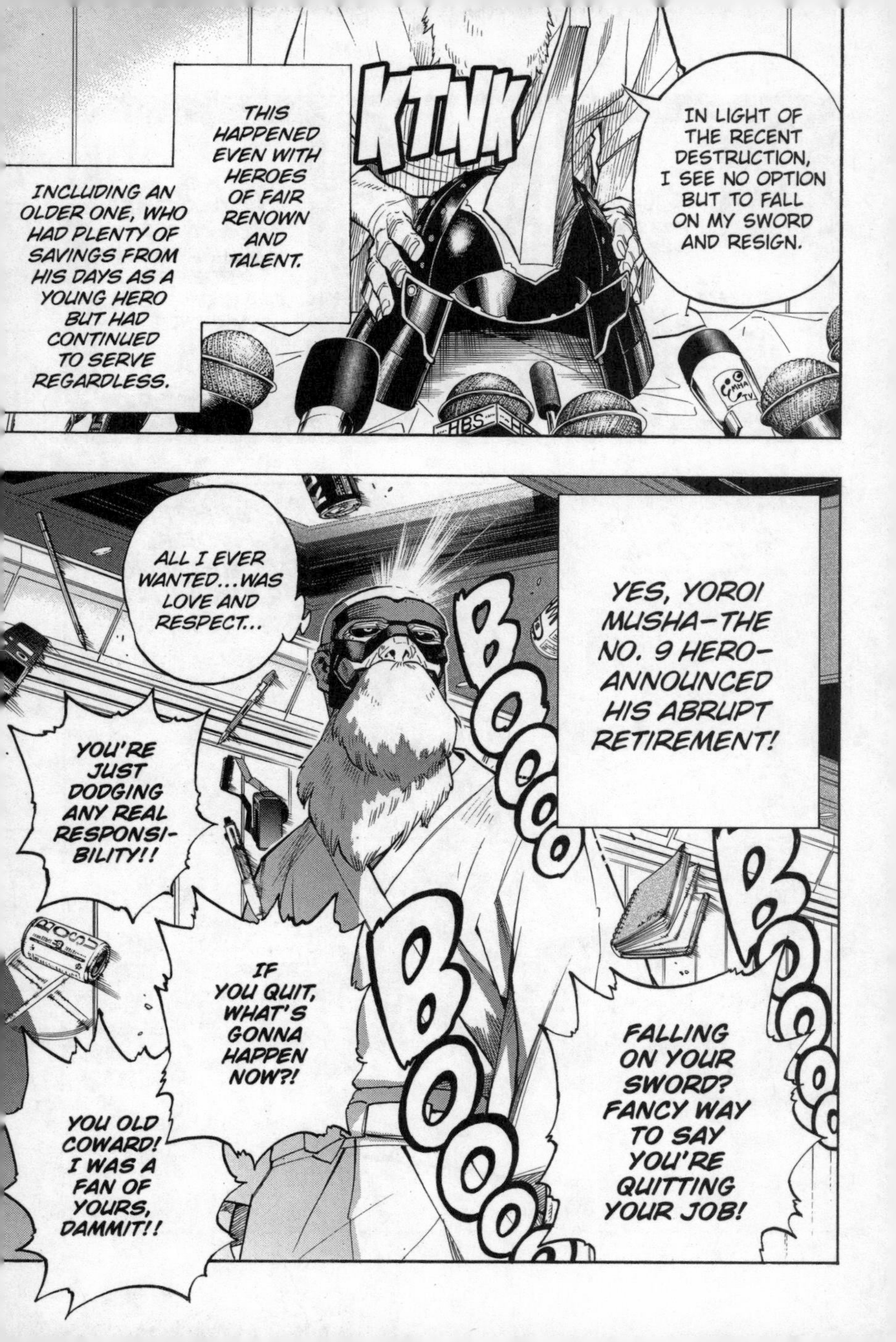
IN LIGHT OF THE RECENT DESTRUCTION, I SEE NO OPTION BUT TO FALL ON MY SWORD AND RESIGN.
KTNK
THIS HAPPENED EVEN WITH HEROES OF FAIR RENOWN AND TALENT.
INCLUDING AN OLDER ONE, WHO HAD PLENTY OF SAVINGS FROM HIS DAYS AS A YOUNG HERO BUT HAD CONTINUED TO SERVE REGARDLESS.
HBS
YES, YOROI MUSHA—THE NO. 9 HERO—ANNOUNCED HIS ABRUPT RETIREMENT!
BOOOOO
ALL I EVER WANTED...WAS LOVE AND RESPECT...
BOOOO
FALLING ON YOUR SWORD? FANCY WAY TO SAY YOU'RE QUITTING YOUR JOB!
BOOOOO
IF YOU QUIT, WHAT'S GONNA HAPPEN NOW?!
YOU'RE JUST DODGING ANY REAL RESPONSI-BILITY!!
YOU OLD COWARD! I WAS A FAN OF YOURS, DAMMIT!!

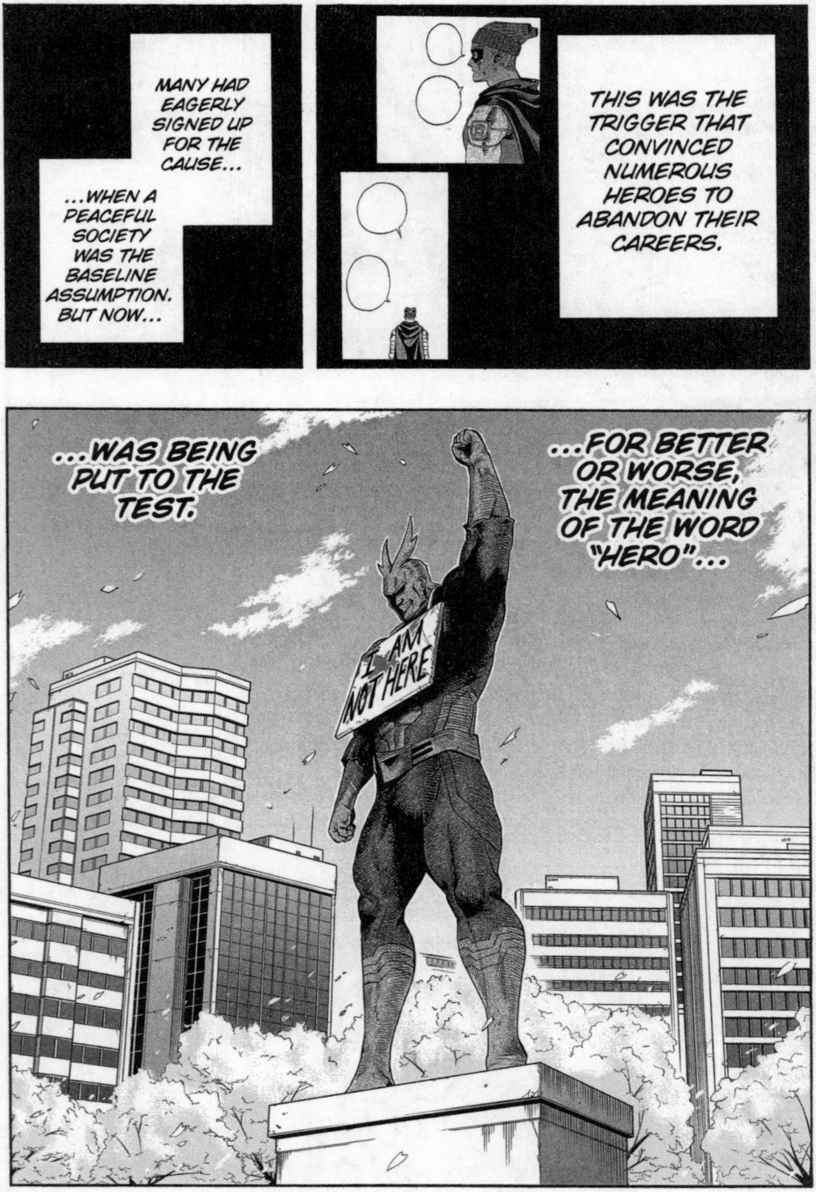
THIS WAS THE TRIGGER THAT CONVINCED NUMEROUS HEROES TO ABANDON THEIR CAREERS.
MANY HAD EAGERLY SIGNED UP FOR THE CAUSE...
...WHEN A PEACEFUL SOCIETY WAS THE BASELINE ASSUMPTION. BUT NOW...
...FOR BETTER OR WORSE, THE MEANING OF THE WORD "HERO"...
I AM NOT HERE
...WAS BEING PUT TO THE TEST.

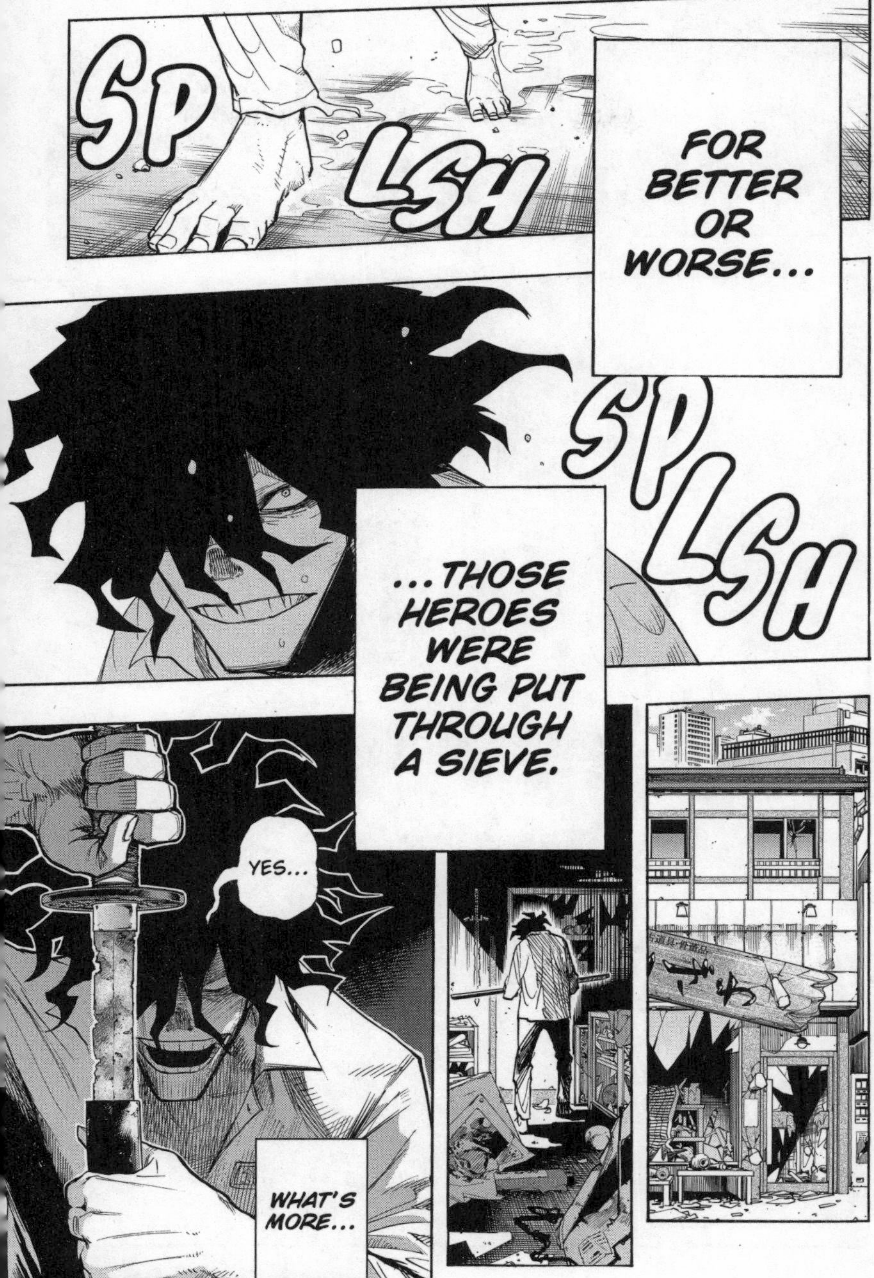
FOR BETTER OR WORSE...
SP LSH
SPLSH
...THOSE HEROES WERE BEING PUT THROUGH A SIEVE.
YES...
WHAT'S MORE...

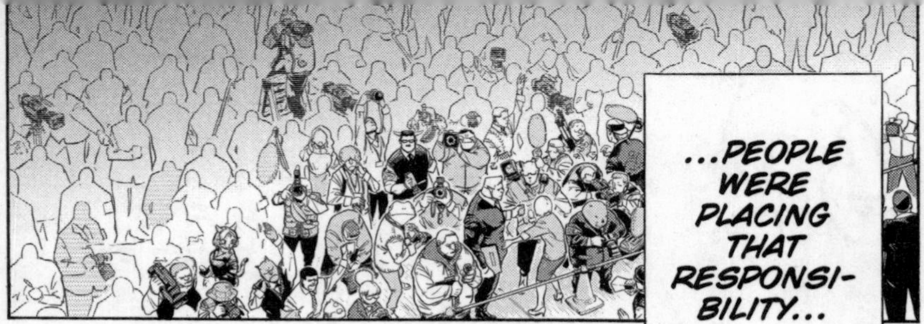
...PEOPLE WERE PLACING THAT RESPONSI-BILITY...
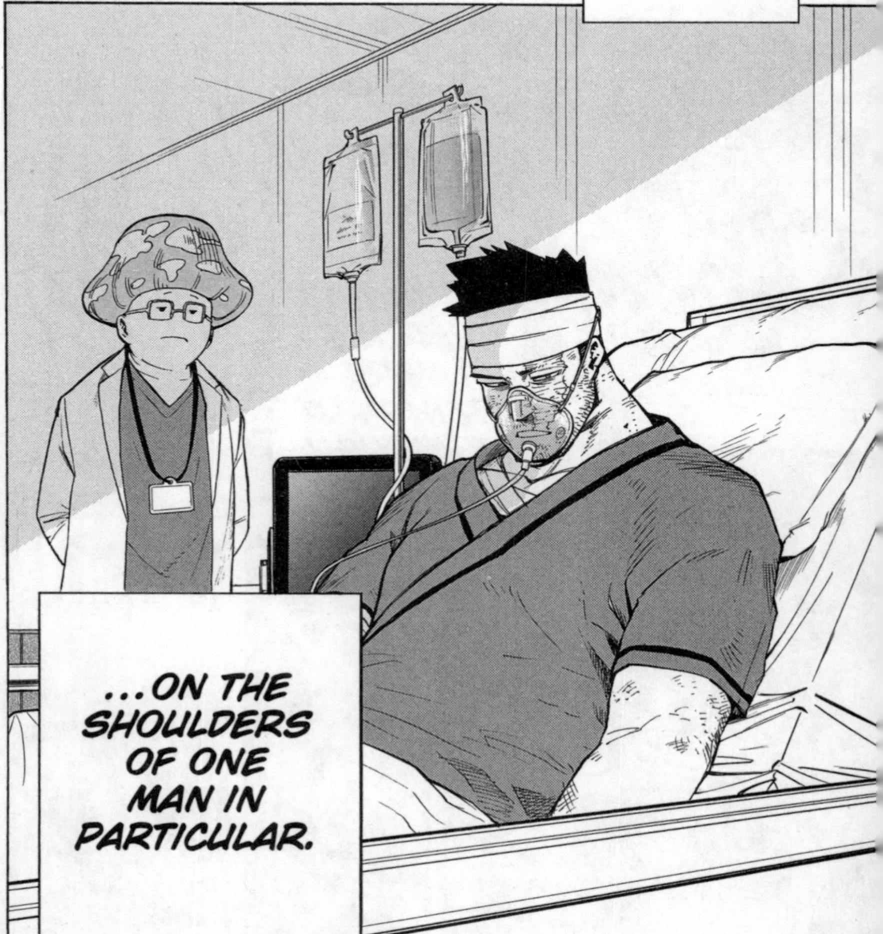
...ON THE SHOULDERS OF ONE MAN IN PARTICULAR.

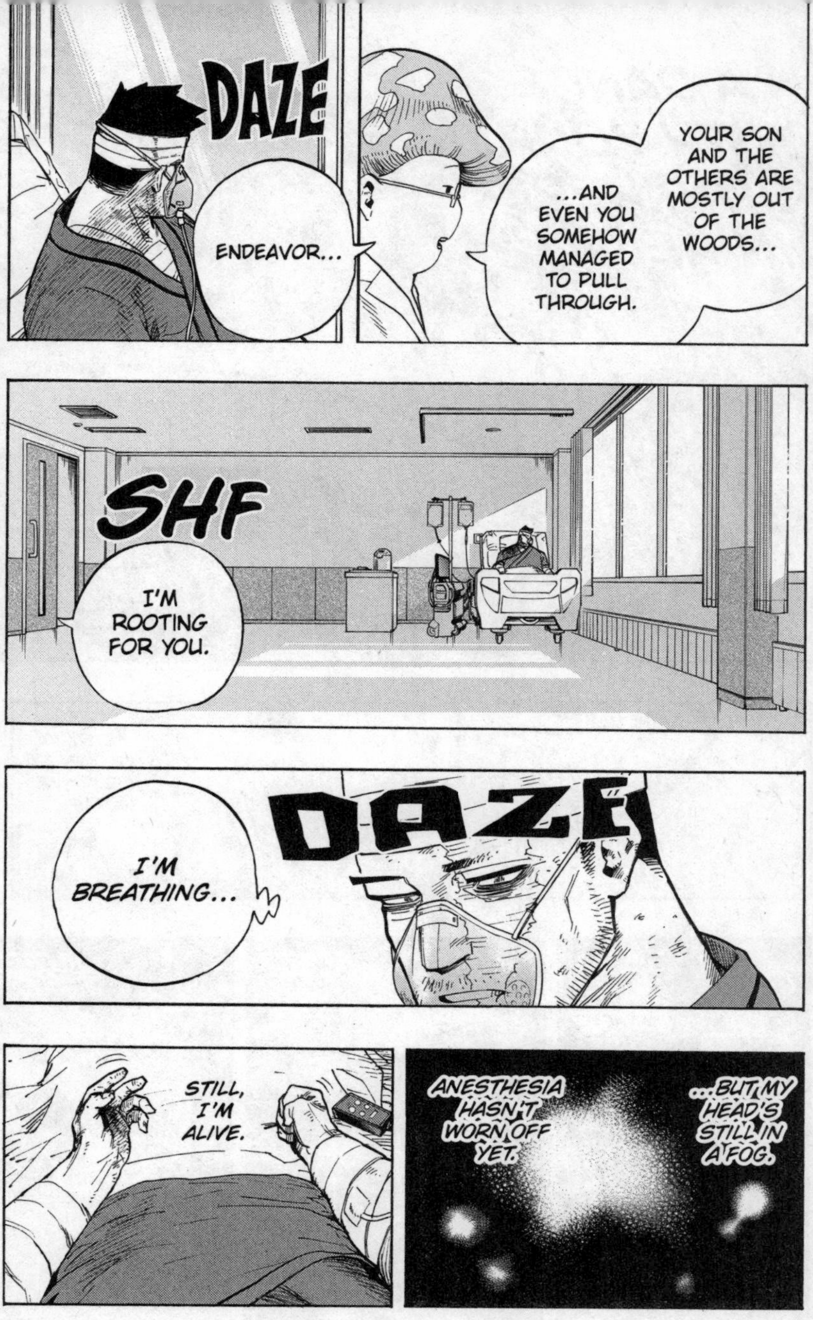
YOUR SON AND THE OTHERS ARE MOSTLY OUT OF THE WOODS...
...AND EVEN YOU SOMEHOW MANAGED TO PULL THROUGH.
DAZE
ENDEAVOR...
SHF
I'M ROOTING FOR YOU.
DAZE
I'M BREATHING...
...BUT MY HEAD'S STILL IN A FOG.
ANESTHESIA HASN'T WORN OFF YET.
STILL, I'M ALIVE.

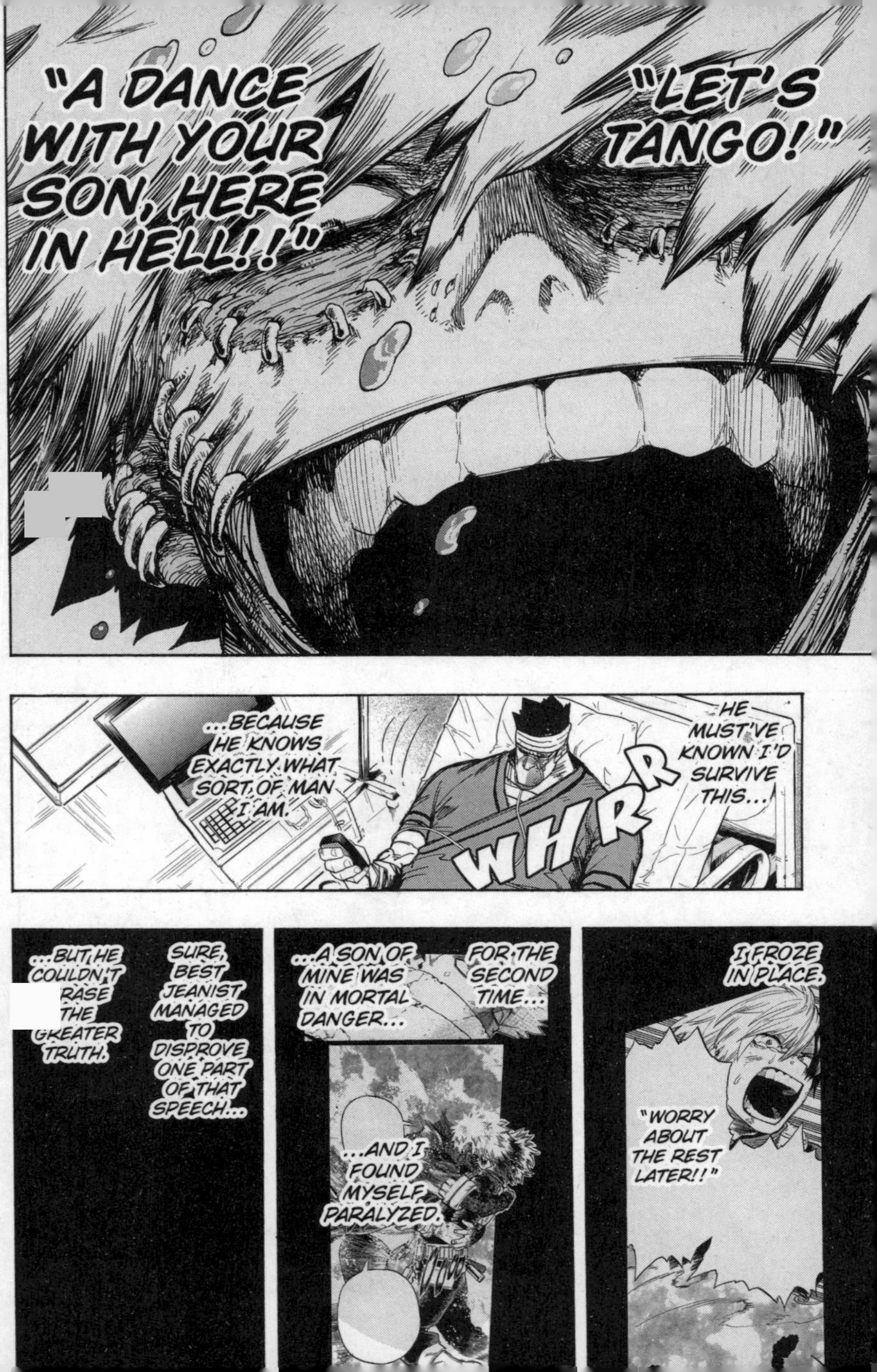
"LET'S TANGO!"
"A DANCE WITH YOUR SON, HERE IN HELL!!"
HE MUST'VE KNOWN I'D SURVIVE THIS...
WHRR
...BECAUSE HE KNOWS EXACTLY WHAT SORT OF MAN I AM.
I FROZE IN PLACE.
"WORRY ABOUT THE REST LATER!!"
FOR THE SECOND TIME...
...A SON OF MINE WAS IN MORTAL DANGER...
...AND I FOUND MYSELF PARALYZED.
SURE, BEST JEANIST MANAGED TO DISPROVE ONE PART OF THAT SPEECH...
...BUT HE COULDN'T RASE THE GREATER TRUTH.

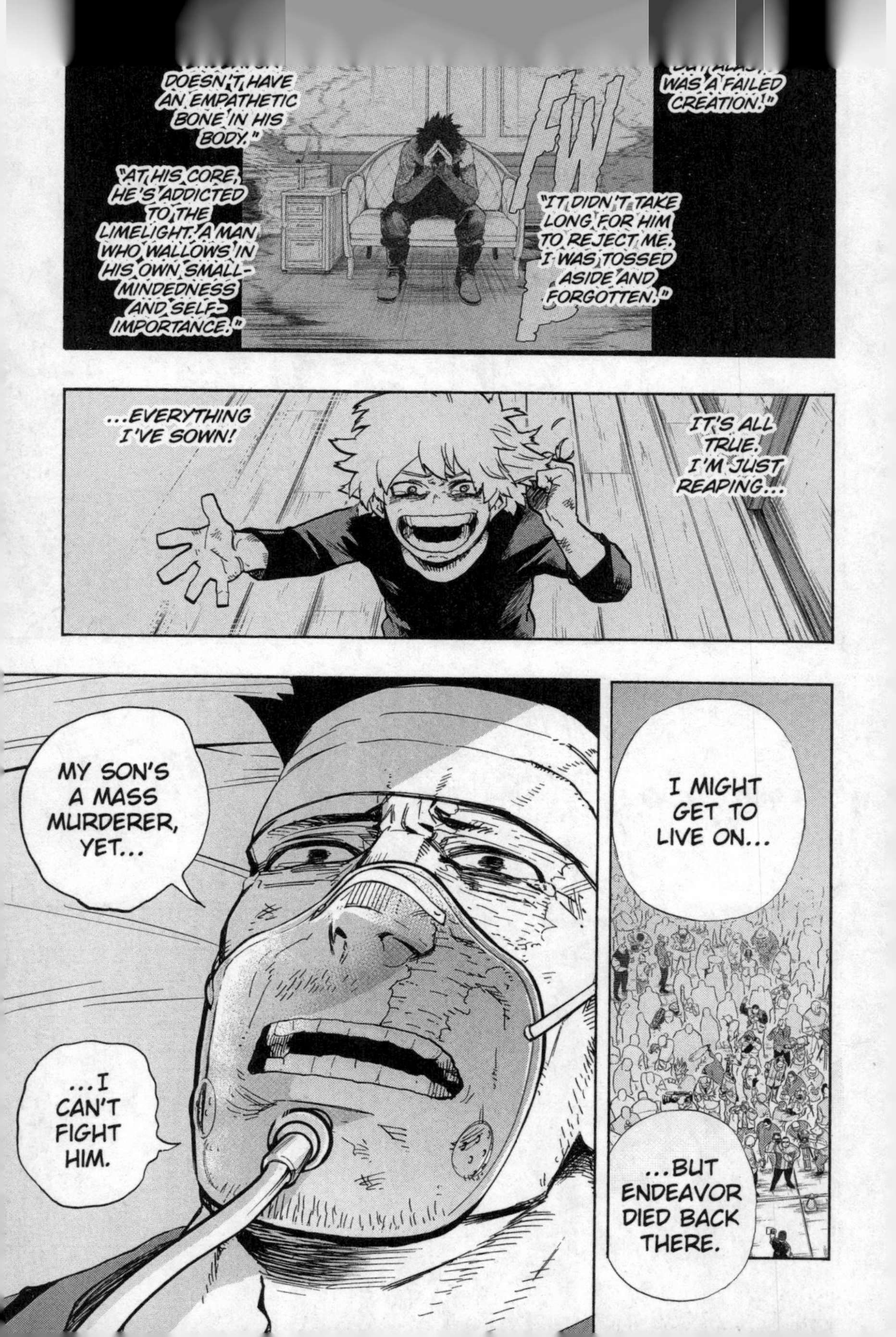
WAS A FAILED CREATION!"
FW
"IT DIDN'T TAKE LONG FOR HIM TO REJECT ME. I WAS TOSSED ASIDE AND FORGOTTEN."
DOESN'T HAVE AN EMPATHETIC BONE IN HIS BODY."
"AT HIS CORE, HE'S ADDICTED TO THE LIMELIGHT. A MAN WHO WALLOWS IN HIS OWN SMALL-MINDEDNESS AND SELF-IMPORTANCE."
IT'S ALL TRUE. I'M JUST REAPING...
...EVERYTHING I'VE SOWN!
I MIGHT GET TO LIVE ON...
...BUT ENDEAVOR DIED BACK THERE.
MY SON'S A MASS MURDERER, YET...
...I CAN'T FIGHT HIM.

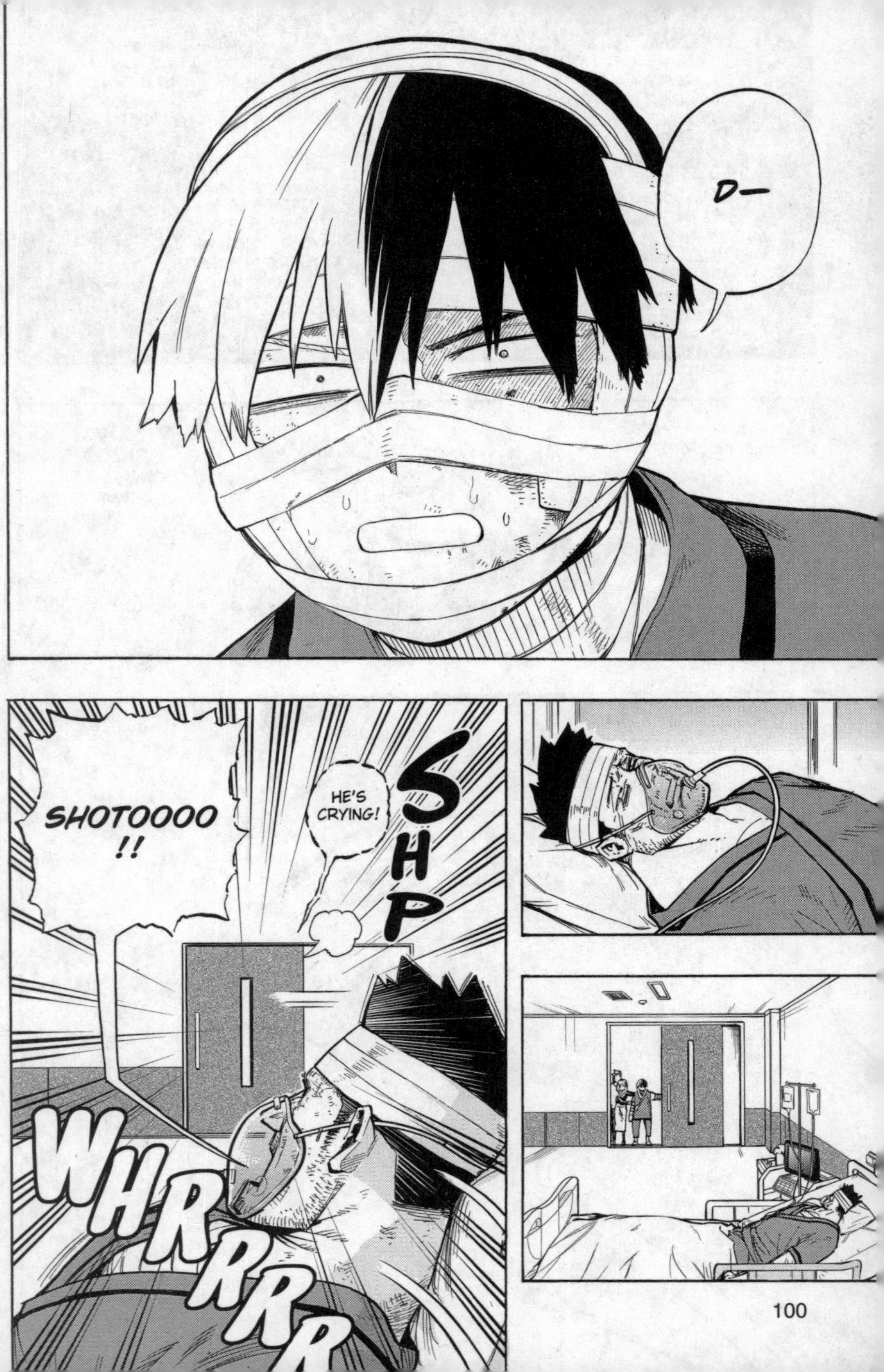
D—
SHP
HE'S CRYING!
SHOTOOOO !!
WHRRRRR

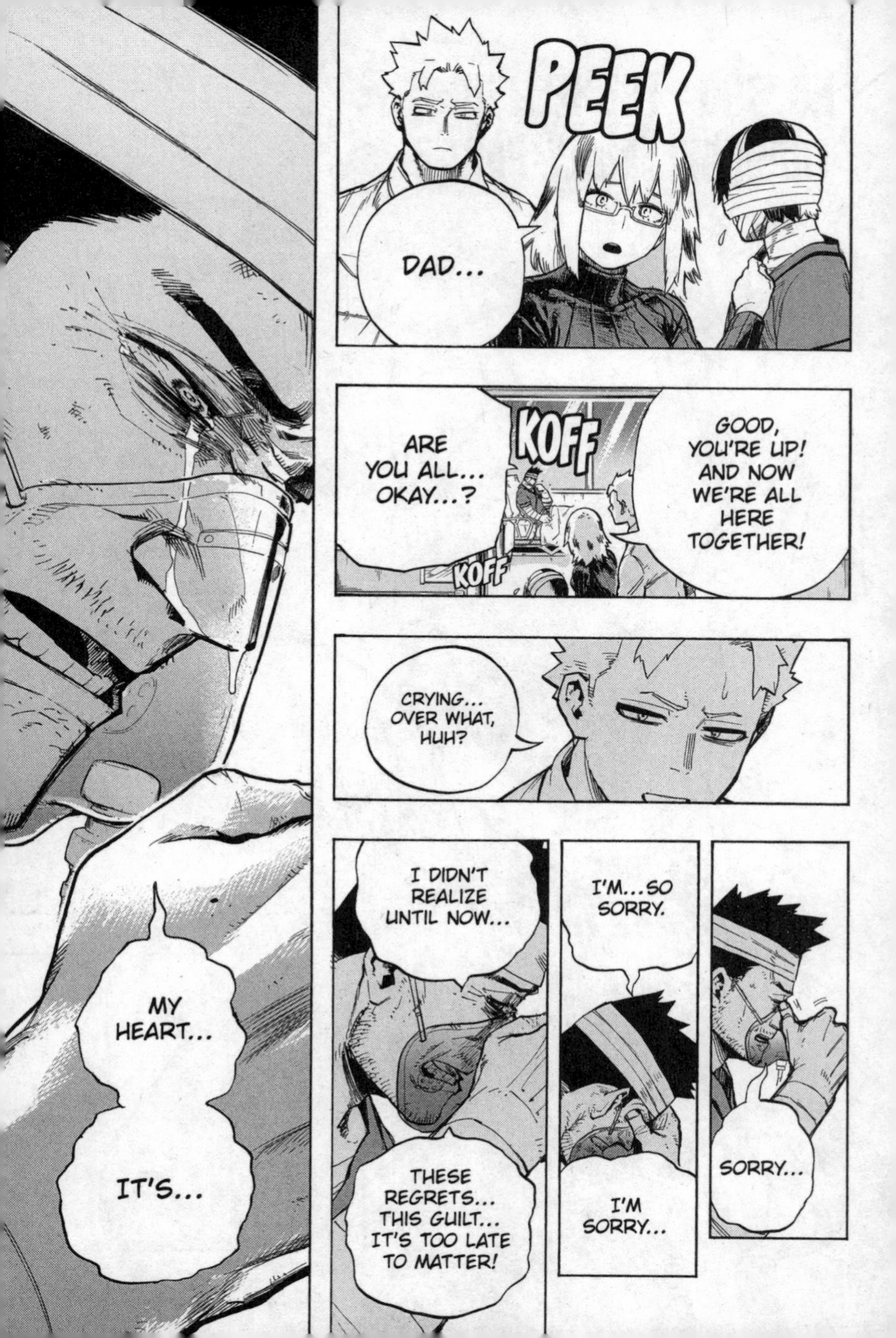
PEEK
DAD...
GOOD, YOU'RE UP! AND NOW WE'RE ALL HERE TOGETHER!
KOFF
ARE YOU ALL... OKAY...?
KOFF
CRYING... OVER WHAT, HUH?
SORRY...
I'M...SO SORRY.
I'M SORRY...
I DIDN'T REALIZE UNTIL NOW...
THESE REGRETS... THIS GUILT... IT'S TOO LATE TO MATTER!
MY HEART...
IT'S...

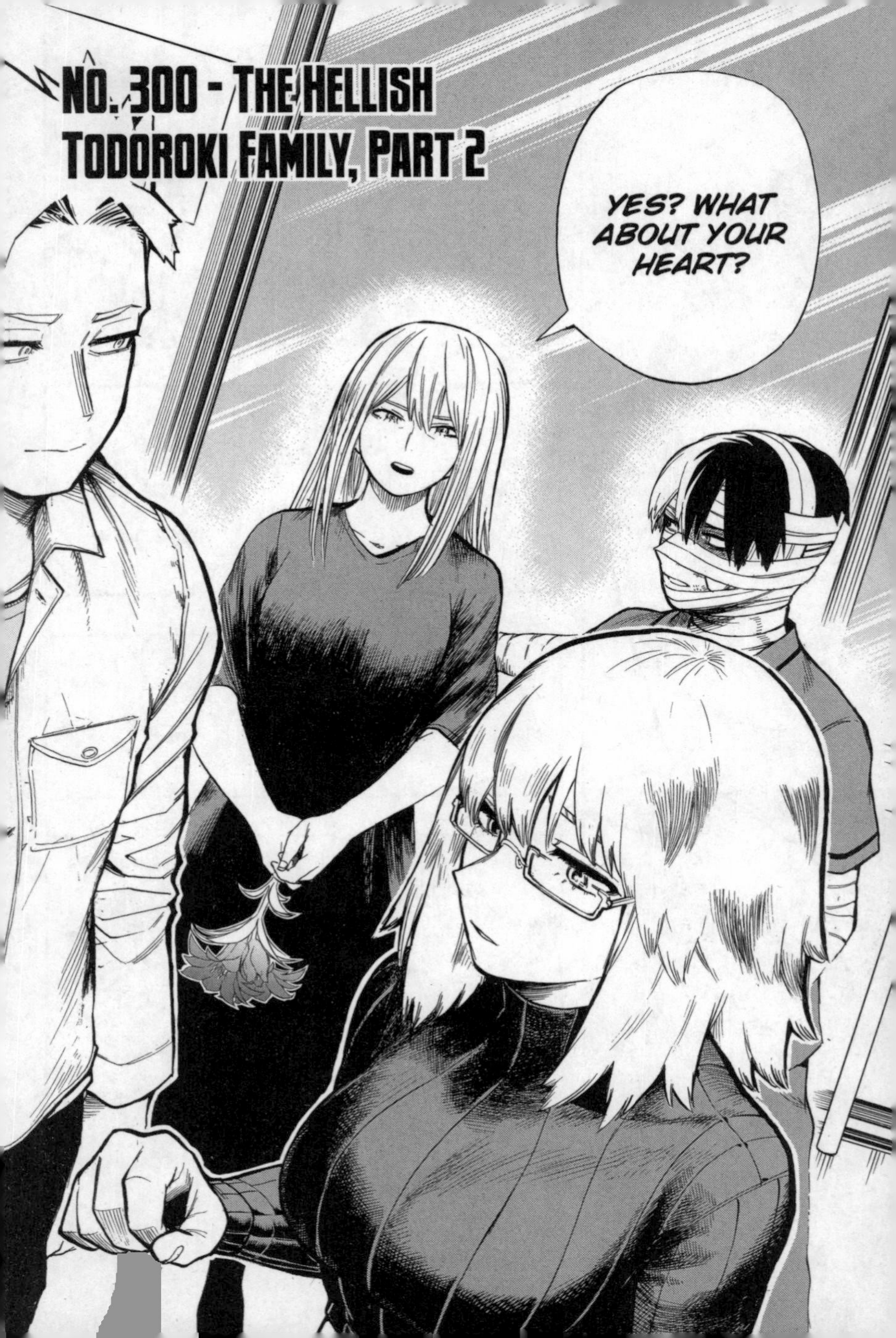
No. 300 - The Hellish Todoroki Family, Part 2
YES? WHAT ABOUT YOUR HEART?

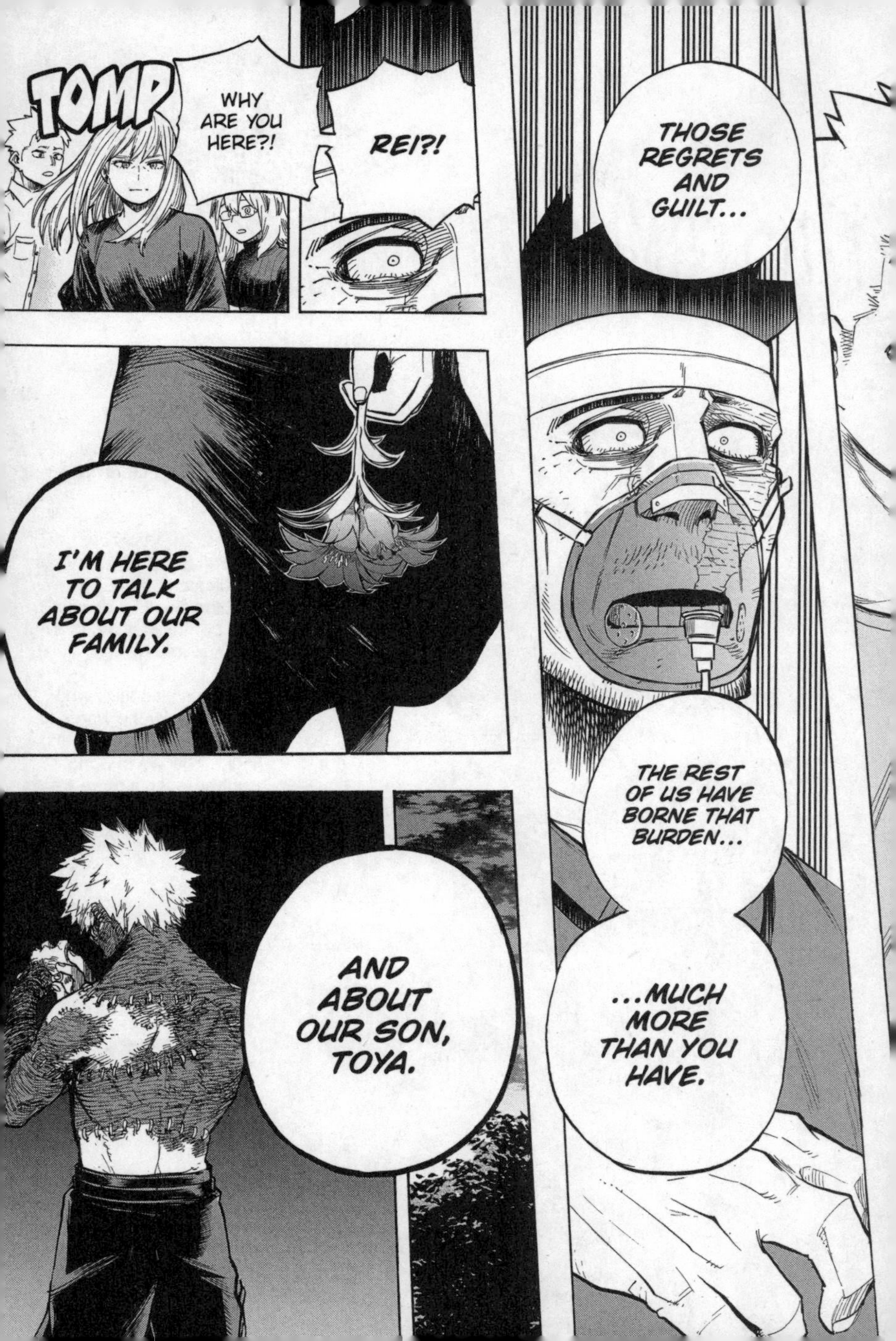
THOSE REGRETS AND GUILT...
THE REST OF US HAVE BORNE THAT BURDEN...
...MUCH MORE THAN YOU HAVE.
REI?!
TOMP
WHY ARE YOU HERE?!
I'M HERE TO TALK ABOUT OUR FAMILY.
AND ABOUT OUR SON, TOYA.

HERO

WASH [AGE 29]
[SUSUGU MITARAI]

THE COMMERCIAL

Birthday: 12/18
Height: 176 cm
Favorite Thing: Children

THE SUPPLEMENT
He dispenses and controls bubbles and suds. The bubbles disinfect anything they surround and can even carry people about.

There's no kid alive who doesn't know the words to that famous commercial jingle "The Wash Song." But hey, even if there were, that's not a problem, since it's so darn catchy.

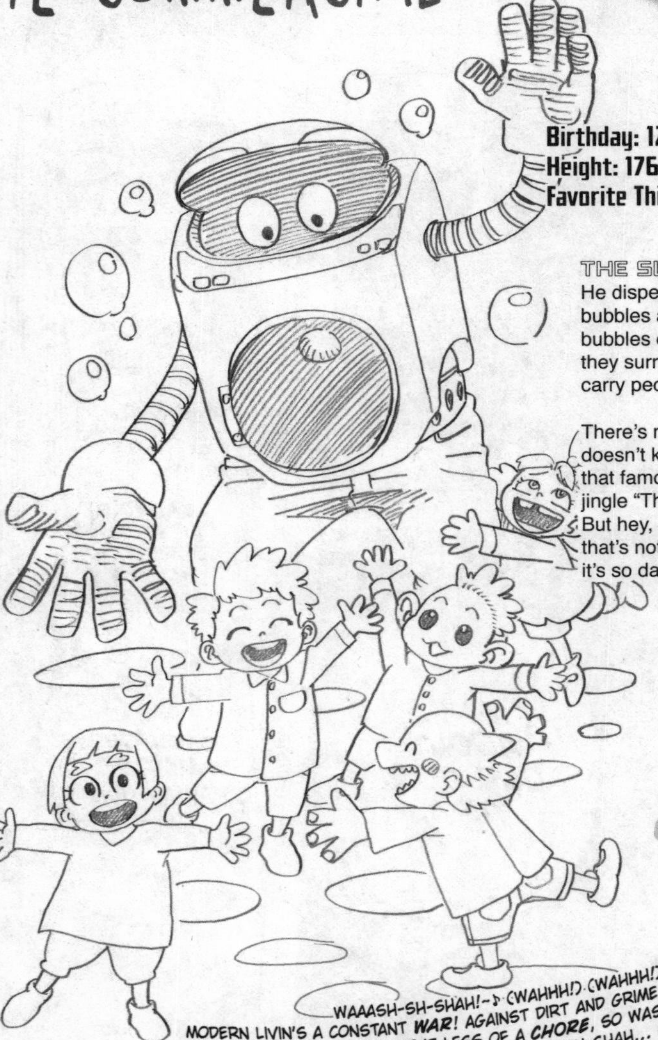
SING ALONG, EVERYONE!
WAAASH-SH-SHAH!~♪ (WAHHH!) (WAHHH!)
MODERN LIVIN'S A CONSTANT WAR! AGAINST DIRT AND GRIME WE CAN'T IGNORE!
OUR CLEANSING SUDS MAKE IT LESS OF A CHORE, SO WASH-SH-SHAH AWAY!
WASH, WASH-SHAH, WASH, WASH-SHAH... (∞)

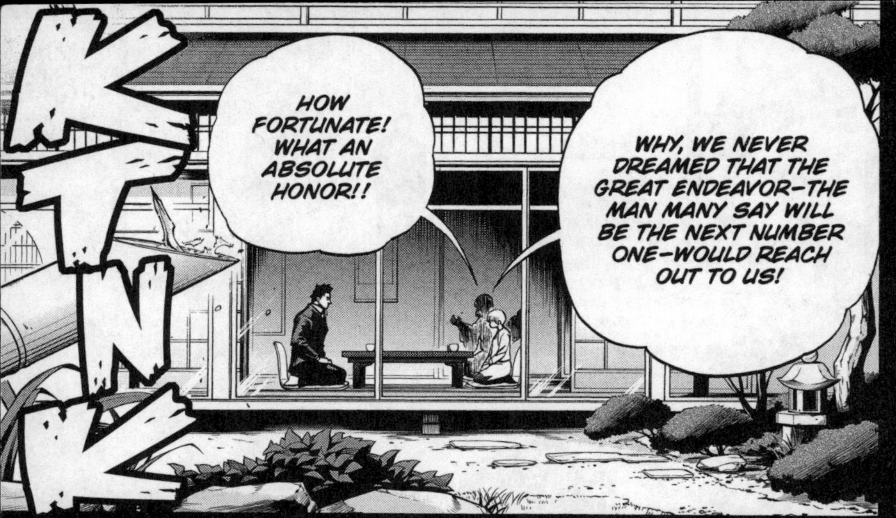
WHY, WE NEVER DREAMED THAT THE GREAT ENDEAVOR—THE MAN MANY SAY WILL BE THE NEXT NUMBER ONE—WOULD REACH OUT TO US!
HOW FORTUNATE! WHAT AN ABSOLUTE HONOR!!
KNK

No. 301 - The Wrong Way to Put Out a Fire, Part 1

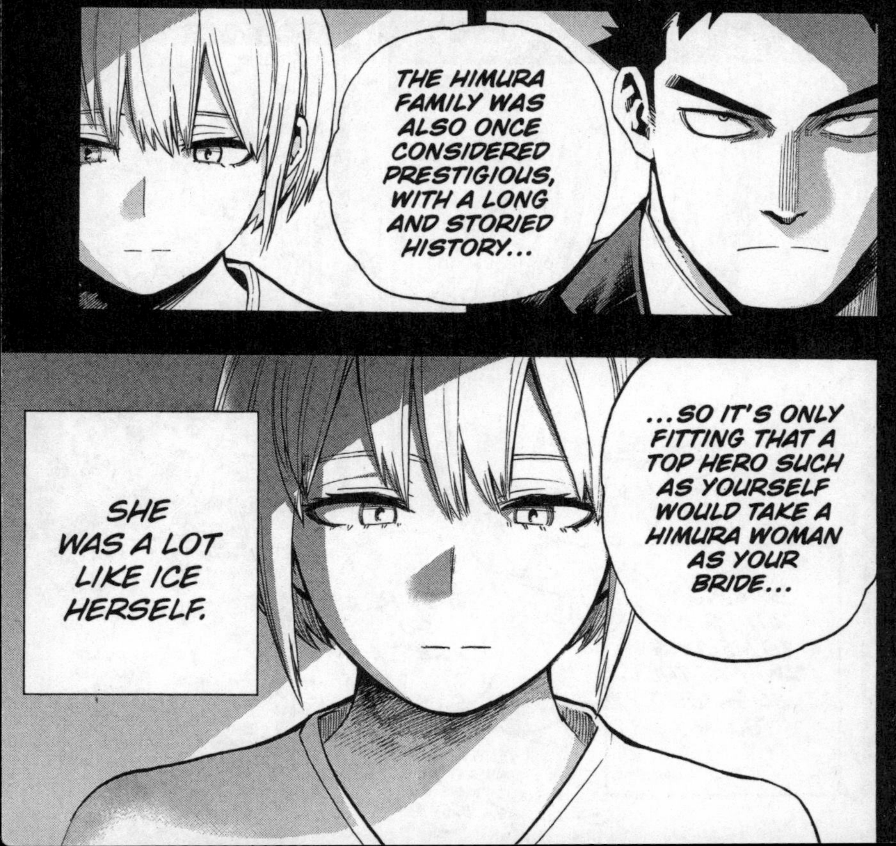
THE HIMURA FAMILY WAS ALSO ONCE CONSIDERED PRESTIGIOUS, WITH A LONG AND STORIED HISTORY...
...SO IT'S ONLY FITTING THAT A TOP HERO SUCH AS YOURSELF WOULD TAKE A HIMURA WOMAN AS YOUR BRIDE...
SHE WAS A LOT LIKE ICE HERSELF.

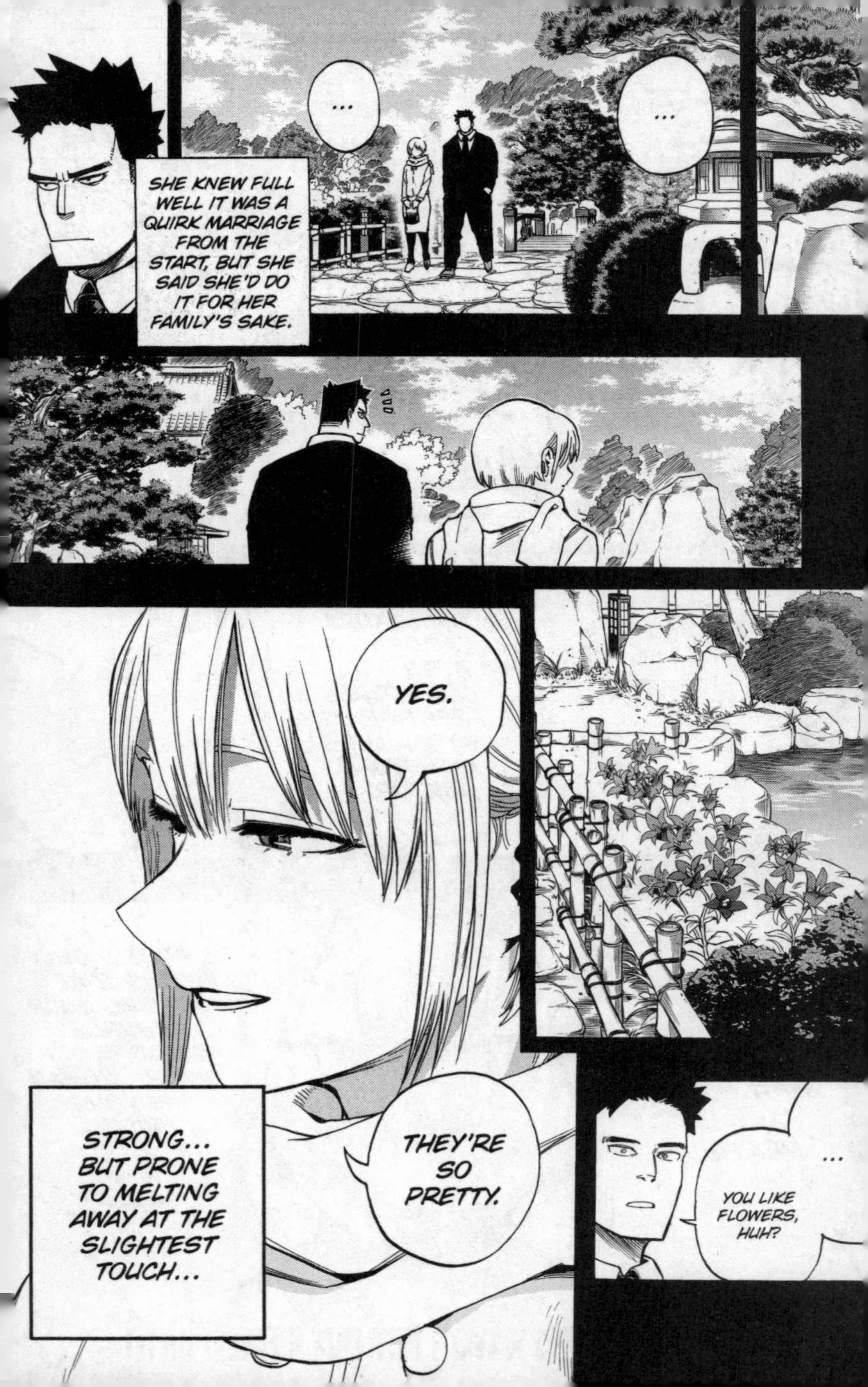
...
...
SHE KNEW FULL WELL IT WAS A QUIRK MARRIAGE FROM THE START, BUT SHE SAID SHE'D DO IT FOR HER FAMILY'S SAKE.
...
YOU LIKE FLOWERS, HUH?
YES.
THEY'RE SO PRETTY.
STRONG... BUT PRONE TO MELTING AWAY AT THE SLIGHTEST TOUCH...

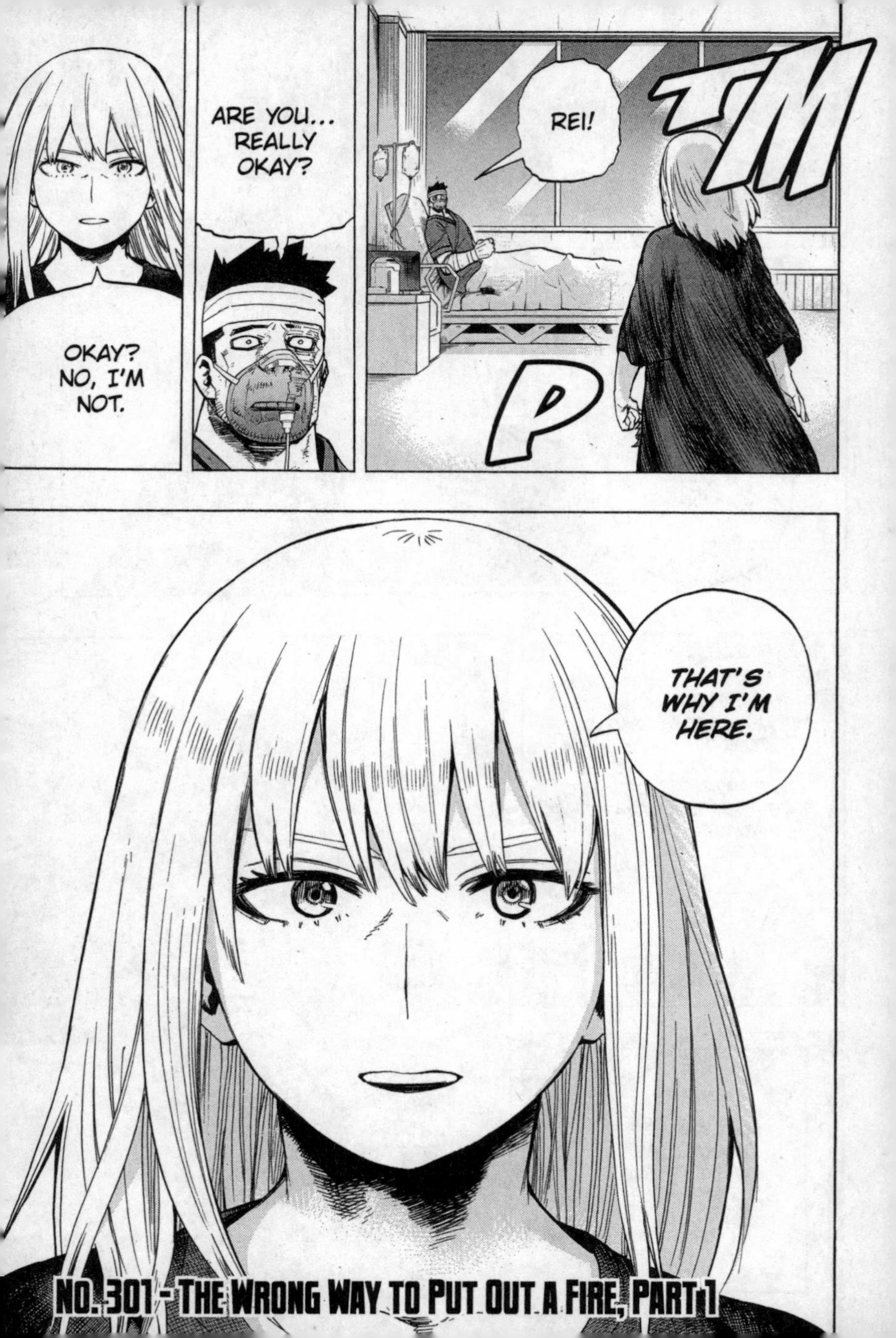

TM
REI!
P
ARE YOU... REALLY OKAY?
OKAY? NO, I'M NOT.
THAT'S WHY I'M HERE.
NO. 301 - THE WRONG WAY TO PUT OUT A FIRE, PART 1

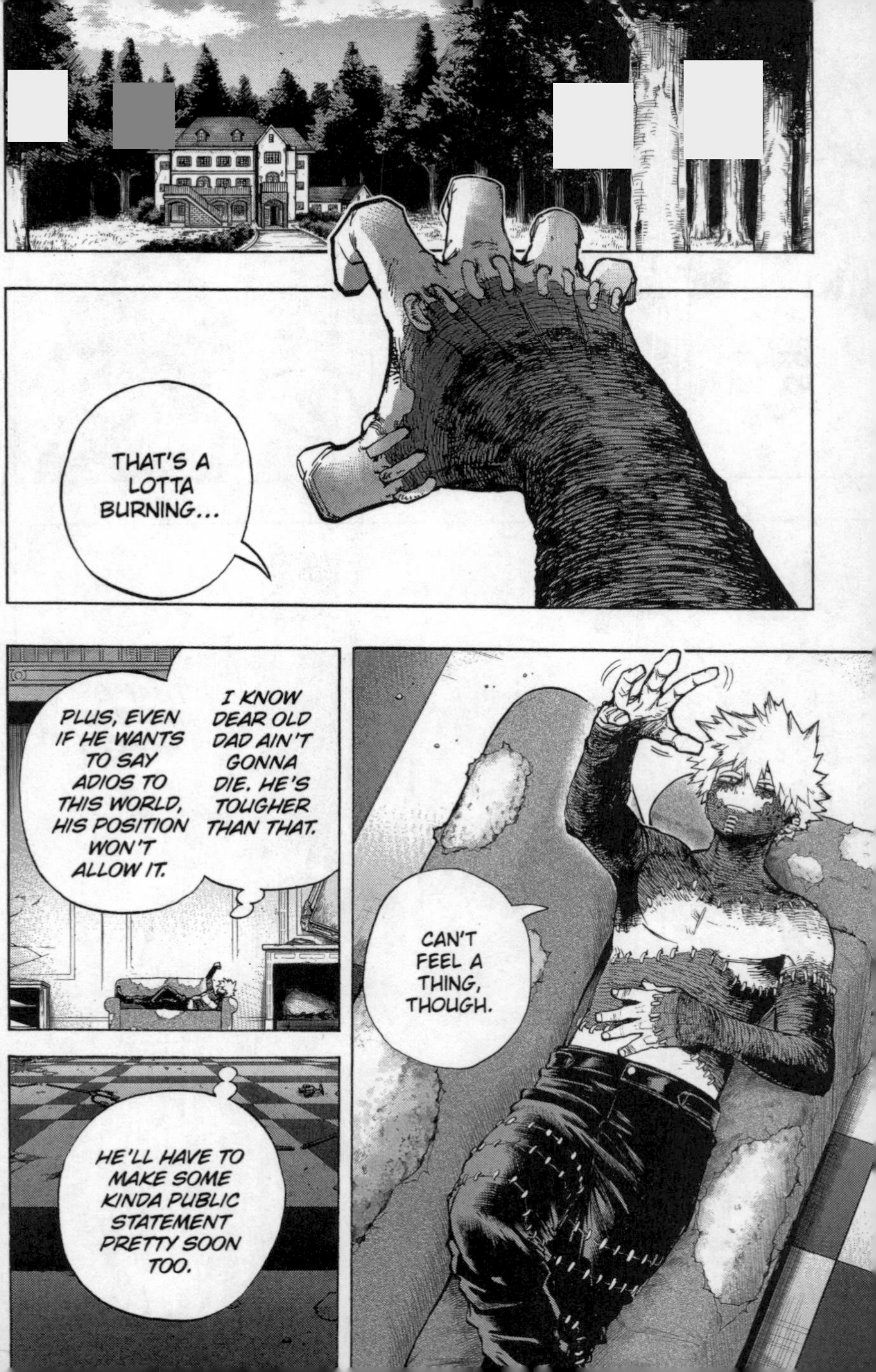
THAT'S A LOTTA BURNING...
CAN'T FEEL A THING, THOUGH.
I KNOW DEAR OLD DAD AIN'T GONNA DIE. HE'S TOUGHER THAN THAT.
PLUS, EVEN IF HE WANTS TO SAY ADIOS TO THIS WORLD, HIS POSITION WON'T ALLOW IT.
HE'LL HAVE TO MAKE SOME KINDA PUBLIC STATEMENT PRETTY SOON TOO.

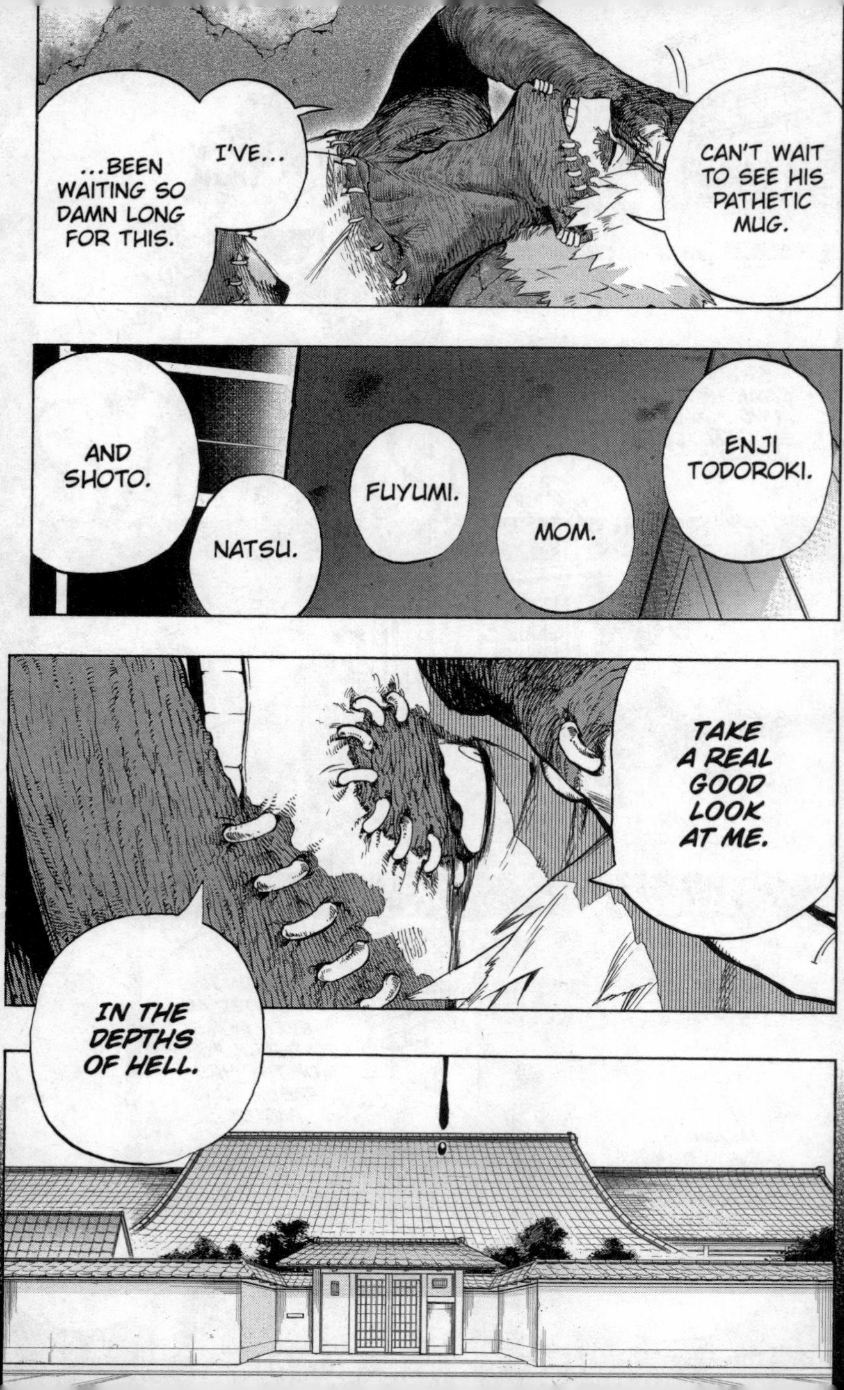
CAN'T WAIT TO SEE HIS PATHETIC MUG.
I'VE...
...BEEN WAITING SO DAMN LONG FOR THIS.
ENJI TODOROKI.
MOM.
FUYUMI.
NATSU.
AND SHOTO.
TAKE A REAL GOOD LOOK AT ME.
IN THE DEPTHS OF HELL.

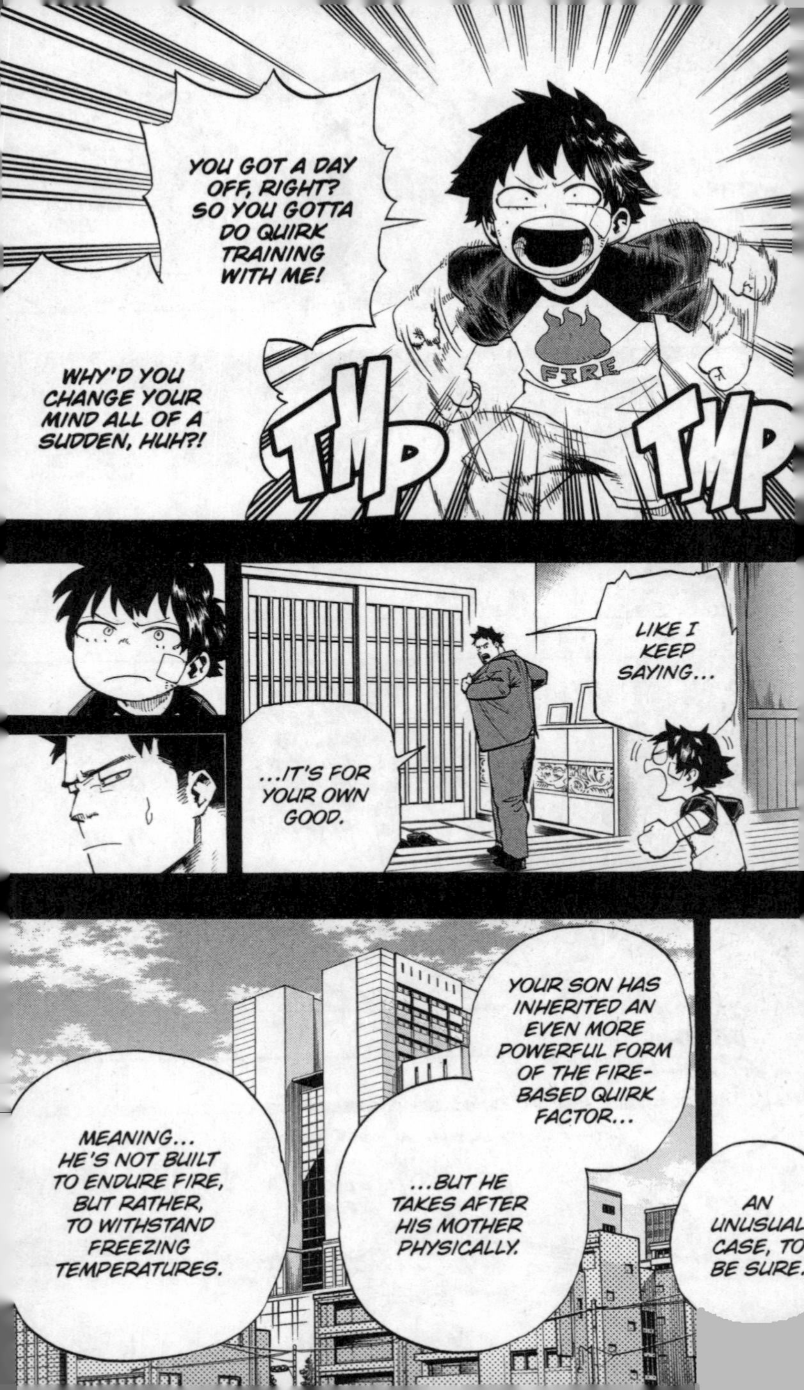
YOU GOT A DAY OFF, RIGHT? SO YOU GOTTA DO QUIRK TRAINING WITH ME!
TMP
FIRE
TMP
WHY'D YOU CHANGE YOUR MIND ALL OF A SUDDEN, HUH?!
LIKE I KEEP SAYING...
...IT'S FOR YOUR OWN GOOD.
YOUR SON HAS INHERITED AN EVEN MORE POWERFUL FORM OF THE FIRE-BASED QUIRK FACTOR...
AN UNUSUAL CASE, TO BE SURE.
...BUT HE TAKES AFTER HIS MOTHER PHYSICALLY.
MEANING... HE'S NOT BUILT TO ENDURE FIRE, BUT RATHER, TO WITHSTAND FREEZING TEMPERATURES.

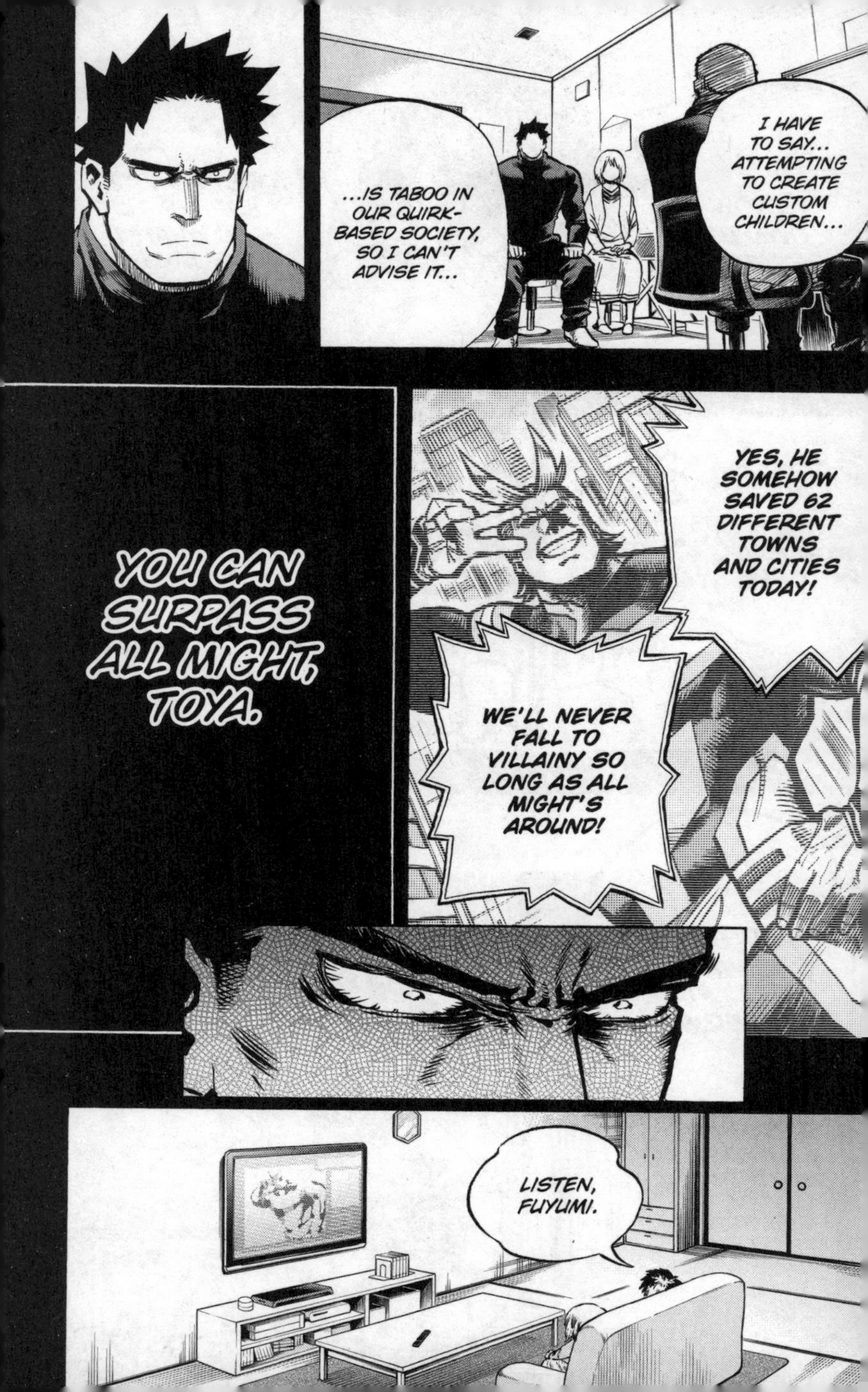
I HAVE TO SAY... ATTEMPTING TO CREATE CUSTOM CHILDREN...
...IS TABOO IN OUR QUIRK-BASED SOCIETY, SO I CAN'T ADVISE IT...
YES, HE SOMEHOW SAVED 62 DIFFERENT TOWNS AND CITIES TODAY!
WE'LL NEVER FALL TO VILLAINY SO LONG AS ALL MIGHT'S AROUND!
YOU CAN SURPASS ALL MIGHT, TOYA.
LISTEN, FUYUMI.

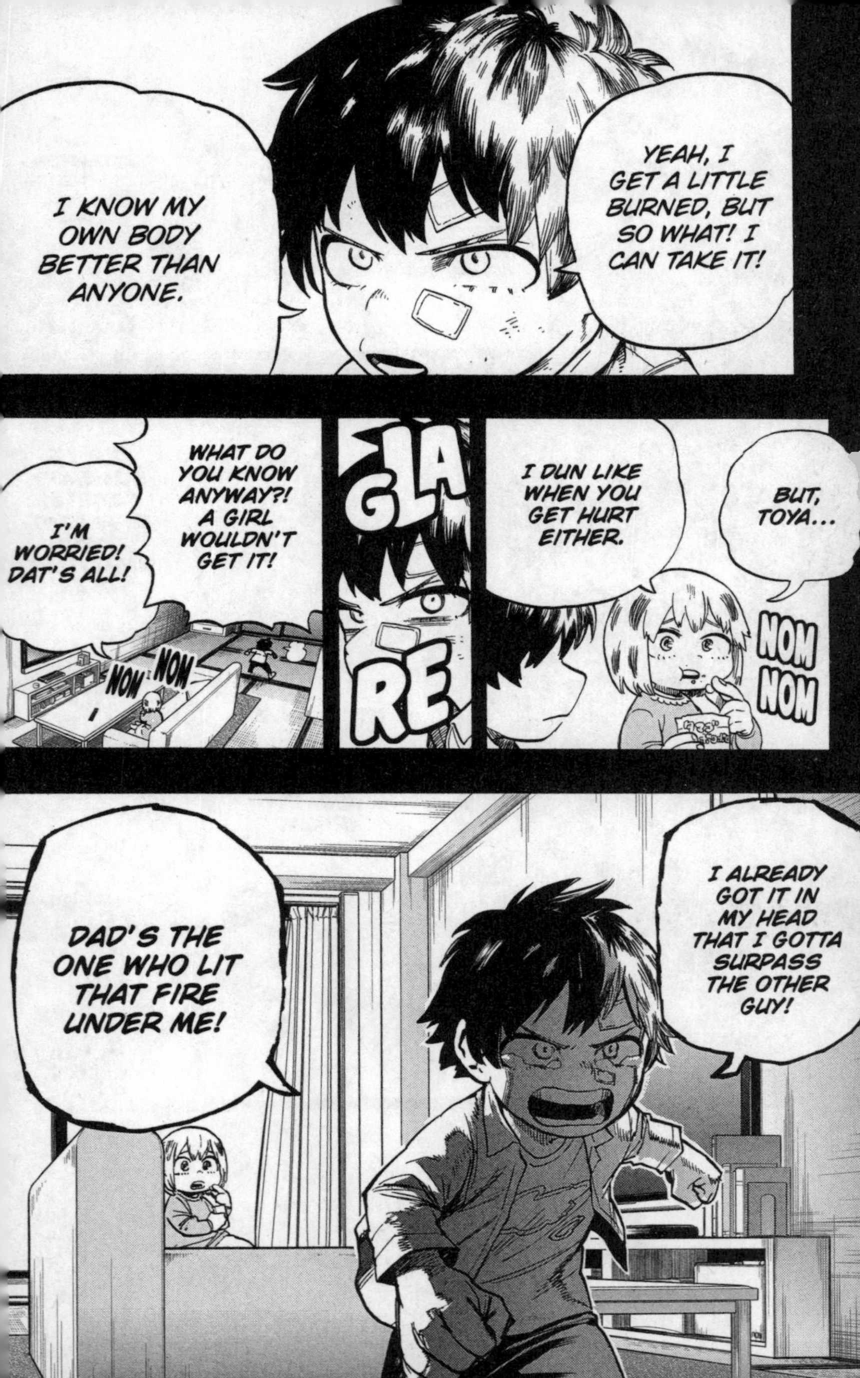
YEAH, I GET A LITTLE BURNED, BUT SO WHAT! I CAN TAKE IT!
I KNOW MY OWN BODY BETTER THAN ANYONE.
BUT, TOYA...
I DUN LIKE WHEN YOU GET HURT EITHER.
NOM NOM
GLARE
WHAT DO YOU KNOW ANYWAY?! A GIRL WOULDN'T GET IT!
I'M WORRIED! DAT'S ALL!
NOM NOM
I ALREADY GOT IT IN MY HEAD THAT I GOTTA SURPASS THE OTHER GUY!
DAD'S THE ONE WHO LIT THAT FIRE UNDER ME!

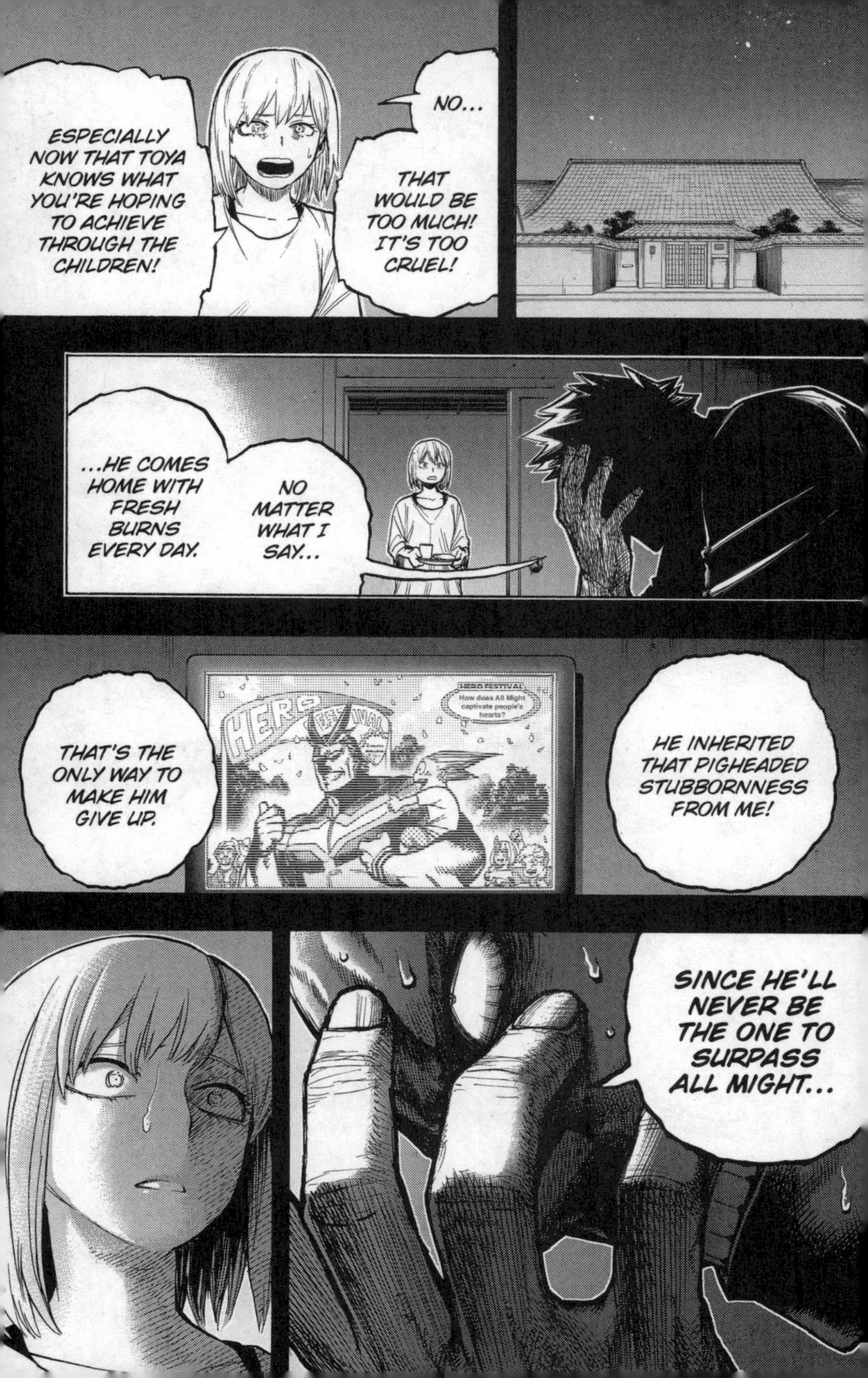
NO... THAT WOULD BE TOO MUCH! IT'S TOO CRUEL!
ESPECIALLY NOW THAT TOYA KNOWS WHAT YOU'RE HOPING TO ACHIEVE THROUGH THE CHILDREN!
NO MATTER WHAT I SAY...
...HE COMES HOME WITH FRESH BURNS EVERY DAY.
HE INHERITED THAT PIGHEADED STUBBORNNESS FROM ME!
HERO FESTIVAL
How does All Might captivate people's hearts?
THAT'S THE ONLY WAY TO MAKE HIM GIVE UP.
SINCE HE'LL NEVER BE THE ONE TO SURPASS ALL MIGHT...

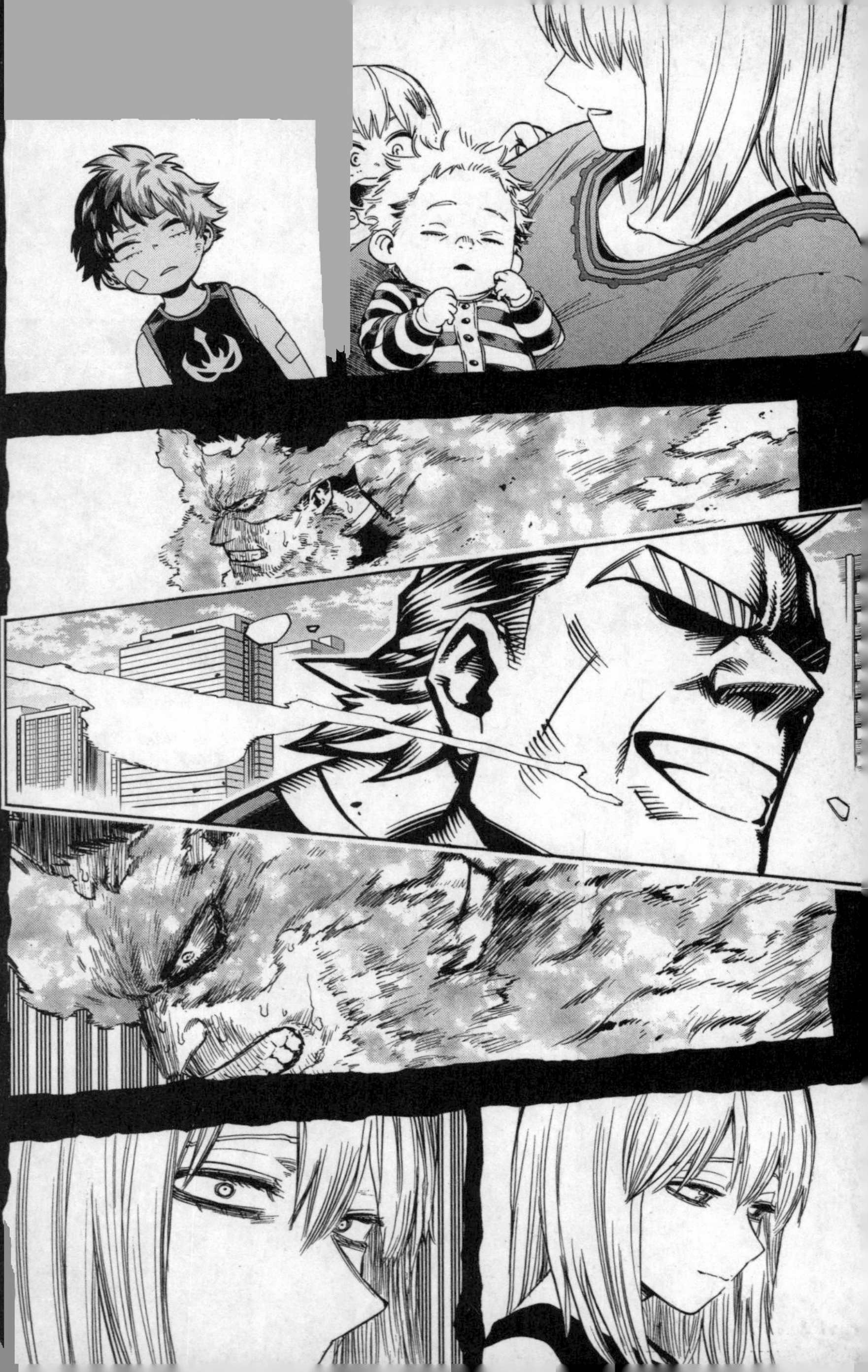

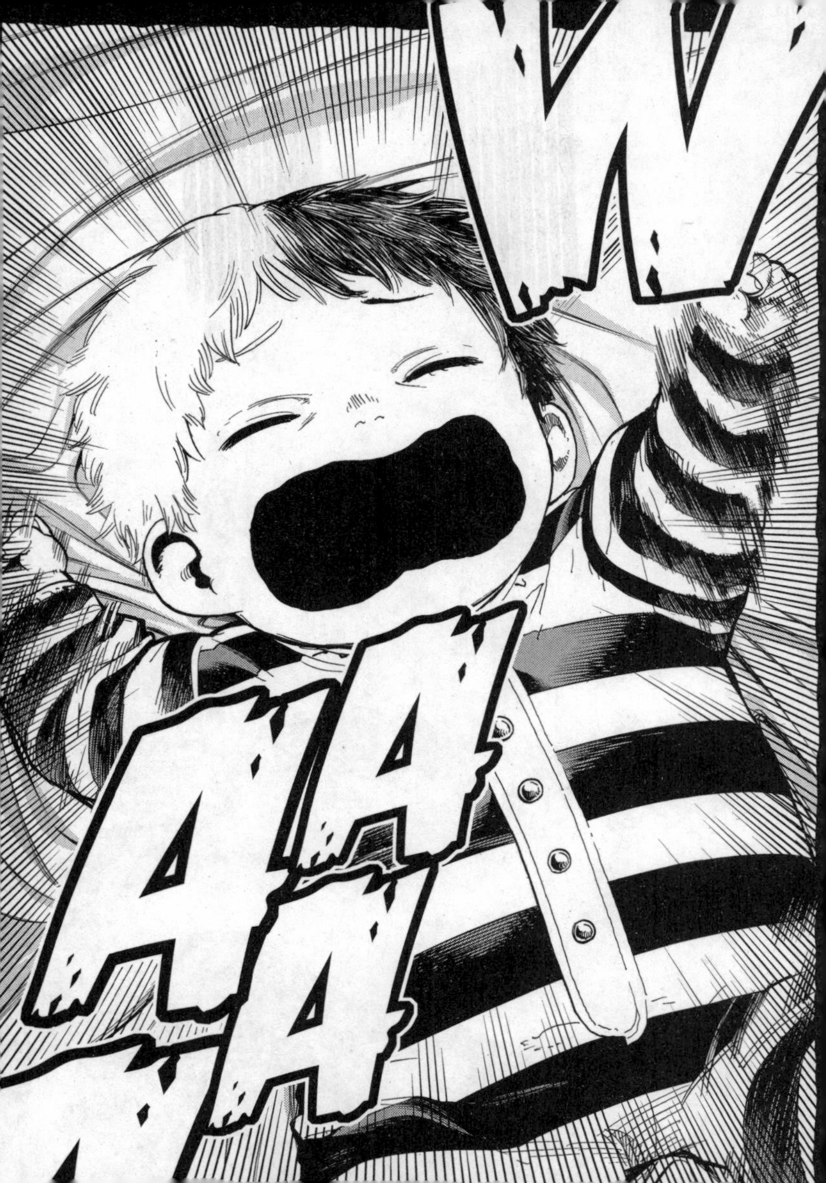
WAAAA

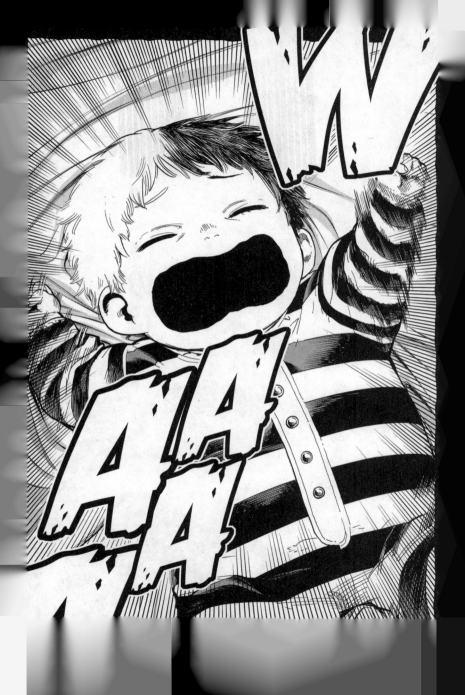

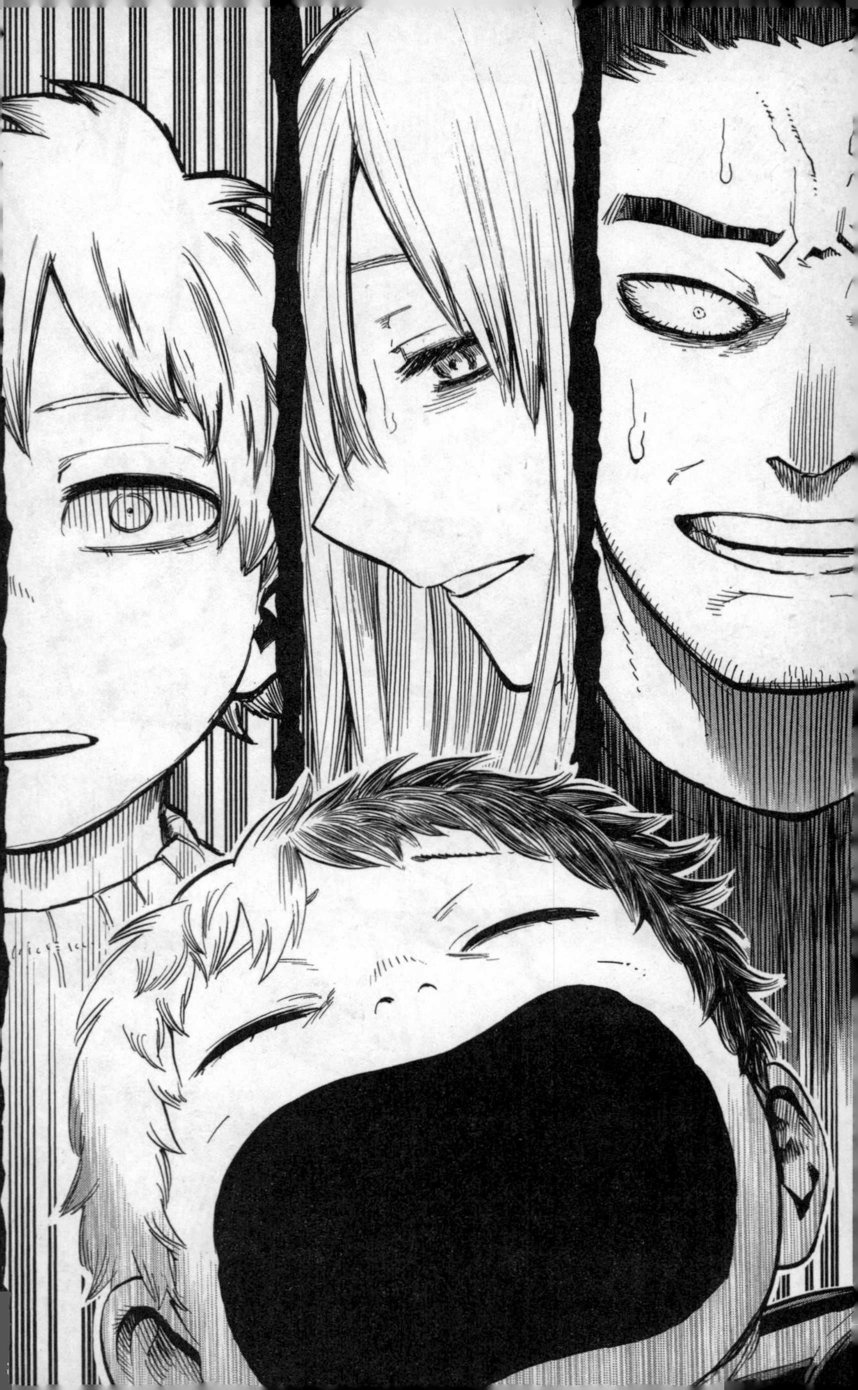

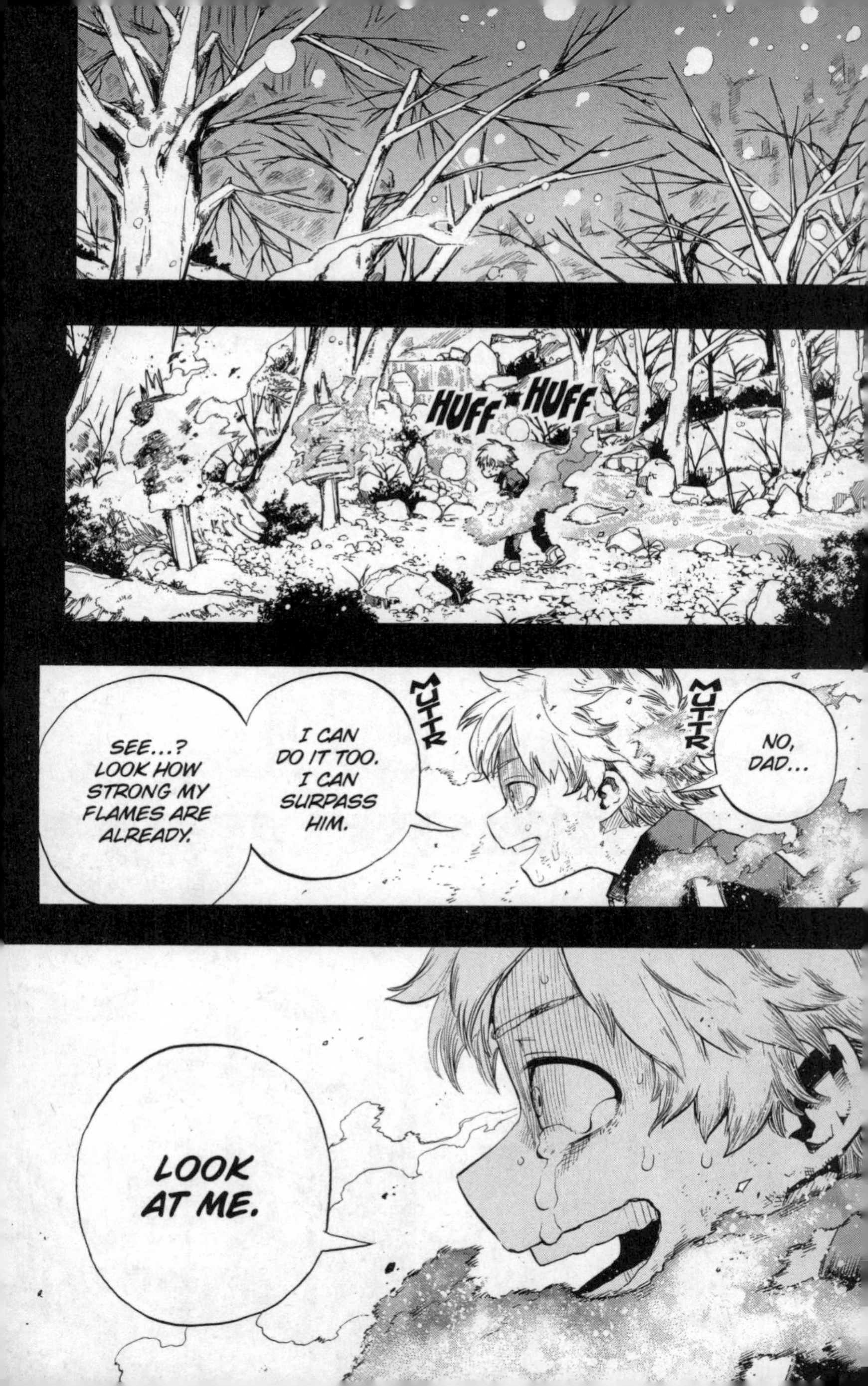
HUFF HUFF
MUTTR
NO, DAD...
MUTTR
I CAN DO IT TOO. I CAN SURPASS HIM.
SEE...? LOOK HOW STRONG MY FLAMES ARE ALREADY.
LOOK AT ME.

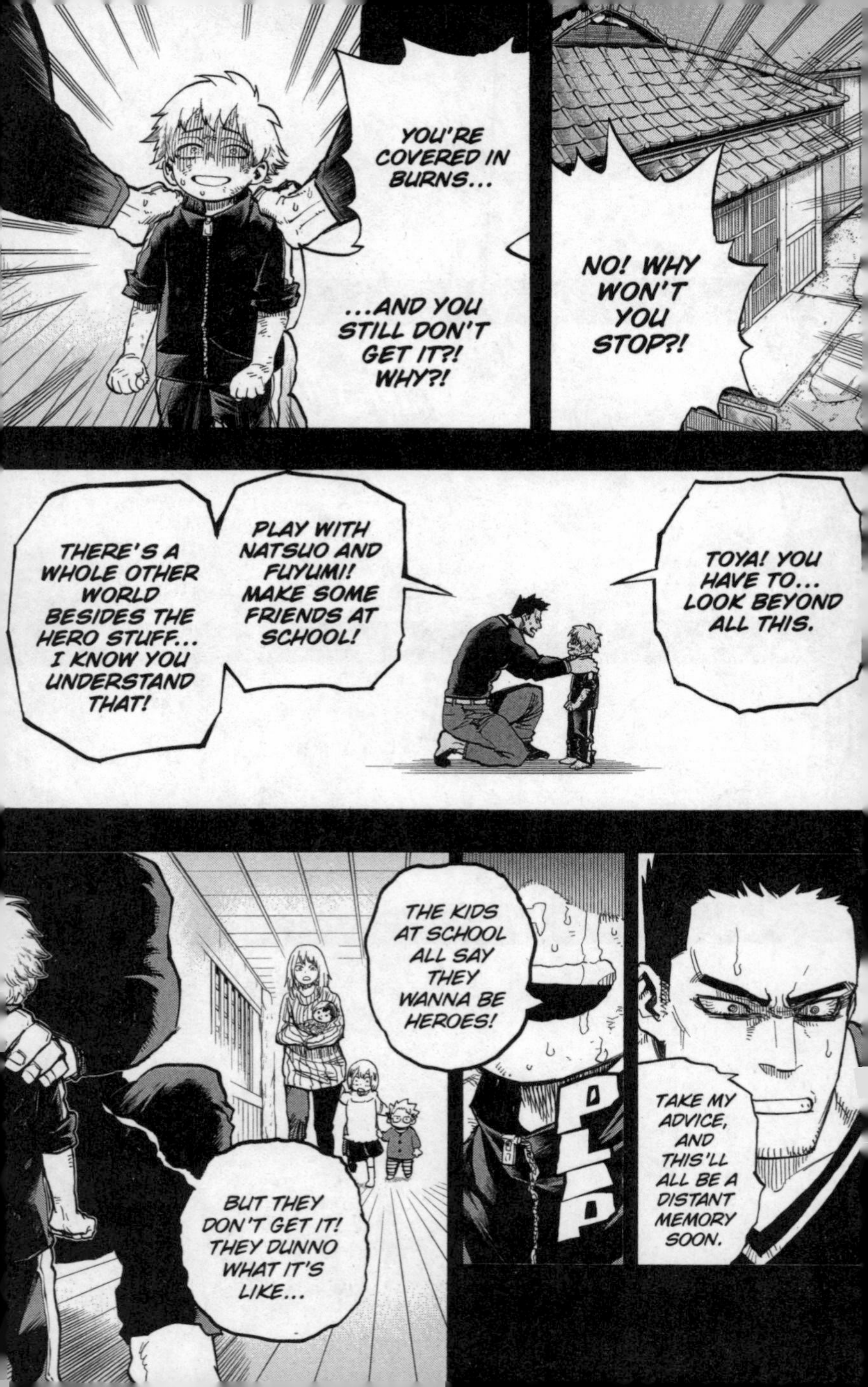
NO! WHY WON'T YOU STOP?!
YOU'RE COVERED IN BURNS...
...AND YOU STILL DON'T GET IT?! WHY?!
TOYA! YOU HAVE TO... LOOK BEYOND ALL THIS.
PLAY WITH NATSUO AND FUYUMI! MAKE SOME FRIENDS AT SCHOOL!
THERE'S A WHOLE OTHER WORLD BESIDES THE HERO STUFF... I KNOW YOU UNDERSTAND THAT!
TAKE MY ADVICE, AND THIS'LL ALL BE A DISTANT MEMORY SOON.
THE KIDS AT SCHOOL ALL SAY THEY WANNA BE HEROES!
PLIP
BUT THEY DON'T GET IT! THEY DUNNO WHAT IT'S LIKE...

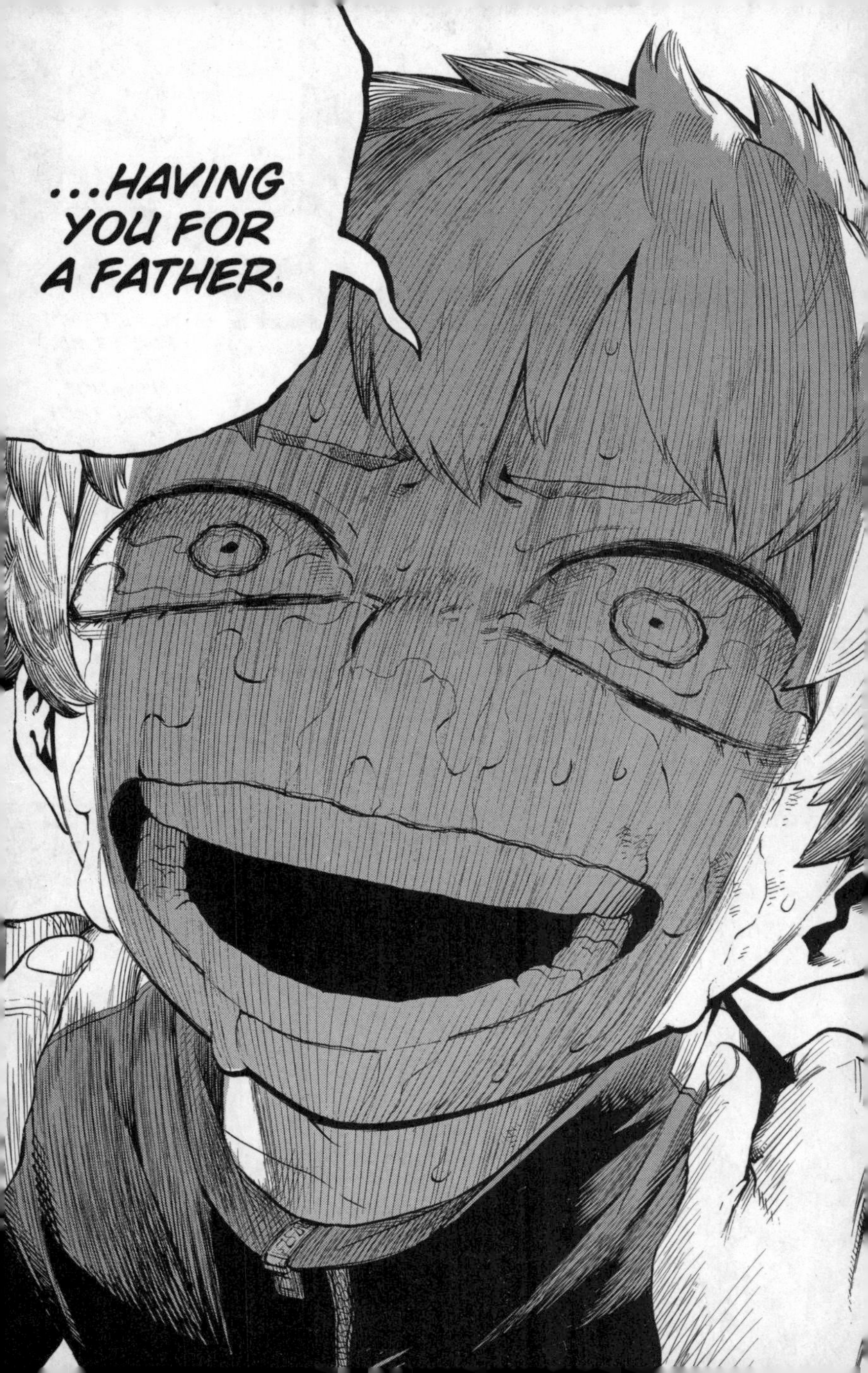
...HAVING YOU FOR A FATHER.

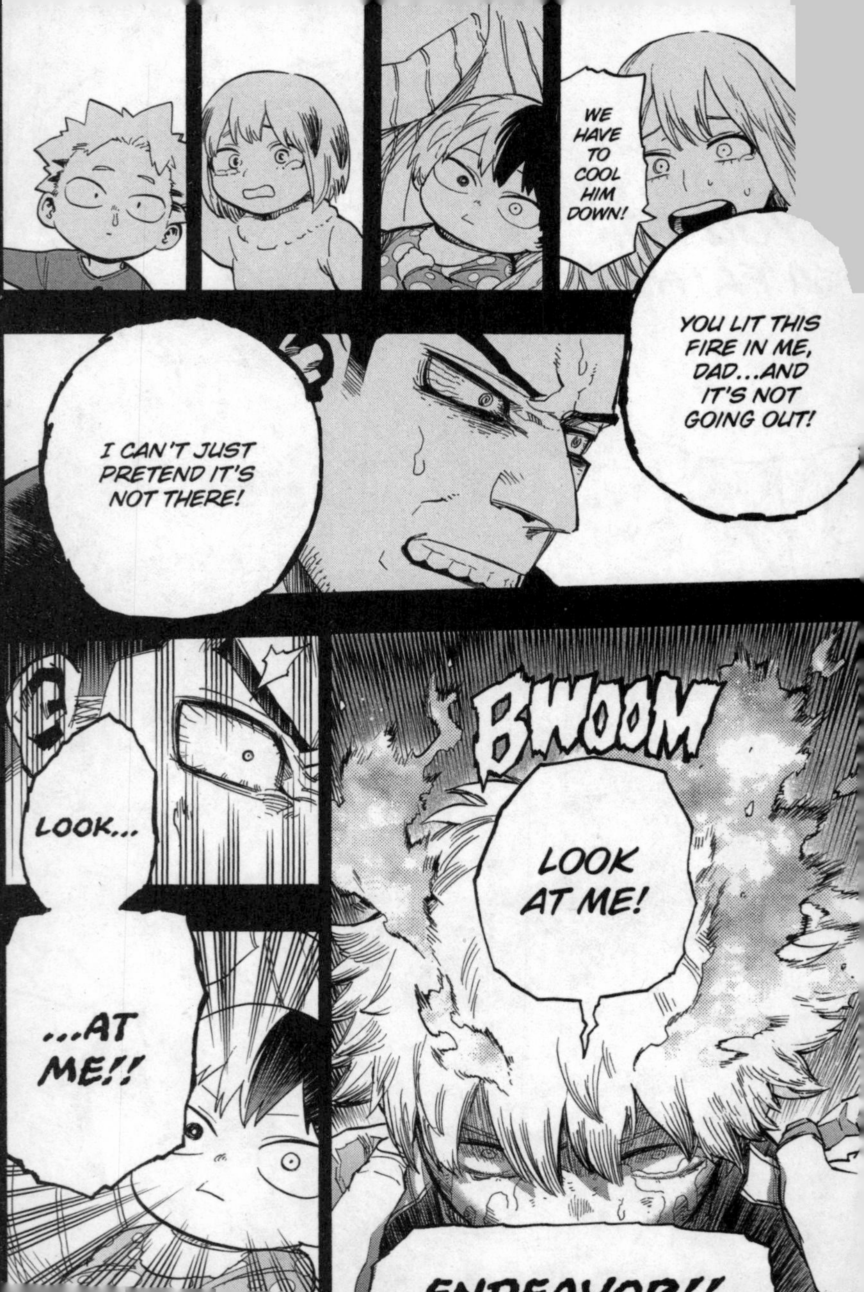
WE HAVE TO COOL HIM DOWN!
YOU LIT THIS FIRE IN ME, DAD...AND IT'S NOT GOING OUT!
I CAN'T JUST PRETEND IT'S NOT THERE!
BWOOM
LOOK AT ME!
ENDEAVOR!!
LOOK...
...AT ME!!

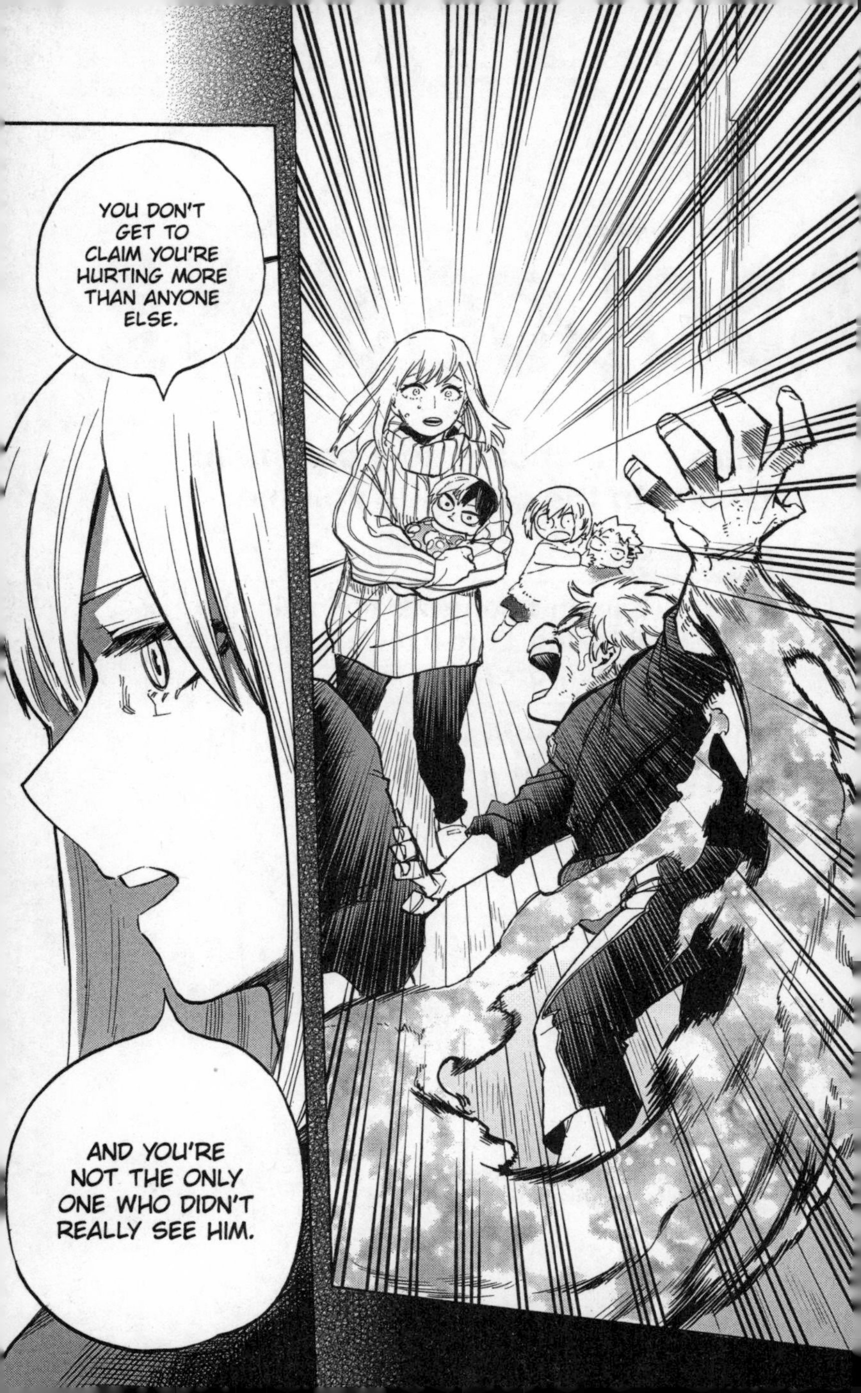
YOU DON'T GET TO CLAIM YOU'RE HURTING MORE THAN ANYONE ELSE.
AND YOU'RE NOT THE ONLY ONE WHO DIDN'T REALLY SEE HIM.

Apology #2

Here's a flashback to a comment I made in the previous volume:

Instant Replay:

> Somewhere in a corner of my brain, I'm always thinking, "Are five-year-old boys enjoying my work?"

To all the five-year-old boys: I'm sorry the story got so dark.

Baby Roki, before developing a capacity for interpersonal differentiation

No. 302 - The Wrong Way to Put Out a Fire, Part 2

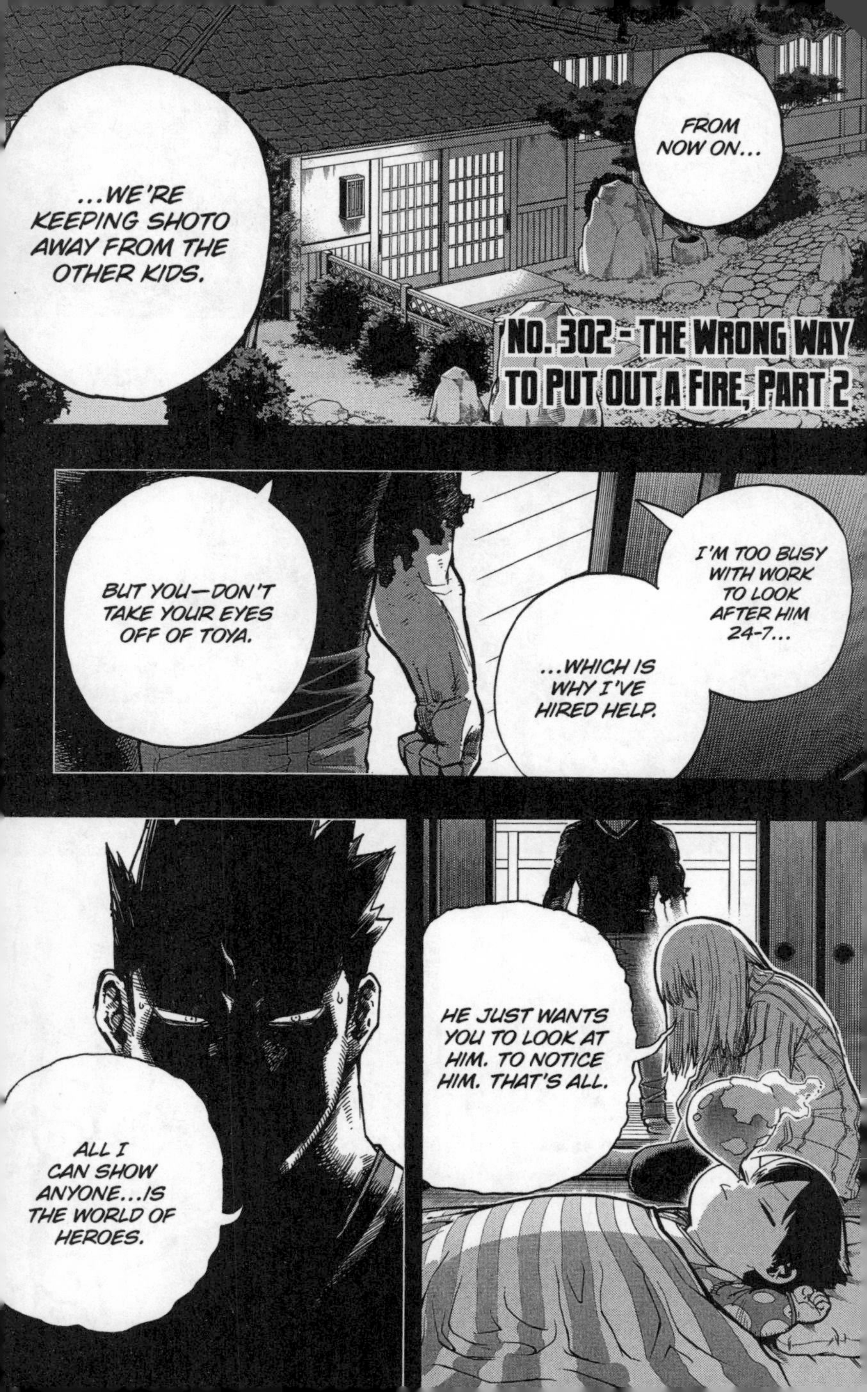
FROM NOW ON...
...WE'RE KEEPING SHOTO AWAY FROM THE OTHER KIDS.
I'M TOO BUSY WITH WORK TO LOOK AFTER HIM 24-7...
...WHICH IS WHY I'VE HIRED HELP.
BUT YOU—DON'T TAKE YOUR EYES OFF OF TOYA.
HE JUST WANTS YOU TO LOOK AT HIM. TO NOTICE HIM. THAT'S ALL.
ALL I CAN SHOW ANYONE...IS THE WORLD OF HEROES.

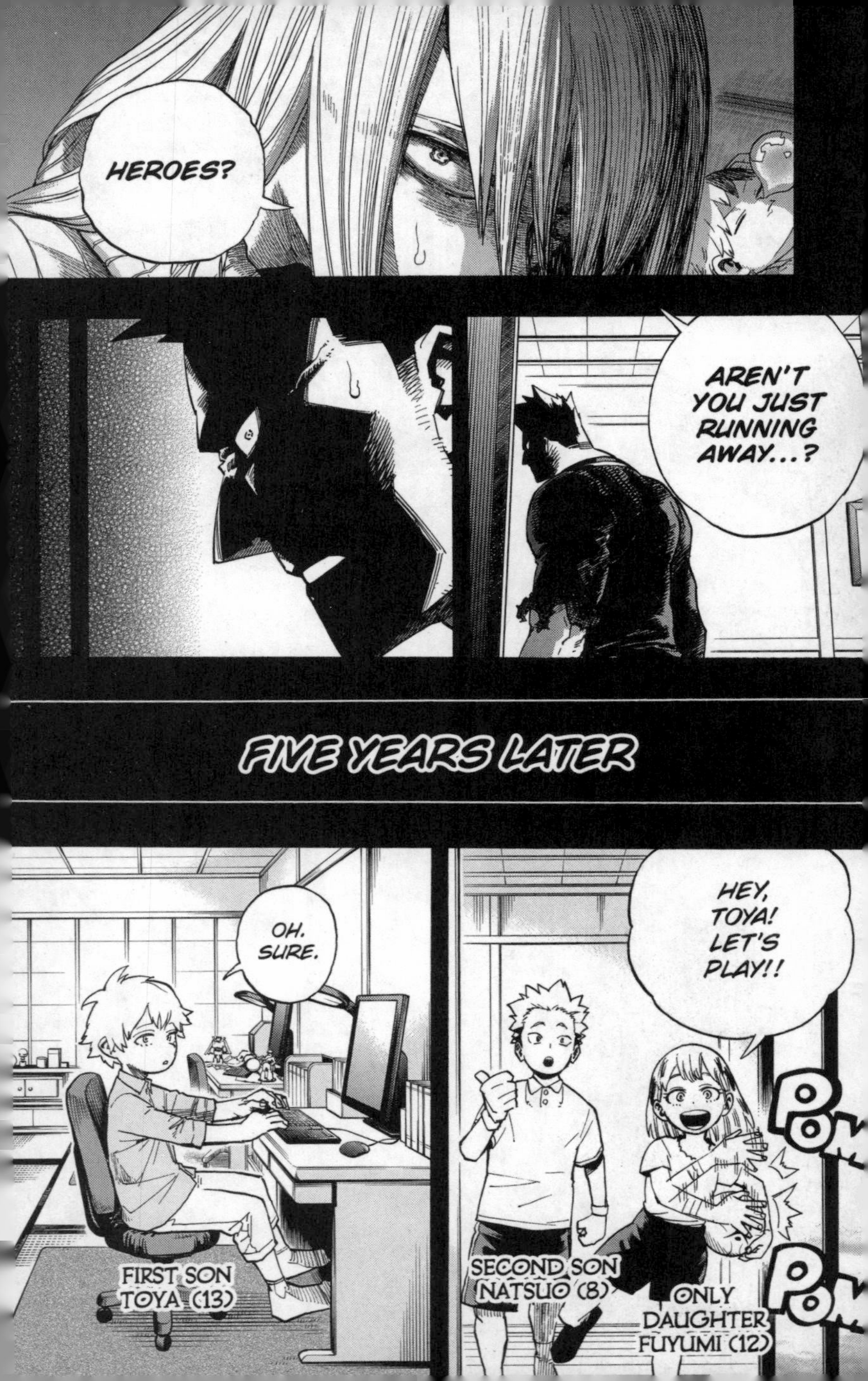
HEROES?
AREN'T YOU JUST RUNNING AWAY...?
FIVE YEARS LATER
HEY, TOYA! LET'S PLAY!!
POM
POM
ONLY DAUGHTER FUYUMI (12)
SECOND SON NATSUO (8)
OH. SURE.
FIRST SON TOYA (13)

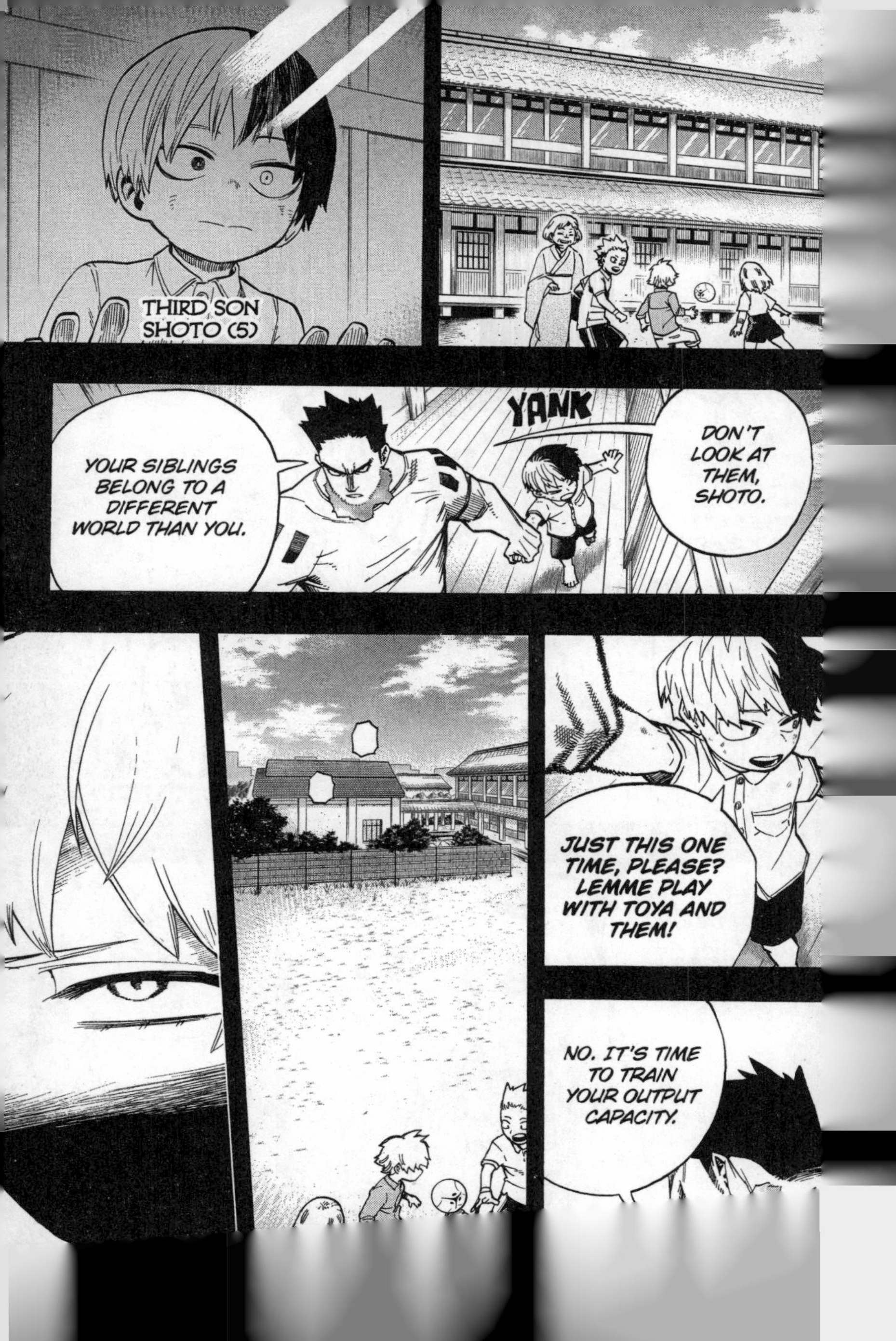
THIRD SON
SHOTO (5)
DON'T LOOK AT THEM, SHOTO.
YANK
YOUR SIBLINGS BELONG TO A DIFFERENT WORLD THAN YOU.
JUST THIS ONE TIME, PLEASE? LEMME PLAY WITH TOYA AND THEM!
NO. IT'S TIME TO TRAIN YOUR OUTPUT CAPACITY.

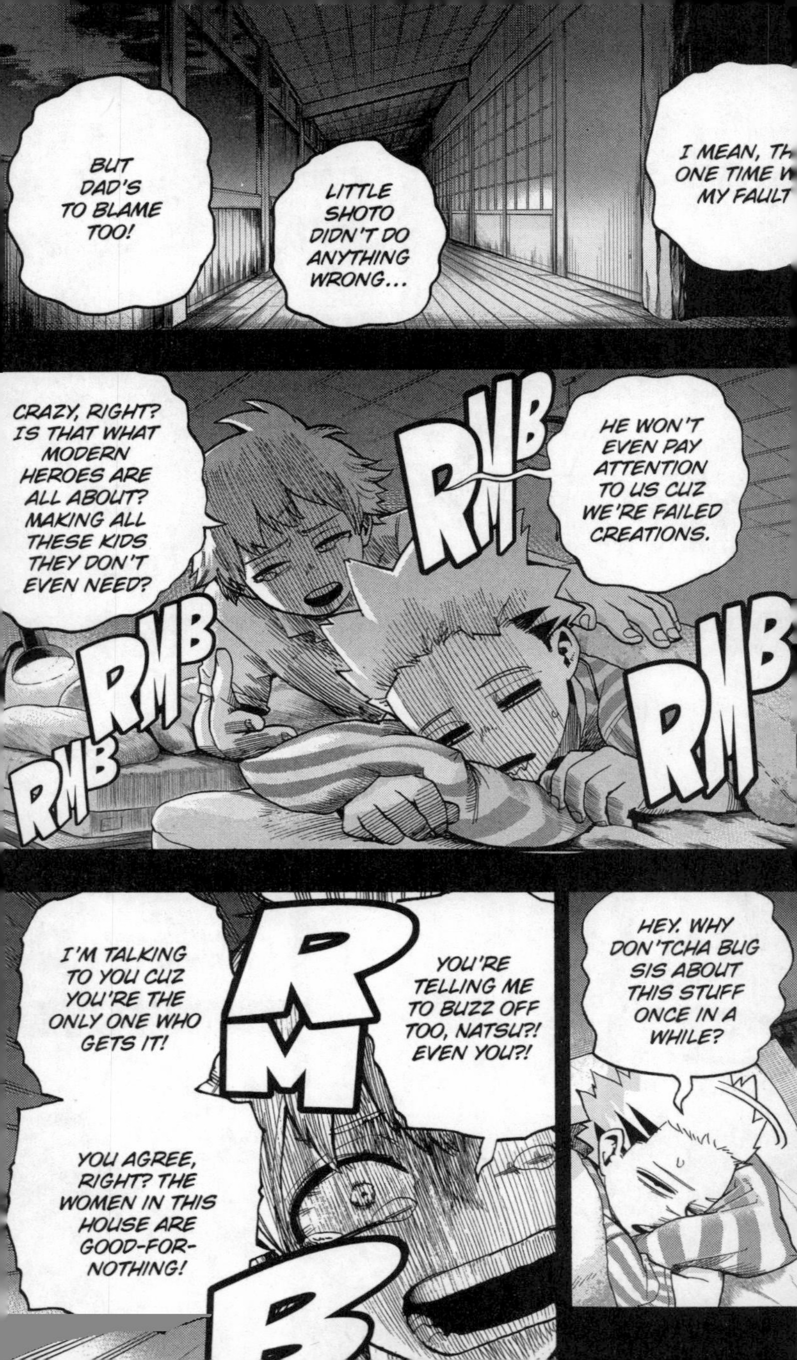
I MEAN, TH ONE TIME W MY FAULT
LITTLE SHOTO DIDN'T DO ANYTHING WRONG...
BUT DAD'S TO BLAME TOO!
HE WON'T EVEN PAY ATTENTION TO US CUZ WE'RE FAILED CREATIONS.
RMB
CRAZY, RIGHT? IS THAT WHAT MODERN HEROES ARE ALL ABOUT? MAKING ALL THESE KIDS THEY DON'T EVEN NEED?
RMB
RMB
RMB
HEY. WHY DON'TCHA BUG SIS ABOUT THIS STUFF ONCE IN A WHILE?
YOU'RE TELLING ME TO BUZZ OFF TOO, NATSU?! EVEN YOU?!
RMB
I'M TALKING TO YOU CUZ YOU'RE THE ONLY ONE WHO GETS IT!
YOU AGREE, RIGHT? THE WOMEN IN THIS HOUSE ARE GOOD-FOR-NOTHING!

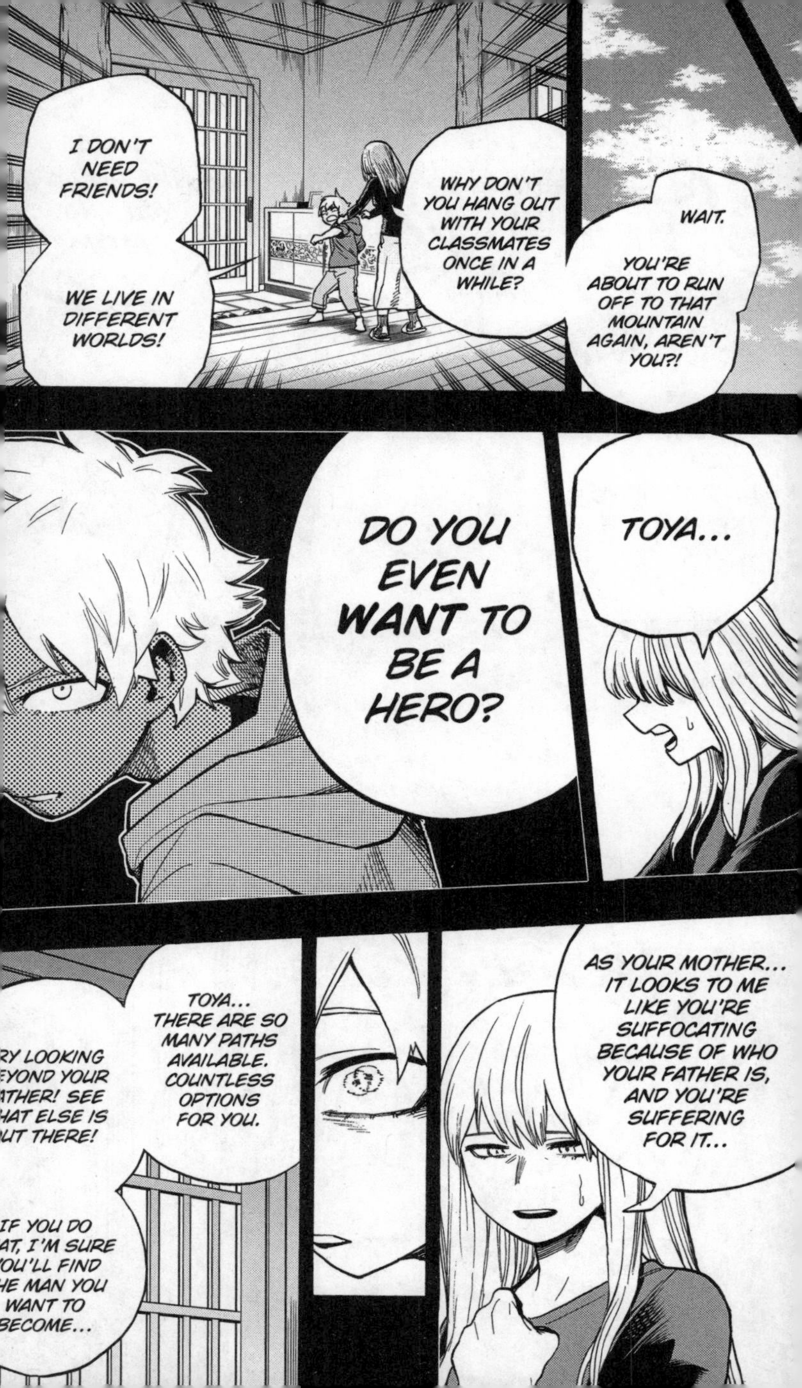
WAIT.
YOU'RE ABOUT TO RUN OFF TO THAT MOUNTAIN AGAIN, AREN'T YOU?!
WHY DON'T YOU HANG OUT WITH YOUR CLASSMATES ONCE IN A WHILE?
I DON'T NEED FRIENDS!
WE LIVE IN DIFFERENT WORLDS!
TOYA...
DO YOU EVEN WANT TO BE A HERO?
AS YOUR MOTHER... IT LOOKS TO ME LIKE YOU'RE SUFFOCATING BECAUSE OF WHO YOUR FATHER IS, AND YOU'RE SUFFERING FOR IT...
TOYA... THERE ARE SO MANY PATHS AVAILABLE. COUNTLESS OPTIONS FOR YOU.
RY LOOKING EYOND YOUR ATHER! SEE HAT ELSE IS UT THERE!
IF YOU DO AT, I'M SURE OU'LL FIND HE MAN YOU WANT TO BECOME...

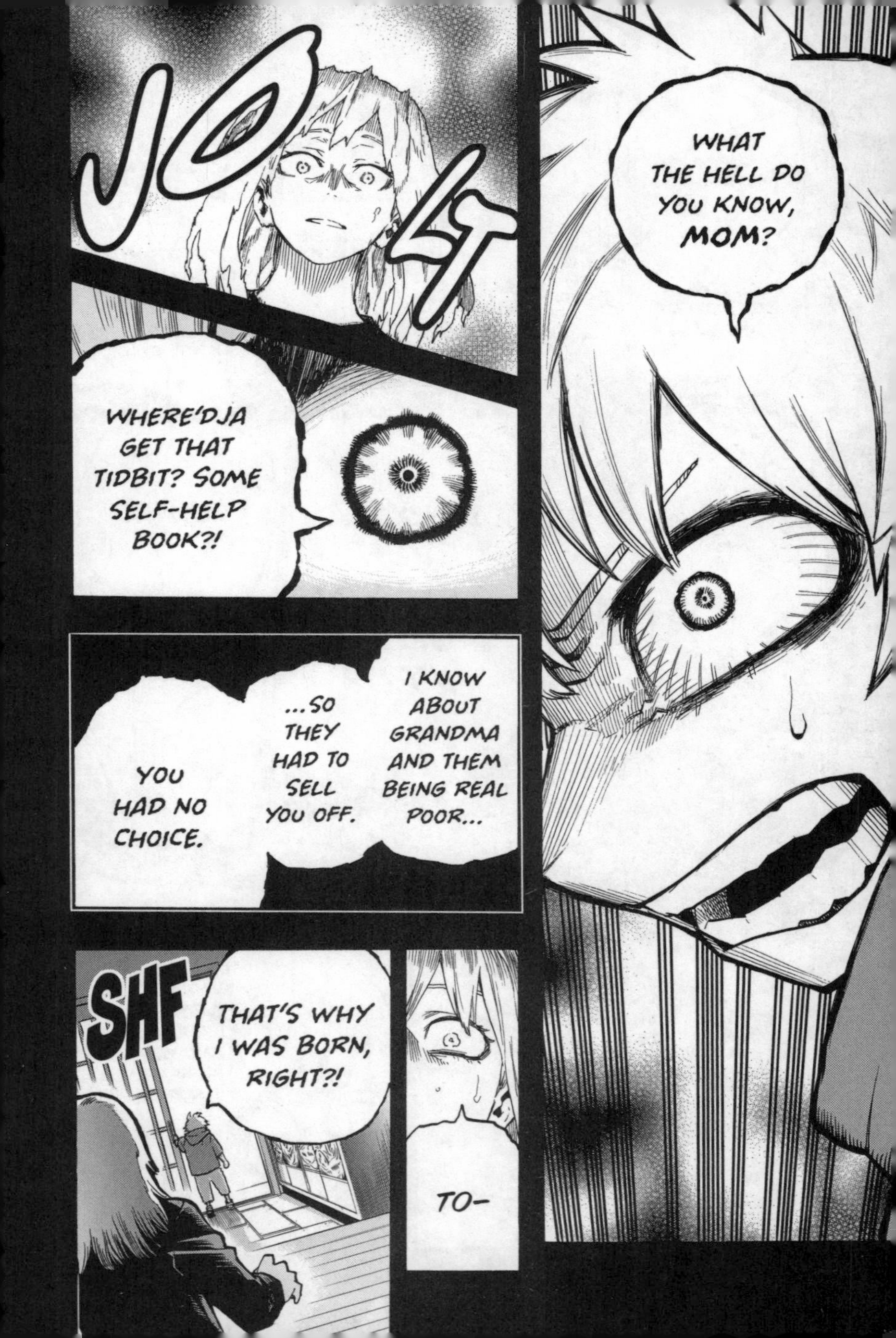
WHAT THE HELL DO YOU KNOW, MOM?
JOLT
WHERE'DJA GET THAT TIDBIT? SOME SELF-HELP BOOK?!
I KNOW ABOUT GRANDMA AND THEM BEING REAL POOR...
...SO THEY HAD TO SELL YOU OFF.
YOU HAD NO CHOICE.
TO-
SHF
THAT'S WHY I WAS BORN, RIGHT?!

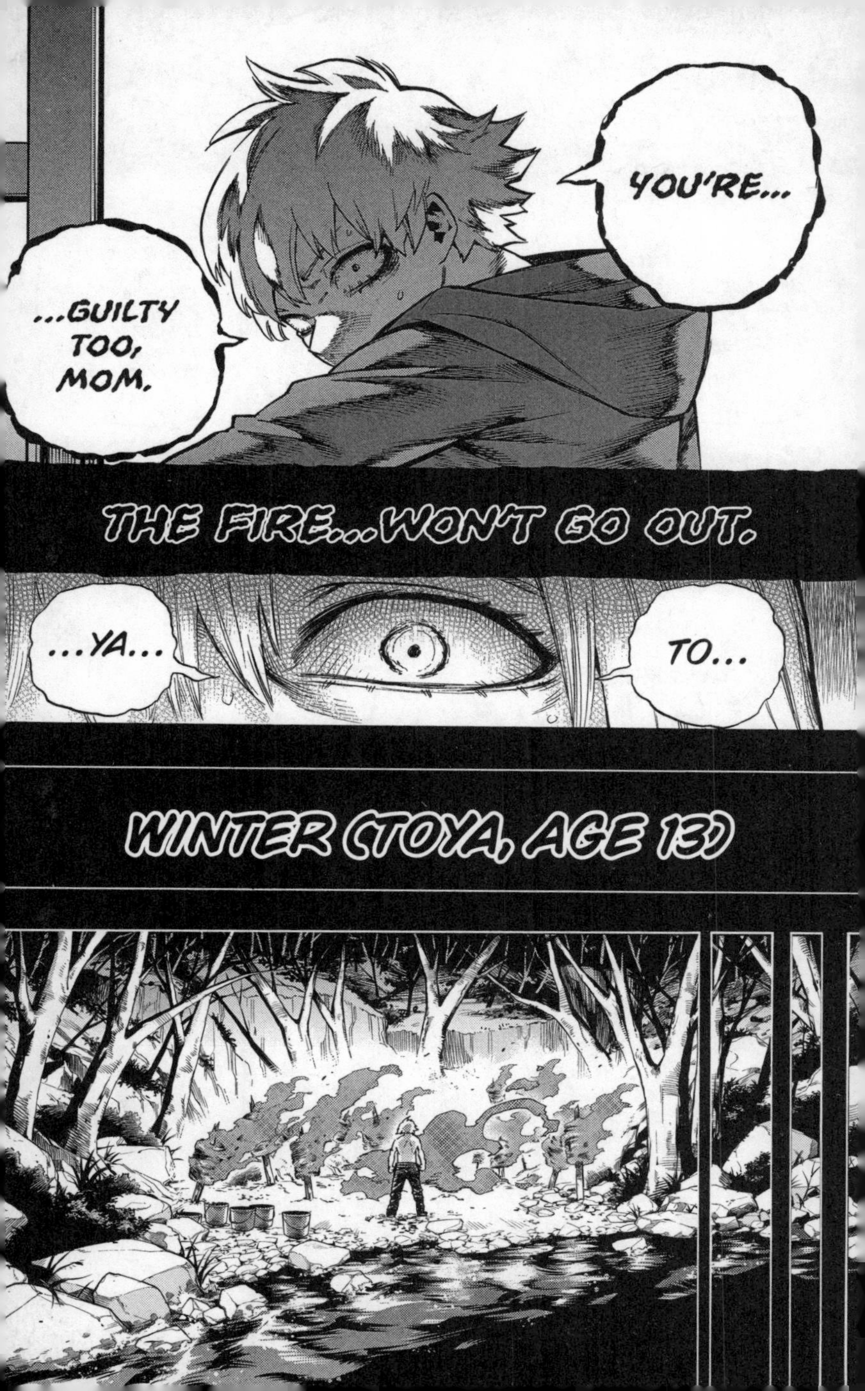
YOU'RE...
...GUILTY TOO, MOM.
THE FIRE...WON'T GO OUT.
TO...
...YA...
WINTER (TOYA, AGE 13)

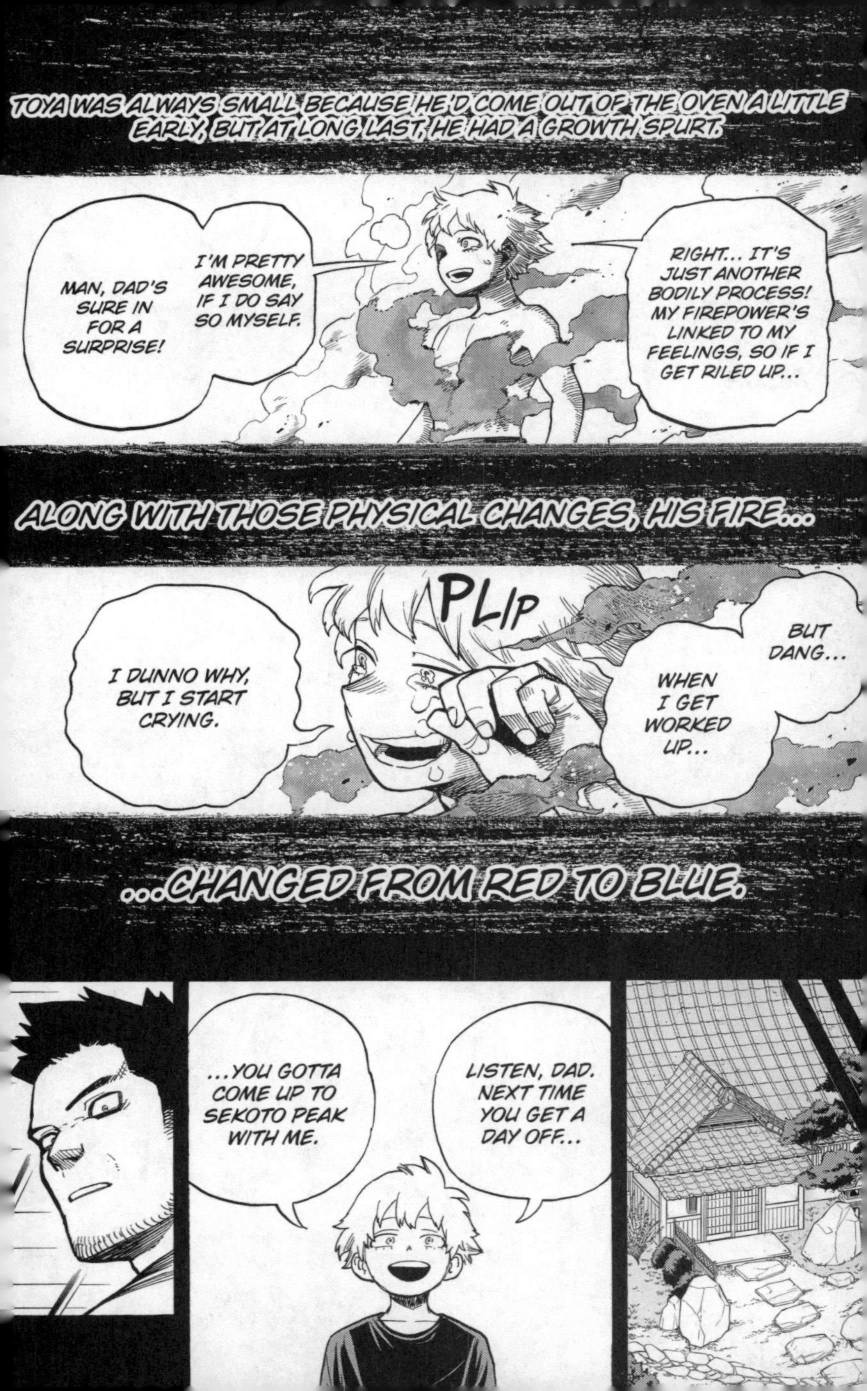
TOYA WAS ALWAYS SMALL BECAUSE HE'D COME OUT OF THE OVEN A LITTLE EARLY, BUT AT LONG LAST, HE HAD A GROWTH SPURT.
RIGHT... IT'S JUST ANOTHER BODILY PROCESS! MY FIREPOWER'S LINKED TO MY FEELINGS, SO IF I GET RILED UP...
I'M PRETTY AWESOME, IF I DO SAY SO MYSELF.
MAN, DAD'S SURE IN FOR A SURPRISE!
ALONG WITH THOSE PHYSICAL CHANGES, HIS FIRE...
BUT DANG...
WHEN I GET WORKED UP...
PLIP
I DUNNO WHY, BUT I START CRYING.
...CHANGED FROM RED TO BLUE.
LISTEN, DAD. NEXT TIME YOU GET A DAY OFF...
...YOU GOTTA COME UP TO SEKOTO PEAK WITH ME.

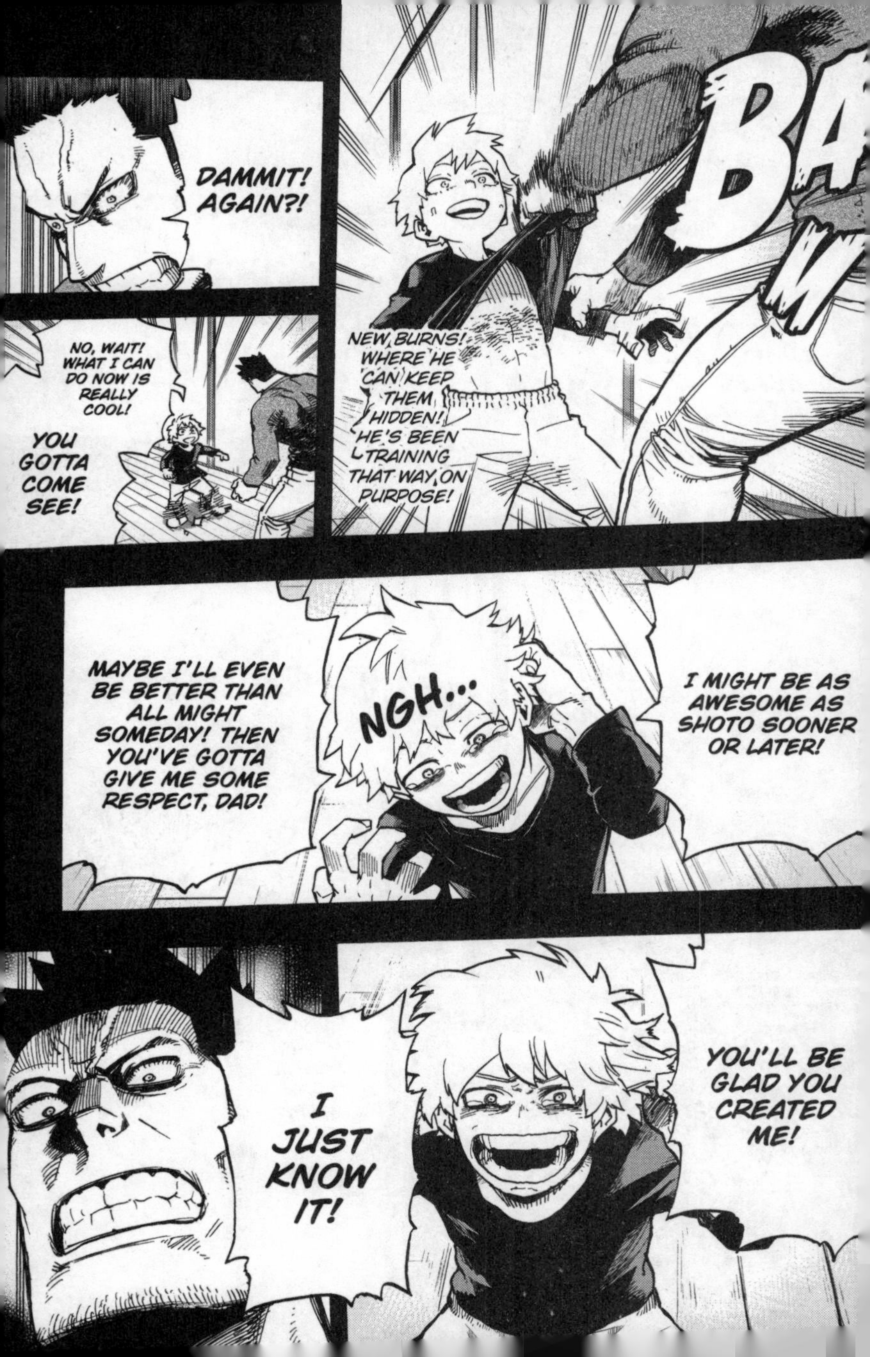
NEW BURNS! WHERE HE CAN KEEP THEM HIDDEN! HE'S BEEN TRAINING THAT WAY ON PURPOSE!
DAMMIT! AGAIN?!
NO, WAIT! WHAT I CAN DO NOW IS REALLY COOL!
YOU GOTTA COME SEE!
I MIGHT BE AS AWESOME AS SHOTO SOONER OR LATER!
NGH...
MAYBE I'LL EVEN BE BETTER THAN ALL MIGHT SOMEDAY! THEN YOU'VE GOTTA GIVE ME SOME RESPECT, DAD!
YOU'LL BE GLAD YOU CREATED ME!
I JUST KNOW IT!

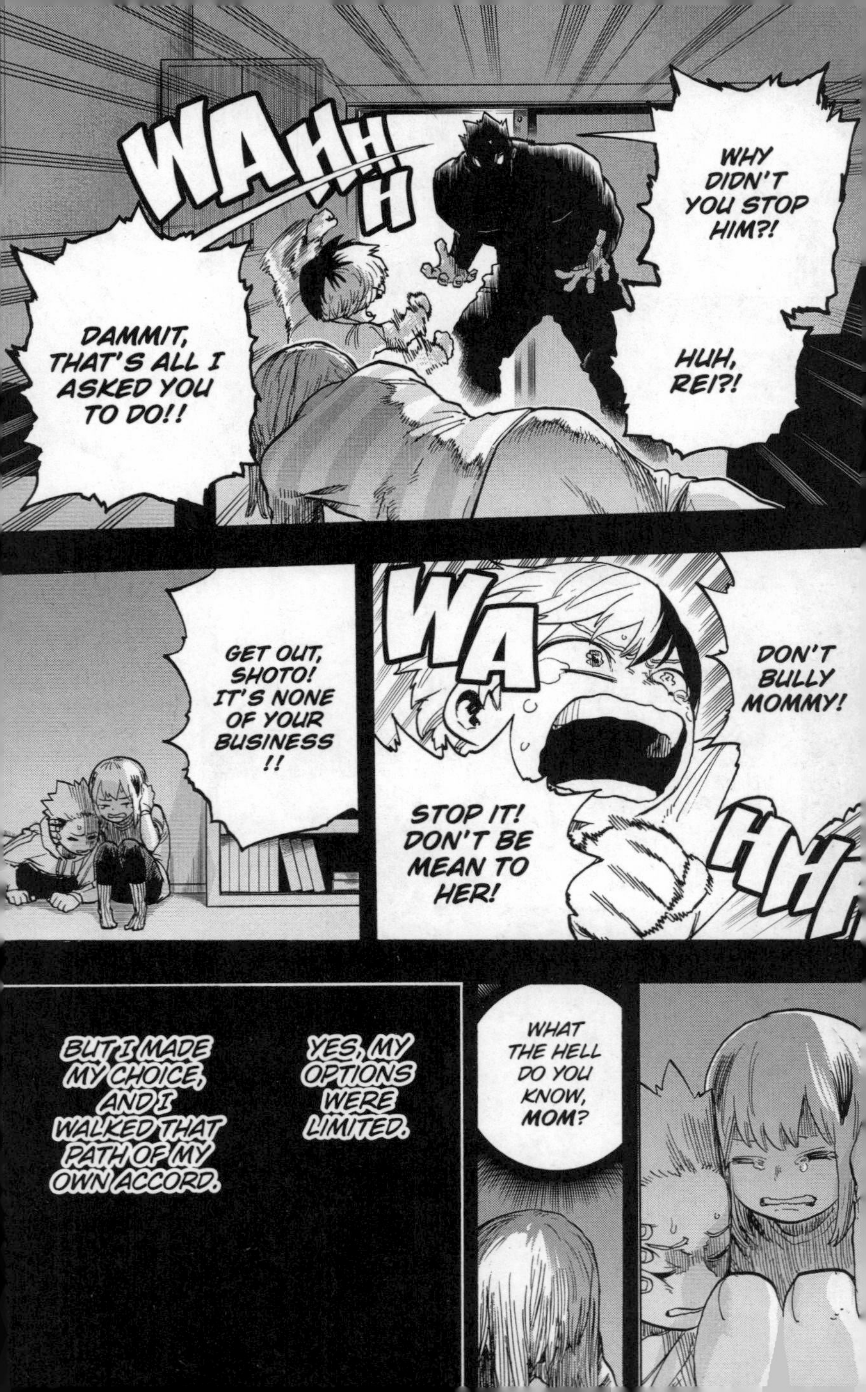
WHY DIDN'T YOU STOP HIM?!
WAHHHH
HUH, REI?!
DAMMIT, THAT'S ALL I ASKED YOU TO DO!!
DON'T BULLY MOMMY!
WA
STOP IT! DON'T BE MEAN TO HER!
HH
GET OUT, SHOTO! IT'S NONE OF YOUR BUSINESS!!
WHAT THE HELL DO YOU KNOW, MOM?
YES, MY OPTIONS WERE LIMITED.
BUT I MADE MY CHOICE, AND I WALKED THAT PATH OF MY OWN ACCORD.

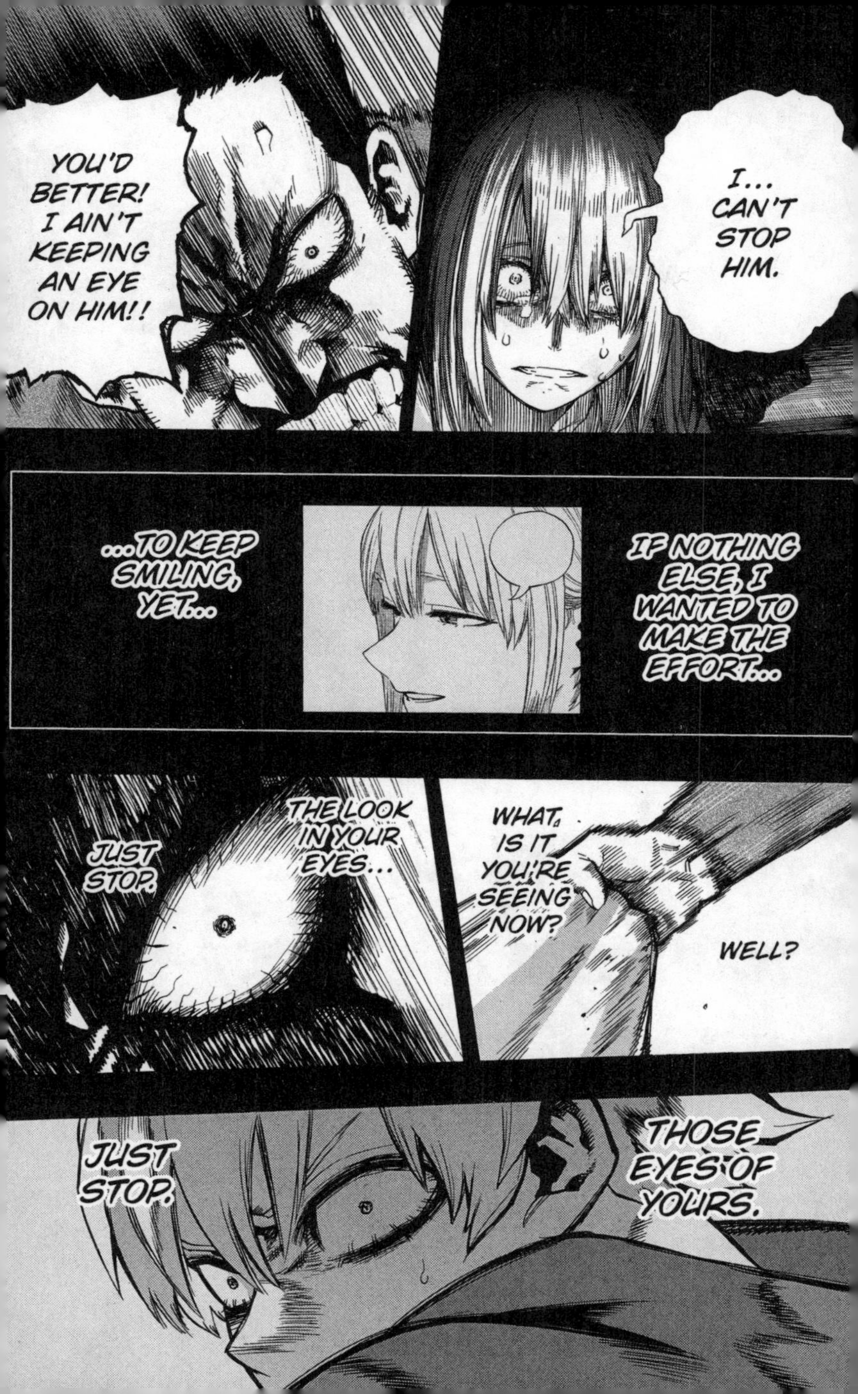
I... CAN'T STOP HIM.
YOU'D BETTER! I AIN'T KEEPING AN EYE ON HIM!!
IF NOTHING ELSE, I WANTED TO MAKE THE EFFORT...
...TO KEEP SMILING, YET...
WHAT IS IT YOU'RE SEEING NOW?
WELL?
THE LOOK IN YOUR EYES...
JUST STOP.
THOSE EYES OF YOURS.
JUST STOP.

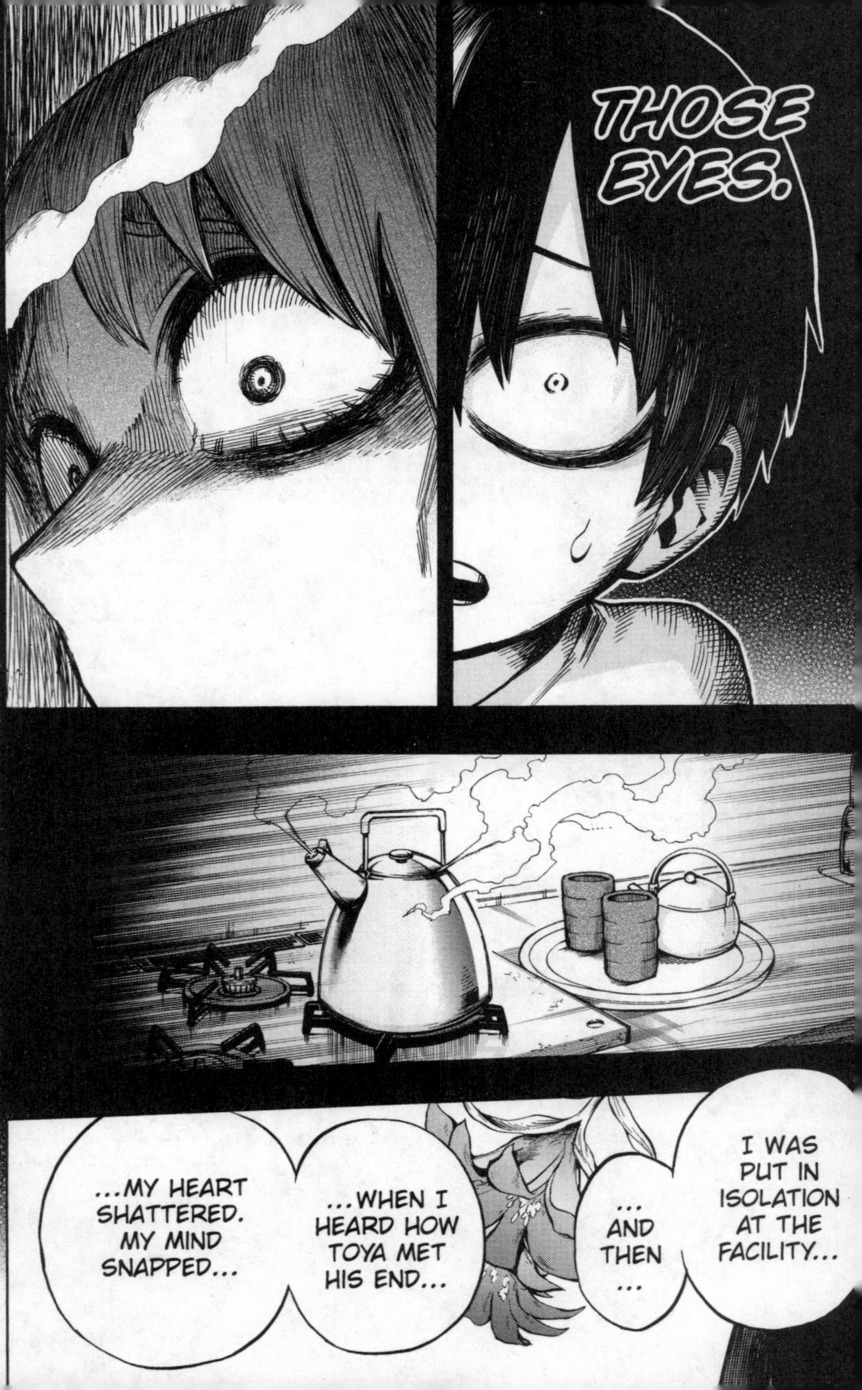
THOSE EYES.
I WAS PUT IN ISOLATION AT THE FACILITY...
...AND THEN...
...WHEN I HEARD HOW TOYA MET HIS END...
...MY HEART SHATTERED. MY MIND SNAPPED...

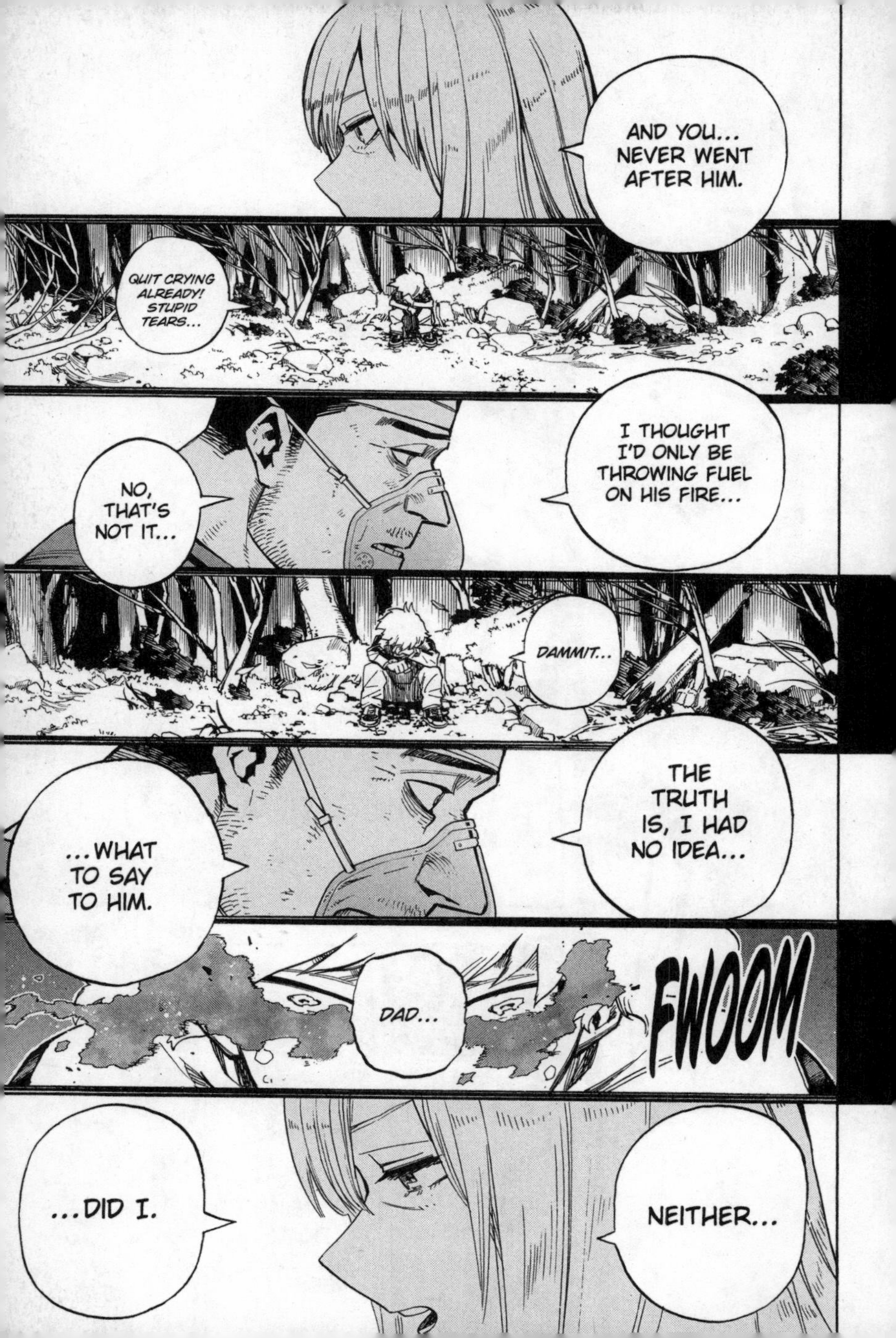
AND YOU... NEVER WENT AFTER HIM.
QUIT CRYING ALREADY! STUPID TEARS...
I THOUGHT I'D ONLY BE THROWING FUEL ON HIS FIRE...
NO, THAT'S NOT IT...
DAMMIT...
THE TRUTH IS, I HAD NO IDEA...
...WHAT TO SAY TO HIM.
FWOOM
DAD...
NEITHER...
...DID I.

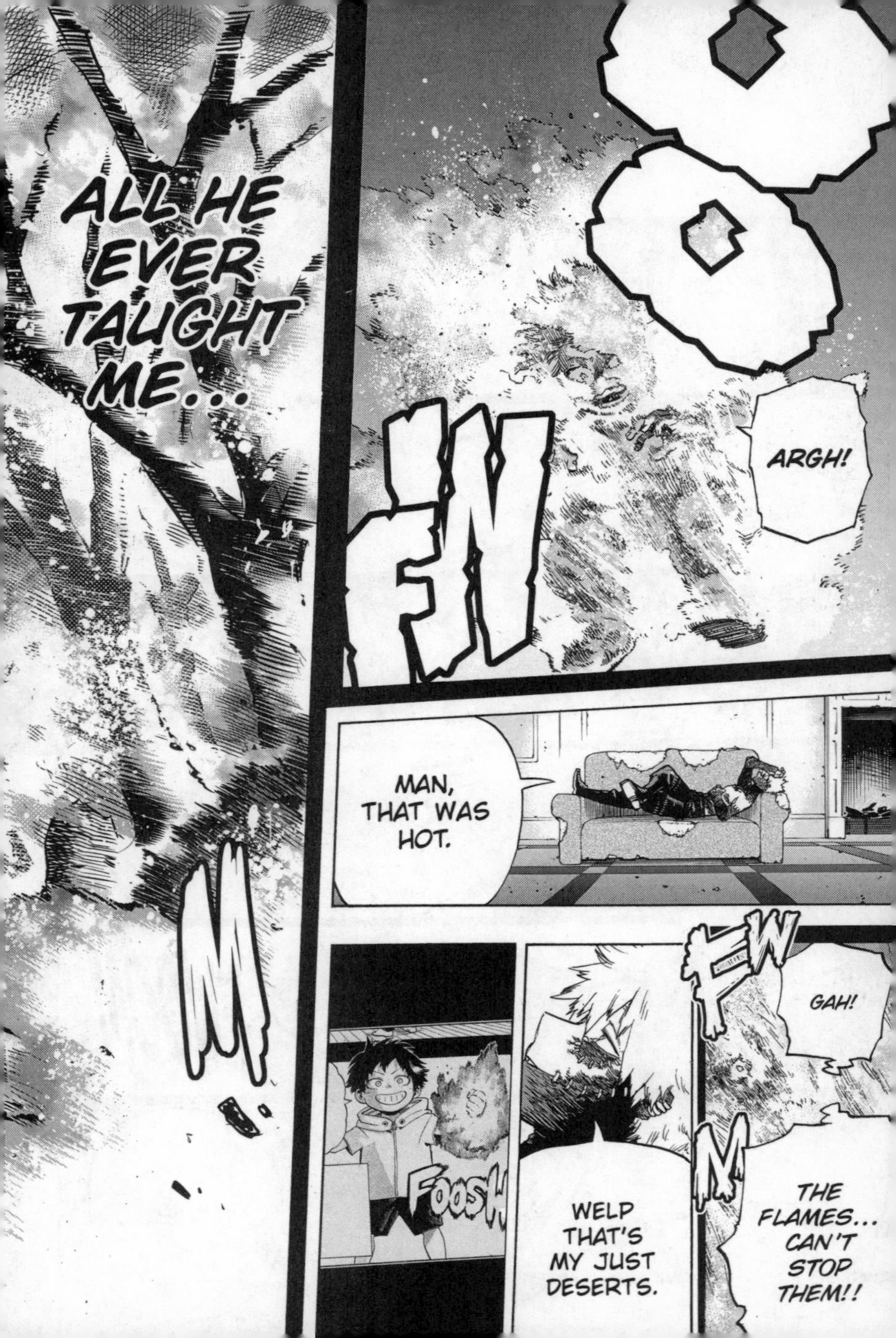
ARGH!
MAN, THAT WAS HOT.
GAH!
THE FLAMES... CAN'T STOP THEM!!
WELP THAT'S MY JUST DESERTS.
FOOSH
ALL HE EVER TAUGHT ME...

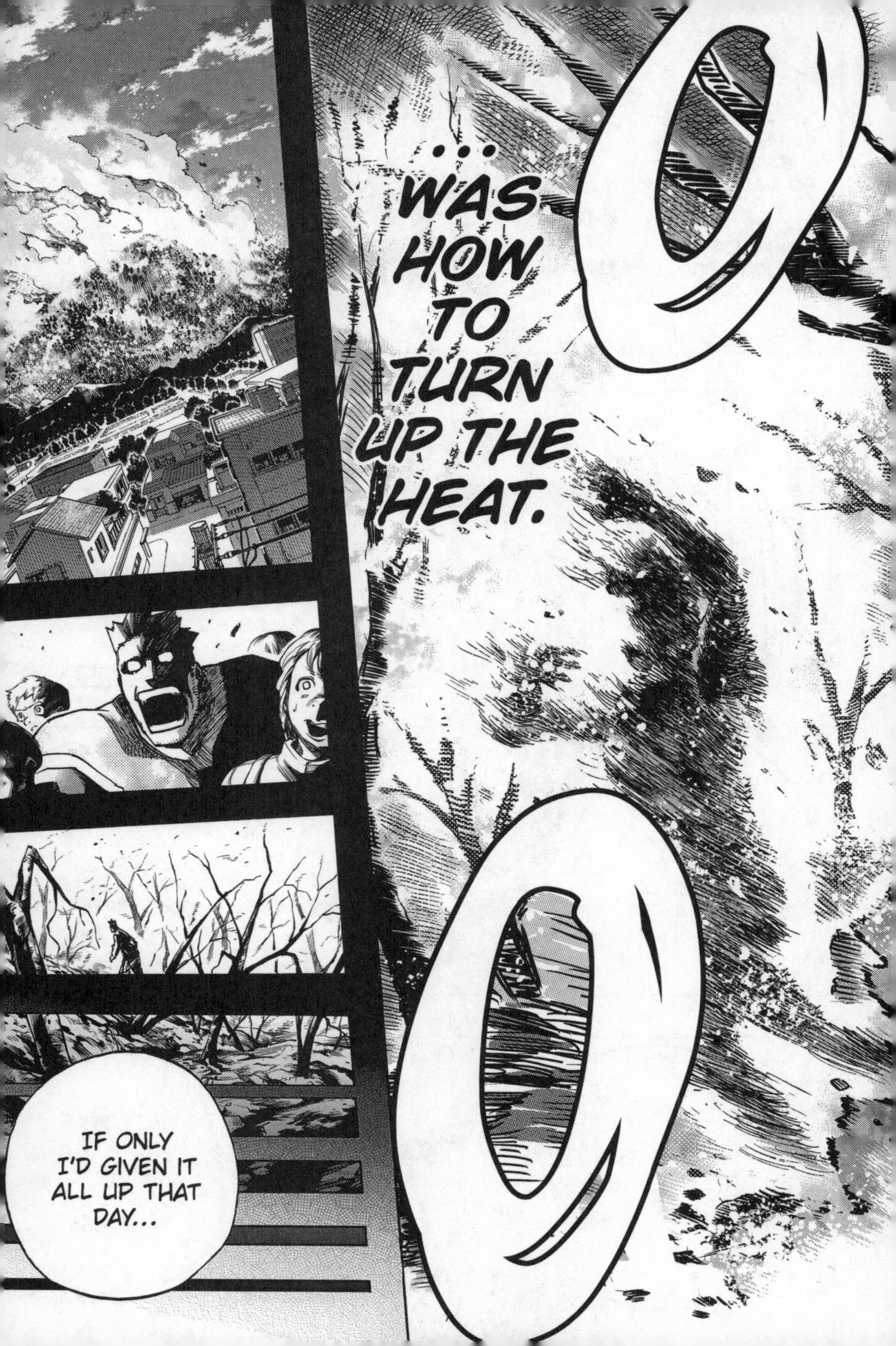
...WAS HOW TO TURN UP THE HEAT.
IF ONLY I'D GIVEN IT ALL UP THAT DAY...

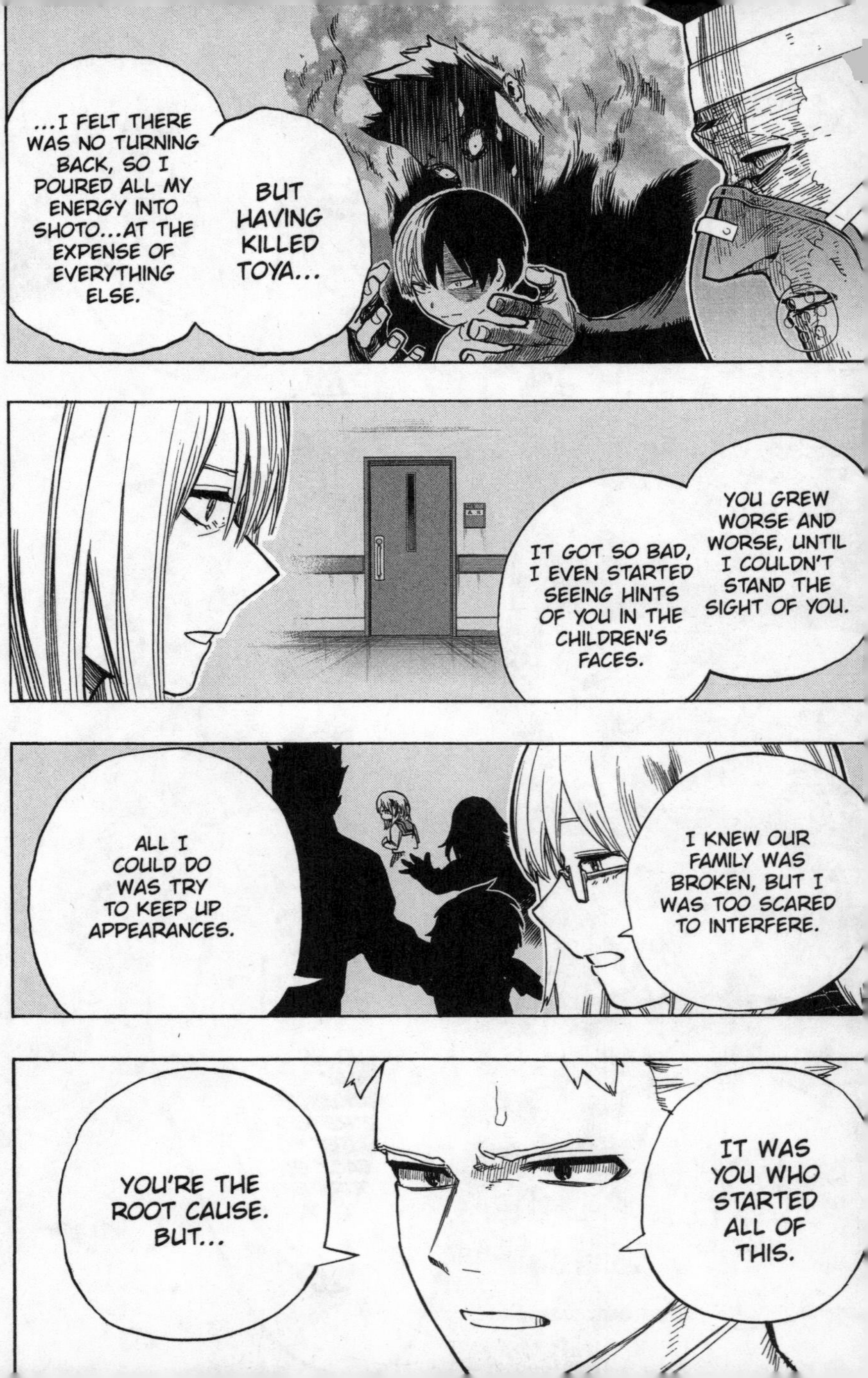
BUT HAVING KILLED TOYA...
...I FELT THERE WAS NO TURNING BACK, SO I POURED ALL MY ENERGY INTO SHOTO...AT THE EXPENSE OF EVERYTHING ELSE.
YOU GREW WORSE AND WORSE, UNTIL I COULDN'T STAND THE SIGHT OF YOU.
IT GOT SO BAD, I EVEN STARTED SEEING HINTS OF YOU IN THE CHILDREN'S FACES.
I KNEW OUR FAMILY WAS BROKEN, BUT I WAS TOO SCARED TO INTERFERE.
ALL I COULD DO WAS TRY TO KEEP UP APPEARANCES.
IT WAS YOU WHO STARTED ALL OF THIS.
YOU'RE THE ROOT CAUSE. BUT...

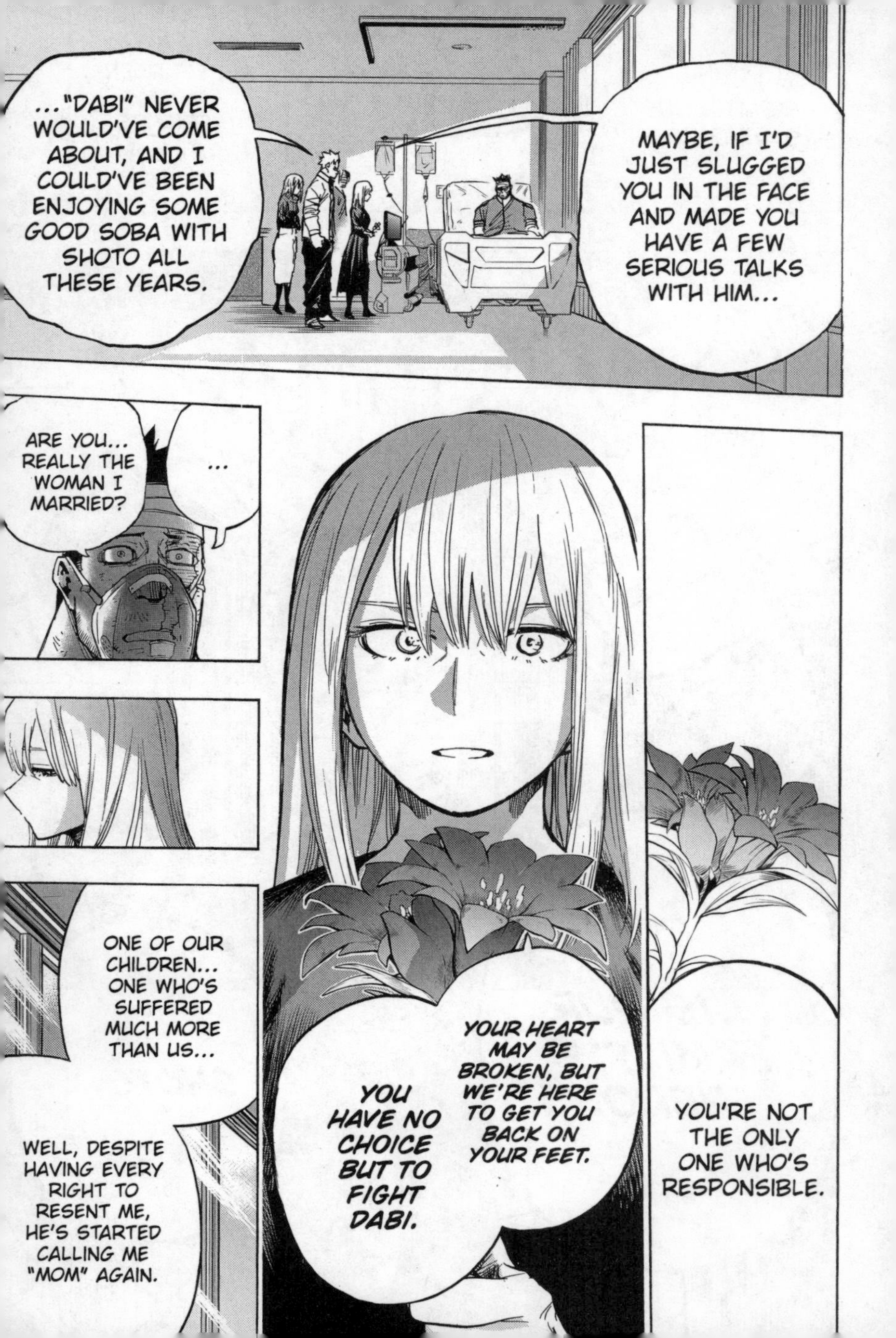
MAYBE, IF I'D JUST SLUGGED YOU IN THE FACE AND MADE YOU HAVE A FEW SERIOUS TALKS WITH HIM...
..."DABI" NEVER WOULD'VE COME ABOUT, AND I COULD'VE BEEN ENJOYING SOME GOOD SOBA WITH SHOTO ALL THESE YEARS.
YOU'RE NOT THE ONLY ONE WHO'S RESPONSIBLE.
YOUR HEART MAY BE BROKEN, BUT WE'RE HERE TO GET YOU BACK ON YOUR FEET.
YOU HAVE NO CHOICE BUT TO FIGHT DABI.
...
ARE YOU... REALLY THE WOMAN I MARRIED?
ONE OF OUR CHILDREN... ONE WHO'S SUFFERED MUCH MORE THAN US...
WELL, DESPITE HAVING EVERY RIGHT TO RESENT ME, HE'S STARTED CALLING ME "MOM" AGAIN.

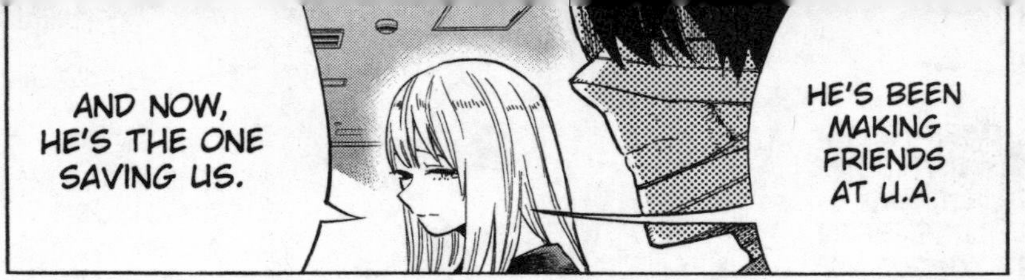
HE'S BEEN MAKING FRIENDS AT U.A.
AND NOW, HE'S THE ONE SAVING US.
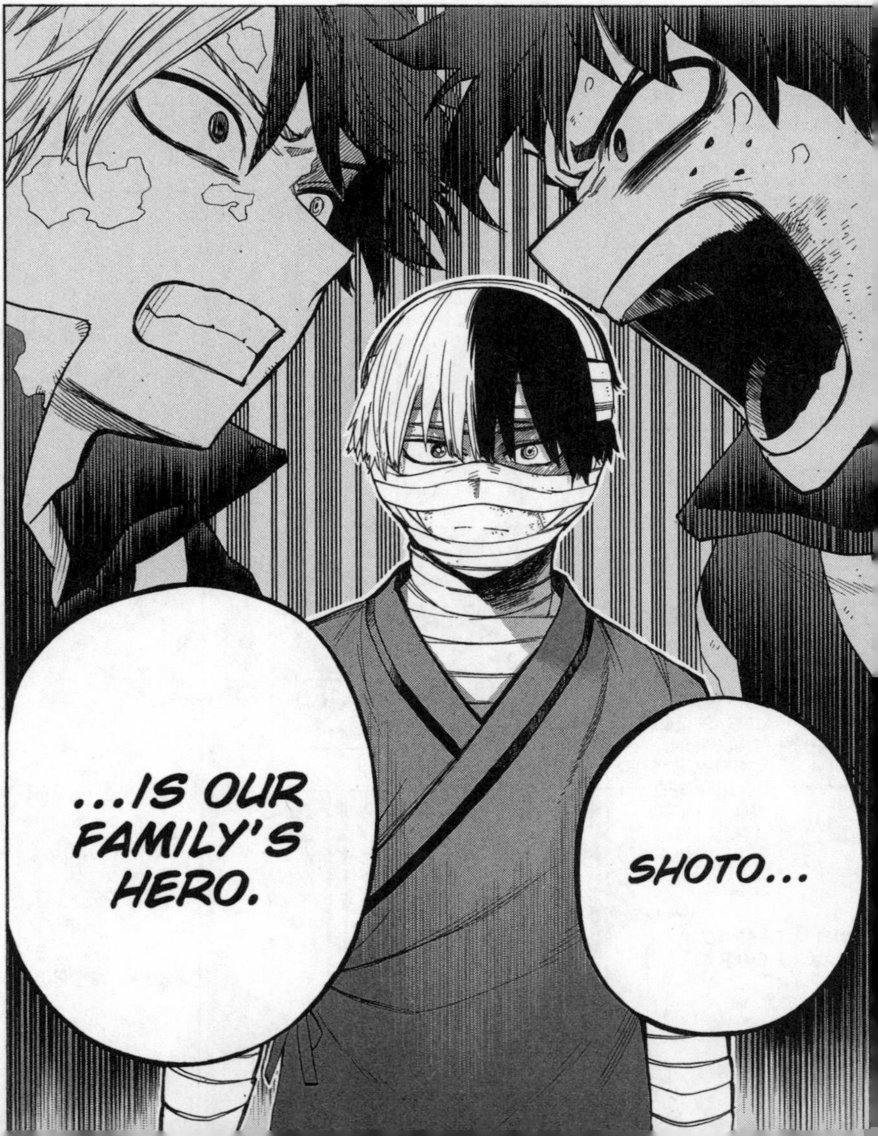
SHOTO...
...IS OUR FAMILY'S HERO.

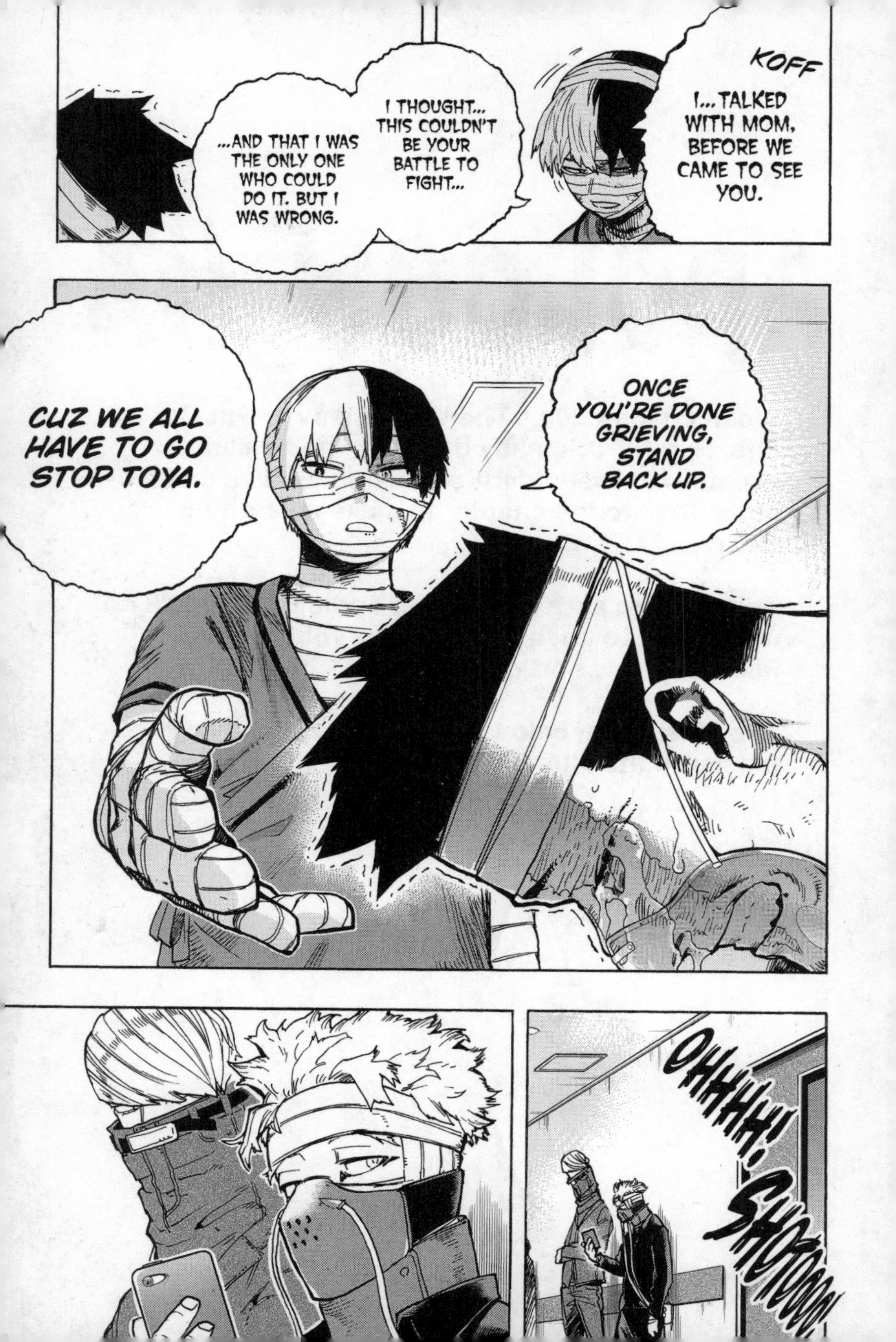
KOFF
I...TALKED WITH MOM, BEFORE WE CAME TO SEE YOU.
I THOUGHT... THIS COULDN'T BE YOUR BATTLE TO FIGHT...
...AND THAT I WAS THE ONLY ONE WHO COULD DO IT. BUT I WAS WRONG.
ONCE YOU'RE DONE GRIEVING, STAND BACK UP.
CUZ WE ALL HAVE TO GO STOP TOYA.
OHHHH!
SHOOOON

APOLOGY #3

When chapter 302, "The Wrong Way to Put Out a Fire, Part 2," originally debuted, the timeline of events was pretty darn confusing. So I've revised and added to the chapter to make everything clearer.

This volume sure has a lot of apologies in it. I'll do my utmost to ensure that future volumes aren't filled with this sort of stuff.

The illustration below shows Todoroki having mastered the ultimate pose.

No. 303 - Top Three

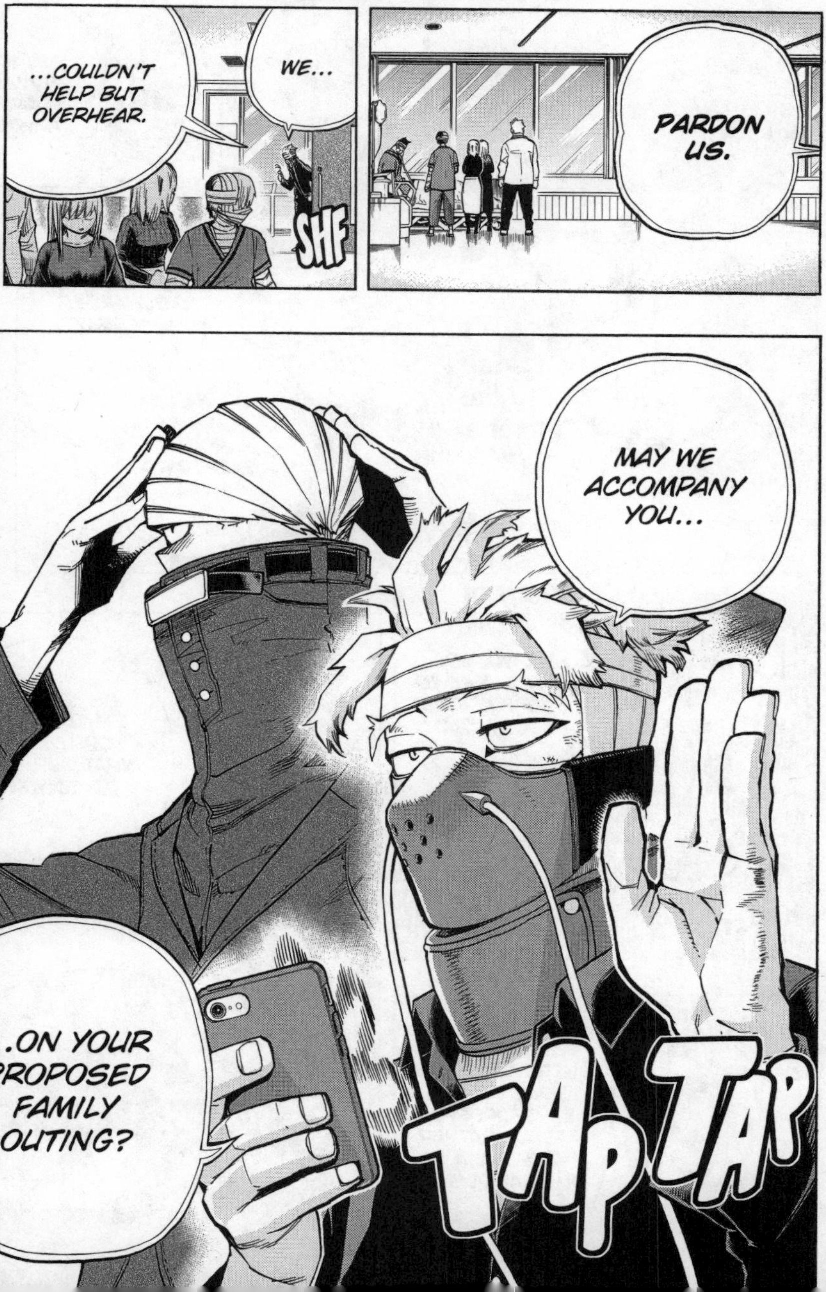
PARDON US.
WE...
...COULDN'T HELP BUT OVERHEAR.
SHF
MAY WE ACCOMPANY YOU...
...ON YOUR PROPOSED FAMILY OUTING?
TAP TAP

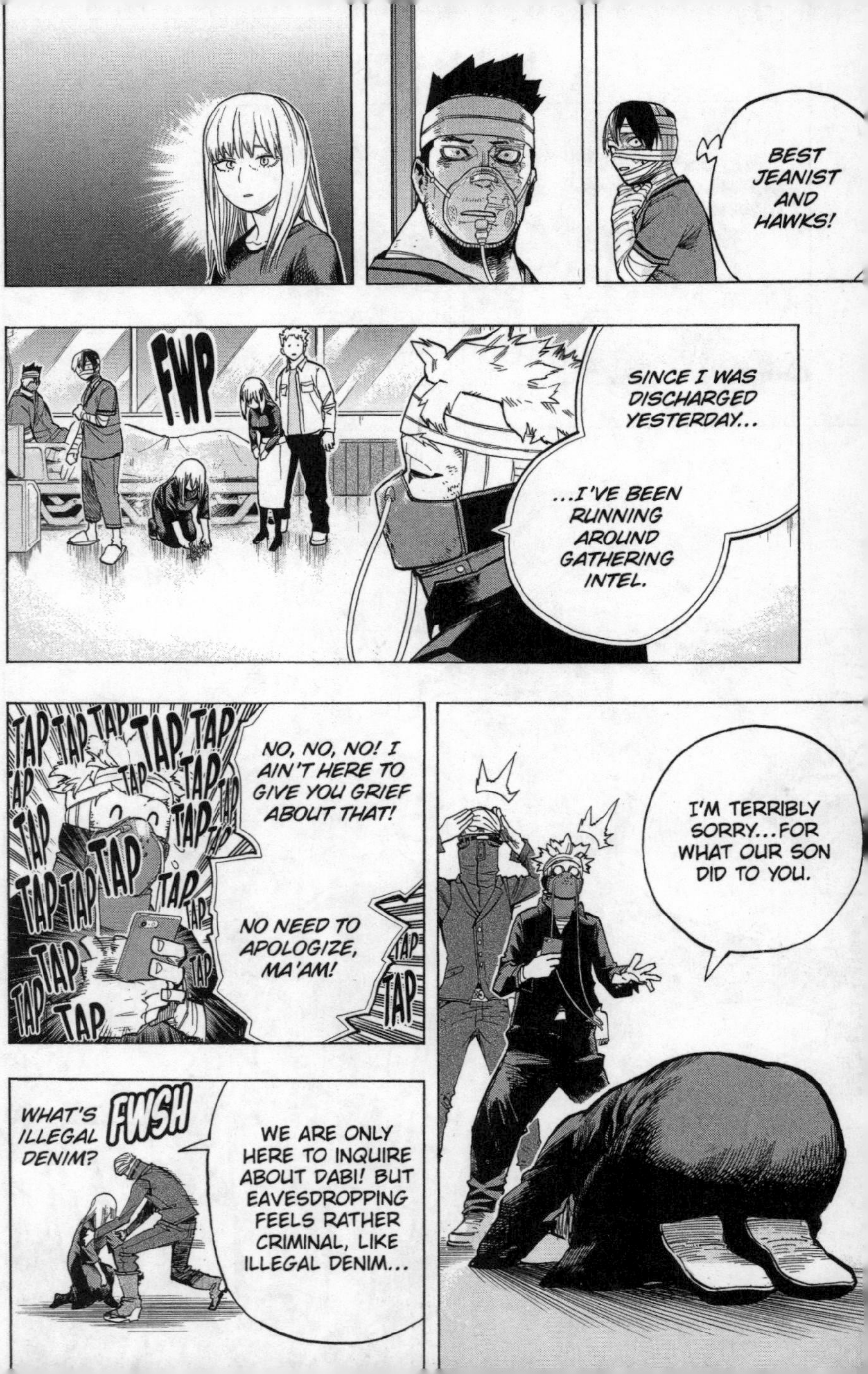
BEST JEANIST AND HAWKS!
SINCE I WAS DISCHARGED YESTERDAY...
...I'VE BEEN RUNNING AROUND GATHERING INTEL.
FWP
I'M TERRIBLY SORRY...FOR WHAT OUR SON DID TO YOU.
NO, NO, NO! I AIN'T HERE TO GIVE YOU GRIEF ABOUT THAT!
NO NEED TO APOLOGIZE, MA'AM!
TAP TAP TAP TAP TAP TAP TAP TAP
WE ARE ONLY HERE TO INQUIRE ABOUT DABI! BUT EAVESDROPPING FEELS RATHER CRIMINAL, LIKE ILLEGAL DENIM...
FWSH
WHAT'S ILLEGAL DENIM?

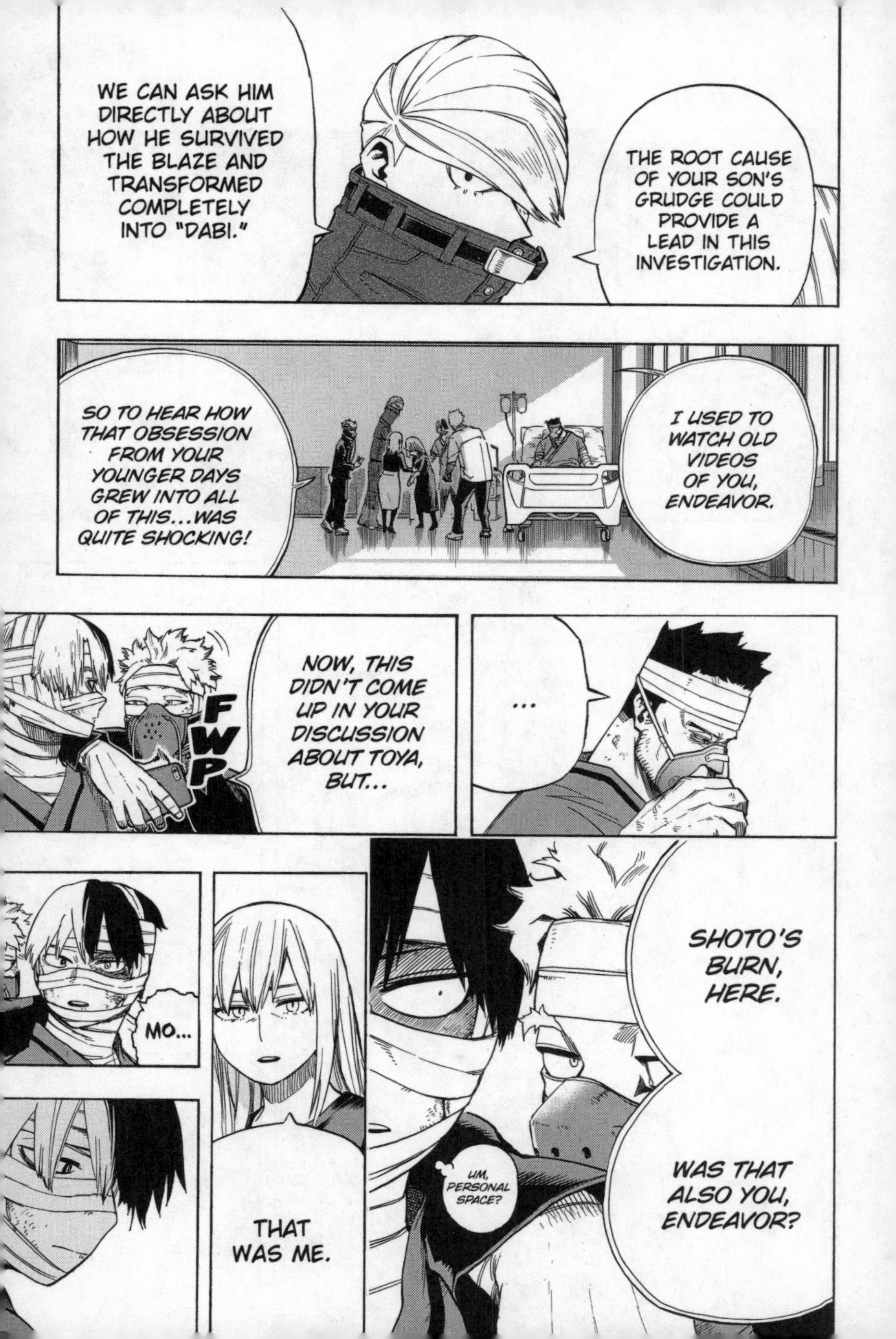
THE ROOT CAUSE OF YOUR SON'S GRUDGE COULD PROVIDE A LEAD IN THIS INVESTIGATION.
WE CAN ASK HIM DIRECTLY ABOUT HOW HE SURVIVED THE BLAZE AND TRANSFORMED COMPLETELY INTO "DABI."
I USED TO WATCH OLD VIDEOS OF YOU, ENDEAVOR.
SO TO HEAR HOW THAT OBSESSION FROM YOUR YOUNGER DAYS GREW INTO ALL OF THIS...WAS QUITE SHOCKING!
...
NOW, THIS DIDN'T COME UP IN YOUR DISCUSSION ABOUT TOYA, BUT...
FWP
SHOTO'S BURN, HERE.
WAS THAT ALSO YOU, ENDEAVOR?
UM, PERSONAL SPACE?
THAT WAS ME.
MO...

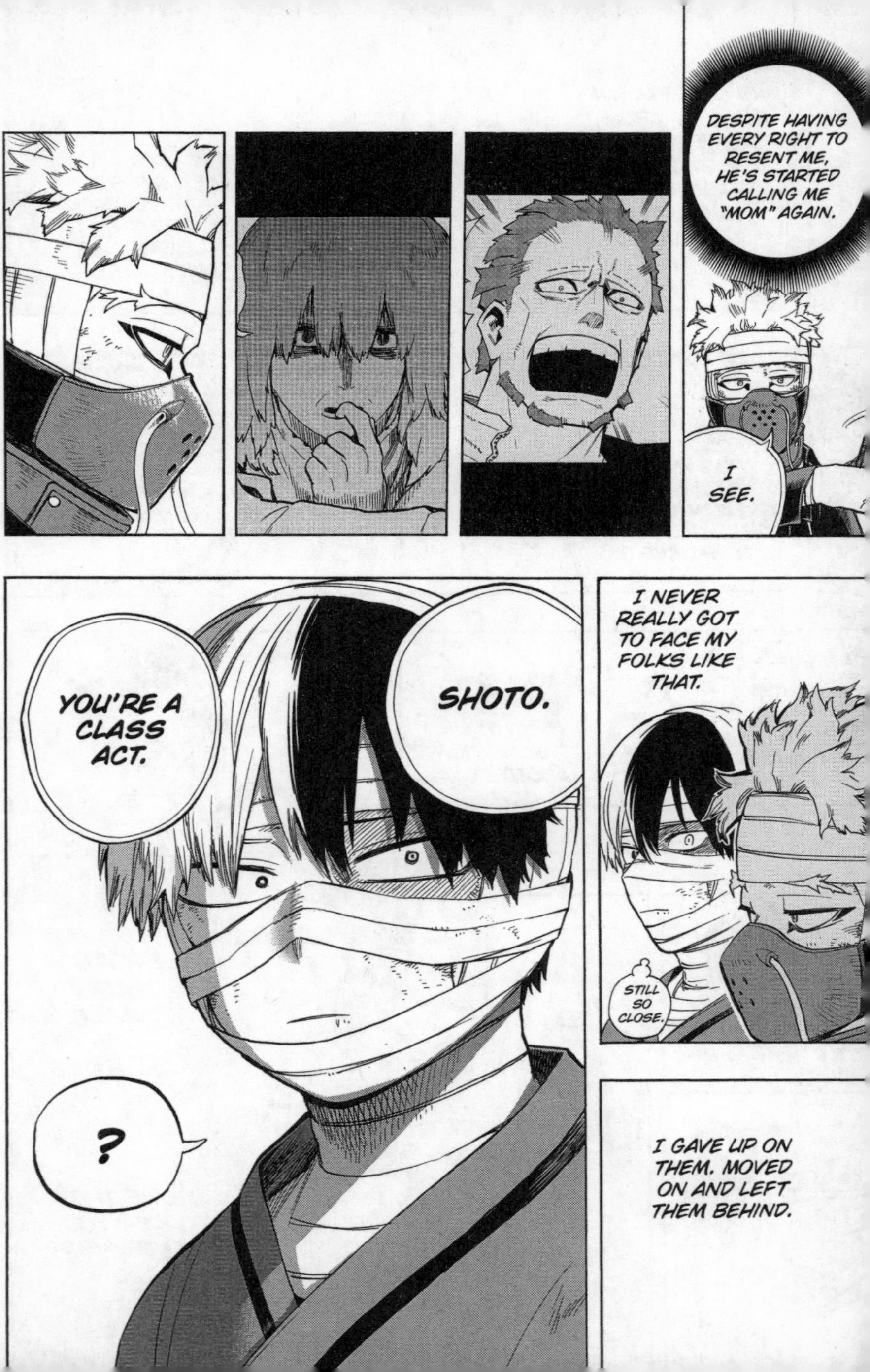
DESPITE HAVING EVERY RIGHT TO RESENT ME, HE'S STARTED CALLING ME "MOM" AGAIN.
I SEE.
I NEVER REALLY GOT TO FACE MY FOLKS LIKE THAT.
STILL SO CLOSE.
I GAVE UP ON THEM. MOVED ON AND LEFT THEM BEHIND.
SHOTO.
YOU'RE A CLASS ACT.
?

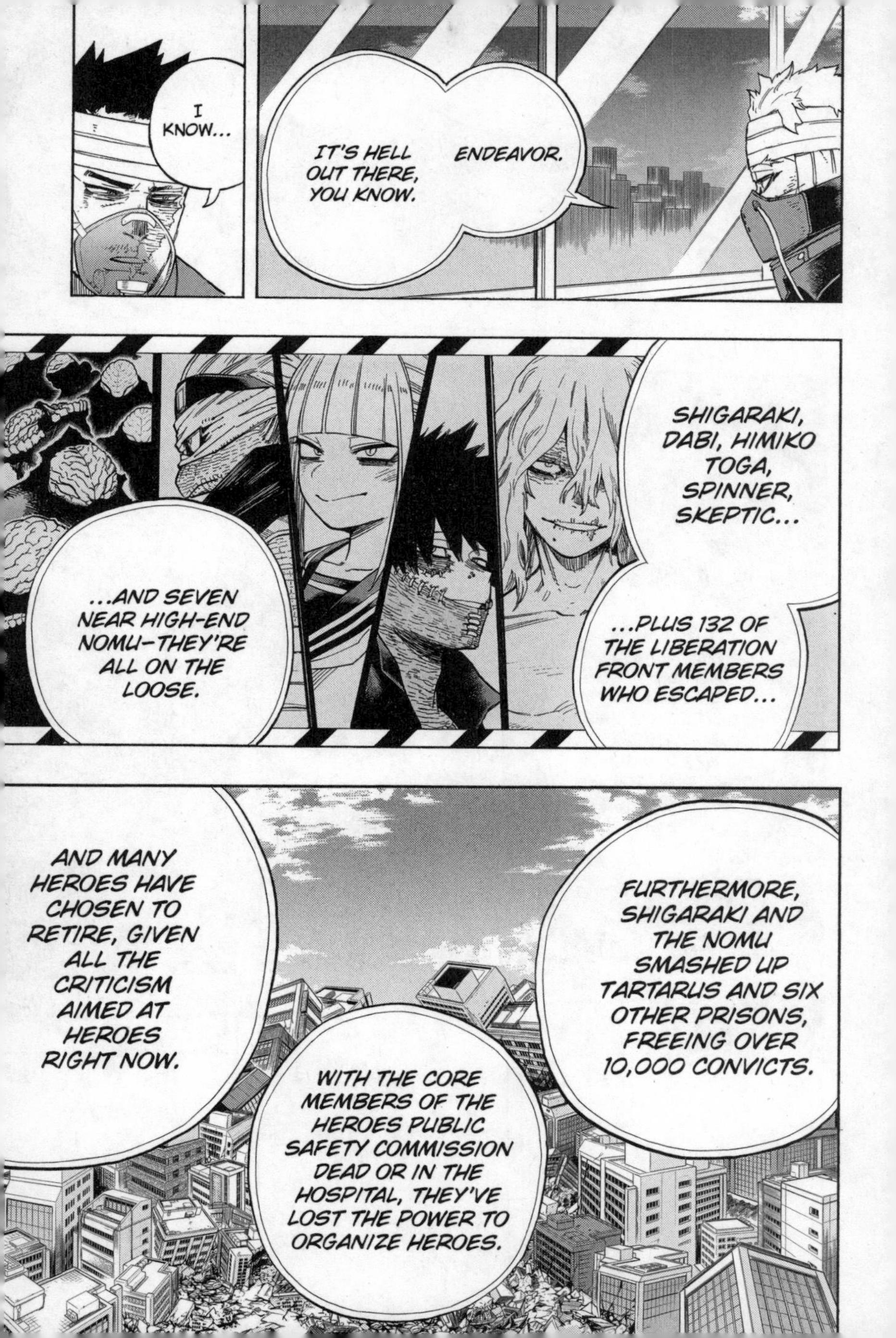
ENDEAVOR.
IT'S HELL OUT THERE, YOU KNOW.
I KNOW...
SHIGARAKI, DABI, HIMIKO TOGA, SPINNER, SKEPTIC...
...PLUS 132 OF THE LIBERATION FRONT MEMBERS WHO ESCAPED...
...AND SEVEN NEAR HIGH-END NOMU–THEY'RE ALL ON THE LOOSE.
FURTHERMORE, SHIGARAKI AND THE NOMU SMASHED UP TARTARUS AND SIX OTHER PRISONS, FREEING OVER 10,000 CONVICTS.
WITH THE CORE MEMBERS OF THE HEROES PUBLIC SAFETY COMMISSION DEAD OR IN THE HOSPITAL, THEY'VE LOST THE POWER TO ORGANIZE HEROES.
AND MANY HEROES HAVE CHOSEN TO RETIRE, GIVEN ALL THE CRITICISM AIMED AT HEROES RIGHT NOW.

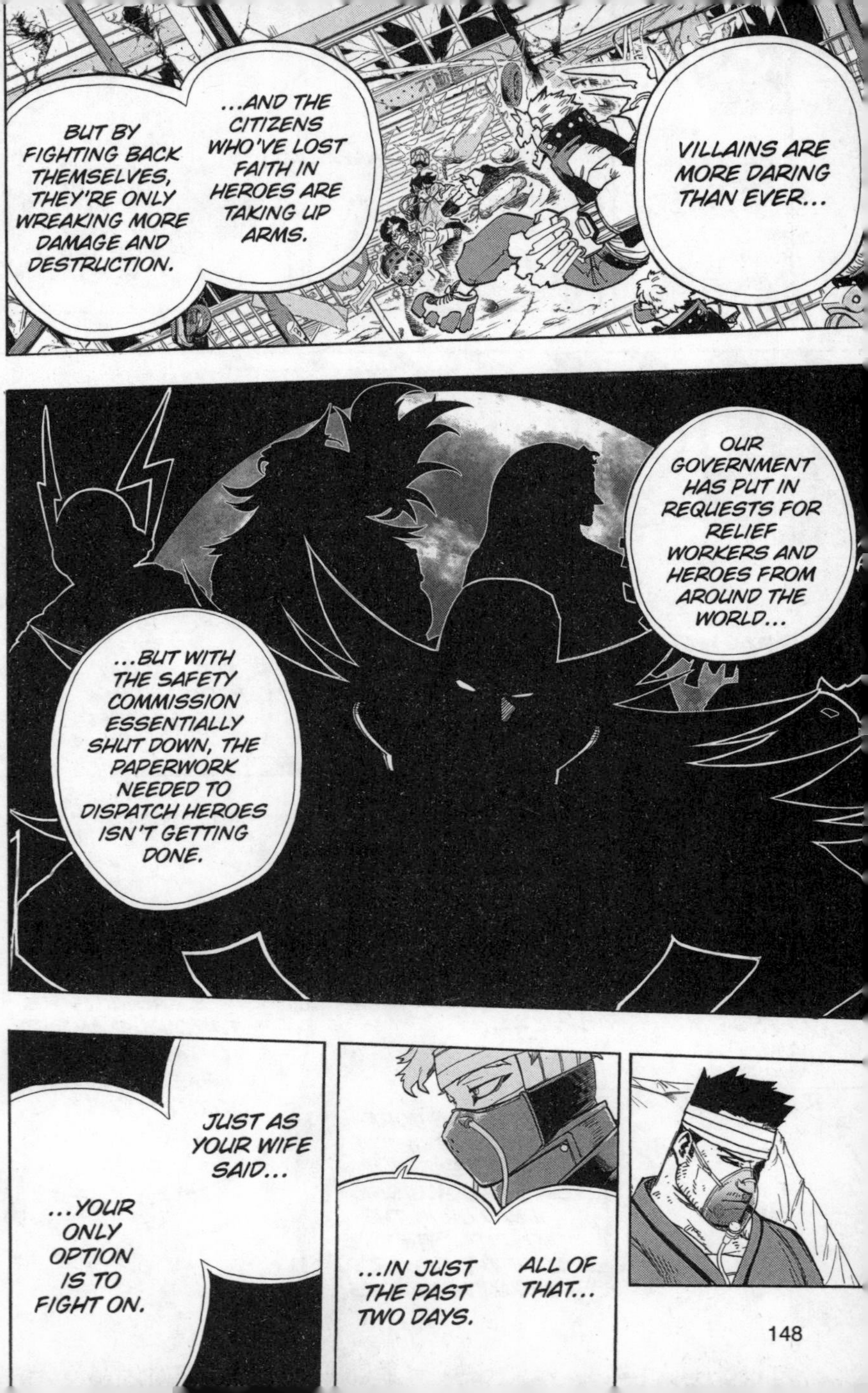
VILLAINS ARE MORE DARING THAN EVER...
...AND THE CITIZENS WHO'VE LOST FAITH IN HEROES ARE TAKING UP ARMS.
BUT BY FIGHTING BACK THEMSELVES, THEY'RE ONLY WREAKING MORE DAMAGE AND DESTRUCTION.
OUR GOVERNMENT HAS PUT IN REQUESTS FOR RELIEF WORKERS AND HEROES FROM AROUND THE WORLD...
...BUT WITH THE SAFETY COMMISSION ESSENTIALLY SHUT DOWN, THE PAPERWORK NEEDED TO DISPATCH HEROES ISN'T GETTING DONE.
ALL OF THAT...
...IN JUST THE PAST TWO DAYS.
JUST AS YOUR WIFE SAID...
...YOUR ONLY OPTION IS TO FIGHT ON.

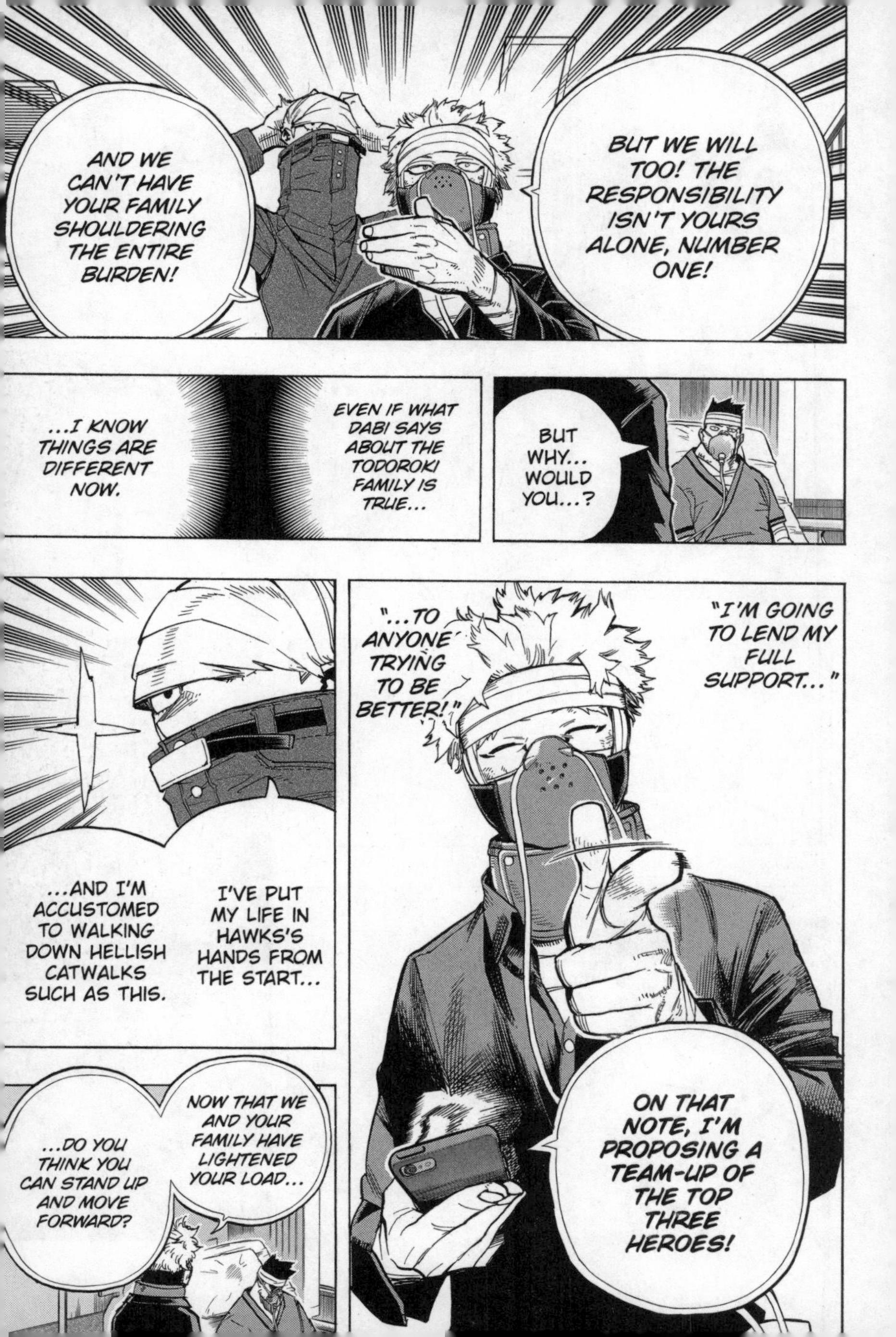
BUT WE WILL TOO! THE RESPONSIBILITY ISN'T YOURS ALONE, NUMBER ONE!
AND WE CAN'T HAVE YOUR FAMILY SHOULDERING THE ENTIRE BURDEN!
BUT WHY... WOULD YOU...?
EVEN IF WHAT DABI SAYS ABOUT THE TODOROKI FAMILY IS TRUE...
...I KNOW THINGS ARE DIFFERENT NOW.
"I'M GOING TO LEND MY FULL SUPPORT..."
"...TO ANYONE TRYING TO BE BETTER!"
ON THAT NOTE, I'M PROPOSING A TEAM-UP OF THE TOP THREE HEROES!
I'VE PUT MY LIFE IN HAWKS'S HANDS FROM THE START...
...AND I'M ACCUSTOMED TO WALKING DOWN HELLISH CATWALKS SUCH AS THIS.
NOW THAT WE AND YOUR FAMILY HAVE LIGHTENED YOUR LOAD...
...DO YOU THINK YOU CAN STAND UP AND MOVE FORWARD?

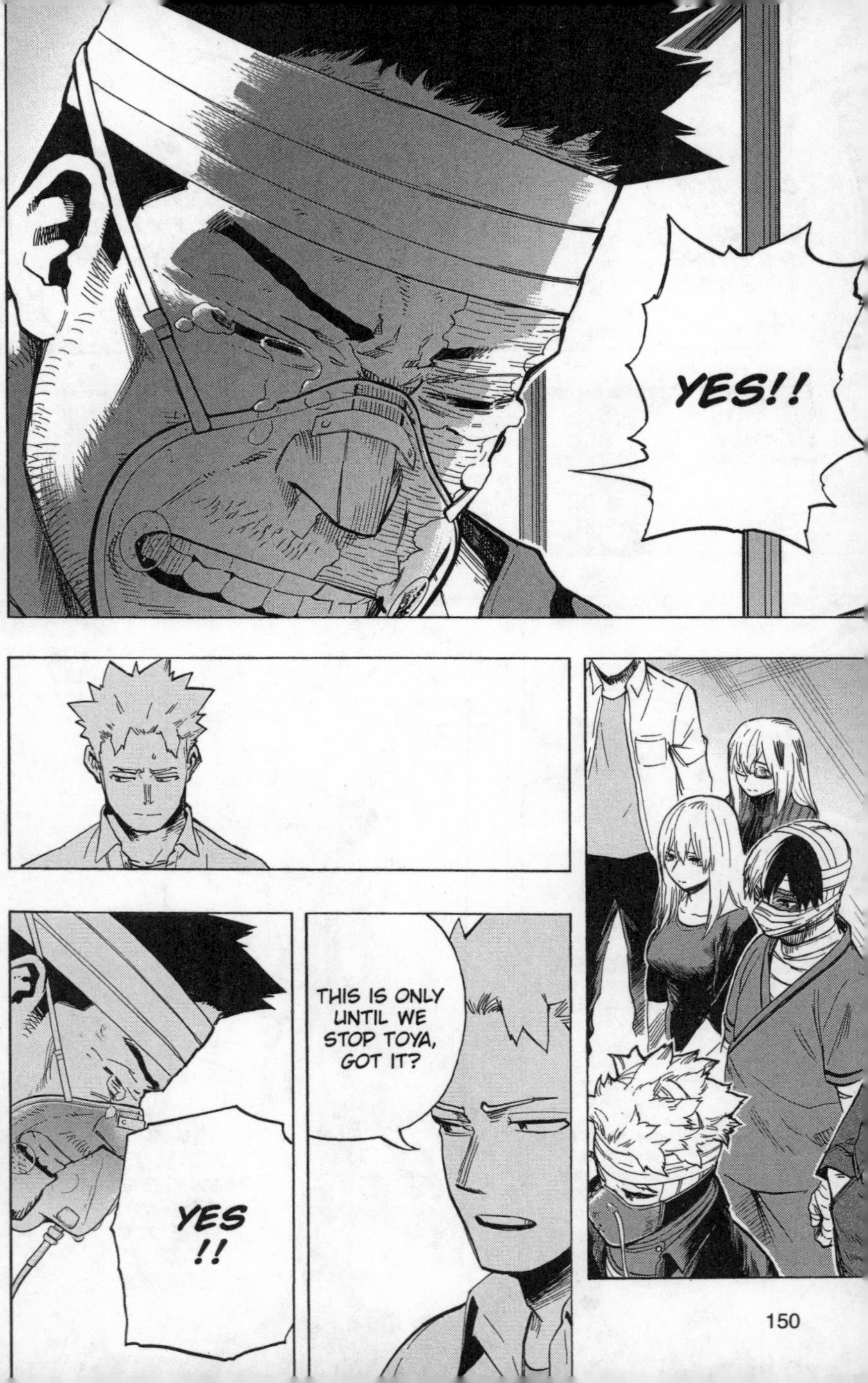
YES!!
THIS IS ONLY UNTIL WE STOP TOYA, GOT IT?
YES !!

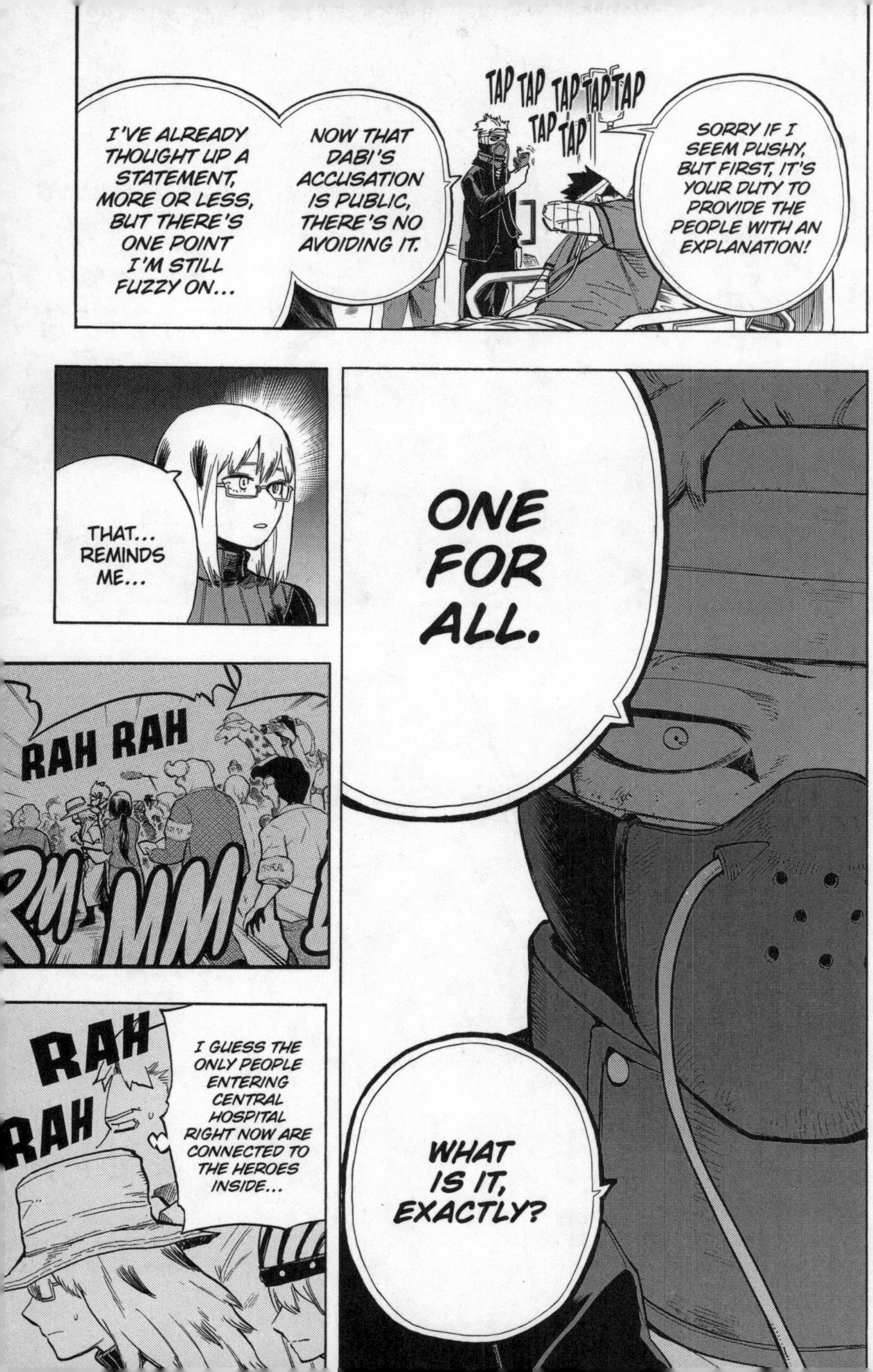
SORRY IF I SEEM PUSHY, BUT FIRST, IT'S YOUR DUTY TO PROVIDE THE PEOPLE WITH AN EXPLANATION!
TAP TAP TAP TAP TAP TAP TAP
NOW THAT DABI'S ACCUSATION IS PUBLIC, THERE'S NO AVOIDING IT.
I'VE ALREADY THOUGHT UP A STATEMENT, MORE OR LESS, BUT THERE'S ONE POINT I'M STILL FUZZY ON...
ONE FOR ALL.
WHAT IS IT, EXACTLY?
THAT... REMINDS ME...
RAH RAH
RUMM
RAH RAH
I GUESS THE ONLY PEOPLE ENTERING CENTRAL HOSPITAL RIGHT NOW ARE CONNECTED TO THE HEROES INSIDE...

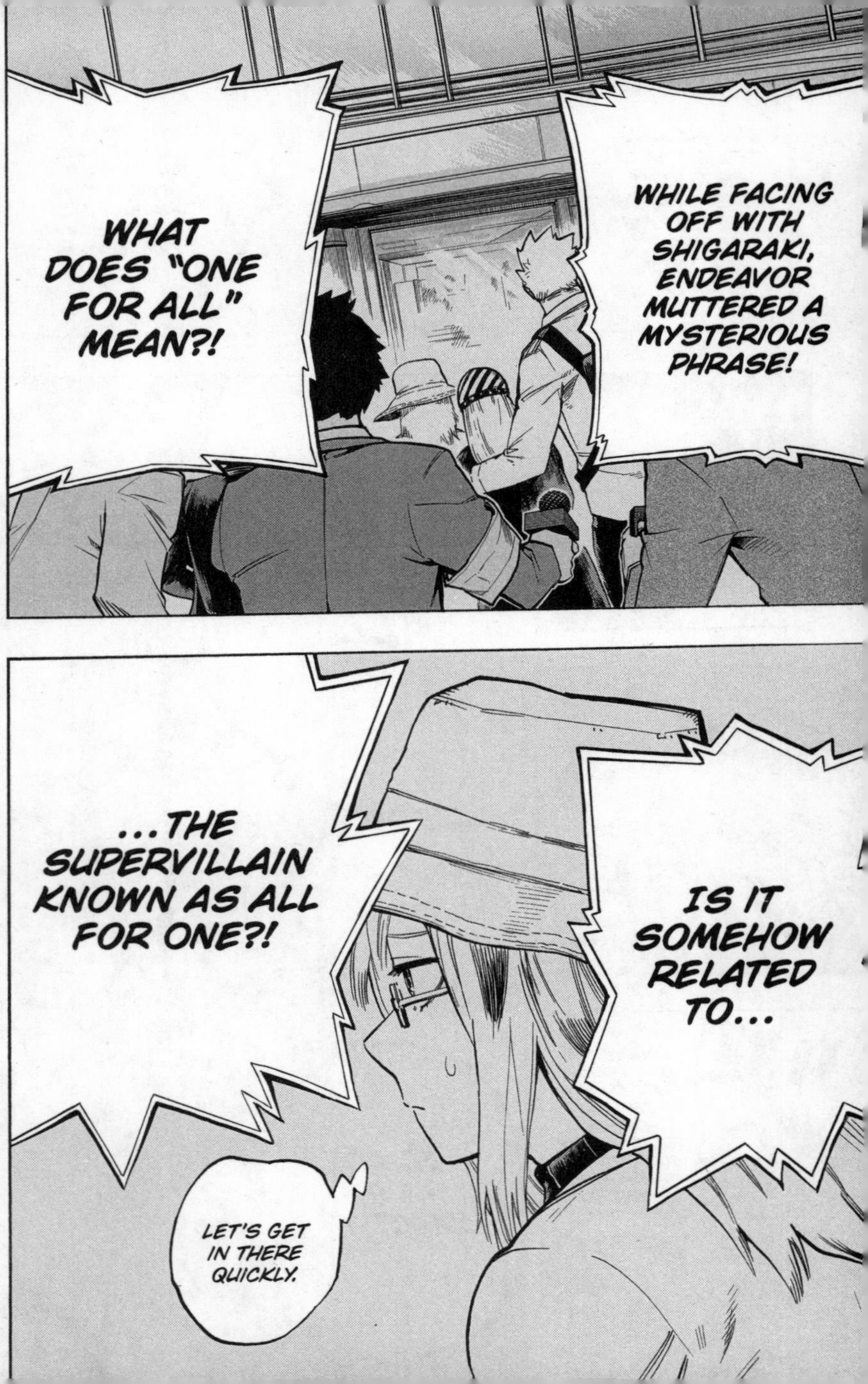
WHILE FACING OFF WITH SHIGARAKI, ENDEAVOR MUTTERED A MYSTERIOUS PHRASE!
WHAT DOES "ONE FOR ALL" MEAN?!
IS IT SOMEHOW RELATED TO...
...THE SUPERVILLAIN KNOWN AS ALL FOR ONE?!
LET'S GET IN THERE QUICKLY.

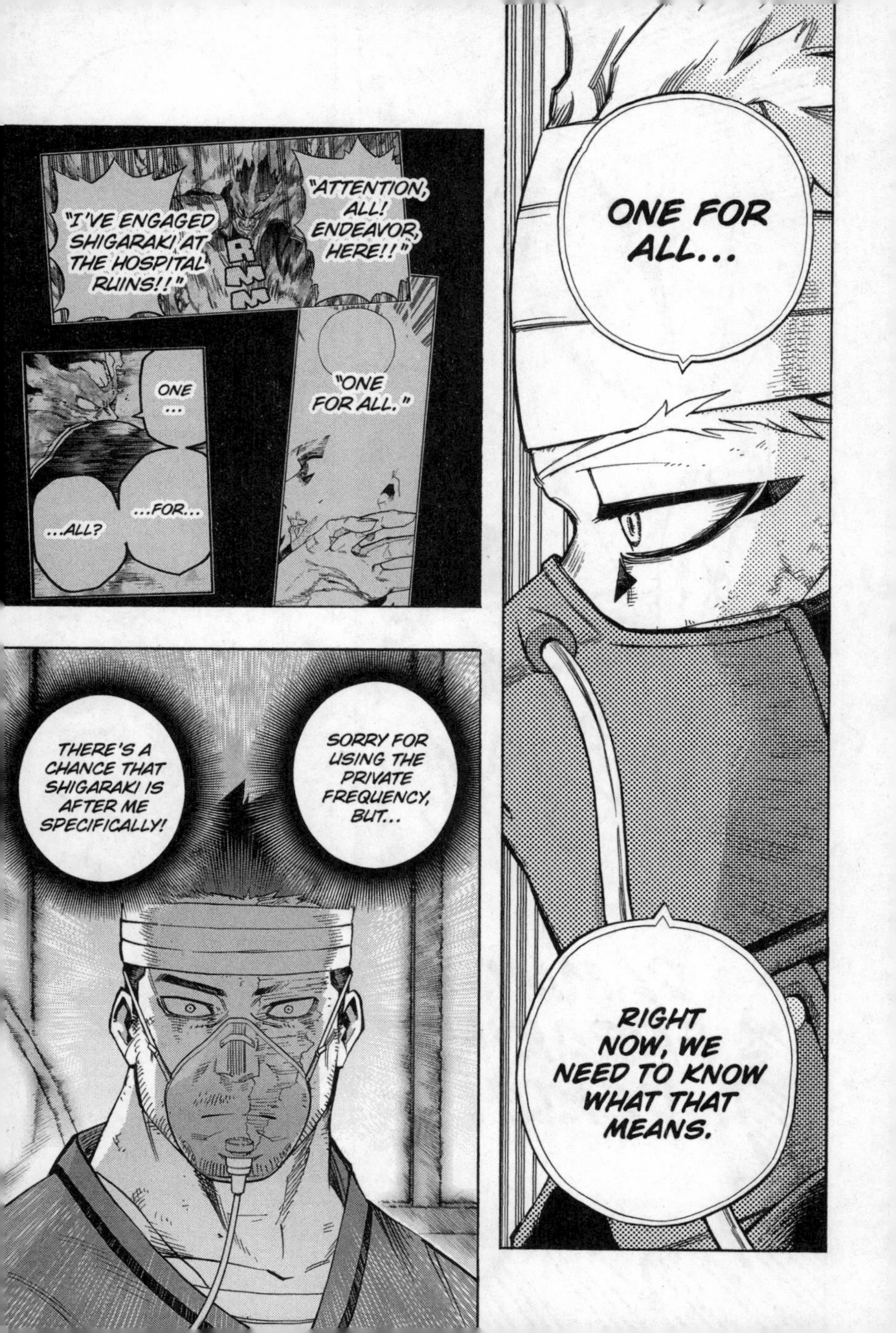
ONE FOR ALL...
RIGHT NOW, WE NEED TO KNOW WHAT THAT MEANS.
"ATTENTION, ALL! ENDEAVOR, HERE!!"
"I'VE ENGAGED SHIGARAKI AT THE HOSPITAL RUINS!!"
RMM
"ONE FOR ALL."
ONE ...
...FOR...
...ALL?
SORRY FOR USING THE PRIVATE FREQUENCY, BUT...
THERE'S A CHANCE THAT SHIGARAKI IS AFTER ME SPECIFICALLY!

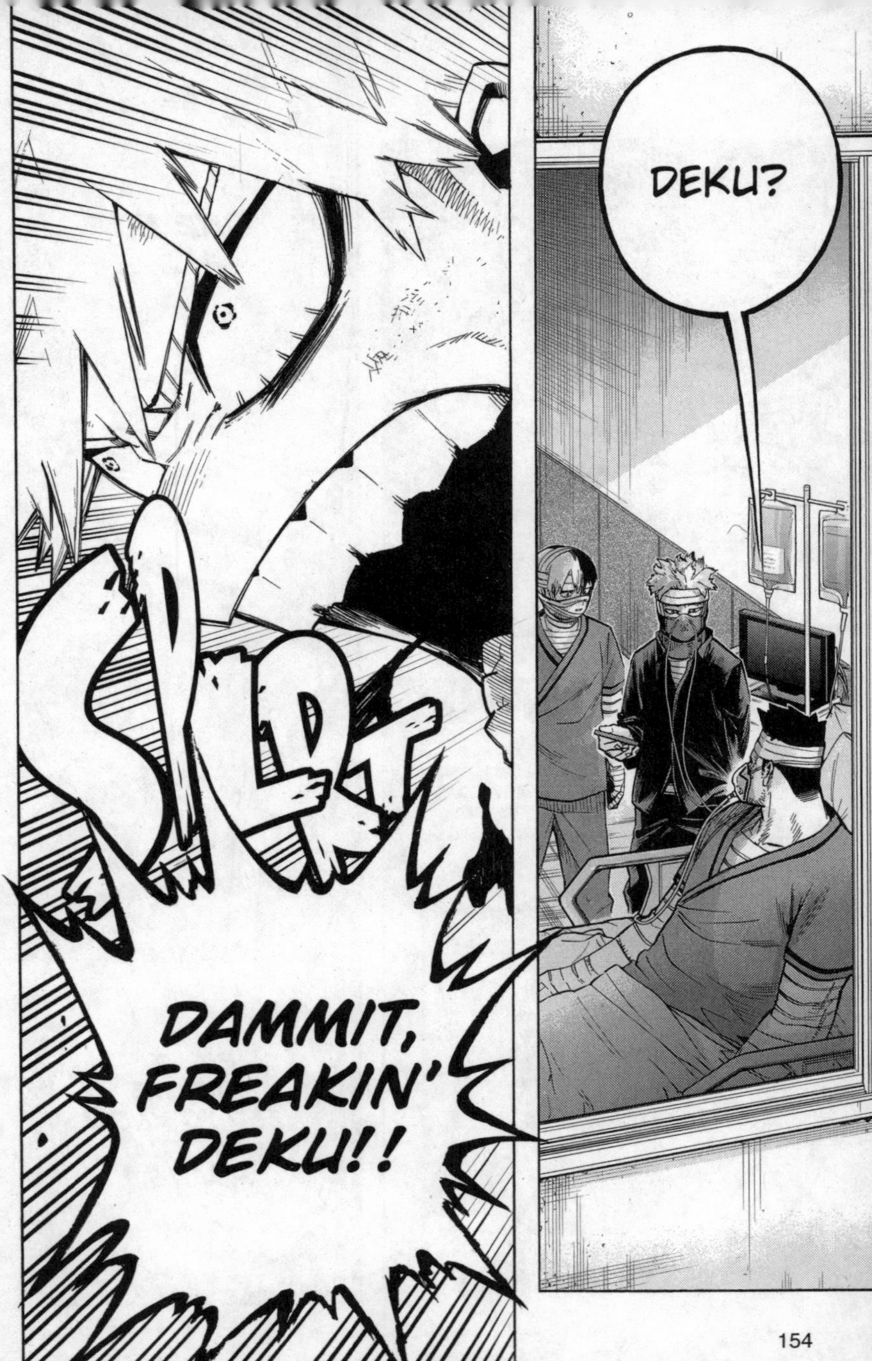
DEKU?
DAMMIT, FREAKIN' DEKU!!

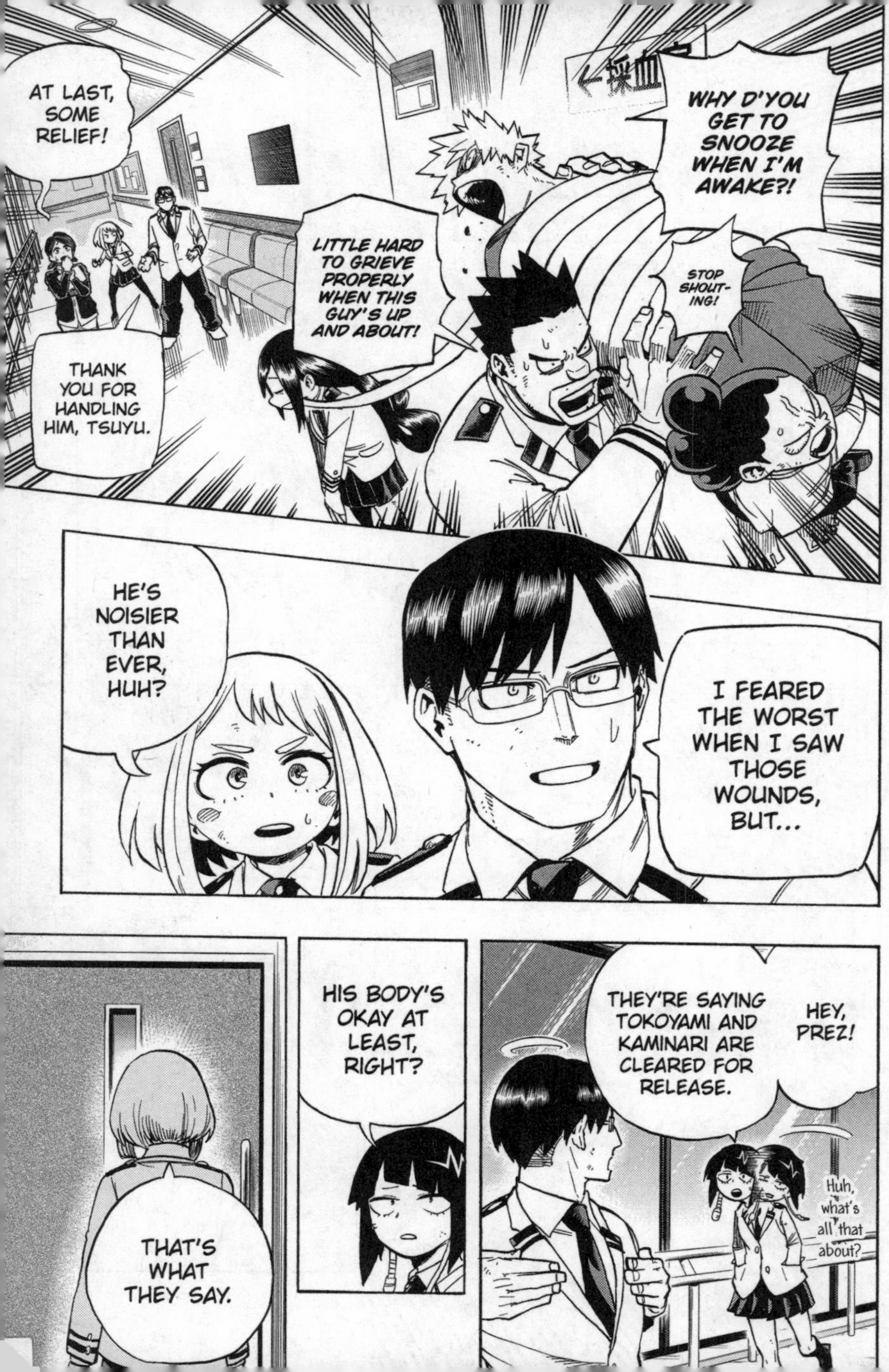

←採血
WHY D'YOU GET TO SNOOZE WHEN I'M AWAKE?!
STOP SHOUTING!
LITTLE HARD TO GRIEVE PROPERLY WHEN THIS GUY'S UP AND ABOUT!
AT LAST, SOME RELIEF!
THANK YOU FOR HANDLING HIM, TSUYU.
I FEARED THE WORST WHEN I SAW THOSE WOUNDS, BUT...
HE'S NOISIER THAN EVER, HUH?
HEY, PREZ!
THEY'RE SAYING TOKOYAMI AND KAMINARI ARE CLEARED FOR RELEASE.
Huh, what's all that about?
HIS BODY'S OKAY AT LEAST, RIGHT?
THAT'S WHAT THEY SAY.

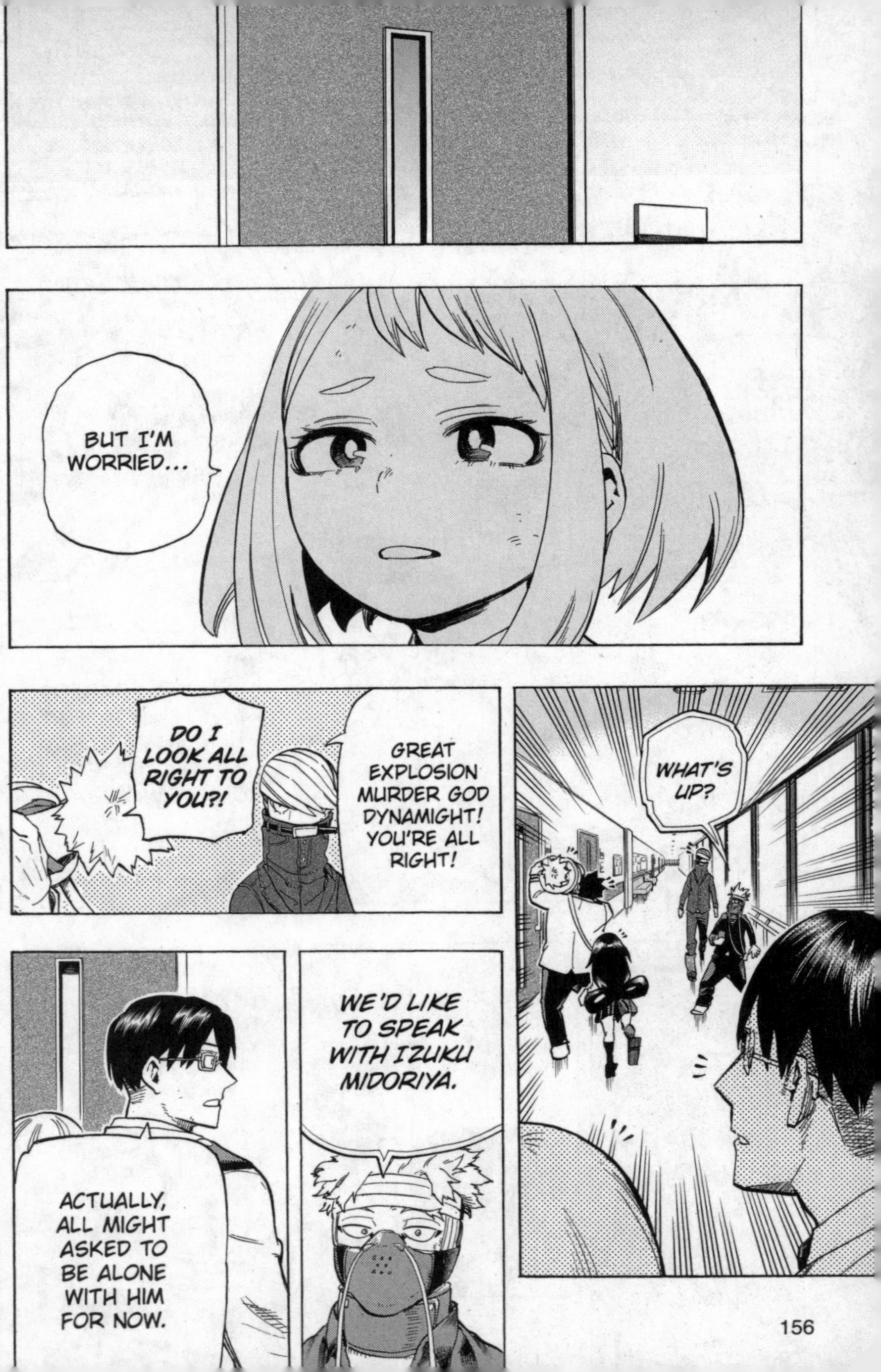
BUT I'M WORRIED...
WHAT'S UP?
GREAT EXPLOSION MURDER GOD DYNAMIGHT! YOU'RE ALL RIGHT!
DO I LOOK ALL RIGHT TO YOU?!
WE'D LIKE TO SPEAK WITH IZUKU MIDORIYA.
ACTUALLY, ALL MIGHT ASKED TO BE ALONE WITH HIM FOR NOW.

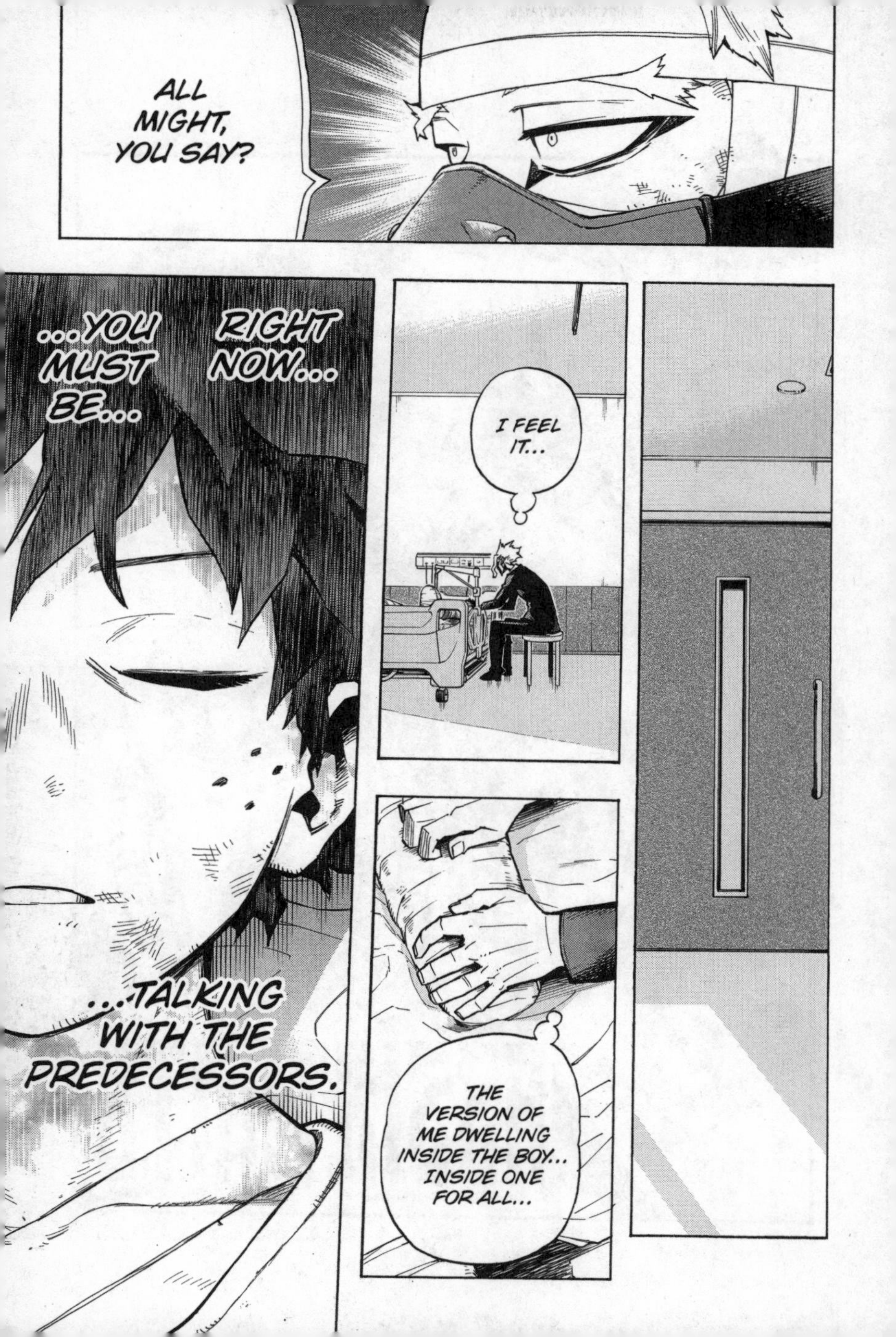
ALL MIGHT, YOU SAY?
I FEEL IT...
THE VERSION OF ME DWELLING INSIDE THE BOY... INSIDE ONE FOR ALL...
RIGHT NOW...
...YOU MUST BE...
...TALKING WITH THE PREDECESSORS.

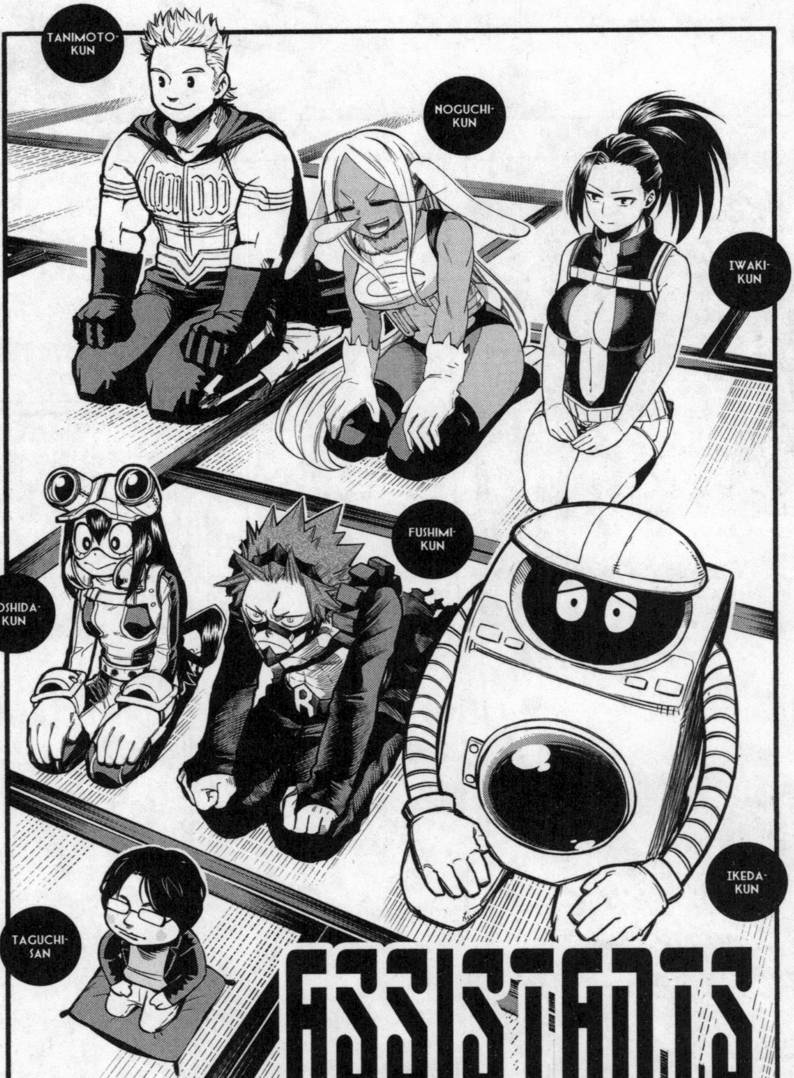
TANIMOTO-KUN
NOGUCHI-KUN
IWAKI-KUN
FUSHIMI-KUN
YOSHIDA-KUN
IKEDA-KUN
TAGUCHI-SAN
ASSISTANTS

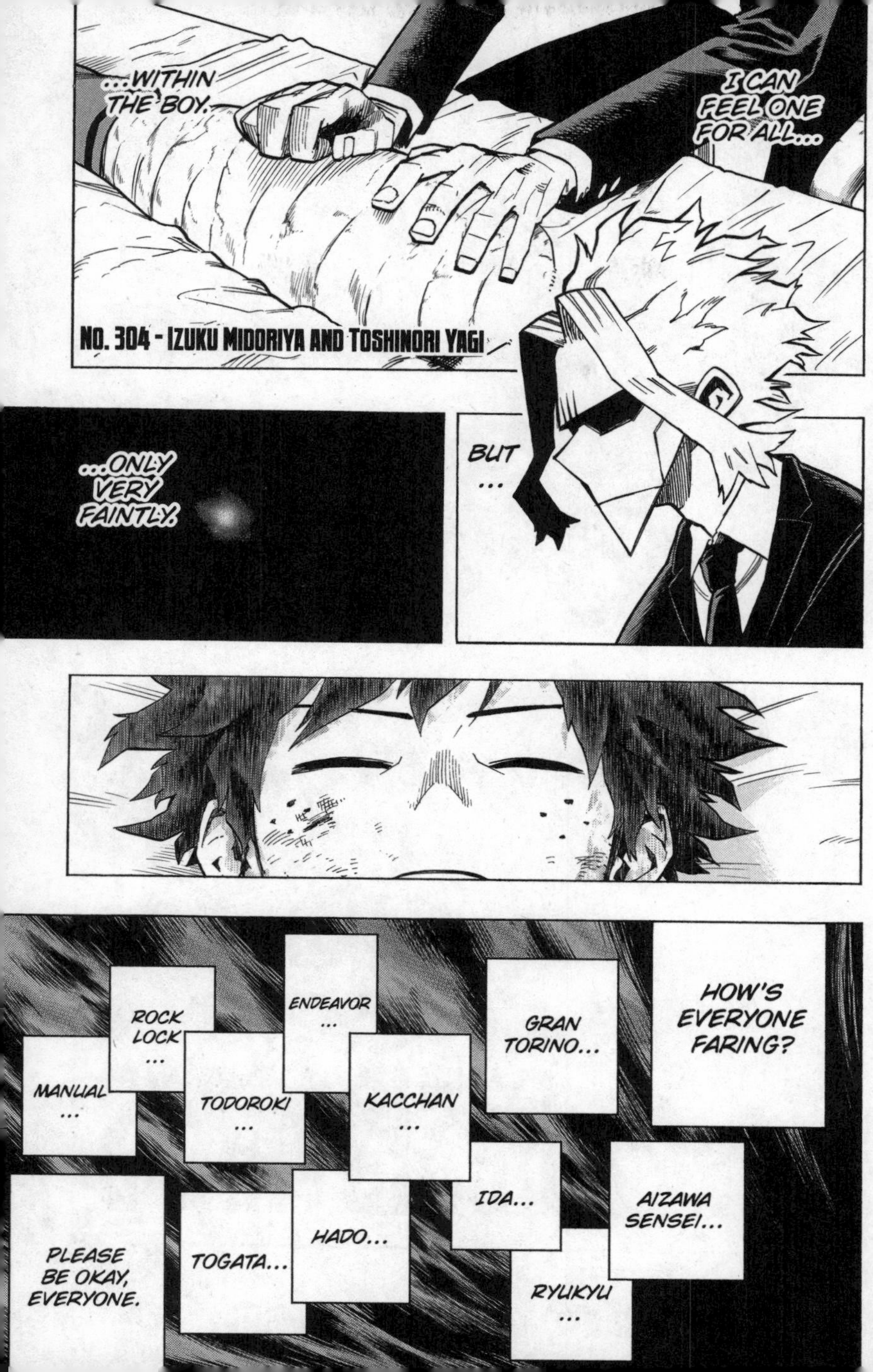
I CAN FEEL ONE FOR ALL...
...WITHIN THE BOY.
No. 304 - Izuku Midoriya and Toshinori Yagi
BUT ...
...ONLY VERY FAINTLY.
HOW'S EVERYONE FARING?
GRAN TORINO...
ENDEAVOR ...
KACCHAN ...
ROCK LOCK ...
TODOROKI ...
MANUAL ...
AIZAWA SENSEI...
IDA...
RYUKYU ...
HADO...
TOGATA...
PLEASE BE OKAY, EVERYONE.

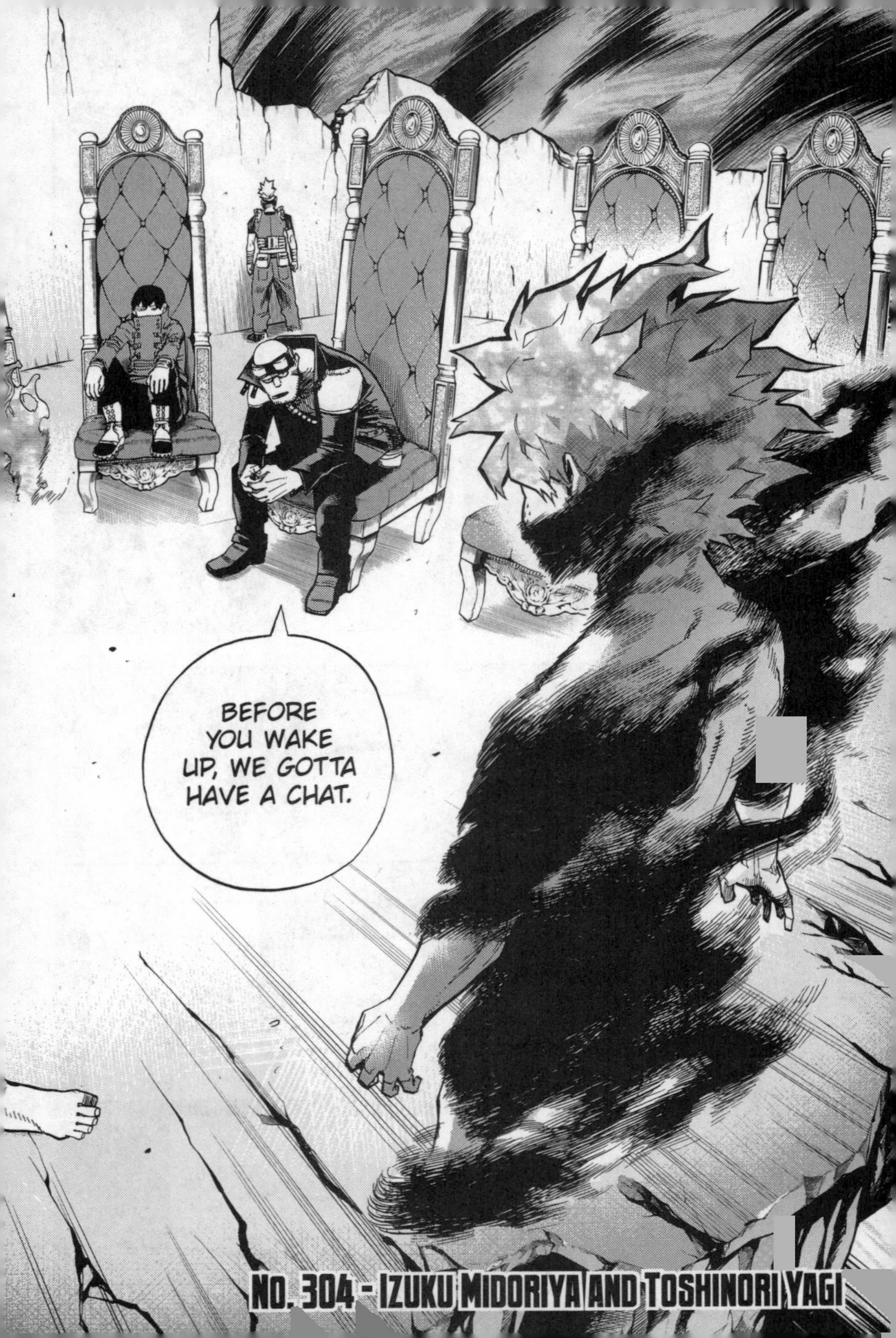
BEFORE YOU WAKE UP, WE GOTTA HAVE A CHAT.
NO. 304 - IZUKU MIDORIYA AND TOSHINORI YAGI

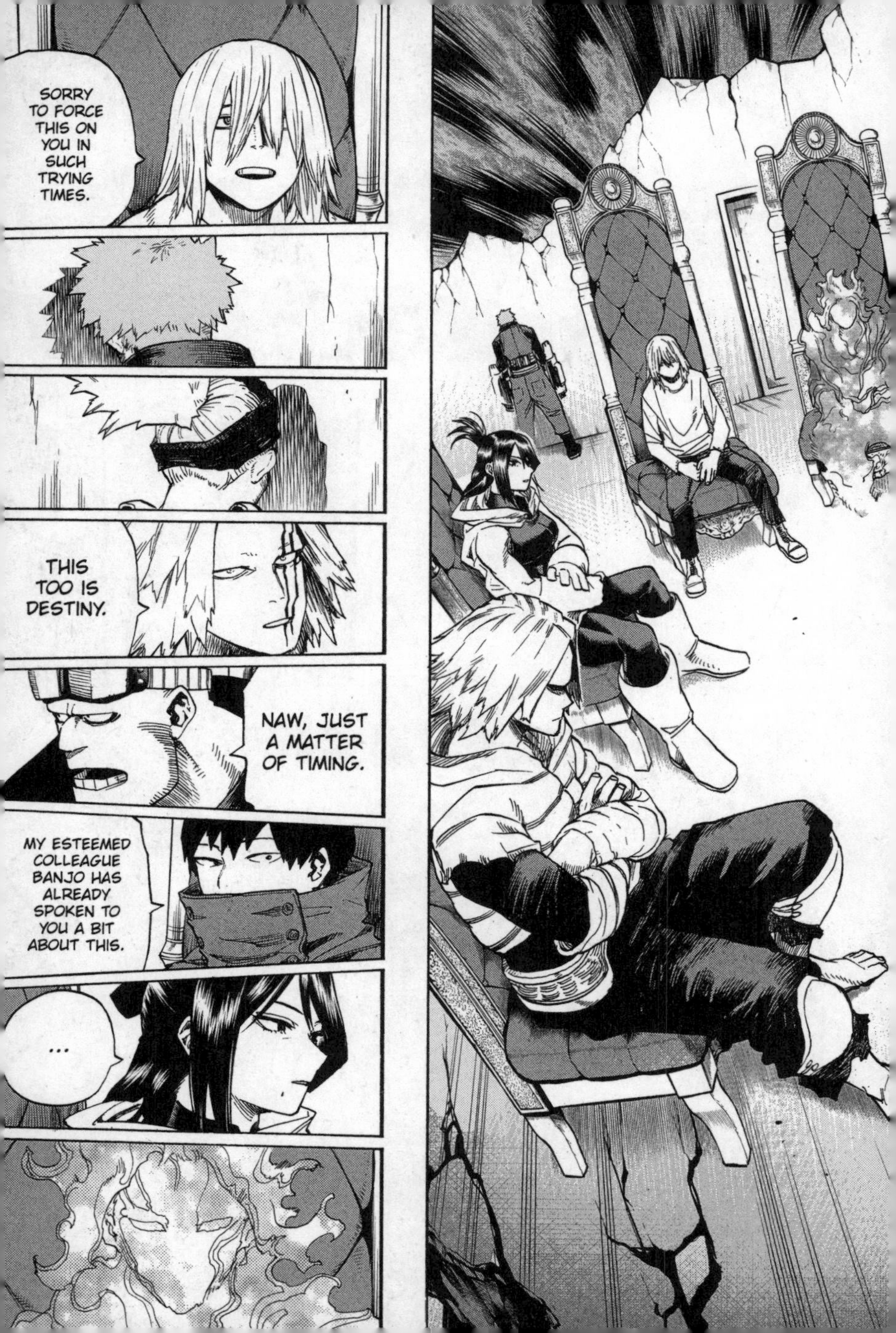
SORRY TO FORCE THIS ON YOU IN SUCH TRYING TIMES.
THIS TOO IS DESTINY.
NAW, JUST A MATTER OF TIMING.
MY ESTEEMED COLLEAGUE BANJO HAS ALREADY SPOKEN TO YOU A BIT ABOUT THIS.
...

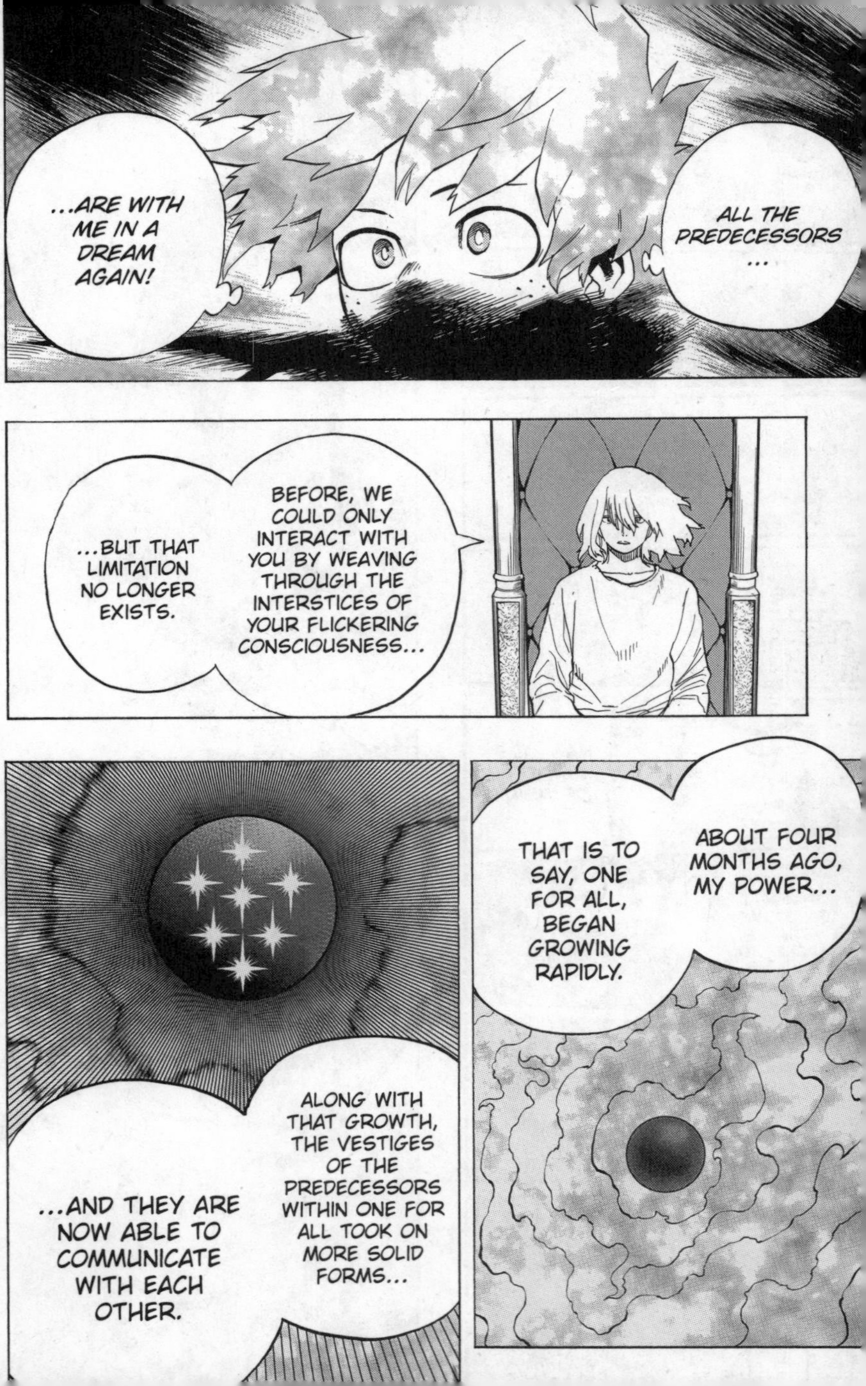
ALL THE PREDECESSORS ...
...ARE WITH ME IN A DREAM AGAIN!
BEFORE, WE COULD ONLY INTERACT WITH YOU BY WEAVING THROUGH THE INTERSTICES OF YOUR FLICKERING CONSCIOUSNESS...
...BUT THAT LIMITATION NO LONGER EXISTS.
ABOUT FOUR MONTHS AGO, MY POWER...
THAT IS TO SAY, ONE FOR ALL, BEGAN GROWING RAPIDLY.
ALONG WITH THAT GROWTH, THE VESTIGES OF THE PREDECESSORS WITHIN ONE FOR ALL TOOK ON MORE SOLID FORMS...
...AND THEY ARE NOW ABLE TO COMMUNICATE WITH EACH OTHER.

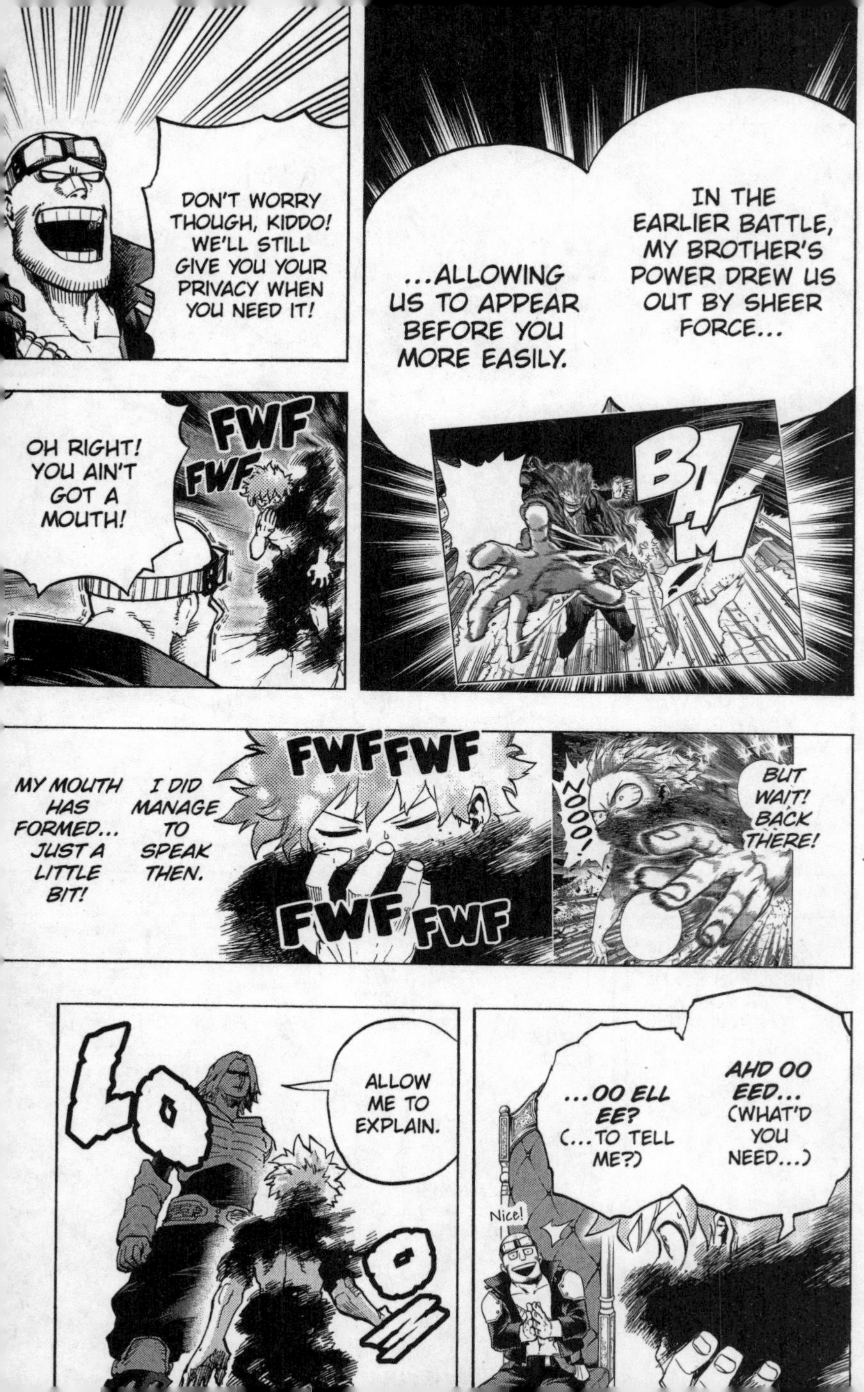
IN THE EARLIER BATTLE, MY BROTHER'S POWER DREW US OUT BY SHEER FORCE...
...ALLOWING US TO APPEAR BEFORE YOU MORE EASILY.
BAM
DON'T WORRY THOUGH, KIDDO! WE'LL STILL GIVE YOU YOUR PRIVACY WHEN YOU NEED IT!
FWF FWF
OH RIGHT! YOU AIN'T GOT A MOUTH!
BUT WAIT! BACK THERE!
ZOOO!
FWFFWF
I DID MANAGE TO SPEAK THEN.
MY MOUTH HAS FORMED... JUST A LITTLE BIT!
FWF FWF
AHD OO EED... (WHAT'D YOU NEED...)
...OO ELL EE? (...TO TELL ME?)
Nice!
ALLOW ME TO EXPLAIN.
LOOM

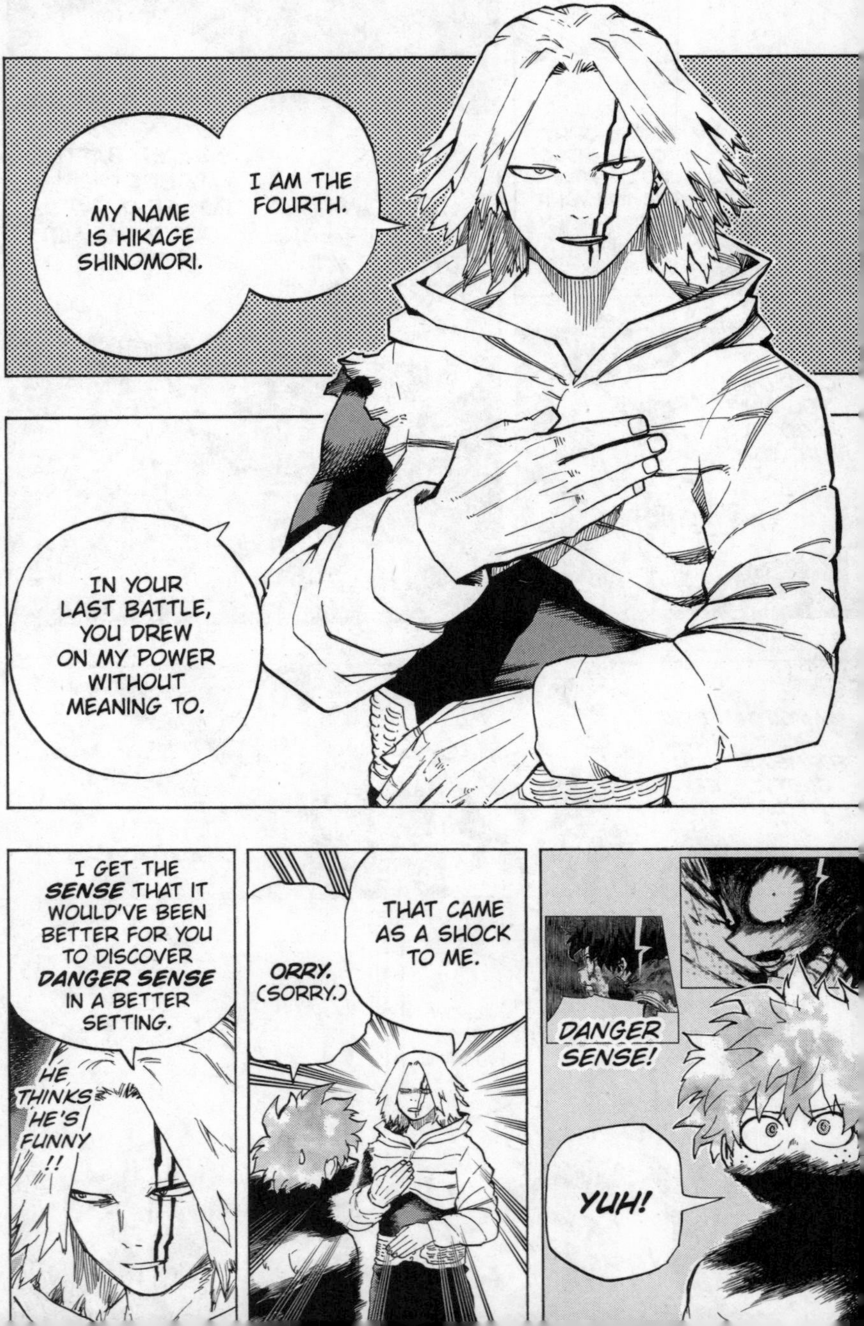

I AM THE FOURTH.
MY NAME IS HIKAGE SHINOMORI.
IN YOUR LAST BATTLE, YOU DREW ON MY POWER WITHOUT MEANING TO.
DANGER SENSE!
YUH!
THAT CAME AS A SHOCK TO ME.
ORRY. (SORRY.)
I GET THE SENSE THAT IT WOULD'VE BEEN BETTER FOR YOU TO DISCOVER DANGER SENSE IN A BETTER SETTING.
HE THINKS HE'S FUNNY!!

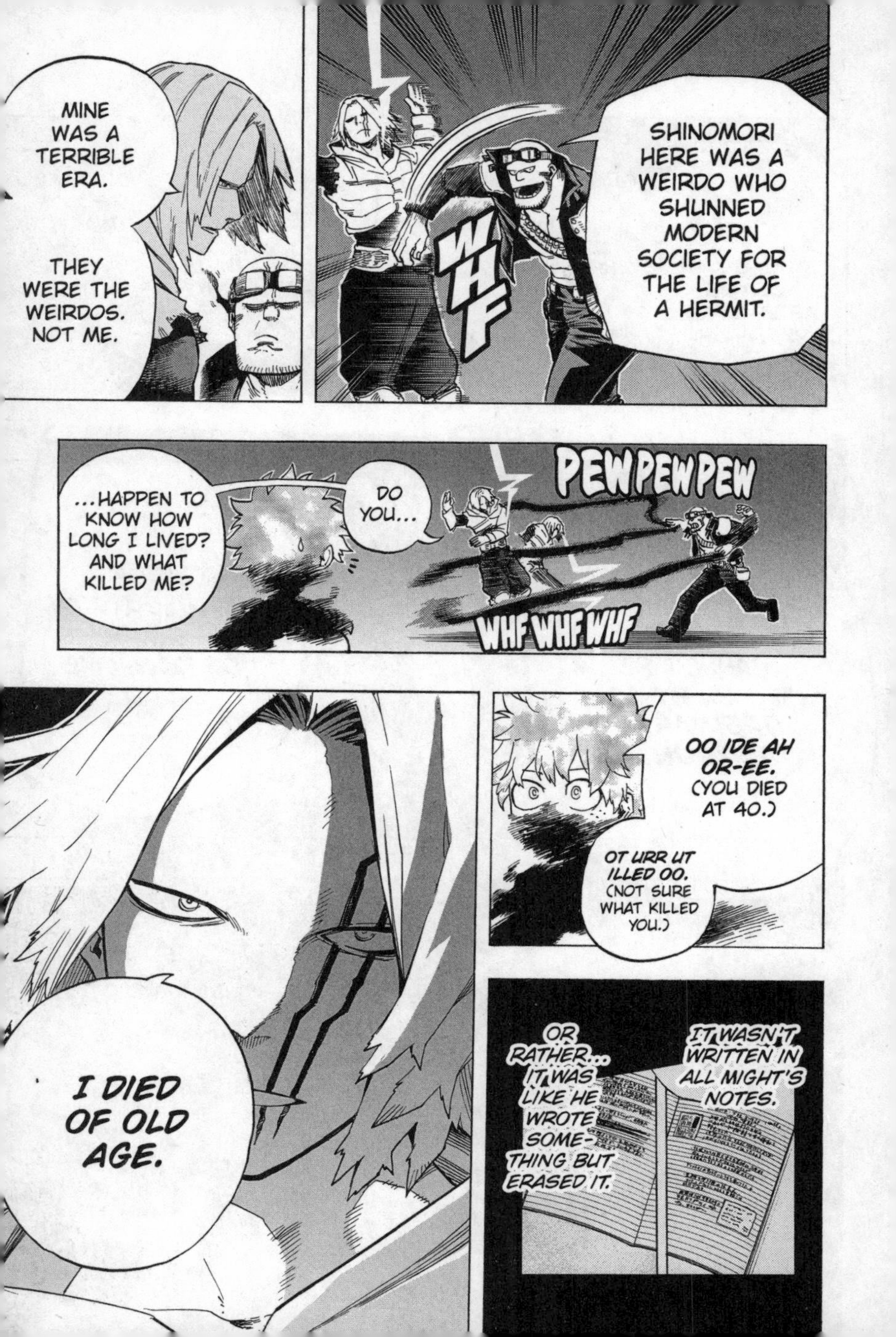
SHINOMORI HERE WAS A WEIRDO WHO SHUNNED MODERN SOCIETY FOR THE LIFE OF A HERMIT.
WHF
MINE WAS A TERRIBLE ERA.
THEY WERE THE WEIRDOS. NOT ME.
PEW PEW PEW
WHF WHF WHF
DO YOU...
...HAPPEN TO KNOW HOW LONG I LIVED? AND WHAT KILLED ME?
OO IDE AH OR-EE. (YOU DIED AT 40.)
OT URR UT ILLED OO. (NOT SURE WHAT KILLED YOU.)
IT WASN'T WRITTEN IN ALL MIGHT'S NOTES.
OR RATHER... IT WAS LIKE HE WROTE SOME-THING BUT ERASED IT.
I DIED OF OLD AGE.

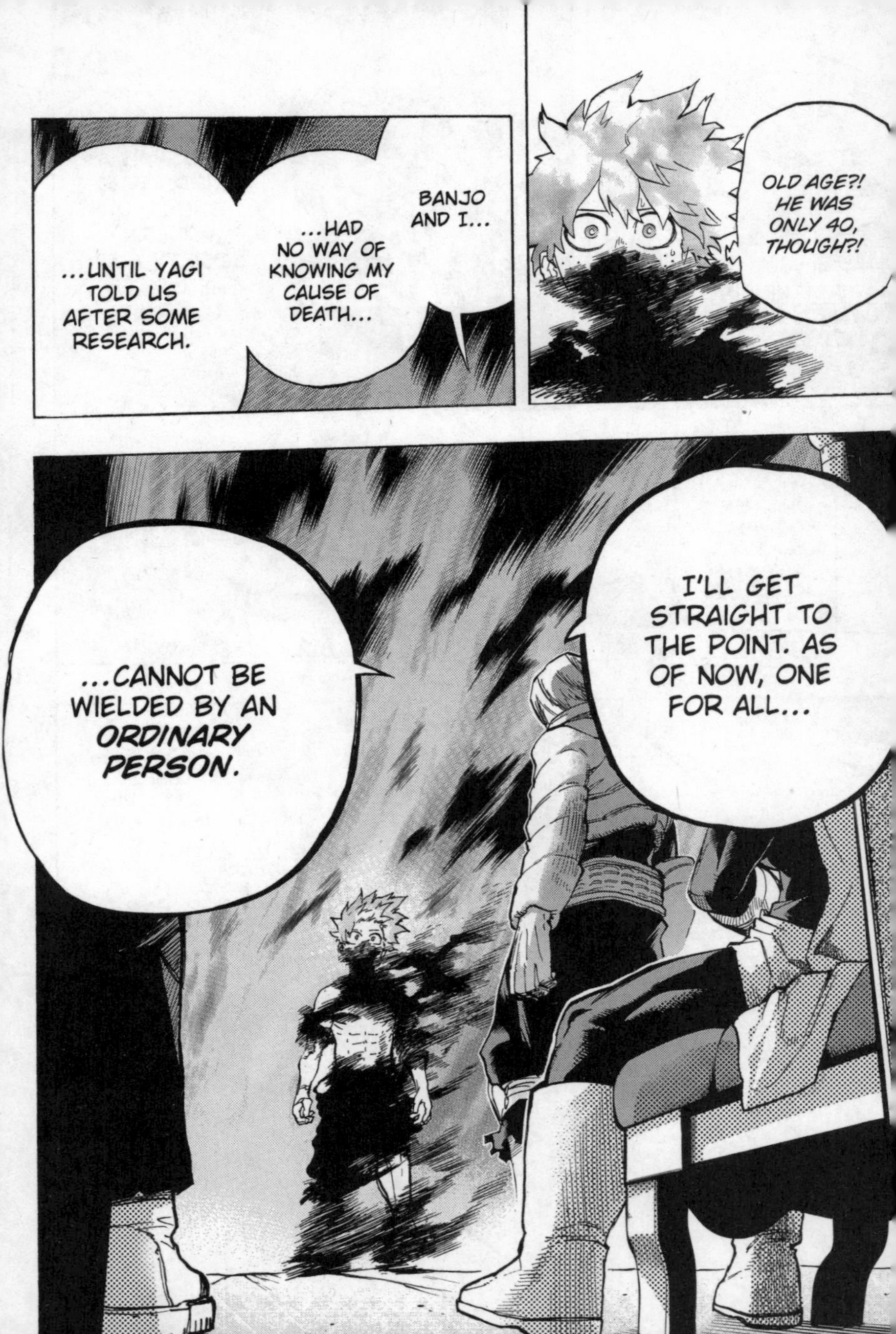
OLD AGE?! HE WAS ONLY 40, THOUGH?!
BANJO AND I...
...HAD NO WAY OF KNOWING MY CAUSE OF DEATH...
...UNTIL YAGI TOLD US AFTER SOME RESEARCH.
I'LL GET STRAIGHT TO THE POINT. AS OF NOW, ONE FOR ALL...
...CANNOT BE WIELDED BY AN *ORDINARY PERSON*.

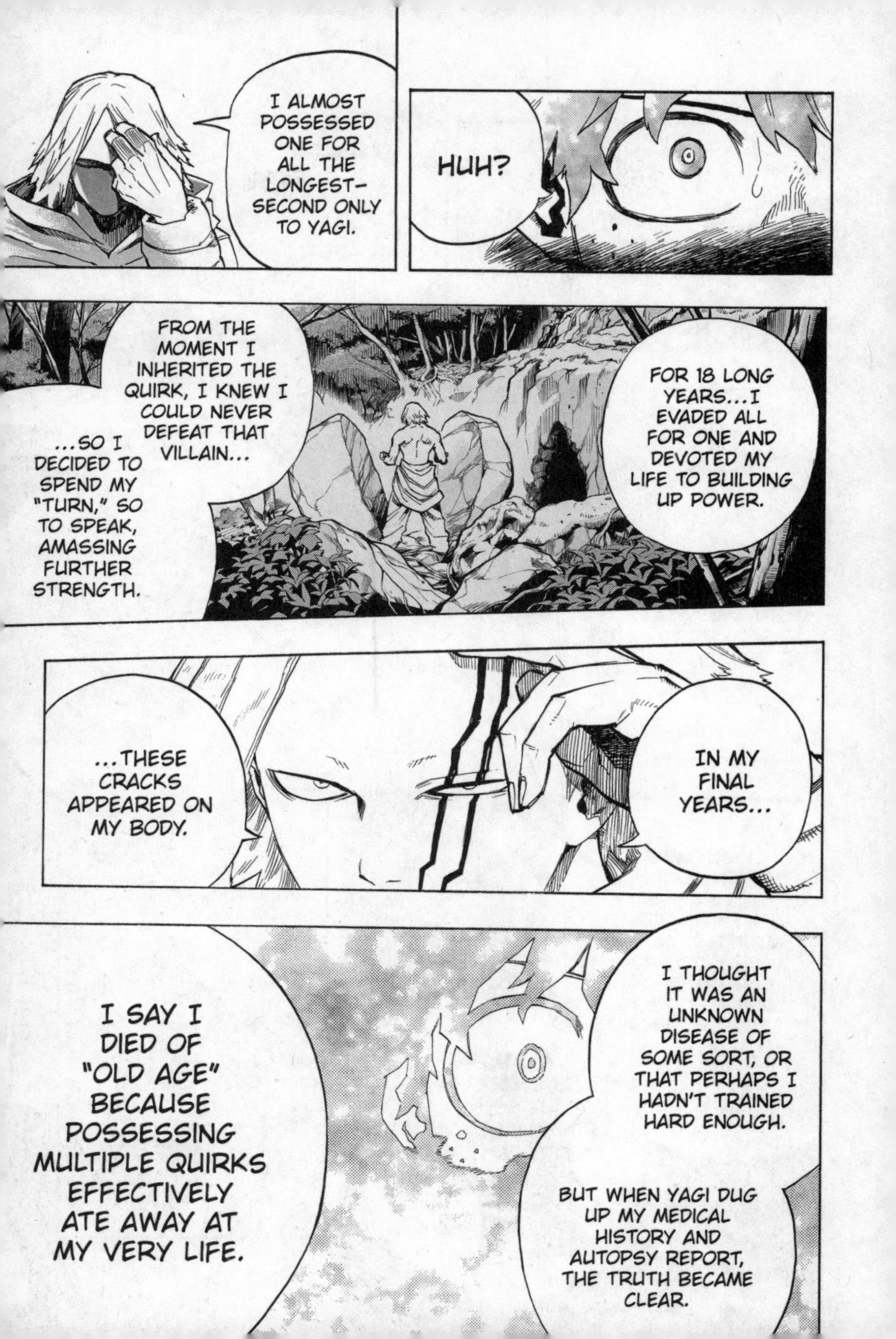
HUH?
I ALMOST POSSESSED ONE FOR ALL THE LONGEST—SECOND ONLY TO YAGI.
FOR 18 LONG YEARS...I EVADED ALL FOR ONE AND DEVOTED MY LIFE TO BUILDING UP POWER.
FROM THE MOMENT I INHERITED THE QUIRK, I KNEW I COULD NEVER DEFEAT THAT VILLAIN...
...SO I DECIDED TO SPEND MY "TURN," SO TO SPEAK, AMASSING FURTHER STRENGTH.
IN MY FINAL YEARS...
...THESE CRACKS APPEARED ON MY BODY.
I THOUGHT IT WAS AN UNKNOWN DISEASE OF SOME SORT, OR THAT PERHAPS I HADN'T TRAINED HARD ENOUGH.
BUT WHEN YAGI DUG UP MY MEDICAL HISTORY AND AUTOPSY REPORT, THE TRUTH BECAME CLEAR.
I SAY I DIED OF "OLD AGE" BECAUSE POSSESSING MULTIPLE QUIRKS EFFECTIVELY ATE AWAY AT MY VERY LIFE.

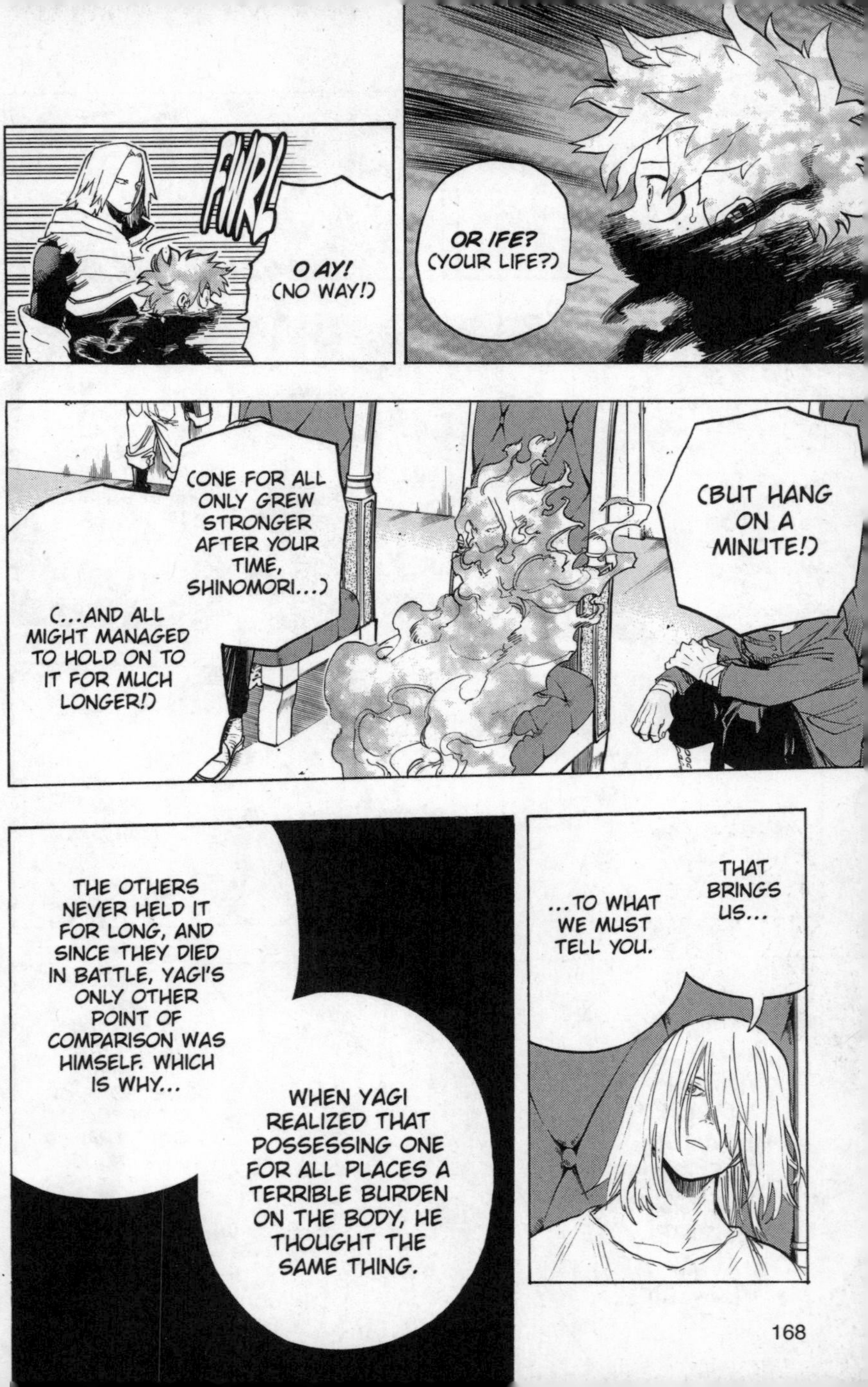
OR IFE? (YOUR LIFE?)
FWIP!
O AY! (NO WAY!)
(BUT HANG ON A MINUTE!)
(ONE FOR ALL ONLY GREW STRONGER AFTER YOUR TIME, SHINOMORI...)
(...AND ALL MIGHT MANAGED TO HOLD ON TO IT FOR MUCH LONGER!)
THAT BRINGS US...
...TO WHAT WE MUST TELL YOU.
THE OTHERS NEVER HELD IT FOR LONG, AND SINCE THEY DIED IN BATTLE, YAGI'S ONLY OTHER POINT OF COMPARISON WAS HIMSELF. WHICH IS WHY...
WHEN YAGI REALIZED THAT POSSESSING ONE FOR ALL PLACES A TERRIBLE BURDEN ON THE BODY, HE THOUGHT THE SAME THING.

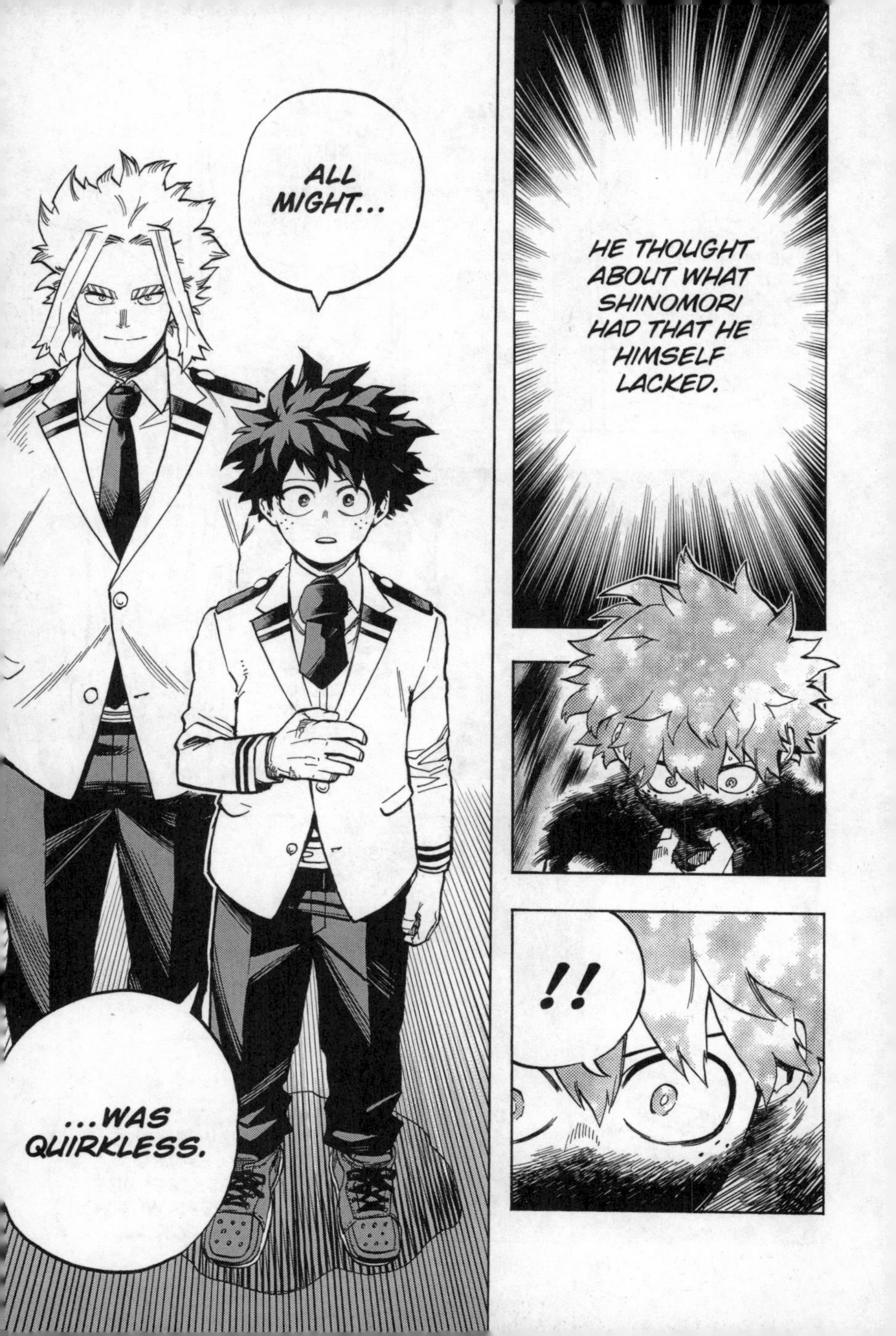
HE THOUGHT ABOUT WHAT SHINOMORI HAD THAT HE HIMSELF LACKED.
!!
ALL MIGHT...
...WAS QUIRKLESS.

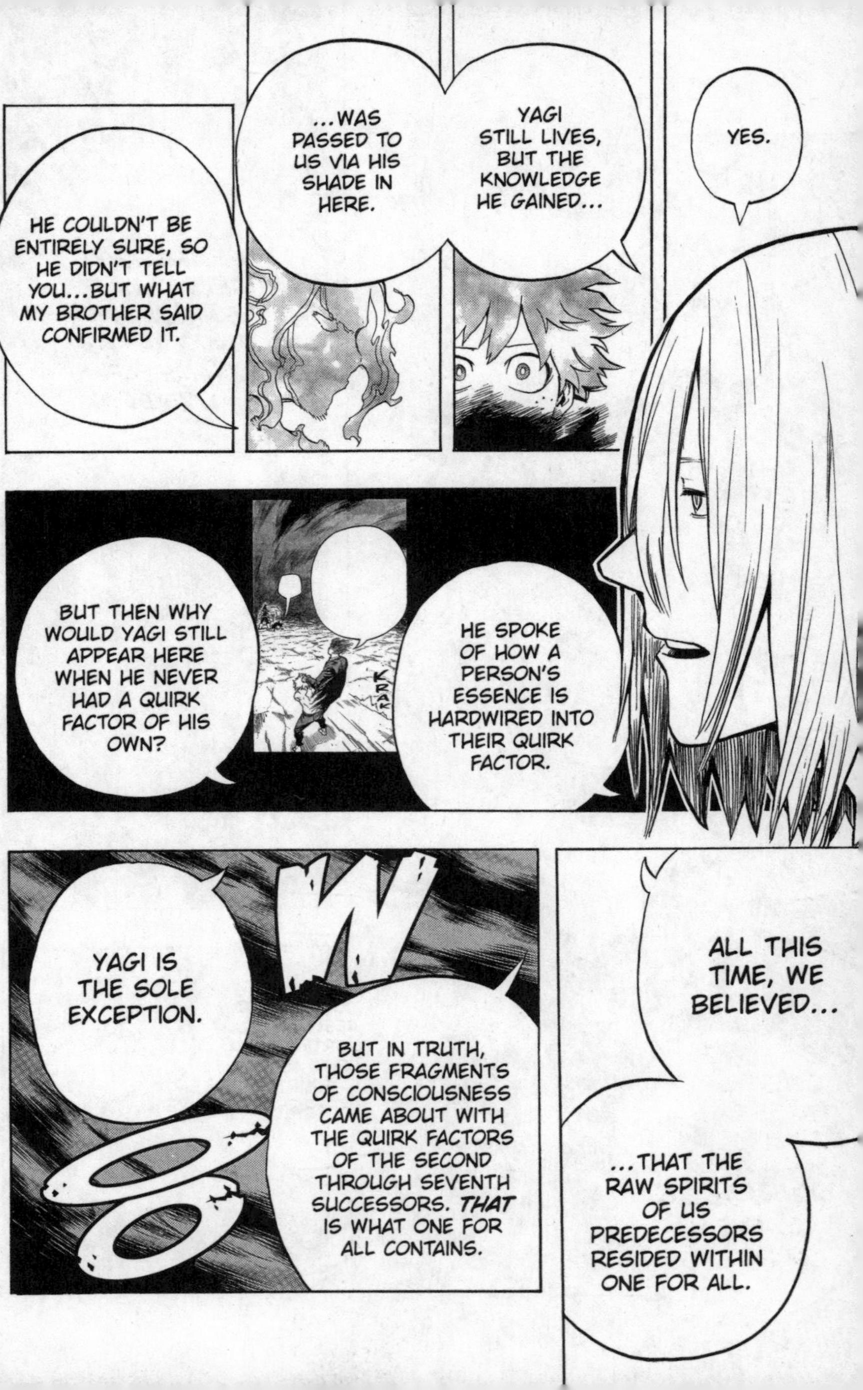
YES.
YAGI STILL LIVES, BUT THE KNOWLEDGE HE GAINED...
...WAS PASSED TO US VIA HIS SHADE IN HERE.
HE COULDN'T BE ENTIRELY SURE, SO HE DIDN'T TELL YOU...BUT WHAT MY BROTHER SAID CONFIRMED IT.
HE SPOKE OF HOW A PERSON'S ESSENCE IS HARDWIRED INTO THEIR QUIRK FACTOR.
KRAK
BUT THEN WHY WOULD YAGI STILL APPEAR HERE WHEN HE NEVER HAD A QUIRK FACTOR OF HIS OWN?
ALL THIS TIME, WE BELIEVED...
...THAT THE RAW SPIRITS OF US PREDECESSORS RESIDED WITHIN ONE FOR ALL.
BUT IN TRUTH, THOSE FRAGMENTS OF CONSCIOUSNESS CAME ABOUT WITH THE QUIRK FACTORS OF THE SECOND THROUGH SEVENTH SUCCESSORS. *THAT* IS WHAT ONE FOR ALL CONTAINS.
YAGI IS THE SOLE EXCEPTION.

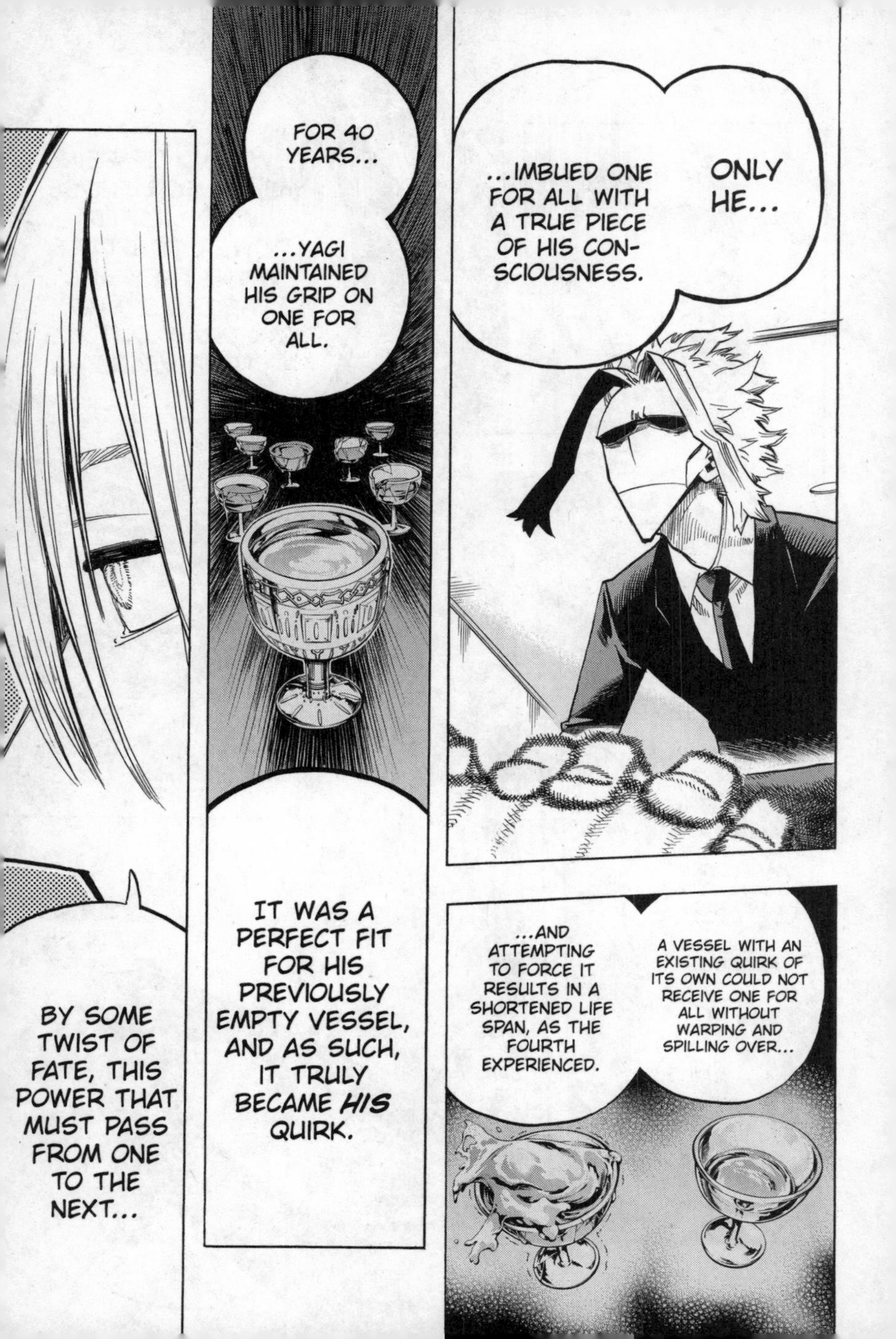
ONLY HE...
...IMBUED ONE FOR ALL WITH A TRUE PIECE OF HIS CON- SCIOUSNESS.
FOR 40 YEARS...
...YAGI MAINTAINED HIS GRIP ON ONE FOR ALL.
A VESSEL WITH AN EXISTING QUIRK OF ITS OWN COULD NOT RECEIVE ONE FOR ALL WITHOUT WARPING AND SPILLING OVER...
...AND ATTEMPTING TO FORCE IT RESULTS IN A SHORTENED LIFE SPAN, AS THE FOURTH EXPERIENCED.
IT WAS A PERFECT FIT FOR HIS PREVIOUSLY EMPTY VESSEL, AND AS SUCH, IT TRULY BECAME *HIS* QUIRK.
BY SOME TWIST OF FATE, THIS POWER THAT MUST PASS FROM ONE TO THE NEXT...

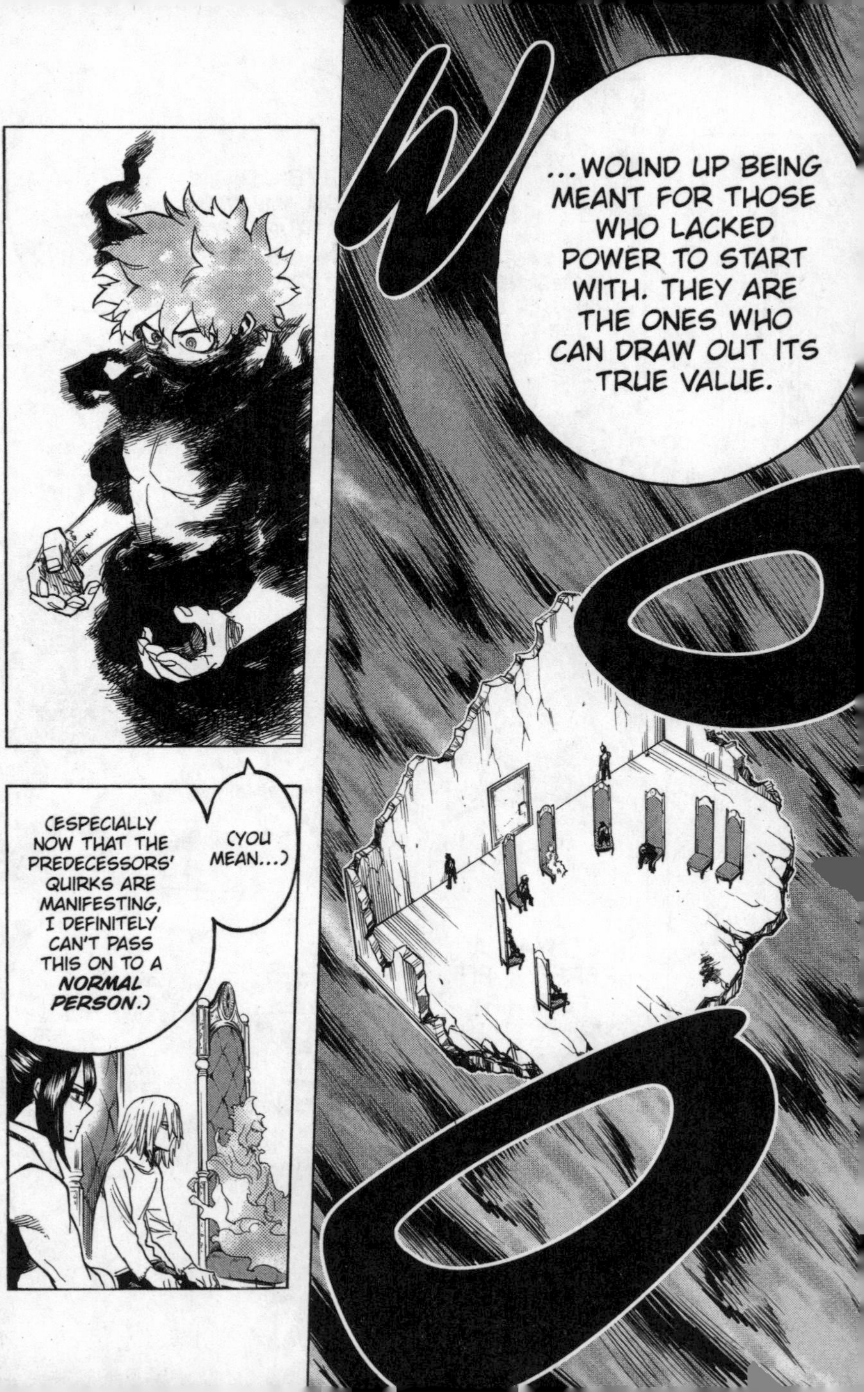
...WOUND UP BEING MEANT FOR THOSE WHO LACKED POWER TO START WITH. THEY ARE THE ONES WHO CAN DRAW OUT ITS TRUE VALUE.
(YOU MEAN...)
(ESPECIALLY NOW THAT THE PREDECESSORS' QUIRKS ARE MANIFESTING, I DEFINITELY CAN'T PASS THIS ON TO A **NORMAL PERSON**.)

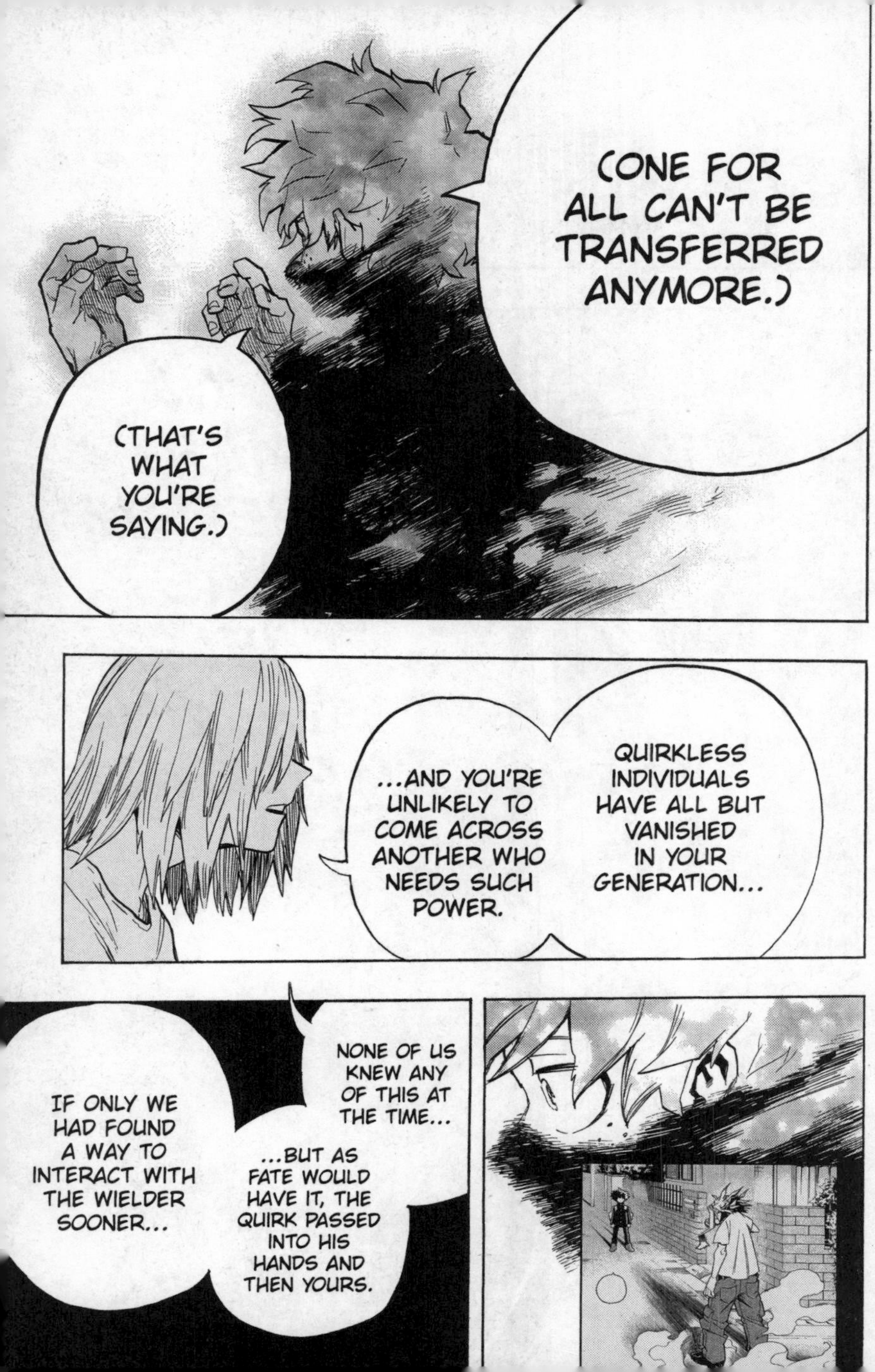
(ONE FOR ALL CAN'T BE TRANSFERRED ANYMORE.)
(THAT'S WHAT YOU'RE SAYING.)
QUIRKLESS INDIVIDUALS HAVE ALL BUT VANISHED IN YOUR GENERATION...
...AND YOU'RE UNLIKELY TO COME ACROSS ANOTHER WHO NEEDS SUCH POWER.
NONE OF US KNEW ANY OF THIS AT THE TIME...
...BUT AS FATE WOULD HAVE IT, THE QUIRK PASSED INTO HIS HANDS AND THEN YOURS.
IF ONLY WE HAD FOUND A WAY TO INTERACT WITH THE WIELDER SOONER...

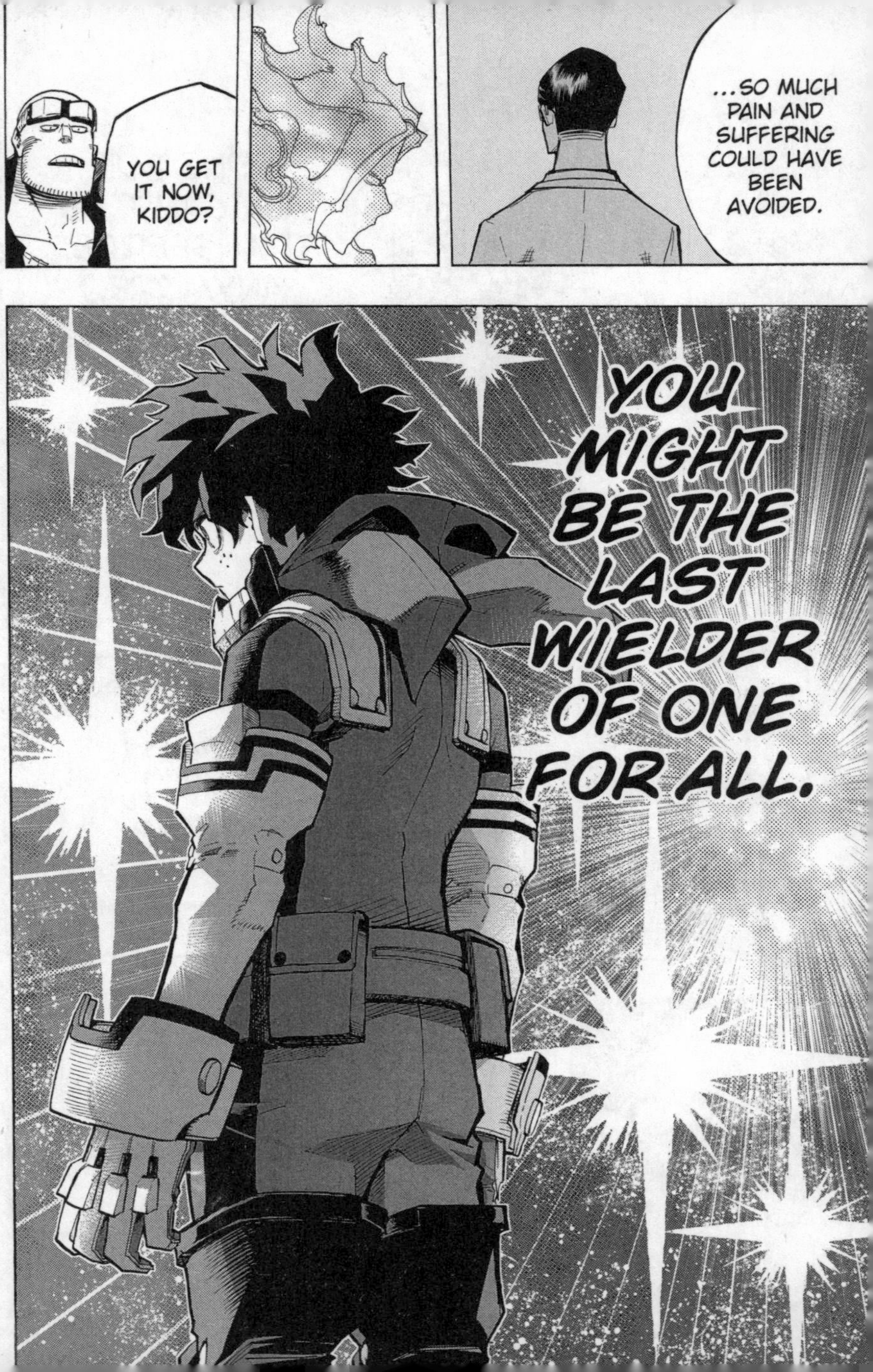
...SO MUCH PAIN AND SUFFERING COULD HAVE BEEN AVOIDED.
YOU GET IT NOW, KIDDO?
YOU MIGHT BE THE LAST WIELDER OF ONE FOR ALL.

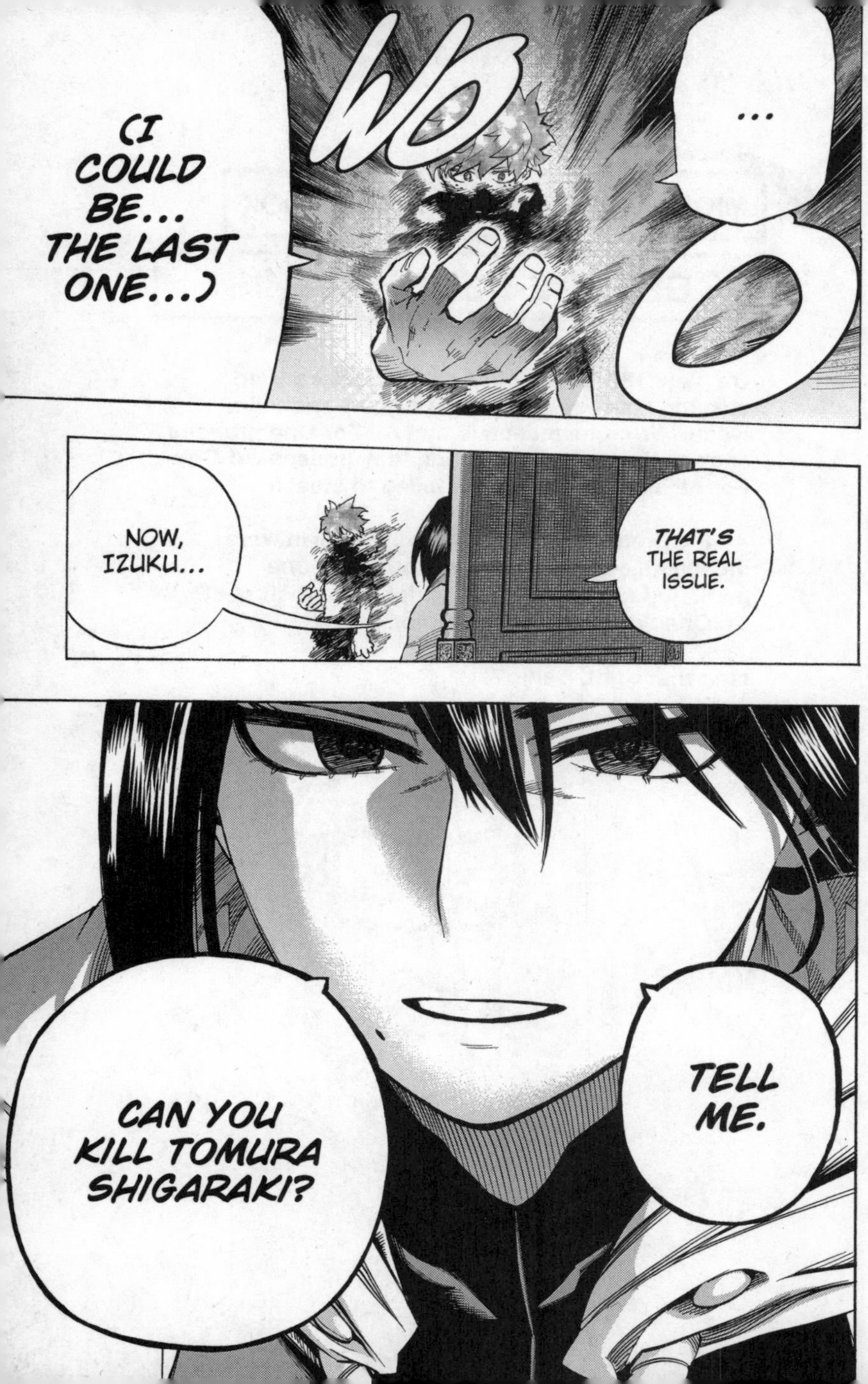
...
(I COULD BE... THE LAST ONE...)
THAT'S THE REAL ISSUE.
NOW, IZUKU...
TELL ME.
CAN YOU KILL TOMURA SHIGARAKI?

MIGHT WANT TO FINISH THE BOOK

BEFORE READING THIS

On page 180, Banjo says, "That bastard tried stealing One For All from us twice—and failed twice!" What he means is that All For One grabbed each of them at a point when they possessed One For All, but both times, he failed to steal it.

All the predecessors besides the Fourth were indeed killed by All For One, but each one managed to pass on the Quirk before their death. So One For All never got stolen away.

Isn't that right, Banjo?!

BINGO.

No. 305 - Izuku Midoriya and Tomura Shigaraki

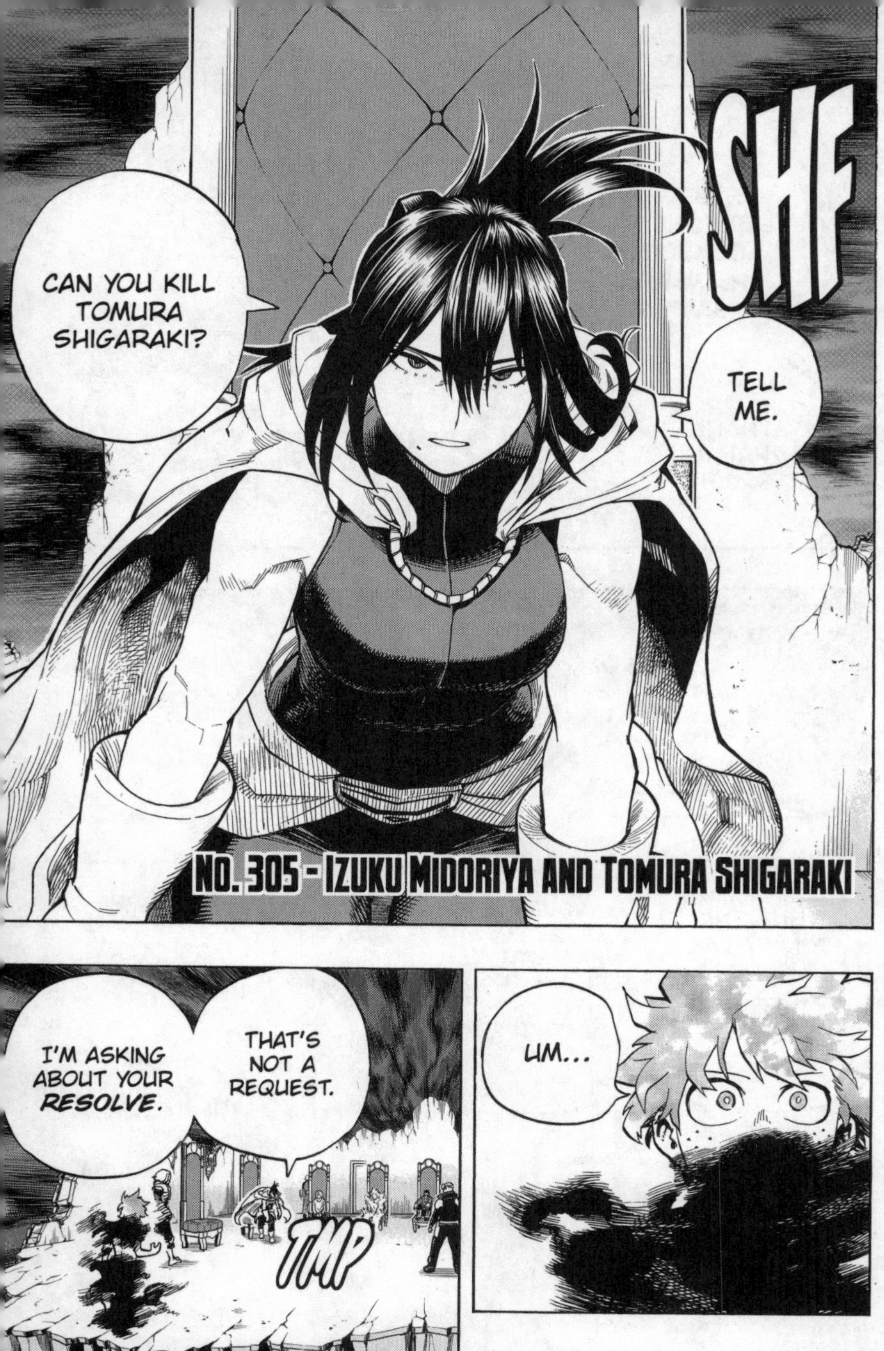

SHF
TELL ME.
CAN YOU KILL TOMURA SHIGARAKI?
No. 305 - Izuku Midoriya and Tomura Shigaraki
UM...
THAT'S NOT A REQUEST.
I'M ASKING ABOUT YOUR *RESOLVE*.
TMP

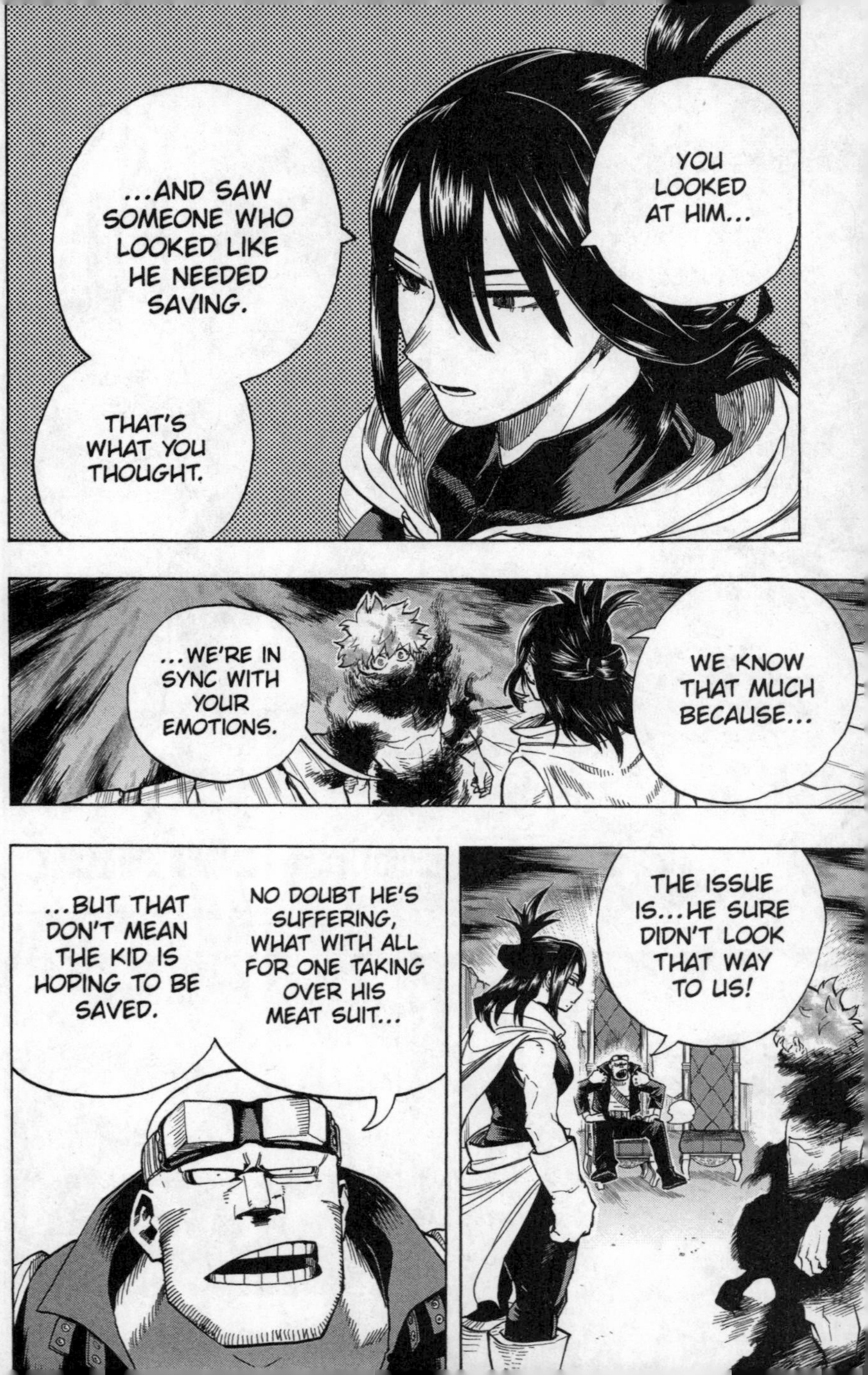
YOU LOOKED AT HIM...
...AND SAW SOMEONE WHO LOOKED LIKE HE NEEDED SAVING.
THAT'S WHAT YOU THOUGHT.
WE KNOW THAT MUCH BECAUSE...
...WE'RE IN SYNC WITH YOUR EMOTIONS.
THE ISSUE IS...HE SURE DIDN'T LOOK THAT WAY TO US!
NO DOUBT HE'S SUFFERING, WHAT WITH ALL FOR ONE TAKING OVER HIS MEAT SUIT...
...BUT THAT DON'T MEAN THE KID IS HOPING TO BE SAVED.

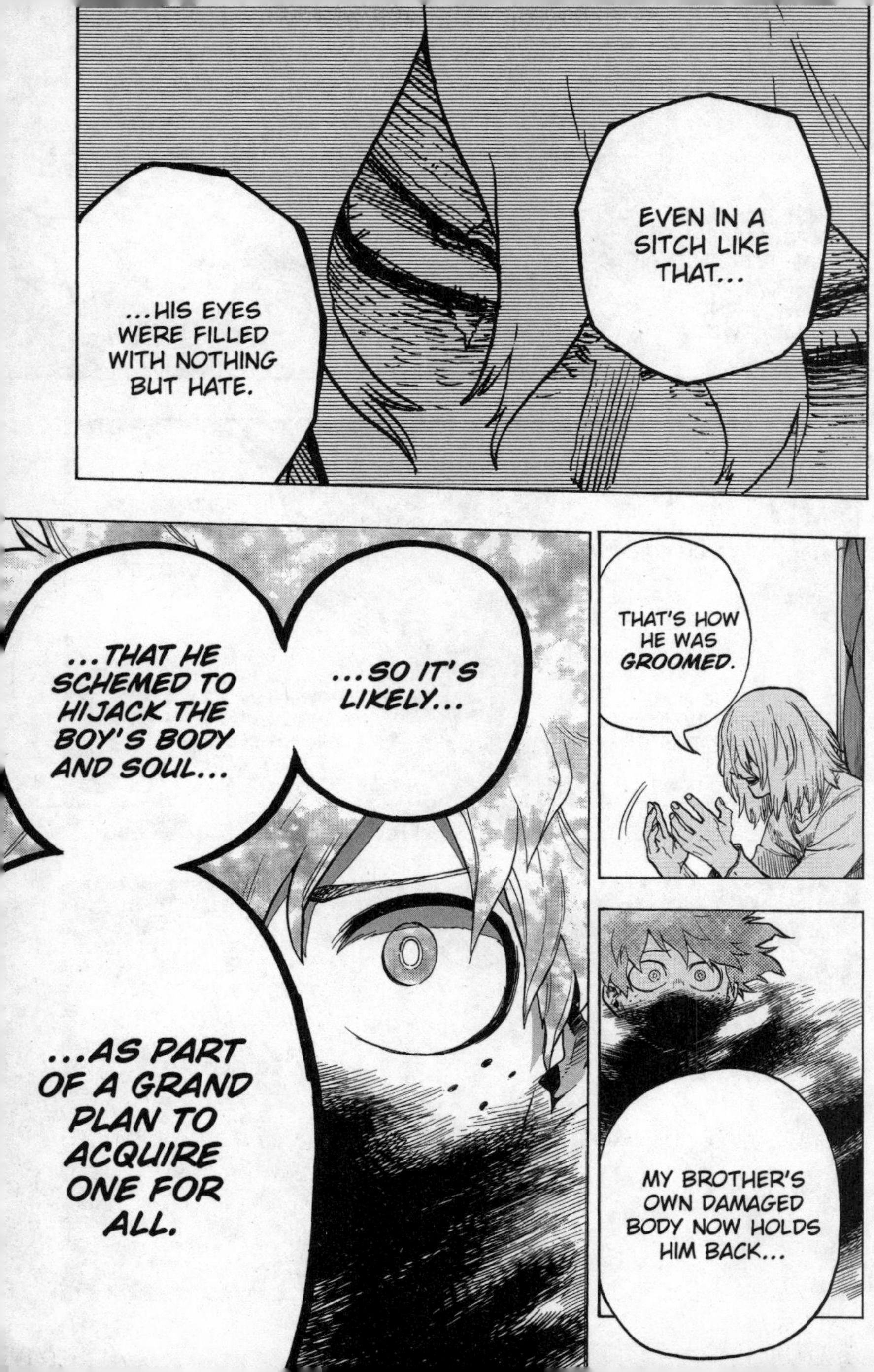
EVEN IN A SITCH LIKE THAT...
...HIS EYES WERE FILLED WITH NOTHING BUT HATE.
THAT'S HOW HE WAS GROOMED.
MY BROTHER'S OWN DAMAGED BODY NOW HOLDS HIM BACK...
...SO IT'S LIKELY...
...THAT HE SCHEMED TO HIJACK THE BOY'S BODY AND SOUL...
...AS PART OF A GRAND PLAN TO ACQUIRE ONE FOR ALL.

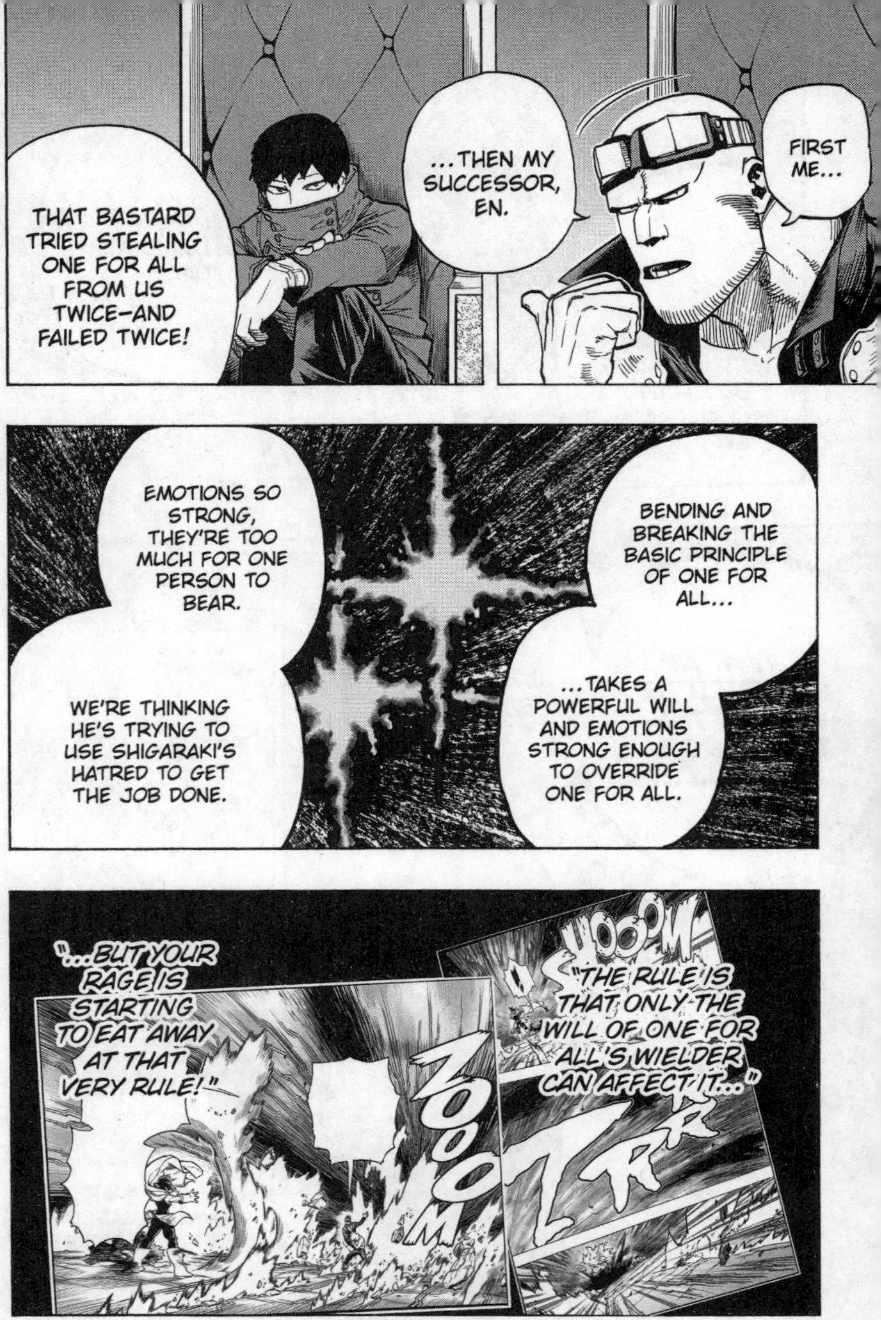
FIRST ME...
...THEN MY SUCCESSOR, EN.
THAT BASTARD TRIED STEALING ONE FOR ALL FROM US TWICE—AND FAILED TWICE!
BENDING AND BREAKING THE BASIC PRINCIPLE OF ONE FOR ALL...
...TAKES A POWERFUL WILL AND EMOTIONS STRONG ENOUGH TO OVERRIDE ONE FOR ALL.
EMOTIONS SO STRONG, THEY'RE TOO MUCH FOR ONE PERSON TO BEAR.
WE'RE THINKING HE'S TRYING TO USE SHIGARAKI'S HATRED TO GET THE JOB DONE.
"THE RULE IS THAT ONLY THE WILL OF ONE FOR ALL'S WIELDER CAN AFFECT IT..."
"...BUT YOUR RAGE IS STARTING TO EAT AWAY AT THAT VERY RULE!"

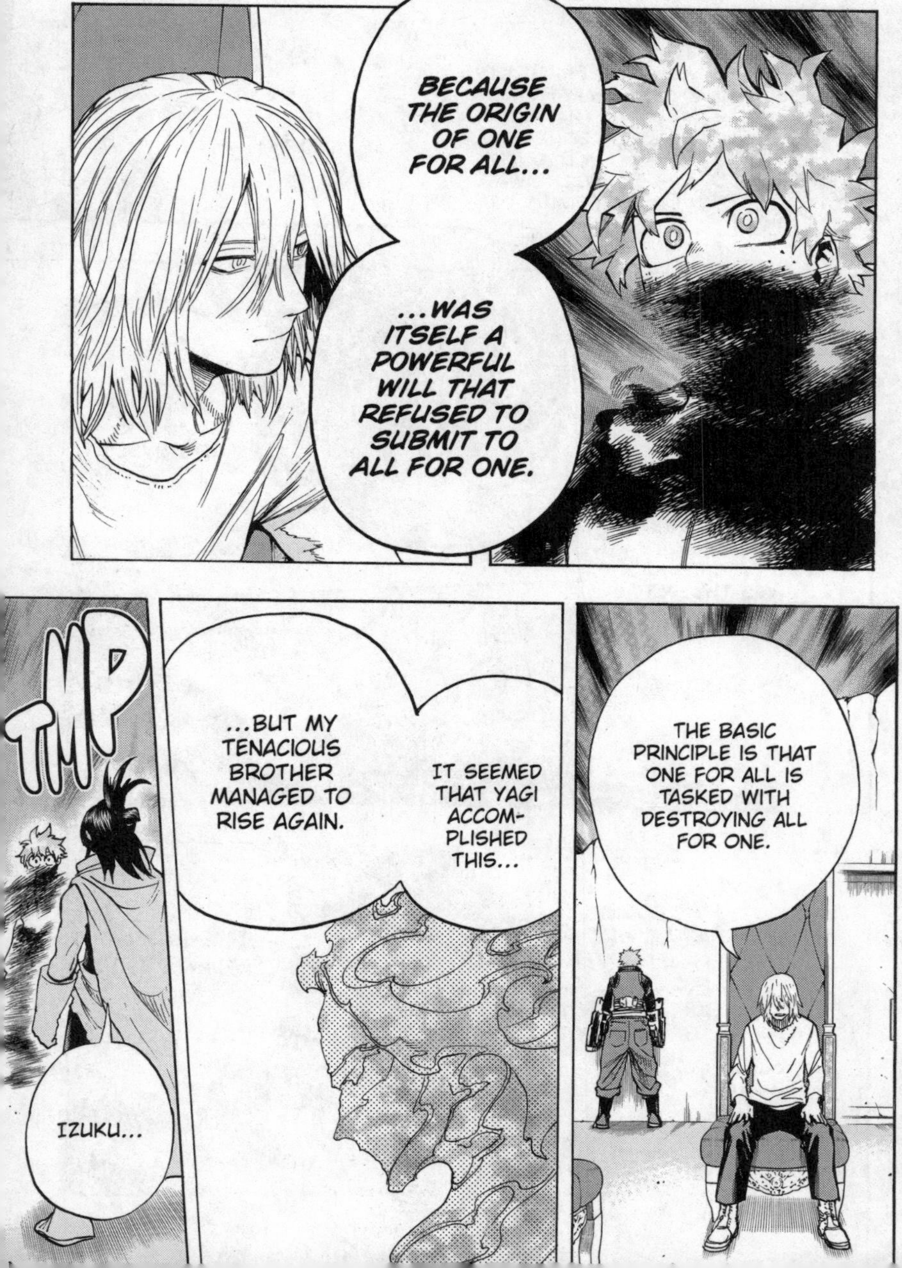
BECAUSE THE ORIGIN OF ONE FOR ALL...
...WAS ITSELF A POWERFUL WILL THAT REFUSED TO SUBMIT TO ALL FOR ONE.
THE BASIC PRINCIPLE IS THAT ONE FOR ALL IS TASKED WITH DESTROYING ALL FOR ONE.
IT SEEMED THAT YAGI ACCOMPLISHED THIS...
...BUT MY TENACIOUS BROTHER MANAGED TO RISE AGAIN.
TMP
IZUKU...

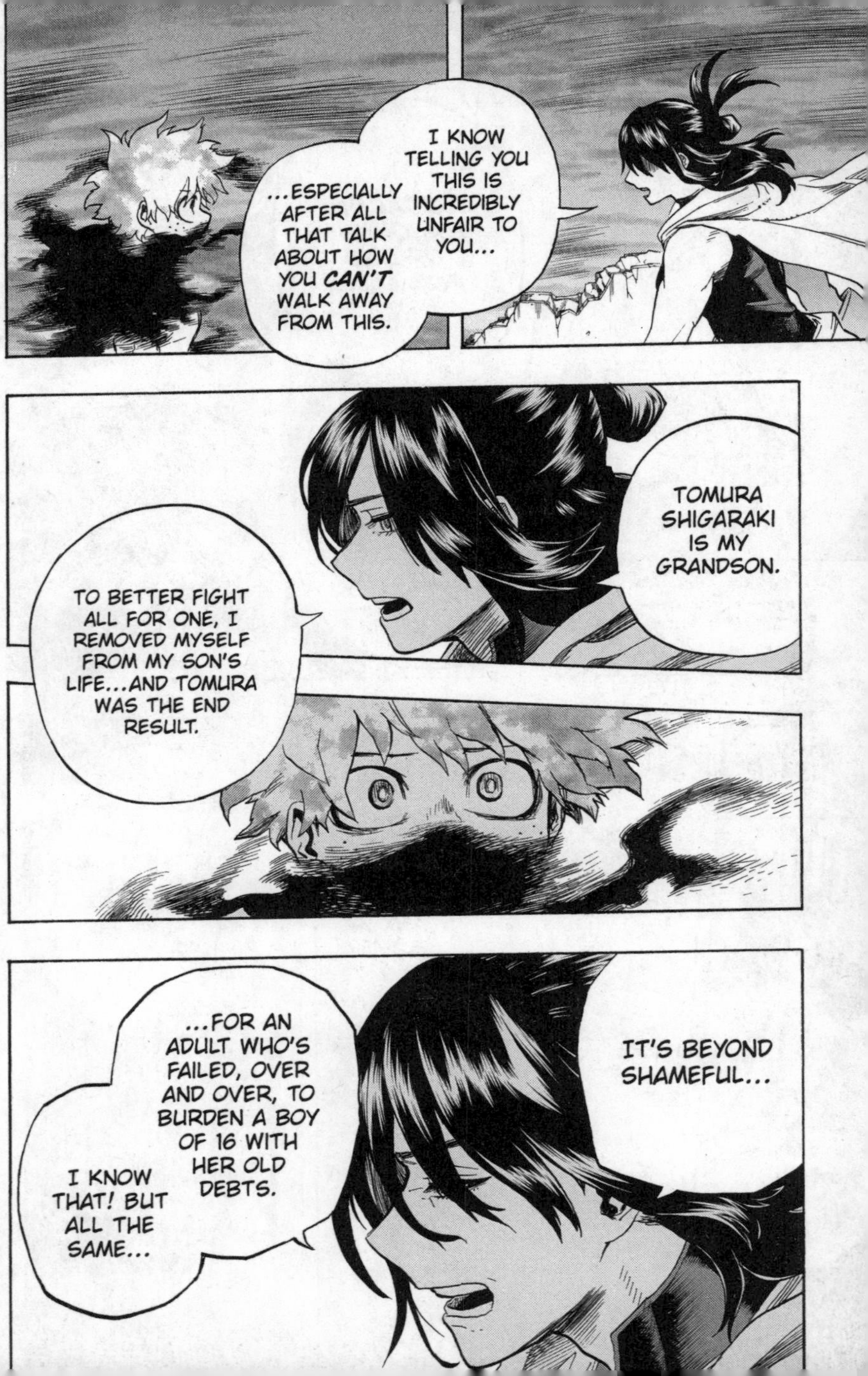
I KNOW TELLING YOU THIS IS INCREDIBLY UNFAIR TO YOU...
...ESPECIALLY AFTER ALL THAT TALK ABOUT HOW YOU *CAN'T* WALK AWAY FROM THIS.
TOMURA SHIGARAKI IS MY GRANDSON.
TO BETTER FIGHT ALL FOR ONE, I REMOVED MYSELF FROM MY SON'S LIFE...AND TOMURA WAS THE END RESULT.
IT'S BEYOND SHAMEFUL...
...FOR AN ADULT WHO'S FAILED, OVER AND OVER, TO BURDEN A BOY OF 16 WITH HER OLD DEBTS.
I KNOW THAT! BUT ALL THE SAME...

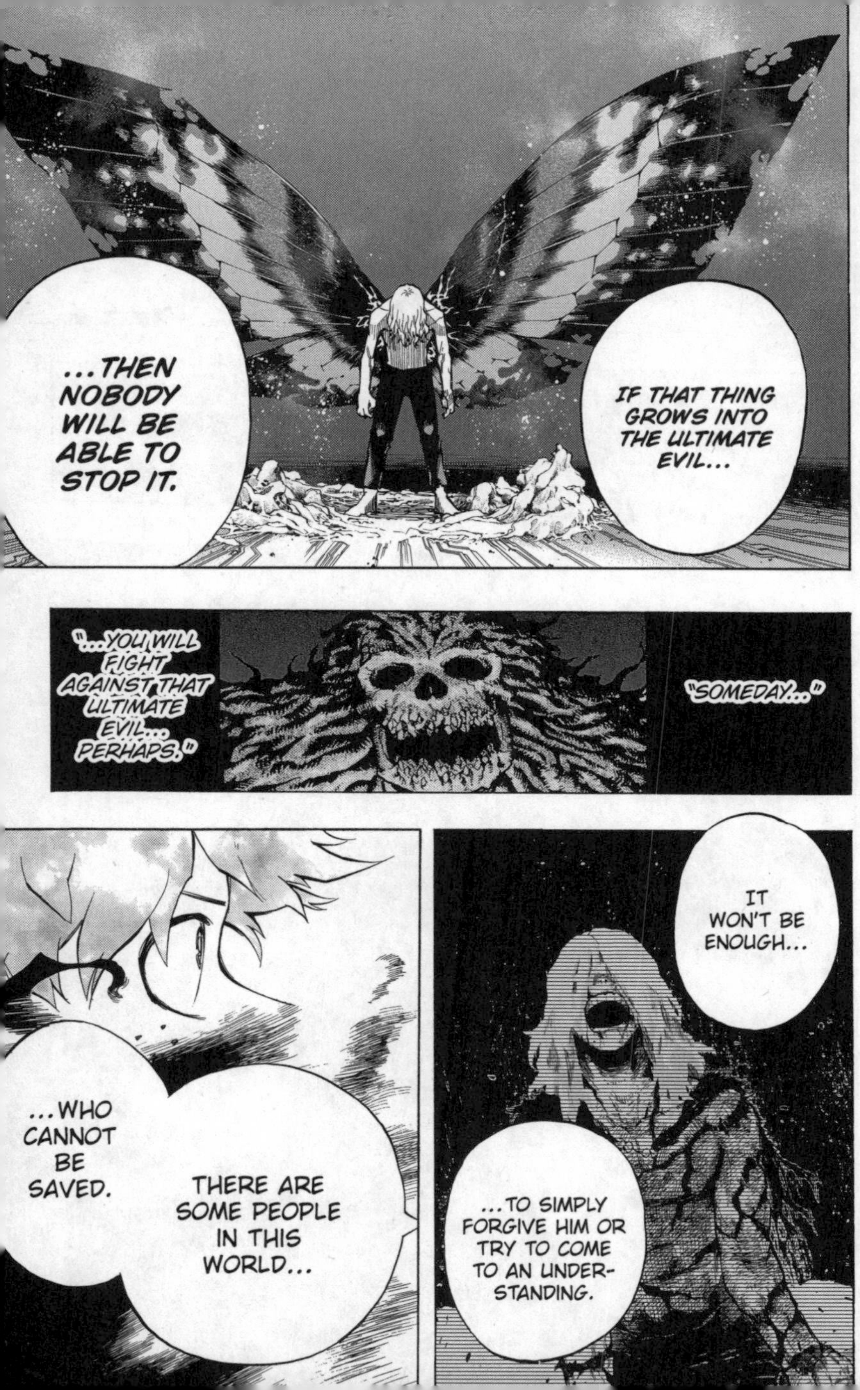
IF THAT THING GROWS INTO THE ULTIMATE EVIL...
...THEN NOBODY WILL BE ABLE TO STOP IT.
"SOMEDAY..."
"...YOU WILL FIGHT AGAINST THAT ULTIMATE EVIL... PERHAPS."
IT WON'T BE ENOUGH...
...TO SIMPLY FORGIVE HIM OR TRY TO COME TO AN UNDER-STANDING.
THERE ARE SOME PEOPLE IN THIS WORLD...
...WHO CANNOT BE SAVED.

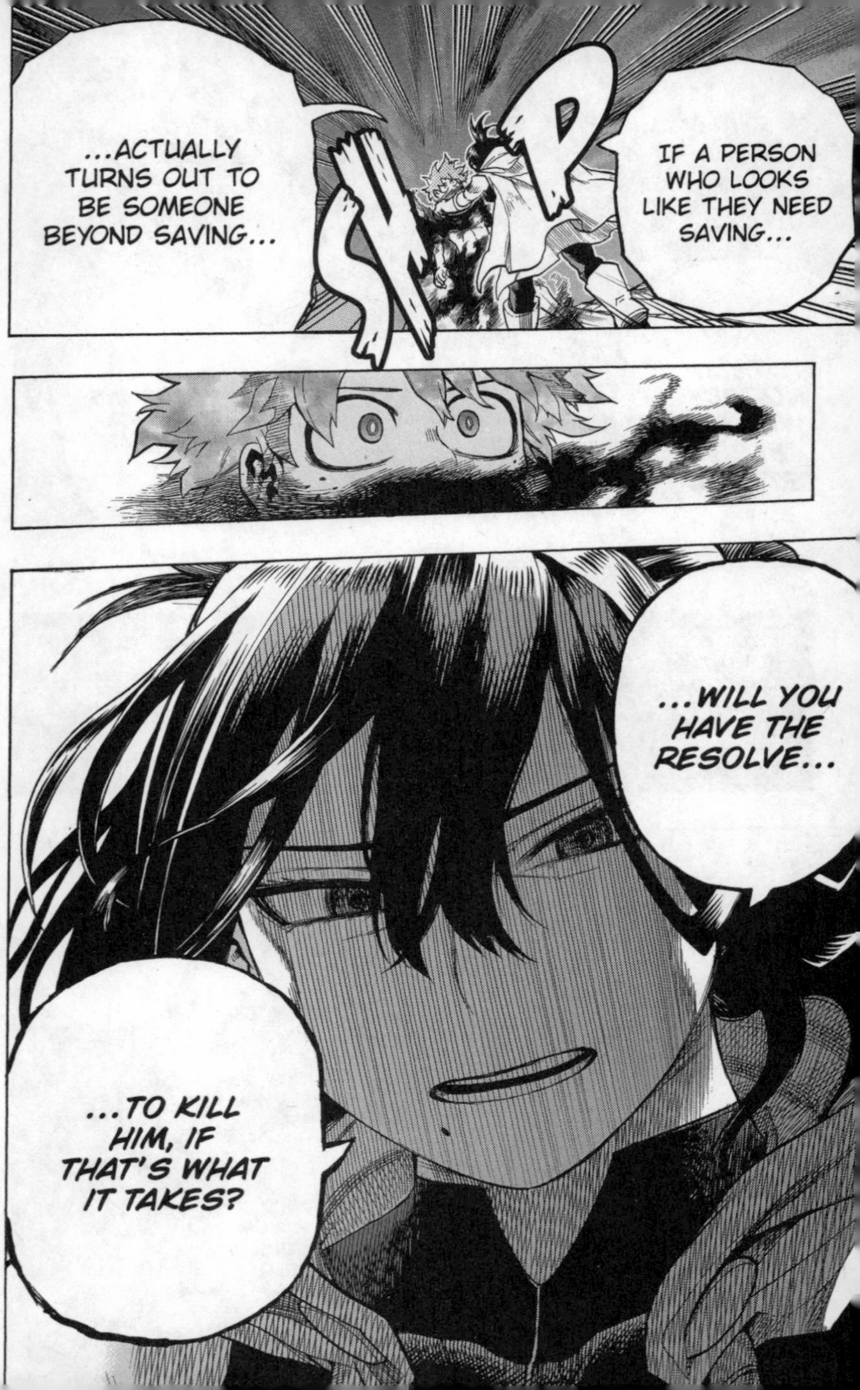
IF A PERSON WHO LOOKS LIKE THEY NEED SAVING...
...ACTUALLY TURNS OUT TO BE SOMEONE BEYOND SAVING...
...WILL YOU HAVE THE RESOLVE...
...TO KILL HIM, IF THAT'S WHAT IT TAKES?

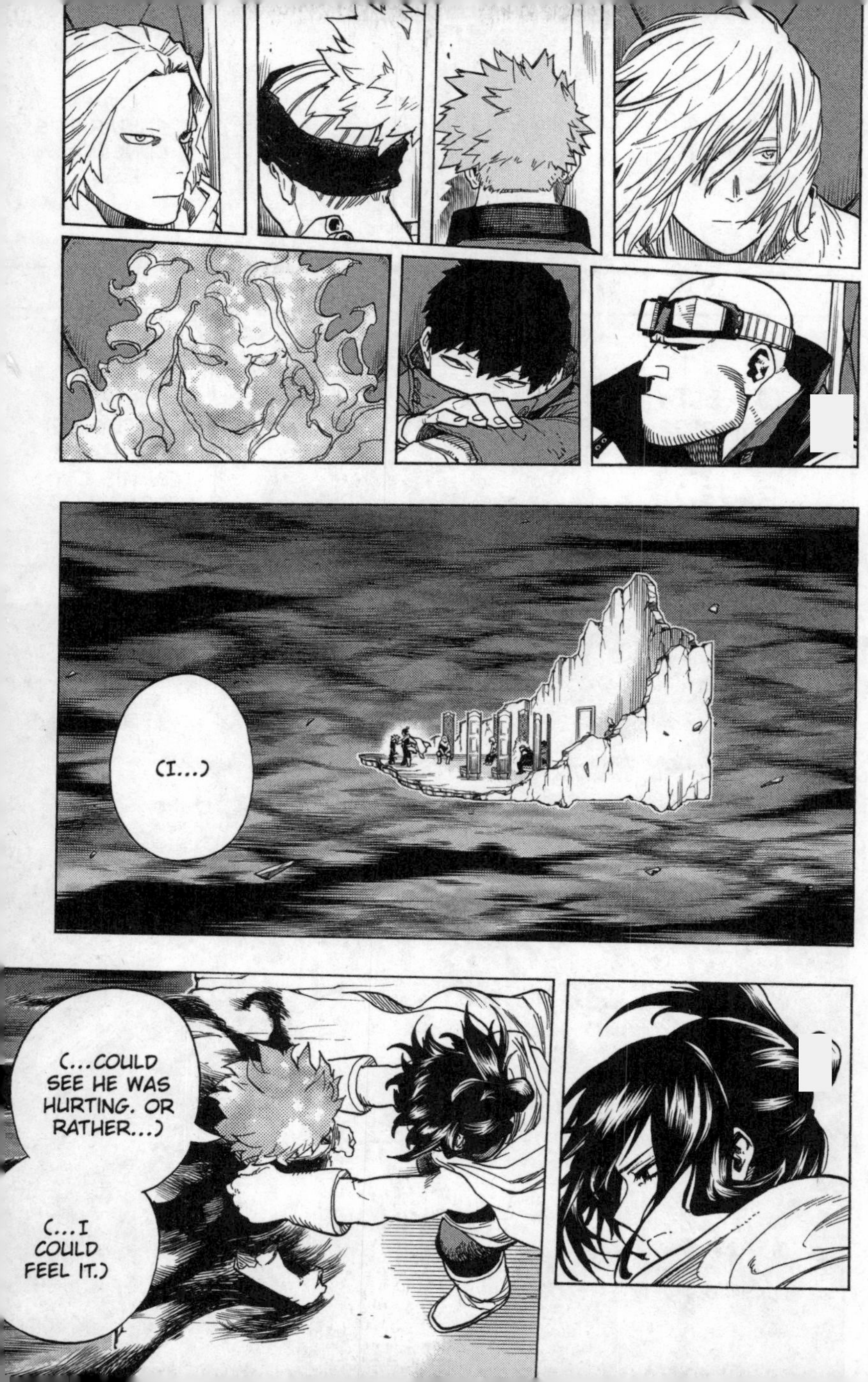
(I...)
(...COULD SEE HE WAS HURTING. OR RATHER...)
(...I COULD FEEL IT.)

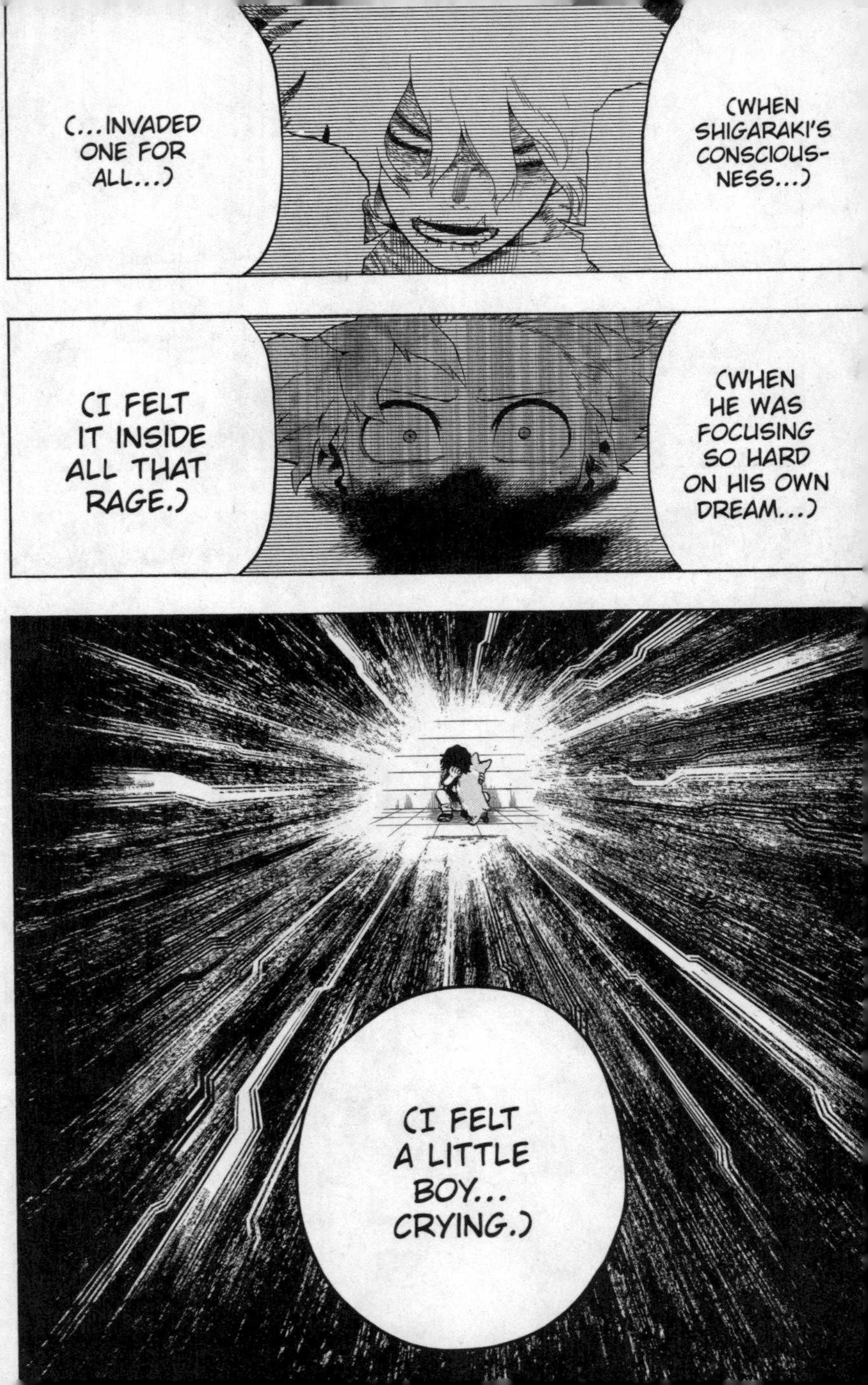
(WHEN SHIGARAKI'S CONSCIOUS-NESS...)
(...INVADED ONE FOR ALL...)
(WHEN HE WAS FOCUSING SO HARD ON HIS OWN DREAM...)
(I FELT IT INSIDE ALL THAT RAGE.)
(I FELT A LITTLE BOY... CRYING.)

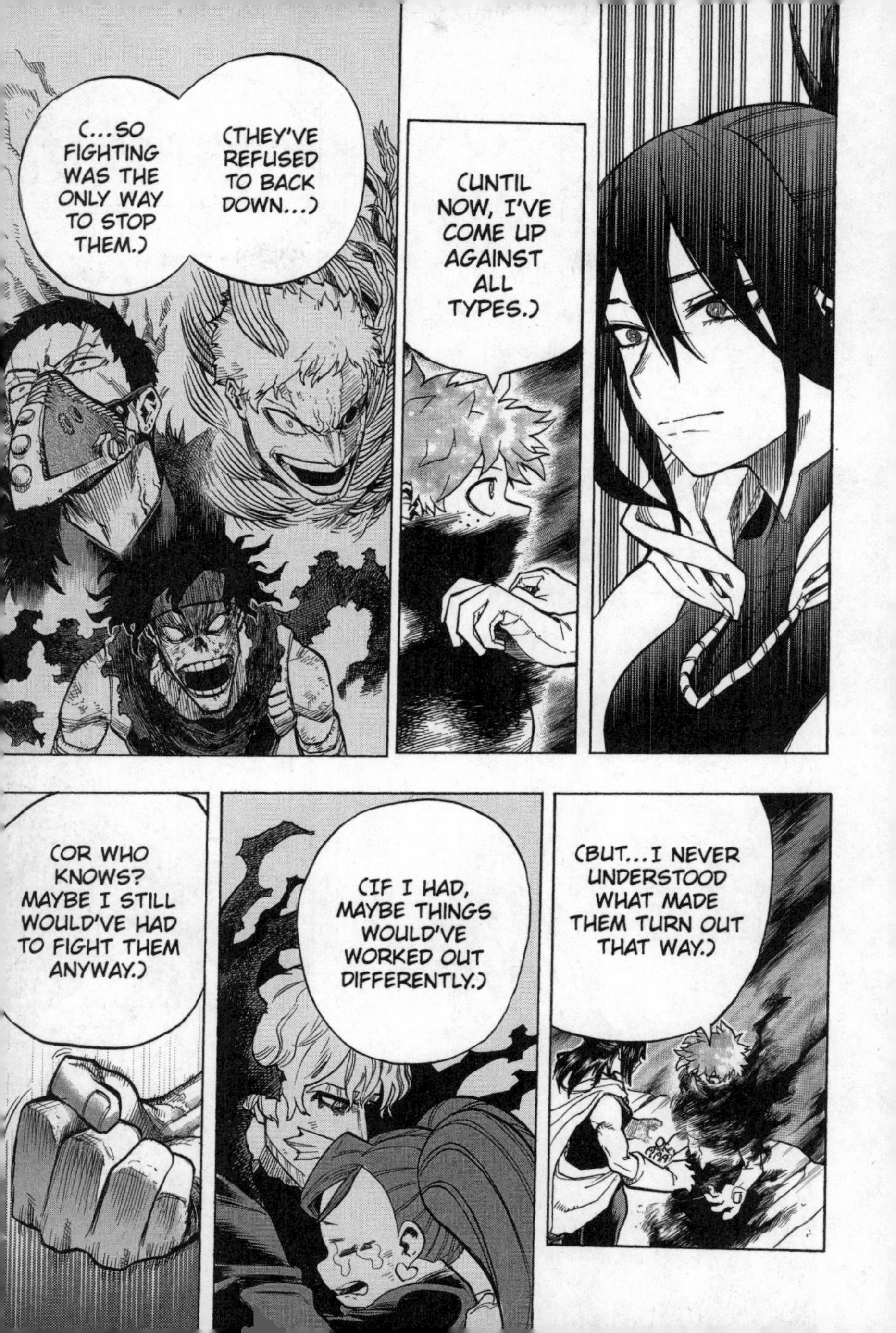
(UNTIL NOW, I'VE COME UP AGAINST ALL TYPES.)
(THEY'VE REFUSED TO BACK DOWN...)
(...SO FIGHTING WAS THE ONLY WAY TO STOP THEM.)
(BUT...I NEVER UNDERSTOOD WHAT MADE THEM TURN OUT THAT WAY.)
(IF I HAD, MAYBE THINGS WOULD'VE WORKED OUT DIFFERENTLY.)
(OR WHO KNOWS? MAYBE I STILL WOULD'VE HAD TO FIGHT THEM ANYWAY.)

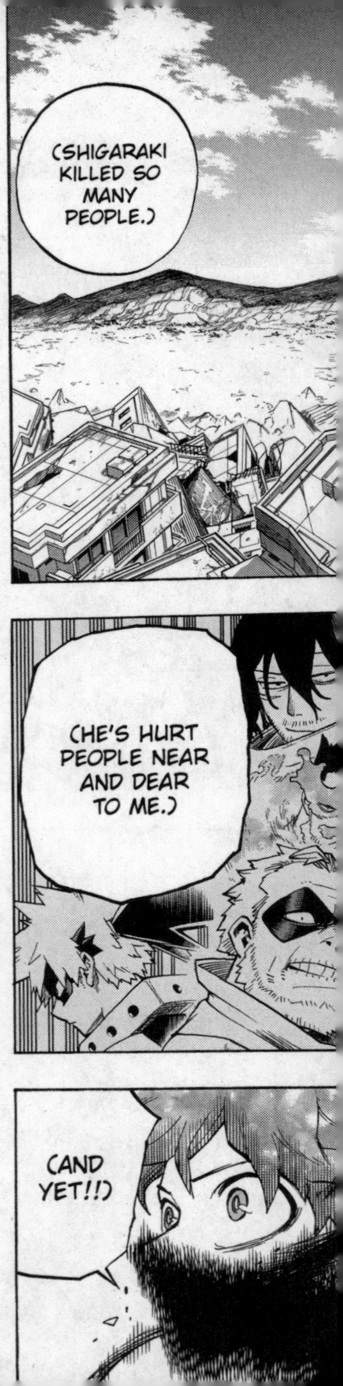
(SHIGARAKI KILLED SO MANY PEOPLE.)
(HE'S HURT PEOPLE NEAR AND DEAR TO ME.)
(AND YET!!)
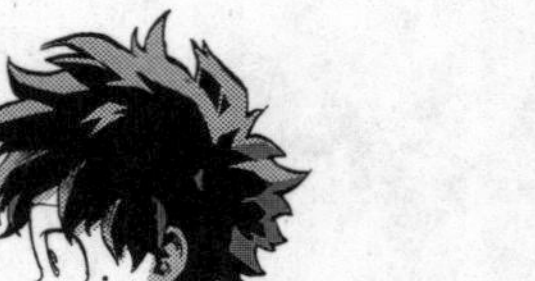

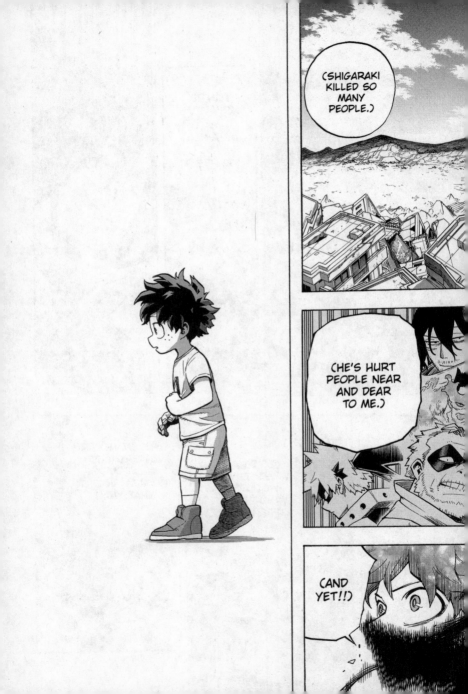

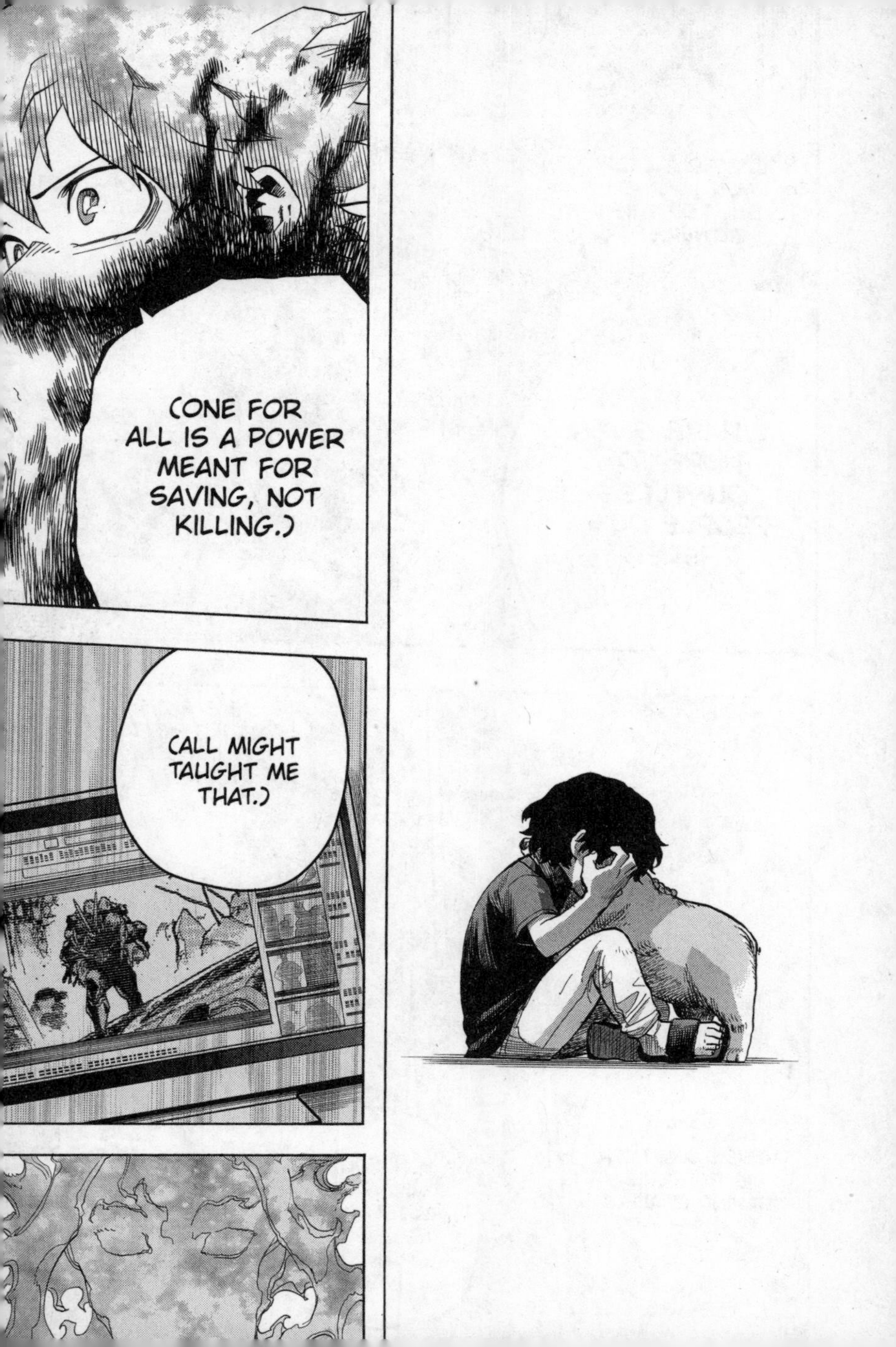
(ONE FOR ALL IS A POWER MEANT FOR SAVING, NOT KILLING.)
(ALL MIGHT TAUGHT ME THAT.)

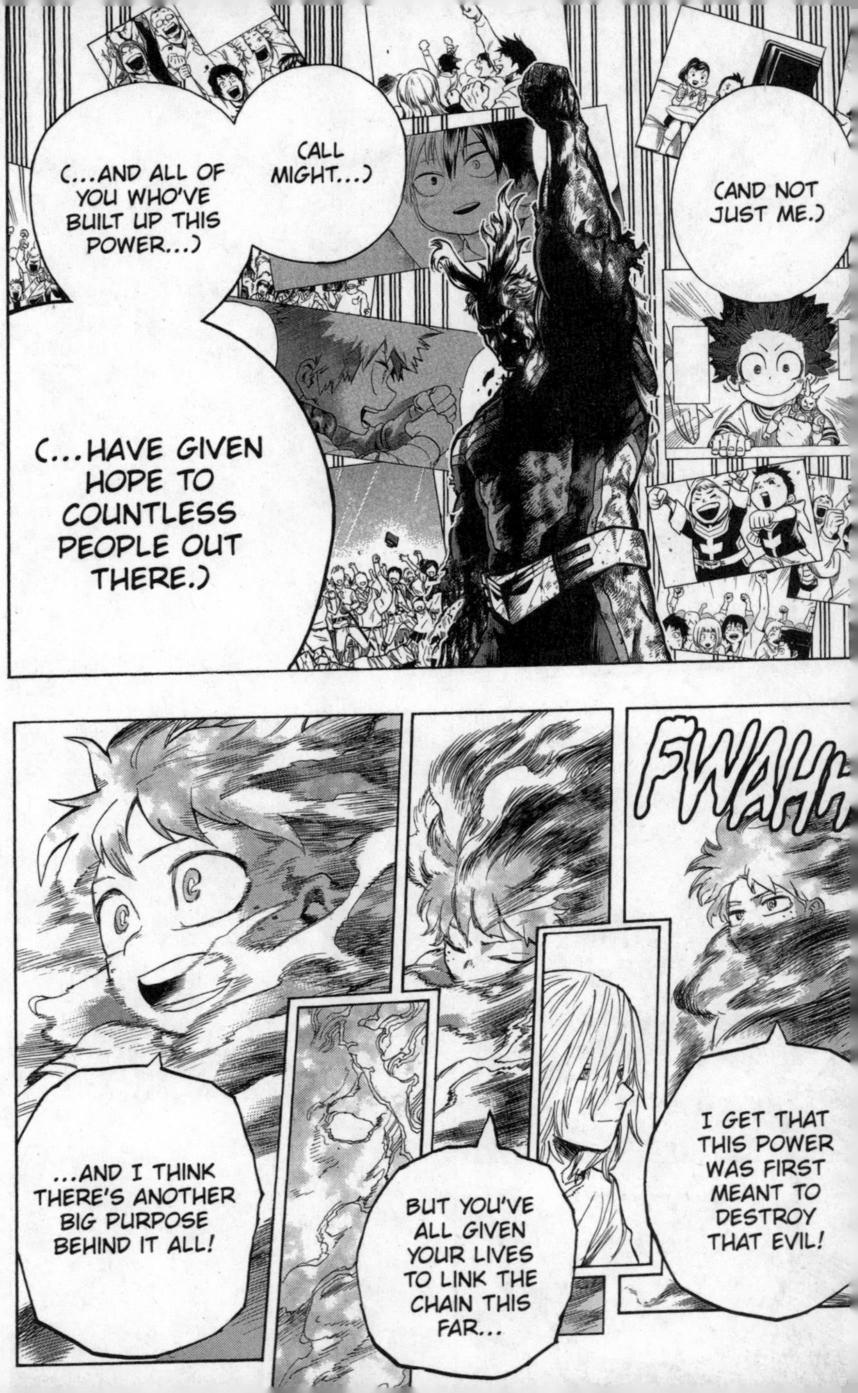
(AND NOT JUST ME.)
(ALL MIGHT...)
(...AND ALL OF YOU WHO'VE BUILT UP THIS POWER...)
(...HAVE GIVEN HOPE TO COUNTLESS PEOPLE OUT THERE.)
FWAHH
I GET THAT THIS POWER WAS FIRST MEANT TO DESTROY THAT EVIL!
BUT YOU'VE ALL GIVEN YOUR LIVES TO LINK THE CHAIN THIS FAR...
...AND I THINK THERE'S ANOTHER BIG PURPOSE BEHIND IT ALL!

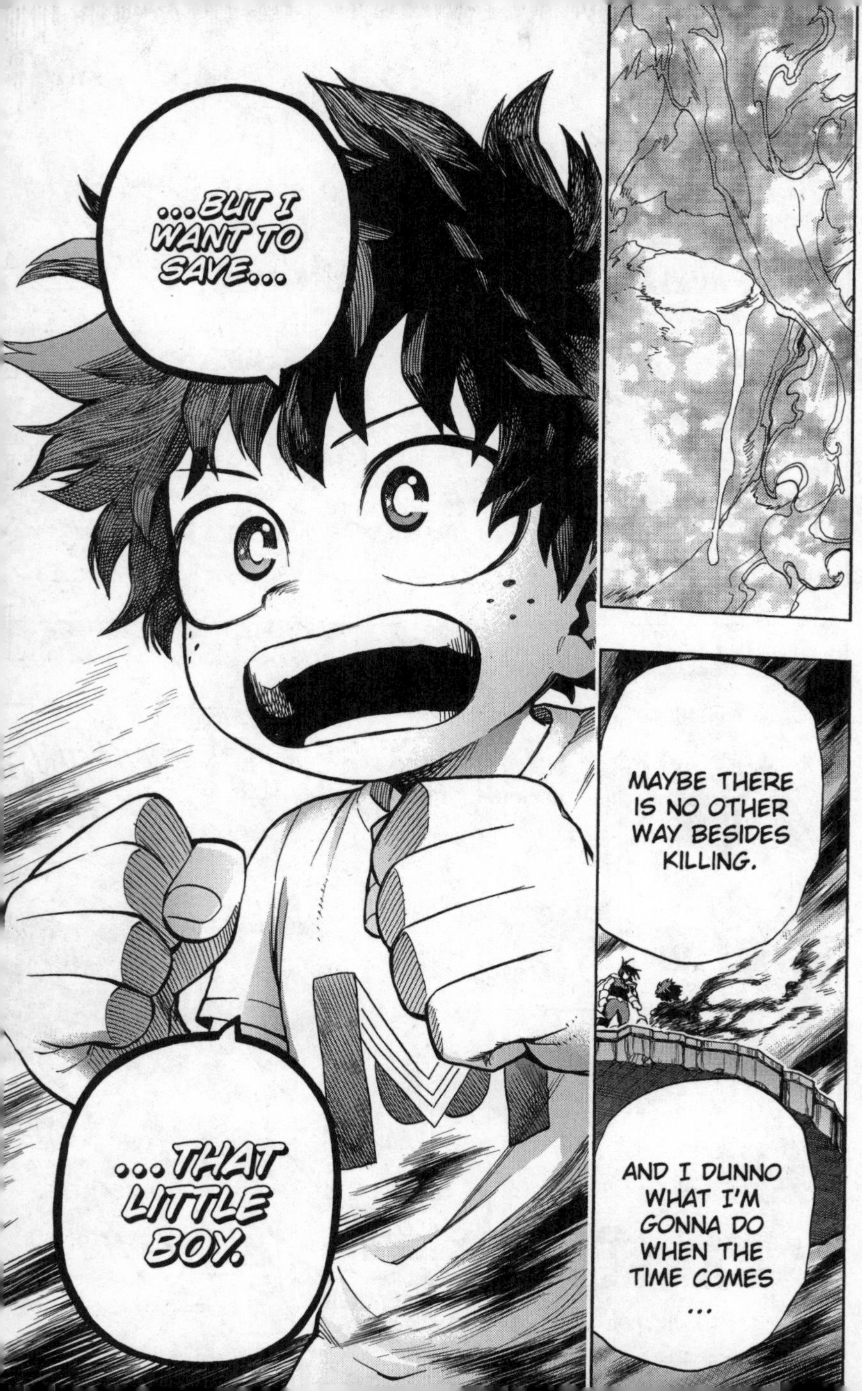
MAYBE THERE IS NO OTHER WAY BESIDES KILLING.
AND I DUNNO WHAT I'M GONNA DO WHEN THE TIME COMES ...
...BUT I WANT TO SAVE...
...THAT LITTLE BOY.

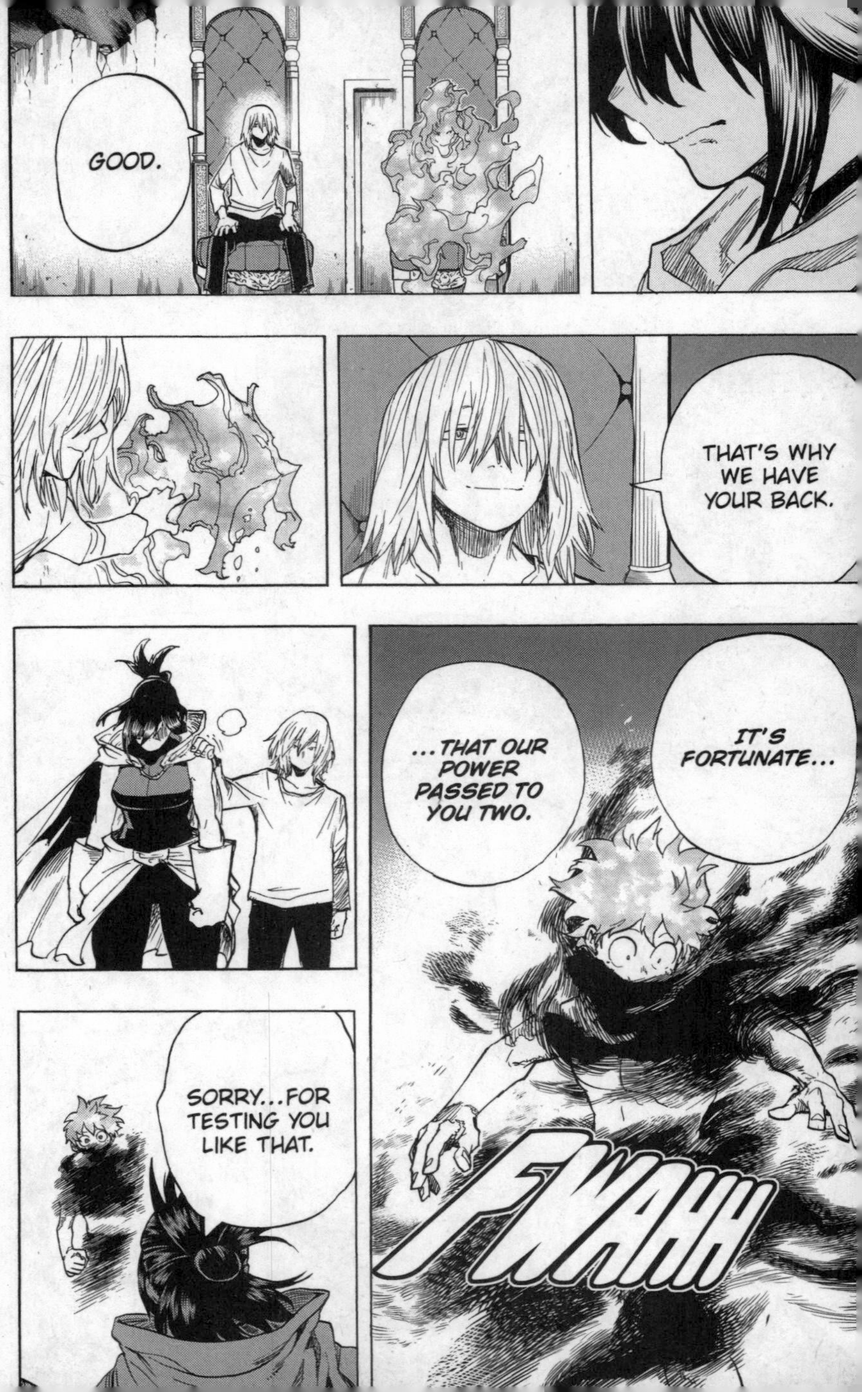
GOOD.
THAT'S WHY WE HAVE YOUR BACK.
IT'S FORTUNATE...
...THAT OUR POWER PASSED TO YOU TWO.
FWAHH
SORRY...FOR TESTING YOU LIKE THAT.

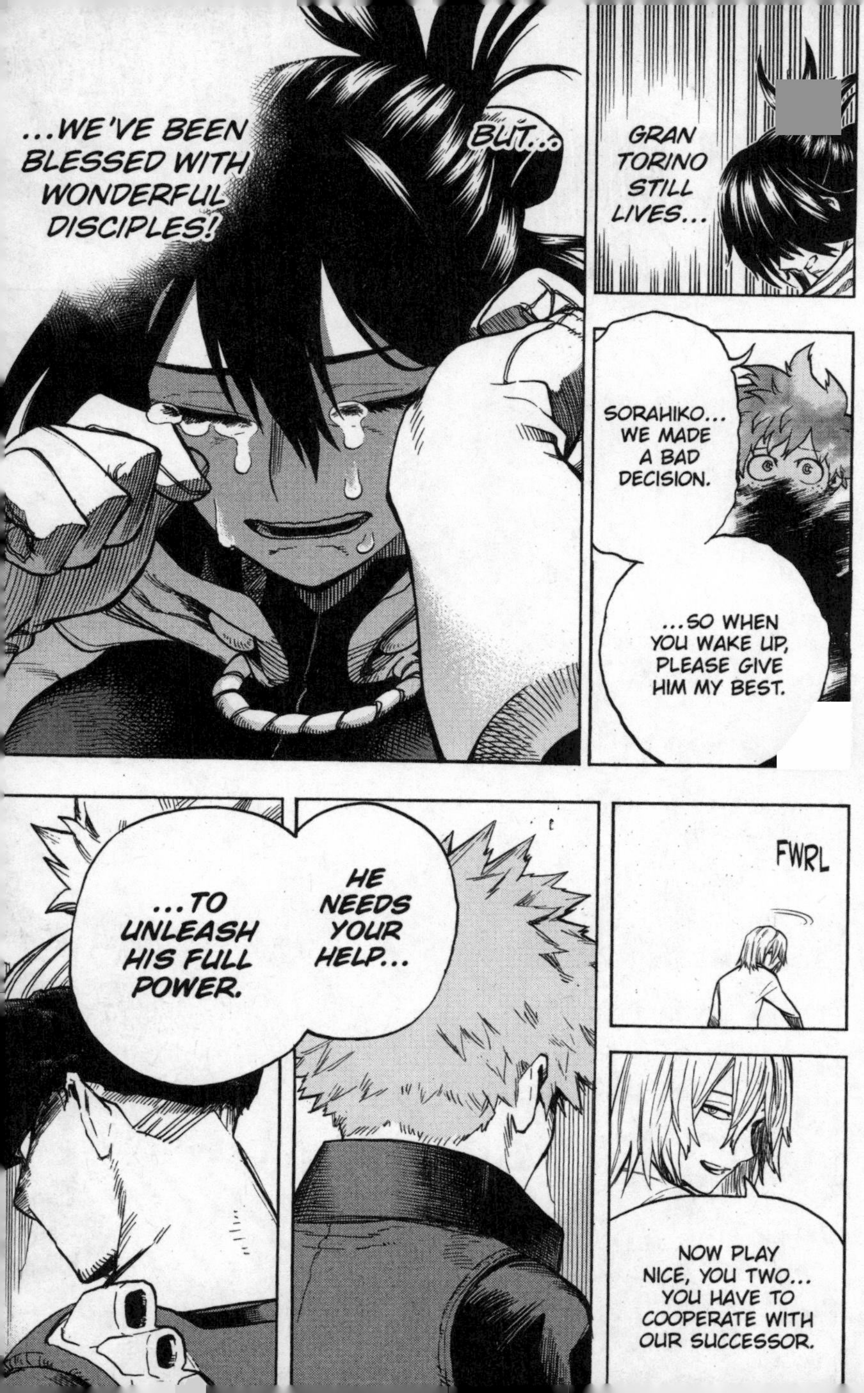
GRAN TORINO STILL LIVES...
SORAHIKO... WE MADE A BAD DECISION.
...SO WHEN YOU WAKE UP, PLEASE GIVE HIM MY BEST.
BUT...
...WE'VE BEEN BLESSED WITH WONDERFUL DISCIPLES!
FWRL
NOW PLAY NICE, YOU TWO... YOU HAVE TO COOPERATE WITH OUR SUCCESSOR.
HE NEEDS YOUR HELP...
...TO UNLEASH HIS FULL POWER.

NO. 306

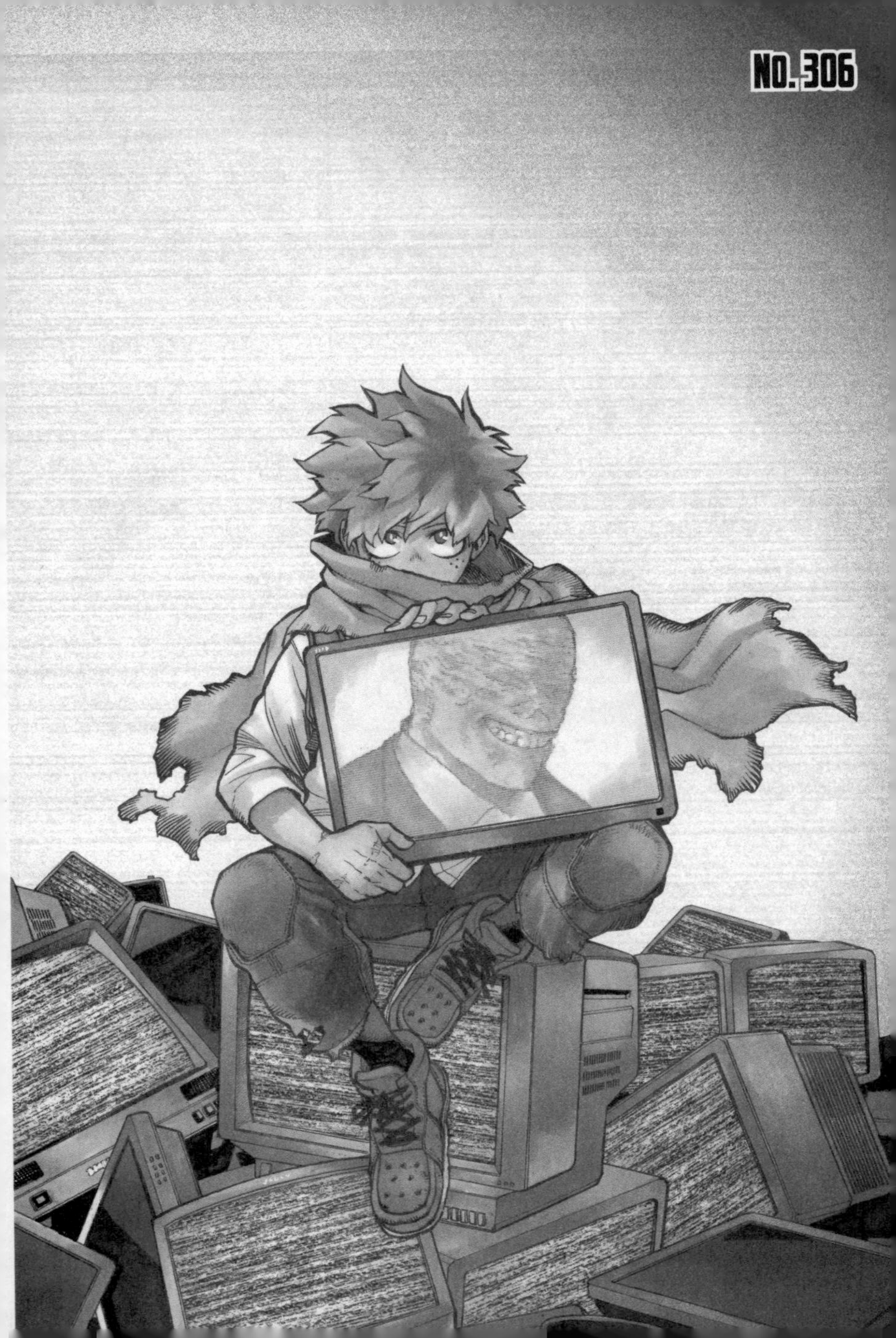

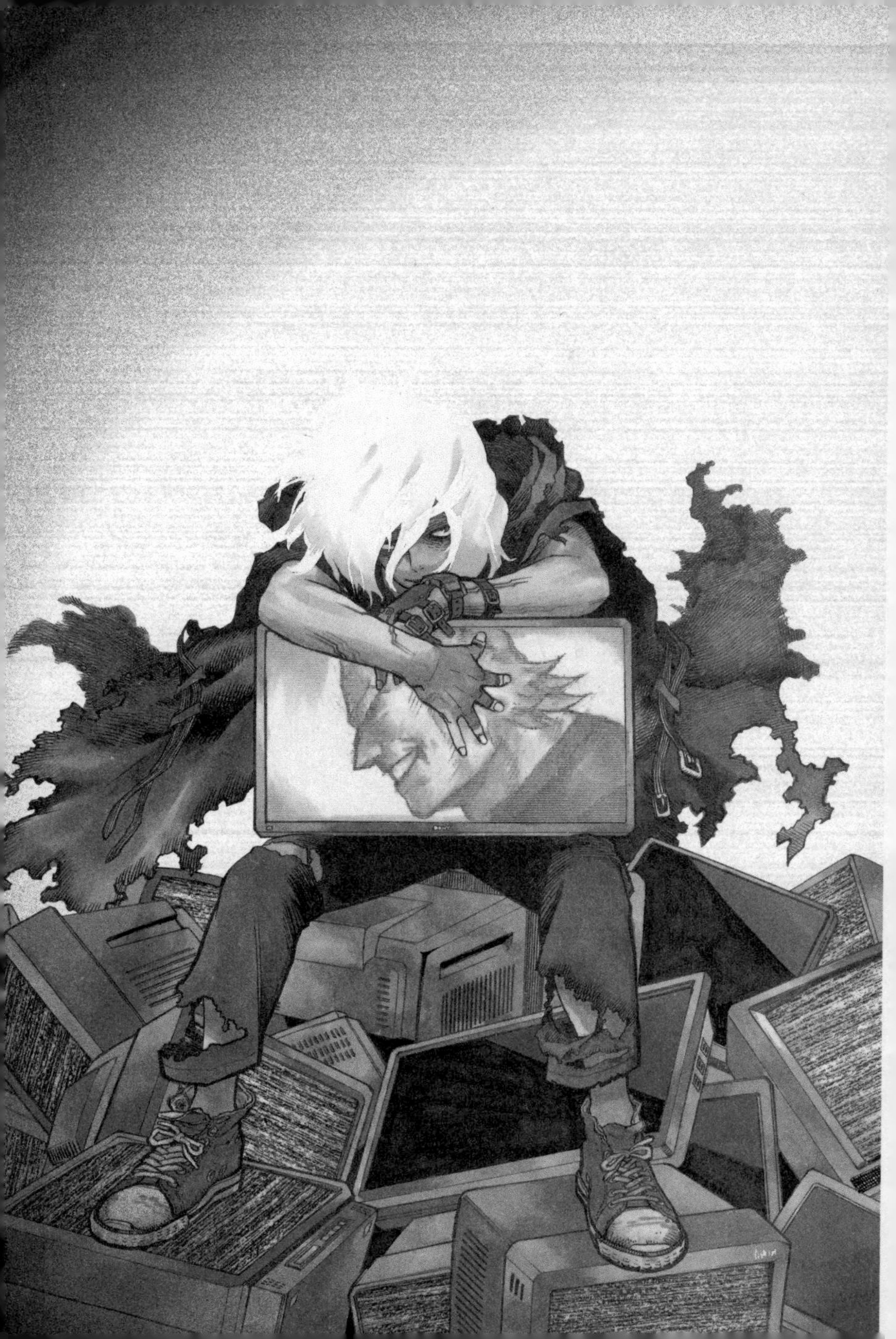

MY HERO ACADEMIA

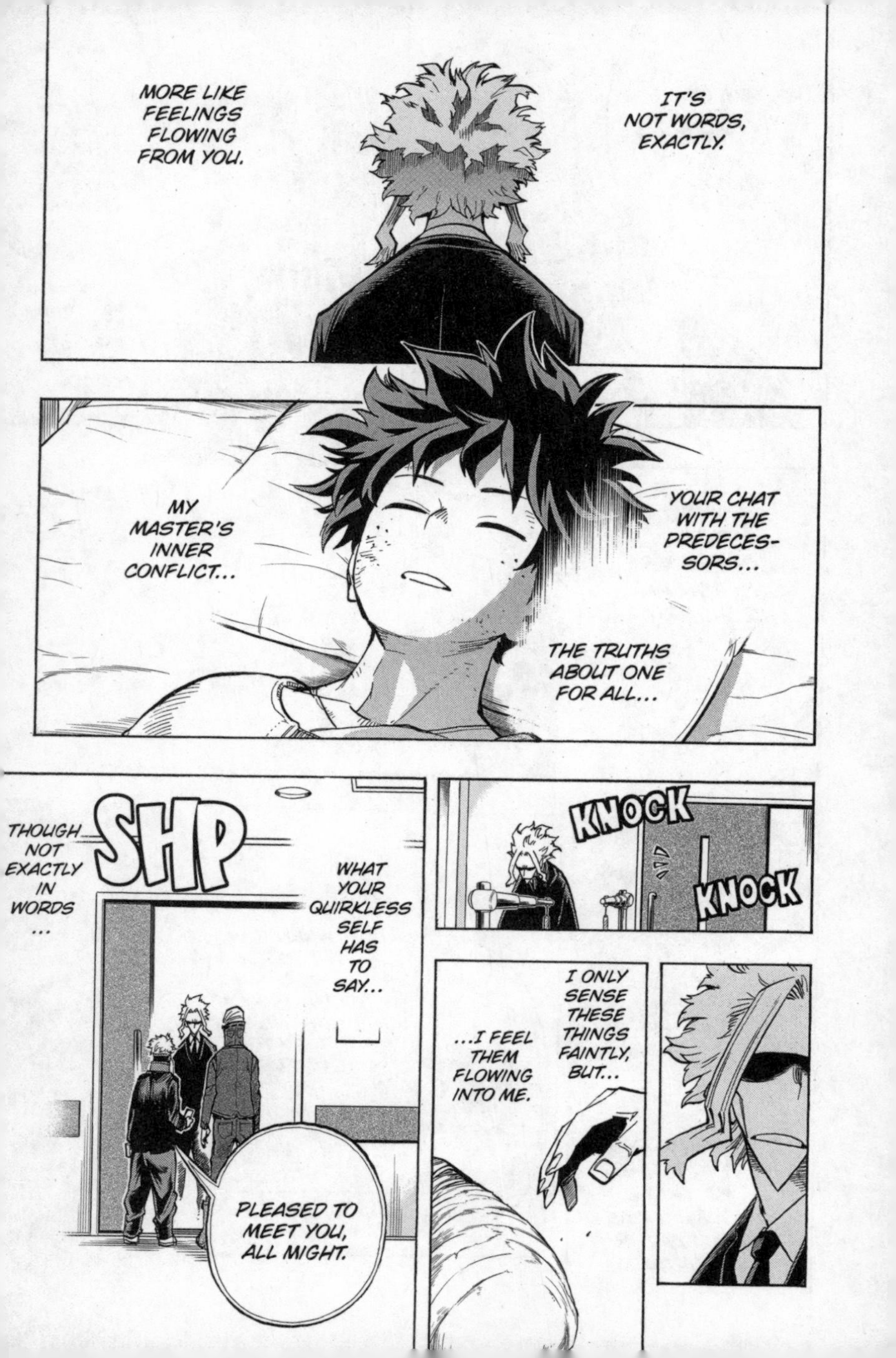
IT'S NOT WORDS, EXACTLY.
MORE LIKE FEELINGS FLOWING FROM YOU.
YOUR CHAT WITH THE PREDECES-SORS...
THE TRUTHS ABOUT ONE FOR ALL...
MY MASTER'S INNER CONFLICT...
KNOCK
KNOCK
I ONLY SENSE THESE THINGS FAINTLY, BUT...
...I FEEL THEM FLOWING INTO ME.
WHAT YOUR QUIRKLESS SELF HAS TO SAY...
THOUGH NOT EXACTLY IN WORDS...
SHP
PLEASED TO MEET YOU, ALL MIGHT.

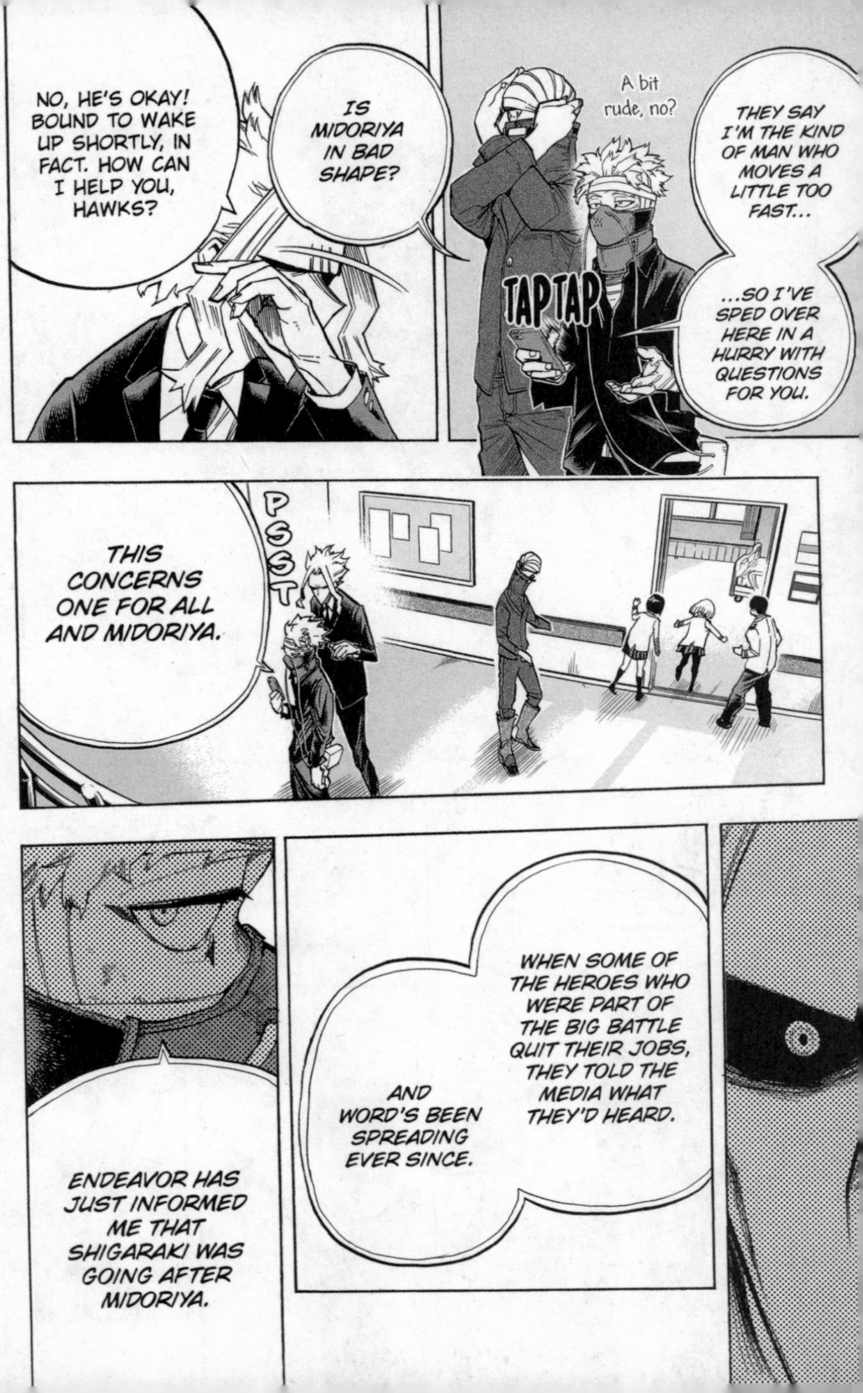
THEY SAY I'M THE KIND OF MAN WHO MOVES A LITTLE TOO FAST...
A bit rude, no?
...SO I'VE SPED OVER HERE IN A HURRY WITH QUESTIONS FOR YOU.
TAPTAP
IS MIDORIYA IN BAD SHAPE?
NO, HE'S OKAY! BOUND TO WAKE UP SHORTLY, IN FACT. HOW CAN I HELP YOU, HAWKS?
PSST
THIS CONCERNS ONE FOR ALL AND MIDORIYA.
WHEN SOME OF THE HEROES WHO WERE PART OF THE BIG BATTLE QUIT THEIR JOBS, THEY TOLD THE MEDIA WHAT THEY'D HEARD.
AND WORD'S BEEN SPREADING EVER SINCE.
ENDEAVOR HAS JUST INFORMED ME THAT SHIGARAKI WAS GOING AFTER MIDORIYA.

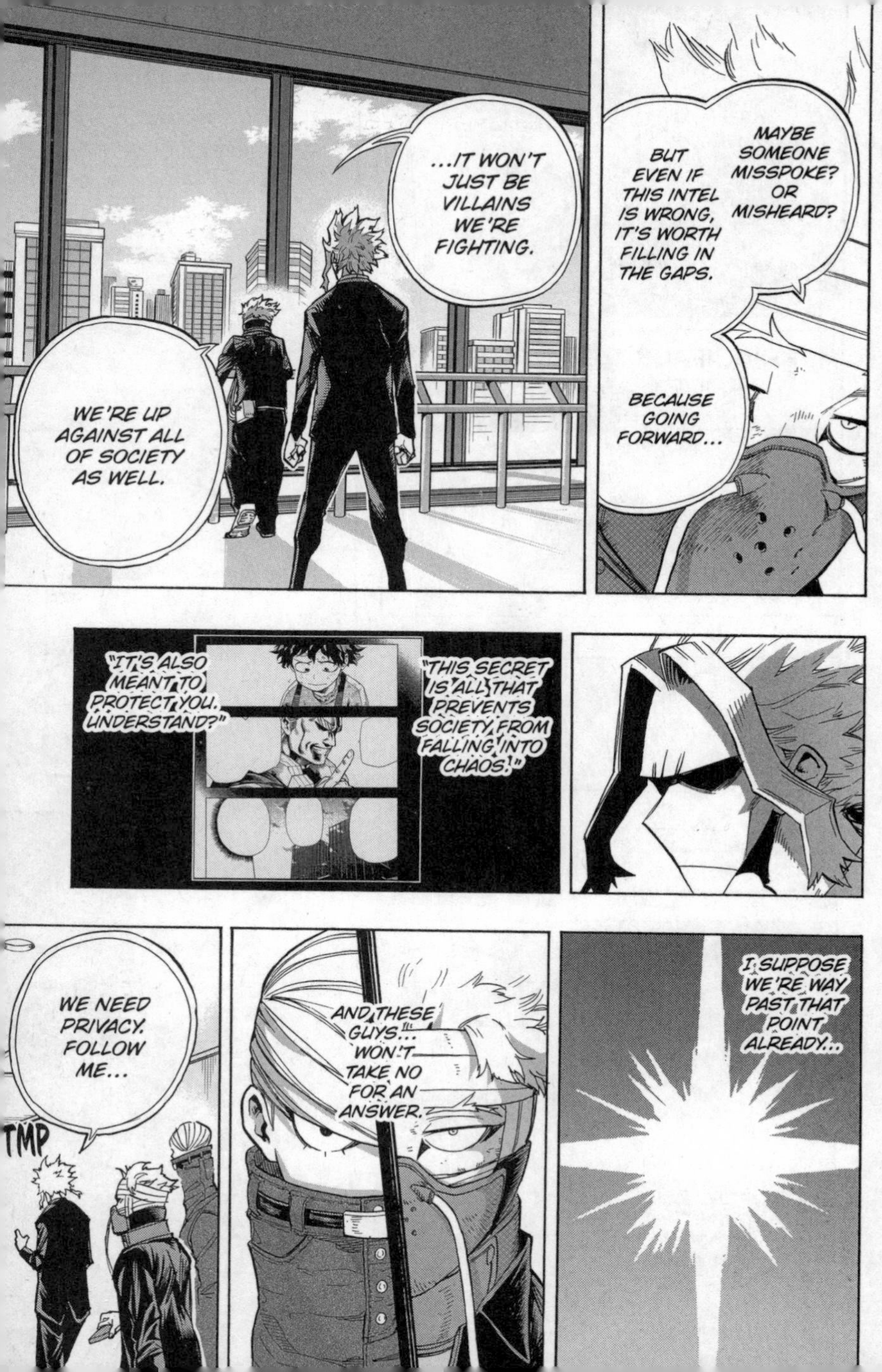
MAYBE SOMEONE MISSPOKE? OR MISHEARD?
BUT EVEN IF THIS INTEL IS WRONG, IT'S WORTH FILLING IN THE GAPS.
BECAUSE GOING FORWARD...
...IT WON'T JUST BE VILLAINS WE'RE FIGHTING.
WE'RE UP AGAINST ALL OF SOCIETY AS WELL.
"THIS SECRET IS ALL THAT PREVENTS SOCIETY FROM FALLING INTO CHAOS."
"IT'S ALSO MEANT TO PROTECT YOU. UNDERSTAND?"
I SUPPOSE WE'RE WAY PAST THAT POINT ALREADY...
AND THESE GUYS... WON'T TAKE NO FOR AN ANSWER.
WE NEED PRIVACY. FOLLOW ME...
TMP

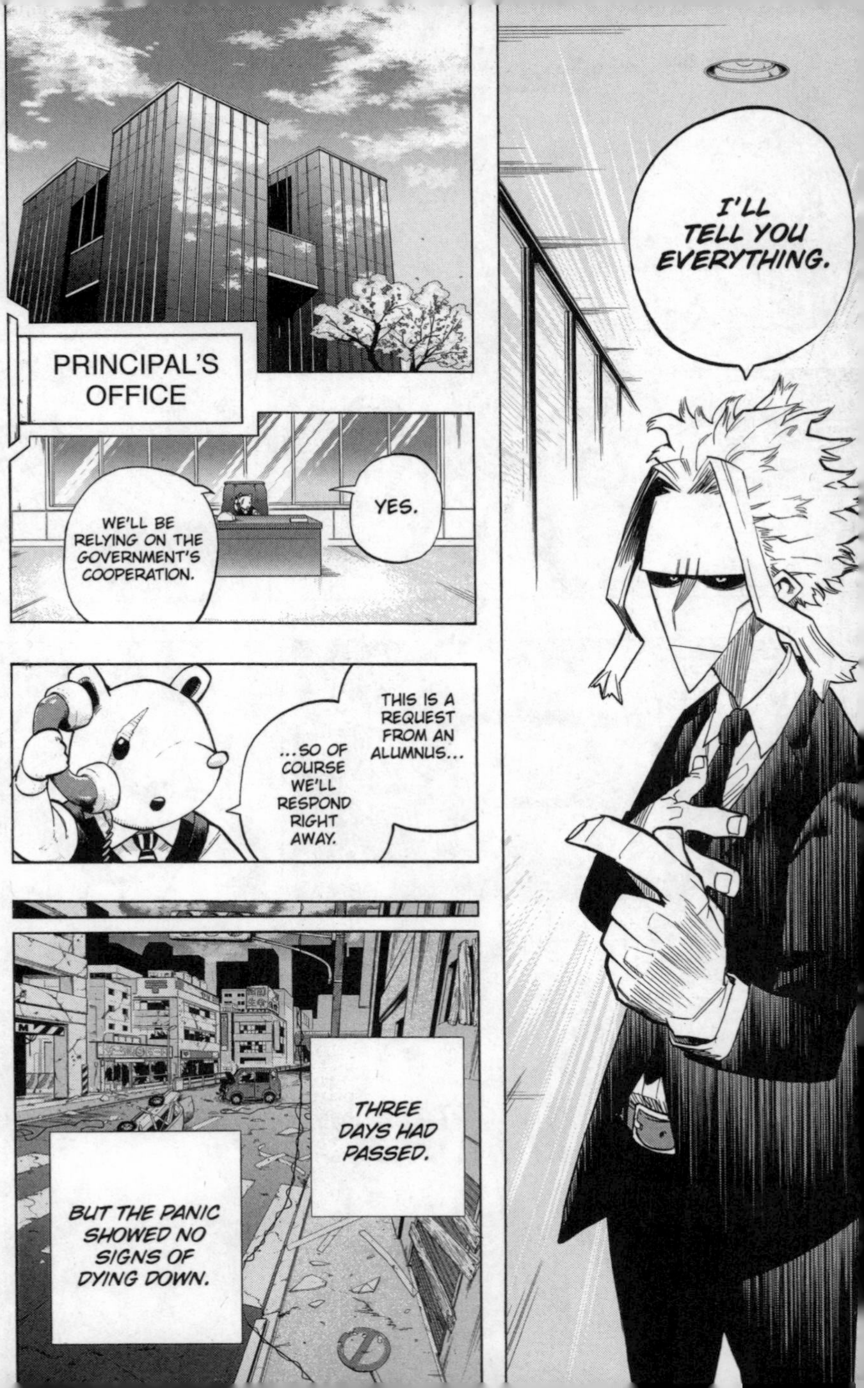
I'LL TELL YOU EVERYTHING.
PRINCIPAL'S OFFICE
YES.
WE'LL BE RELYING ON THE GOVERNMENT'S COOPERATION.
THIS IS A REQUEST FROM AN ALUMNUS...
...SO OF COURSE WE'LL RESPOND RIGHT AWAY.
THREE DAYS HAD PASSED.
BUT THE PANIC SHOWED NO SIGNS OF DYING DOWN.

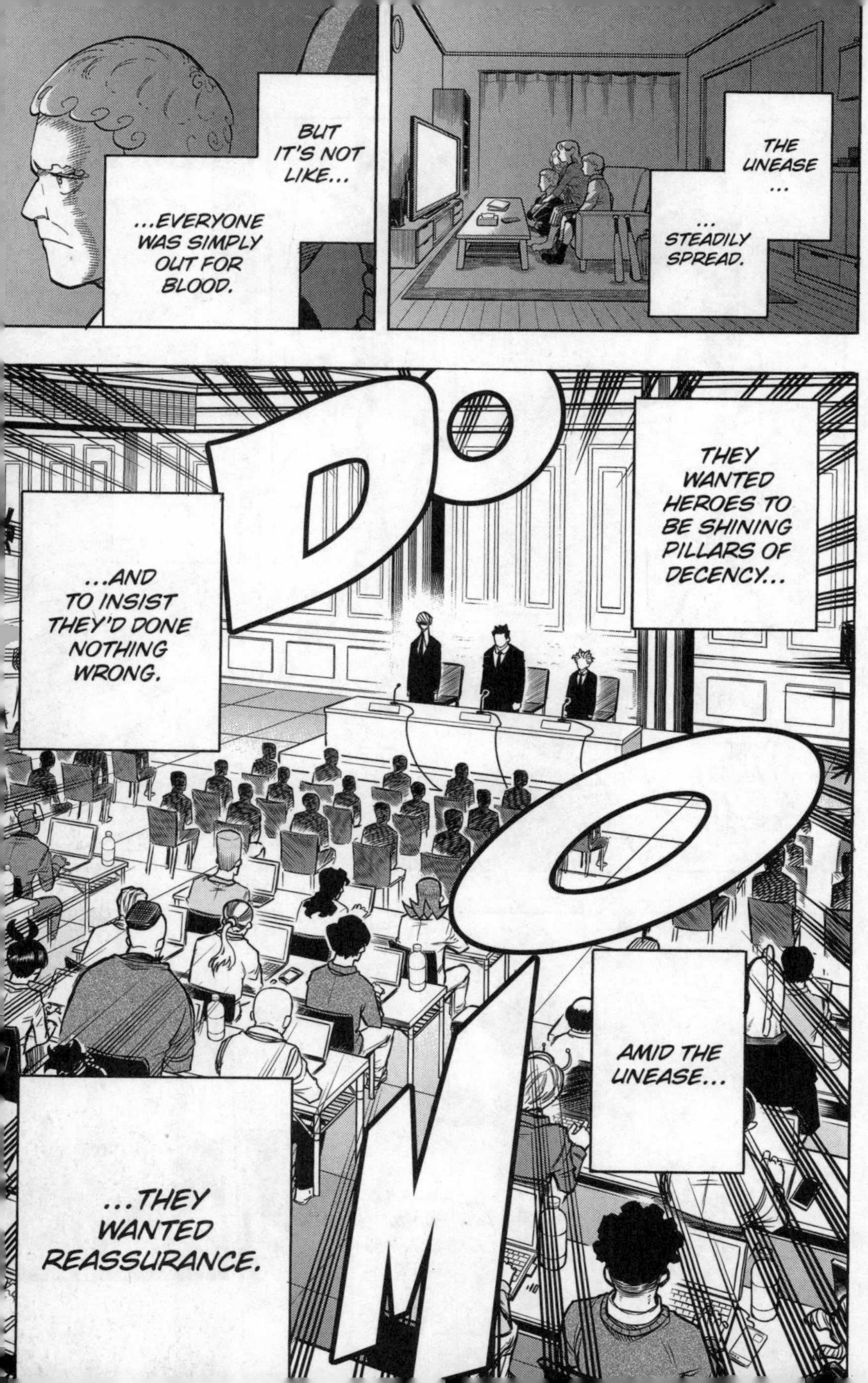
THE UNEASE ...
... STEADILY SPREAD.
BUT IT'S NOT LIKE...
...EVERYONE WAS SIMPLY OUT FOR BLOOD.
THEY WANTED HEROES TO BE SHINING PILLARS OF DECENCY...
...AND TO INSIST THEY'D DONE NOTHING WRONG.
DOOM
AMID THE UNEASE...
...THEY WANTED REASSURANCE.

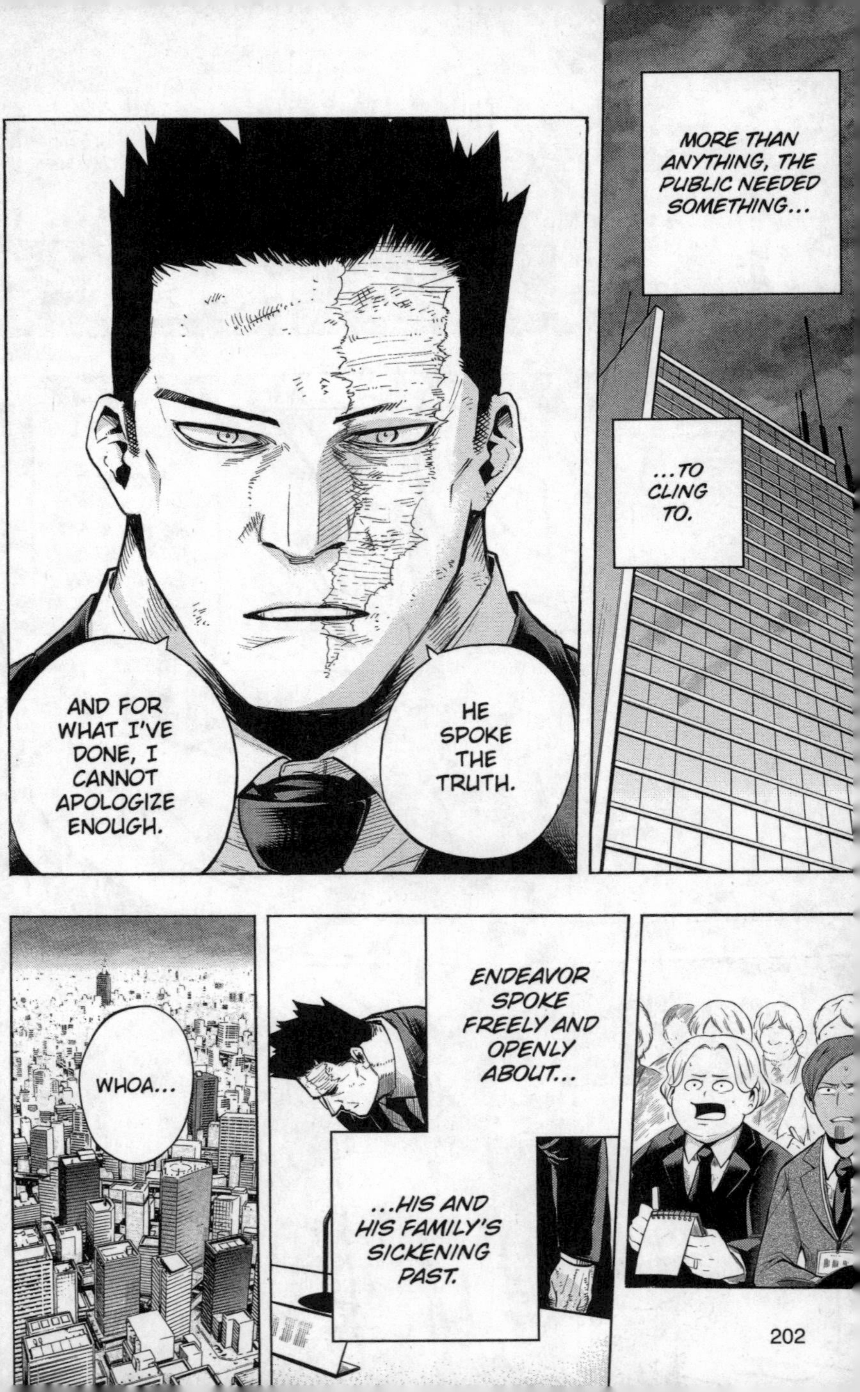
MORE THAN ANYTHING, THE PUBLIC NEEDED SOMETHING...
...TO CLING TO.
HE SPOKE THE TRUTH.
AND FOR WHAT I'VE DONE, I CANNOT APOLOGIZE ENOUGH.
ENDEAVOR SPOKE FREELY AND OPENLY ABOUT...
...HIS AND HIS FAMILY'S SICKENING PAST.
WHOA...

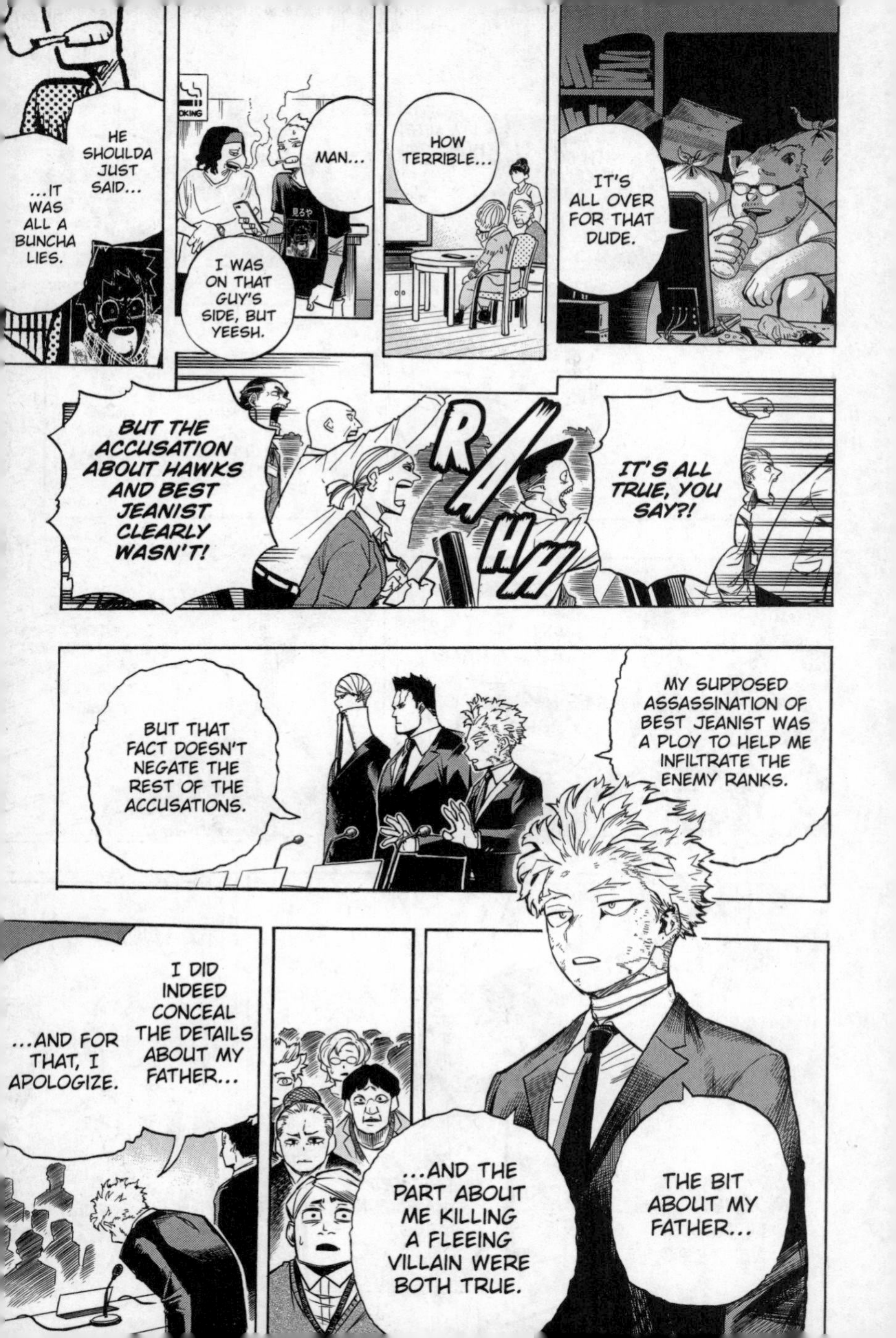
IT'S ALL OVER FOR THAT DUDE.
HOW TERRIBLE...
MAN...
I WAS ON THAT GUY'S SIDE, BUT YEESH.
HE SHOULDA JUST SAID...
...IT WAS ALL A BUNCHA LIES.
IT'S ALL TRUE, YOU SAY?!
RAHH
BUT THE ACCUSATION ABOUT HAWKS AND BEST JEANIST CLEARLY WASN'T!
MY SUPPOSED ASSASSINATION OF BEST JEANIST WAS A PLOY TO HELP ME INFILTRATE THE ENEMY RANKS.
BUT THAT FACT DOESN'T NEGATE THE REST OF THE ACCUSATIONS.
THE BIT ABOUT MY FATHER...
...AND THE PART ABOUT ME KILLING A FLEEING VILLAIN WERE BOTH TRUE.
I DID INDEED CONCEAL THE DETAILS ABOUT MY FATHER...
...AND FOR THAT, I APOLOGIZE.

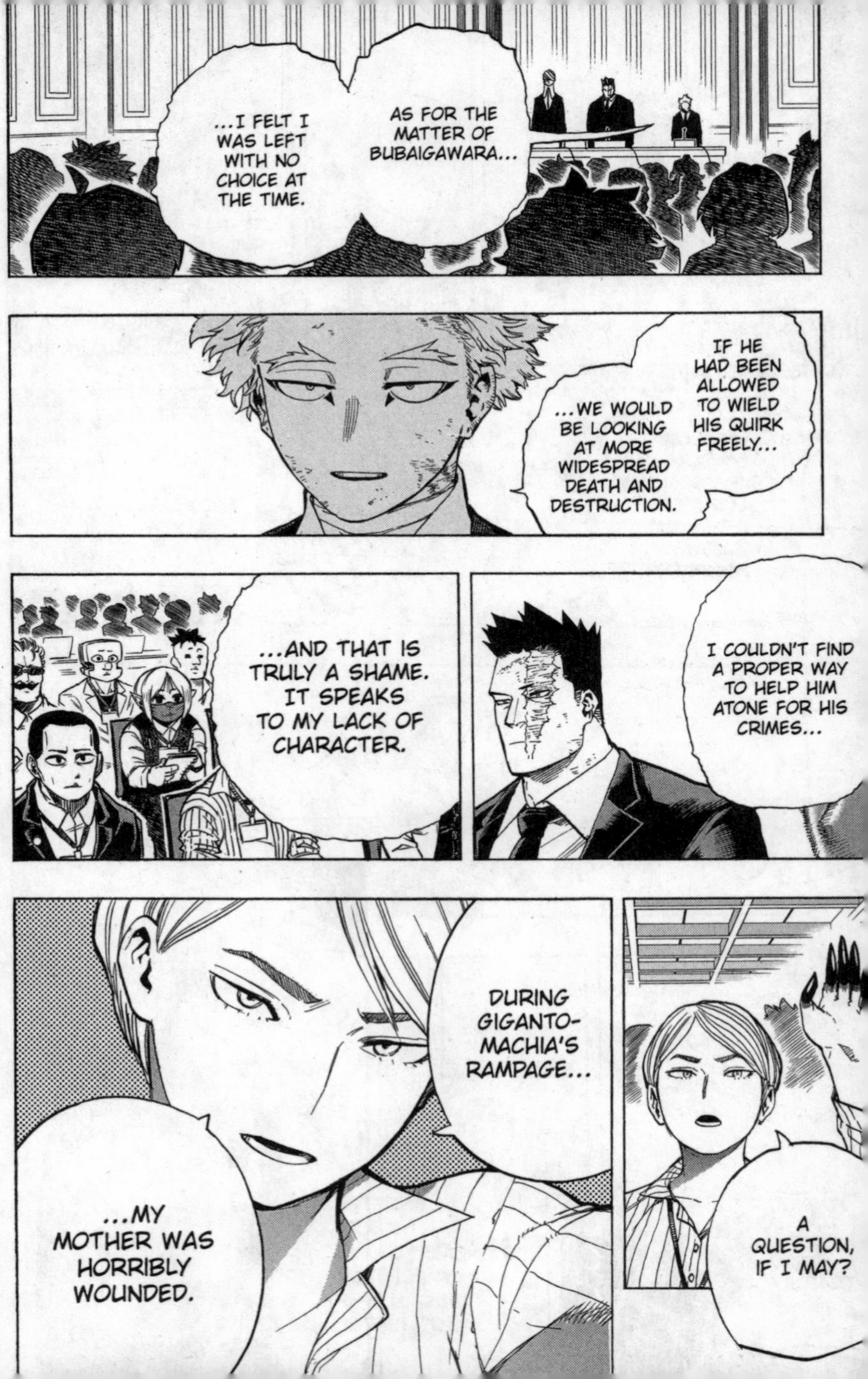

AS FOR THE MATTER OF BUBAIGAWARA...
...I FELT I WAS LEFT WITH NO CHOICE AT THE TIME.
IF HE HAD BEEN ALLOWED TO WIELD HIS QUIRK FREELY...
...WE WOULD BE LOOKING AT MORE WIDESPREAD DEATH AND DESTRUCTION.
I COULDN'T FIND A PROPER WAY TO HELP HIM ATONE FOR HIS CRIMES...
...AND THAT IS TRULY A SHAME. IT SPEAKS TO MY LACK OF CHARACTER.
A QUESTION, IF I MAY?
DURING GIGANTO-MACHIA'S RAMPAGE...
...MY MOTHER WAS HORRIBLY WOUNDED.

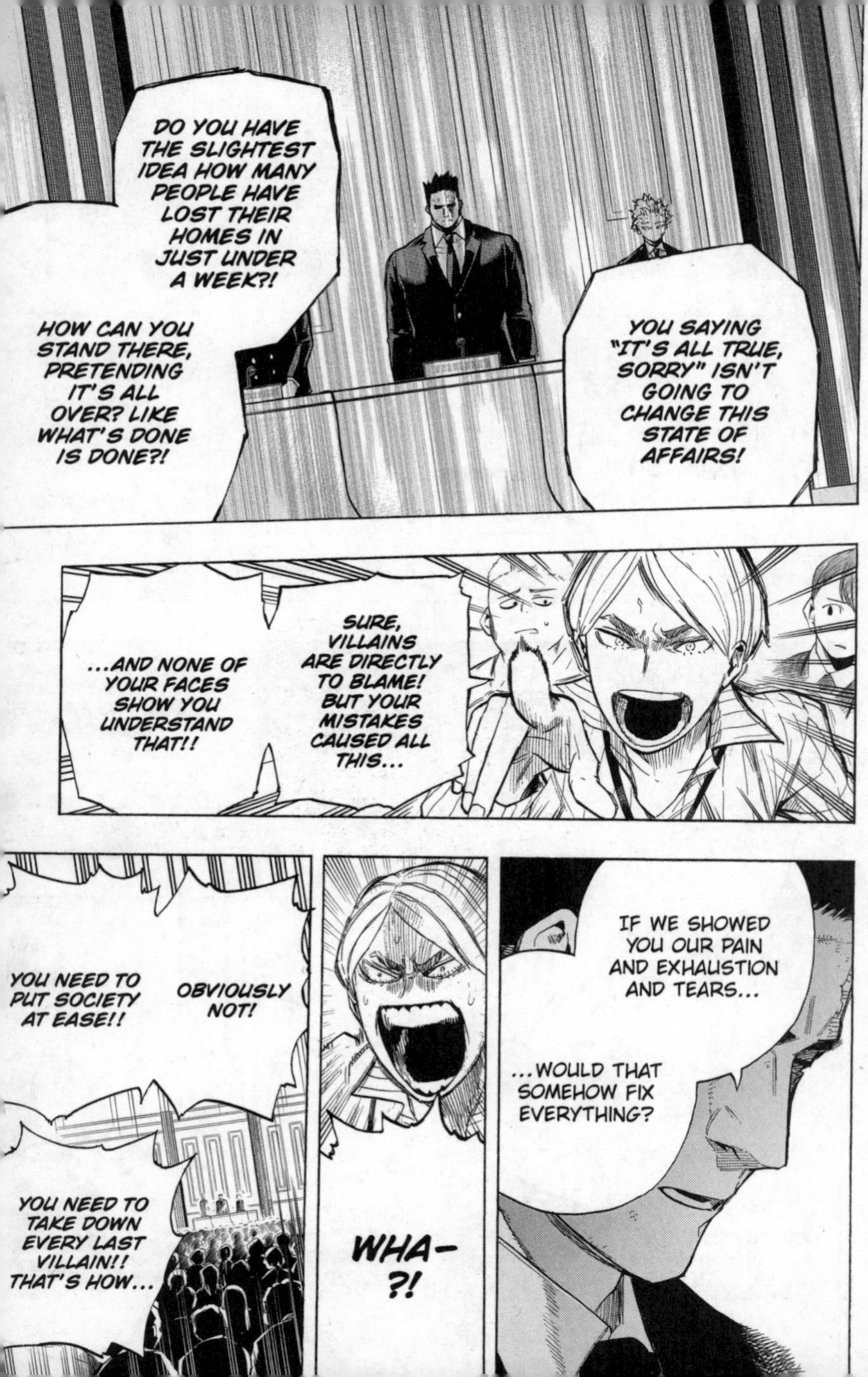
DO YOU HAVE THE SLIGHTEST IDEA HOW MANY PEOPLE HAVE LOST THEIR HOMES IN JUST UNDER A WEEK?!
HOW CAN YOU STAND THERE, PRETENDING IT'S ALL OVER? LIKE WHAT'S DONE IS DONE?!
YOU SAYING "IT'S ALL TRUE, SORRY" ISN'T GOING TO CHANGE THIS STATE OF AFFAIRS!
SURE, VILLAINS ARE DIRECTLY TO BLAME! BUT YOUR MISTAKES CAUSED ALL THIS...
...AND NONE OF YOUR FACES SHOW YOU UNDERSTAND THAT!!
IF WE SHOWED YOU OUR PAIN AND EXHAUSTION AND TEARS...
...WOULD THAT SOMEHOW FIX EVERYTHING?
WHA- ?!
OBVIOUSLY NOT!
YOU NEED TO PUT SOCIETY AT EASE!!
YOU NEED TO TAKE DOWN EVERY LAST VILLAIN!! THAT'S HOW...

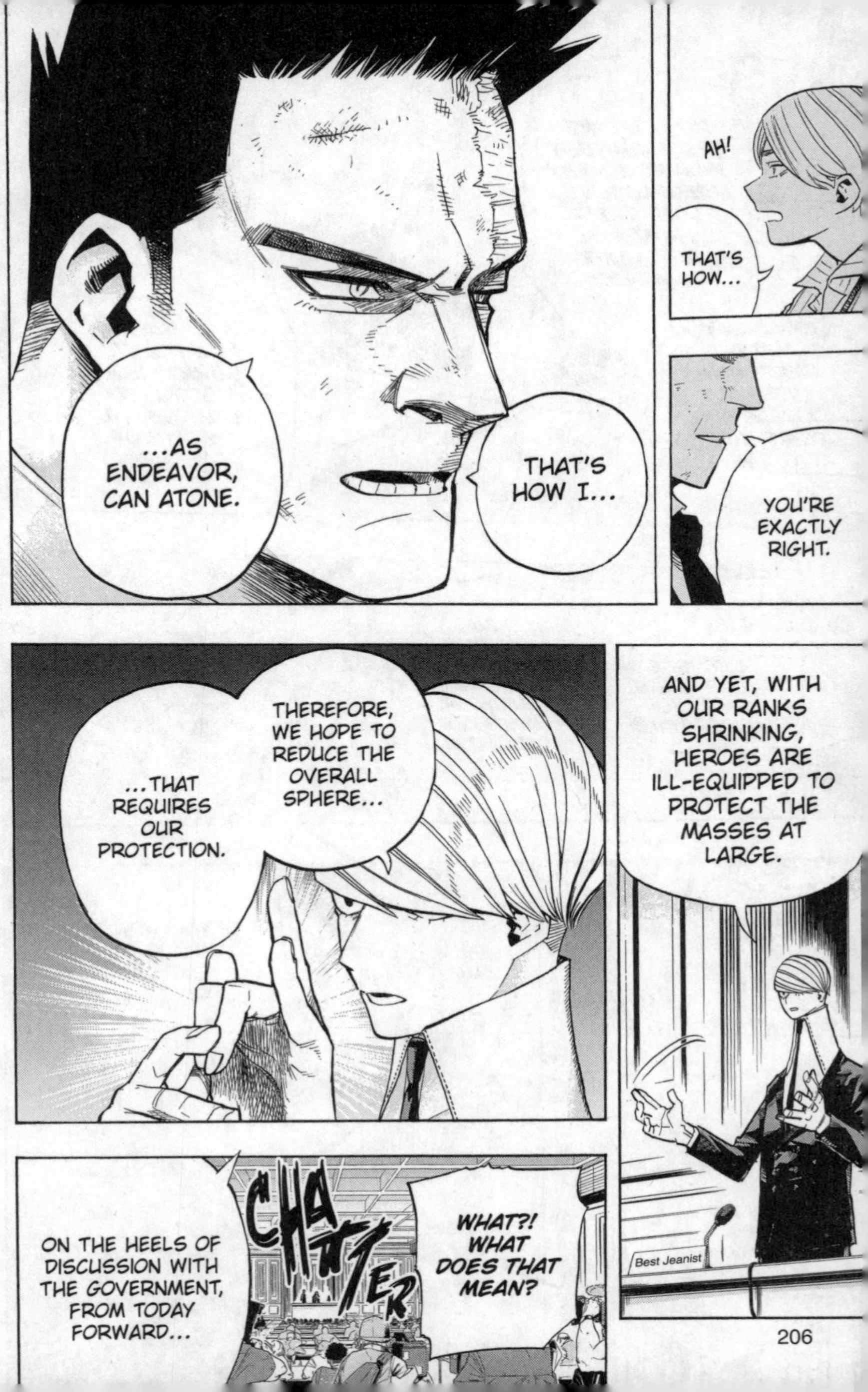
AH!
THAT'S HOW...
YOU'RE EXACTLY RIGHT.
THAT'S HOW I...
...AS ENDEAVOR, CAN ATONE.
AND YET, WITH OUR RANKS SHRINKING, HEROES ARE ILL-EQUIPPED TO PROTECT THE MASSES AT LARGE.
Best Jeanist
THEREFORE, WE HOPE TO REDUCE THE OVERALL SPHERE...
...THAT REQUIRES OUR PROTECTION.
WHAT?! WHAT DOES THAT MEAN?
CHATTER
ON THE HEELS OF DISCUSSION WITH THE GOVERNMENT, FROM TODAY FORWARD...

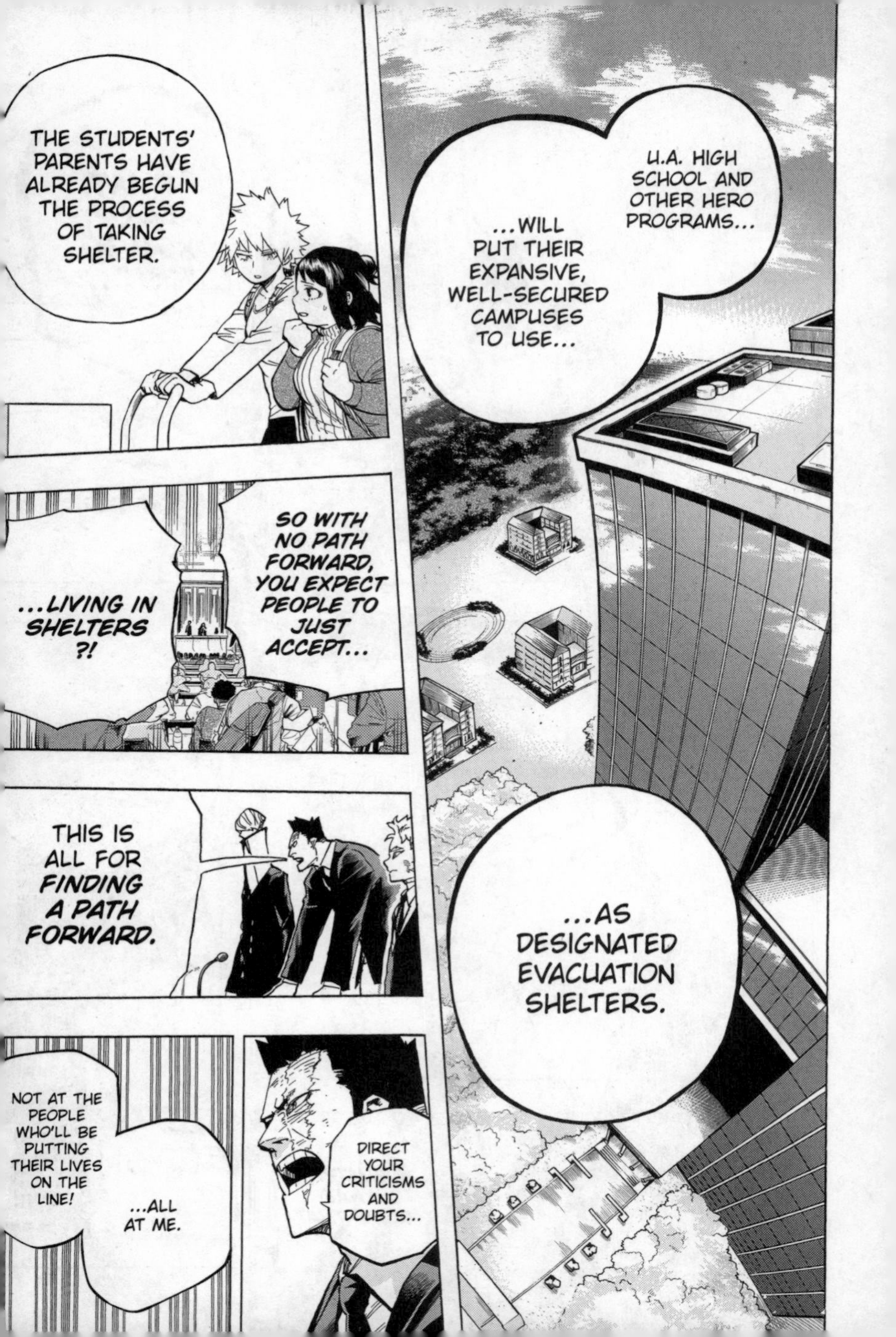
U.A. HIGH SCHOOL AND OTHER HERO PROGRAMS...
...WILL PUT THEIR EXPANSIVE, WELL-SECURED CAMPUSES TO USE...
...AS DESIGNATED EVACUATION SHELTERS.
THE STUDENTS' PARENTS HAVE ALREADY BEGUN THE PROCESS OF TAKING SHELTER.
SO WITH NO PATH FORWARD, YOU EXPECT PEOPLE TO JUST ACCEPT...
...LIVING IN SHELTERS?!
THIS IS ALL FOR FINDING A PATH FORWARD.
DIRECT YOUR CRITICISMS AND DOUBTS...
...ALL AT ME.
NOT AT THE PEOPLE WHO'LL BE PUTTING THEIR LIVES ON THE LINE!

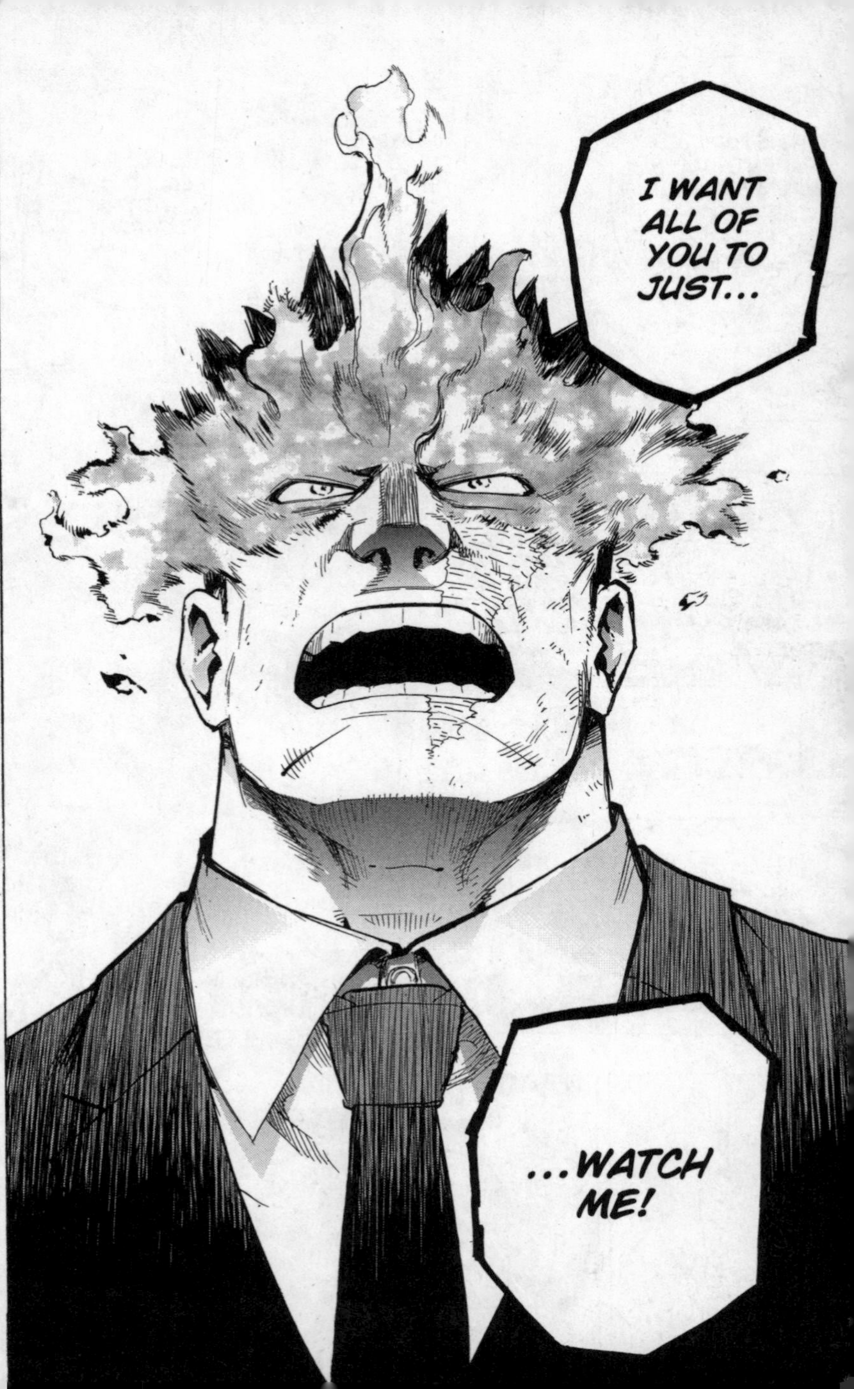
I WANT ALL OF YOU TO JUST...
...WATCH ME!

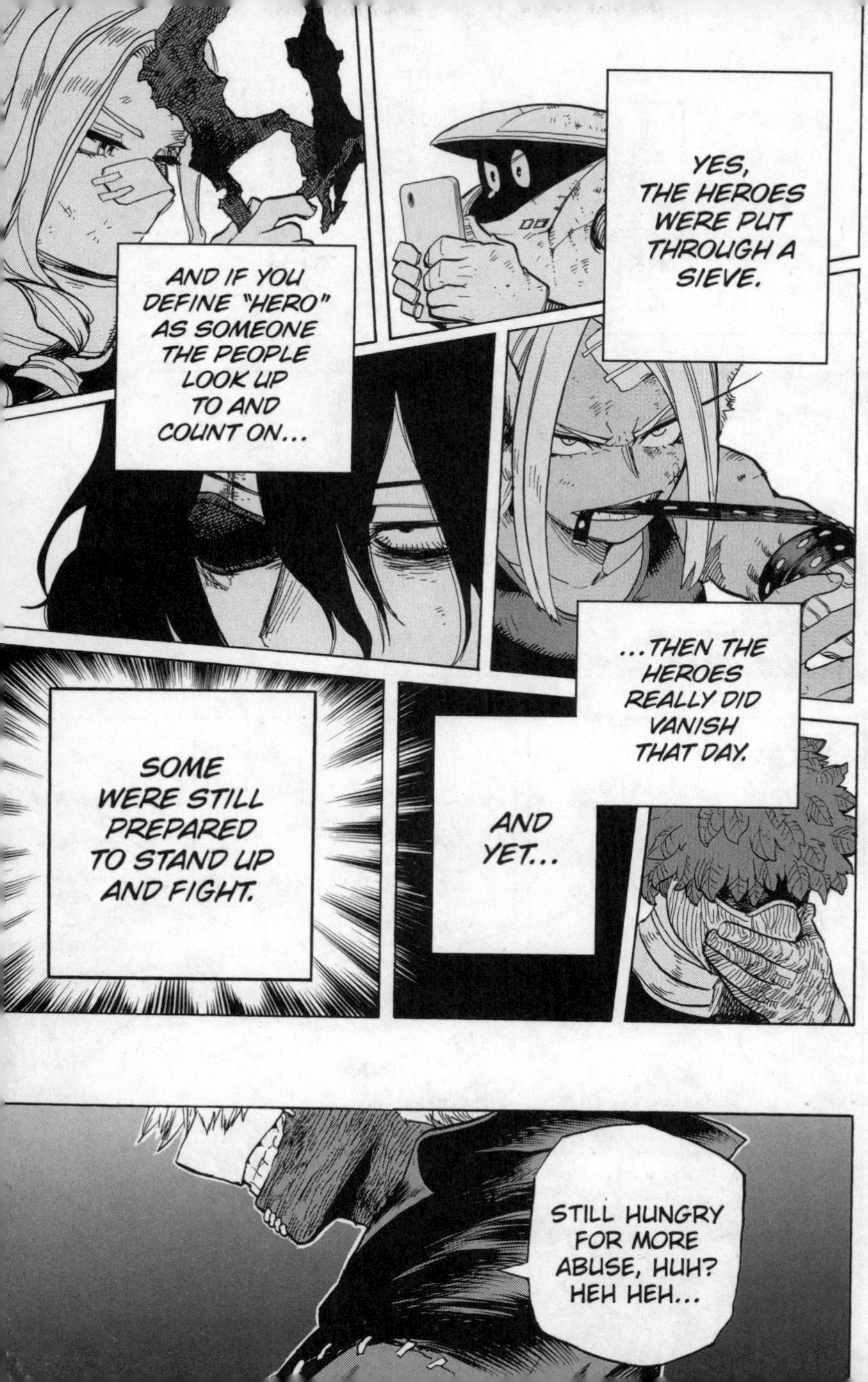
YES, THE HEROES WERE PUT THROUGH A SIEVE.
AND IF YOU DEFINE "HERO" AS SOMEONE THE PEOPLE LOOK UP TO AND COUNT ON...
...THEN THE HEROES REALLY DID VANISH THAT DAY.
AND YET...
SOME WERE STILL PREPARED TO STAND UP AND FIGHT.
STILL HUNGRY FOR MORE ABUSE, HUH? HEH HEH...

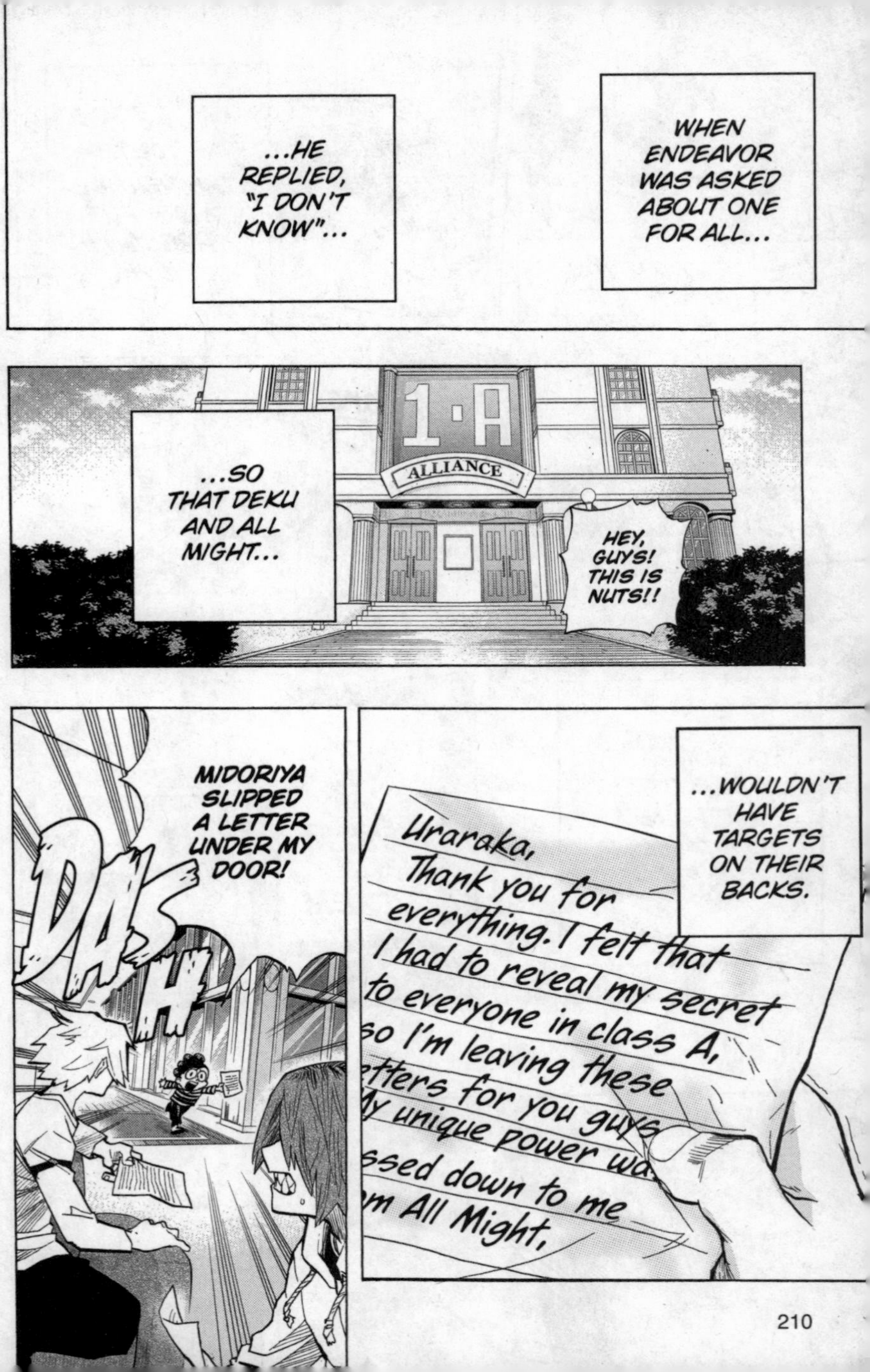
WHEN ENDEAVOR WAS ASKED ABOUT ONE FOR ALL...
...HE REPLIED, "I DON'T KNOW"...
1-A
ALLIANCE
...SO THAT DEKU AND ALL MIGHT...
HEY, GUYS! THIS IS NUTS!!
...WOULDN'T HAVE TARGETS ON THEIR BACKS.
Uraraka,
Thank you for
everything. I felt that
I had to reveal my secret
to everyone in class A,
so I'm leaving these
etters for you guys
My unique power wa
ssed down to me
m All Might,
MIDORIYA SLIPPED A LETTER UNDER MY DOOR!
DASH

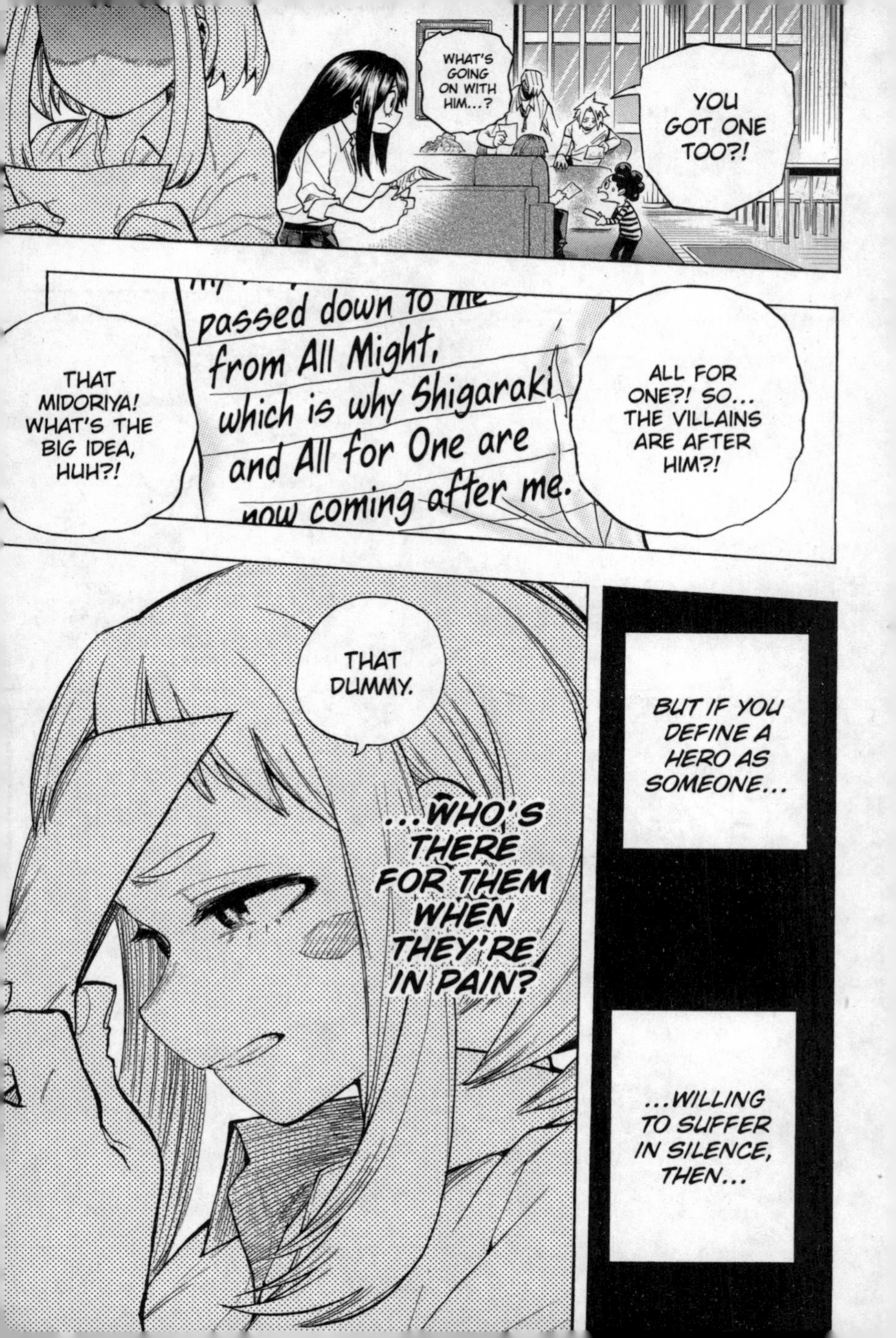
YOU GOT ONE TOO?!
WHAT'S GOING ON WITH HIM...?
ALL FOR ONE?! SO... THE VILLAINS ARE AFTER HIM?!
passed down to me from All Might, which is why Shigaraki and All for One are now coming after me.
THAT MIDORIYA! WHAT'S THE BIG IDEA, HUH?!
BUT IF YOU DEFINE A HERO AS SOMEONE...
...WILLING TO SUFFER IN SILENCE, THEN...
THAT DUMMY.
...WHO'S THERE FOR THEM WHEN THEY'RE IN PAIN?

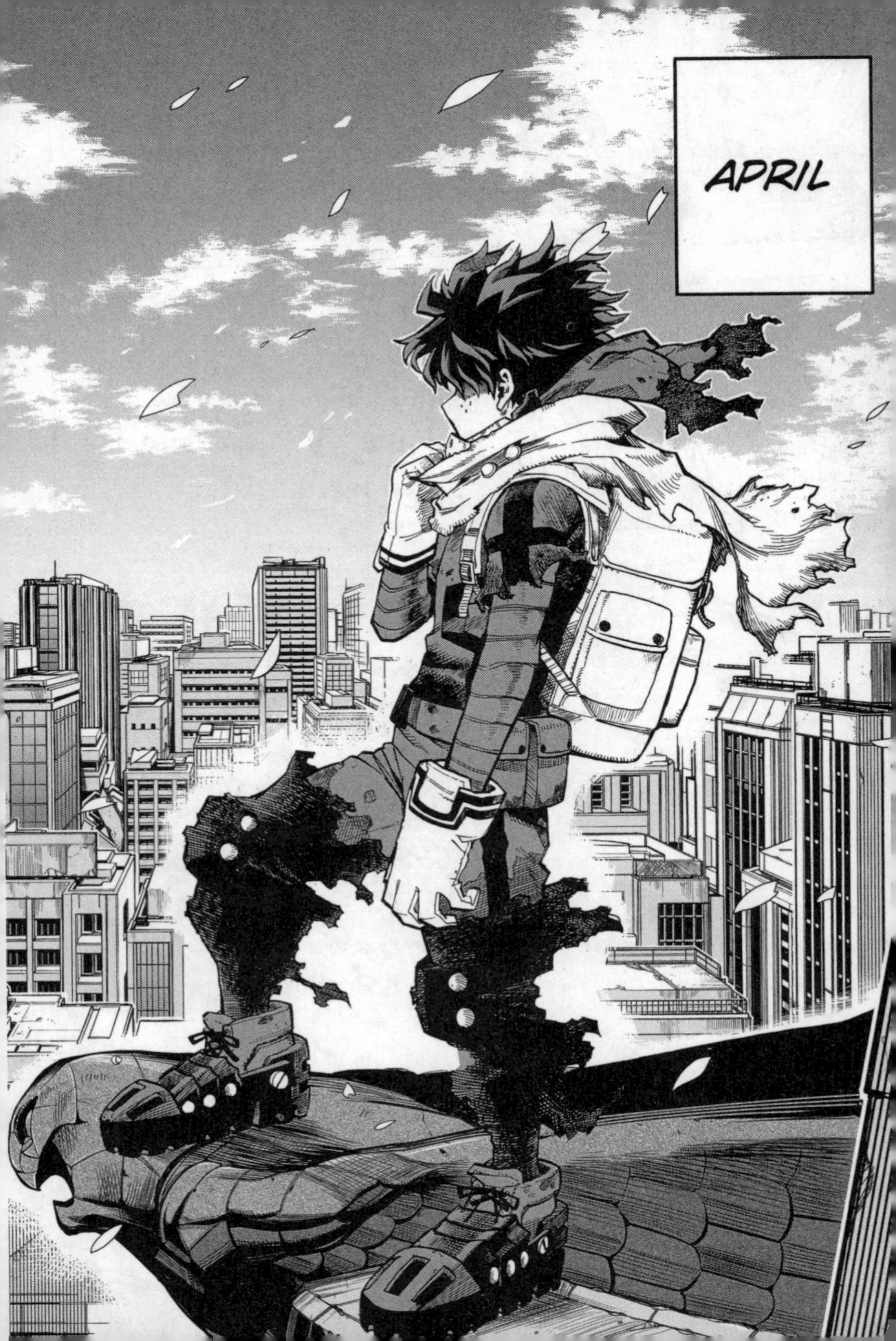
APRIL

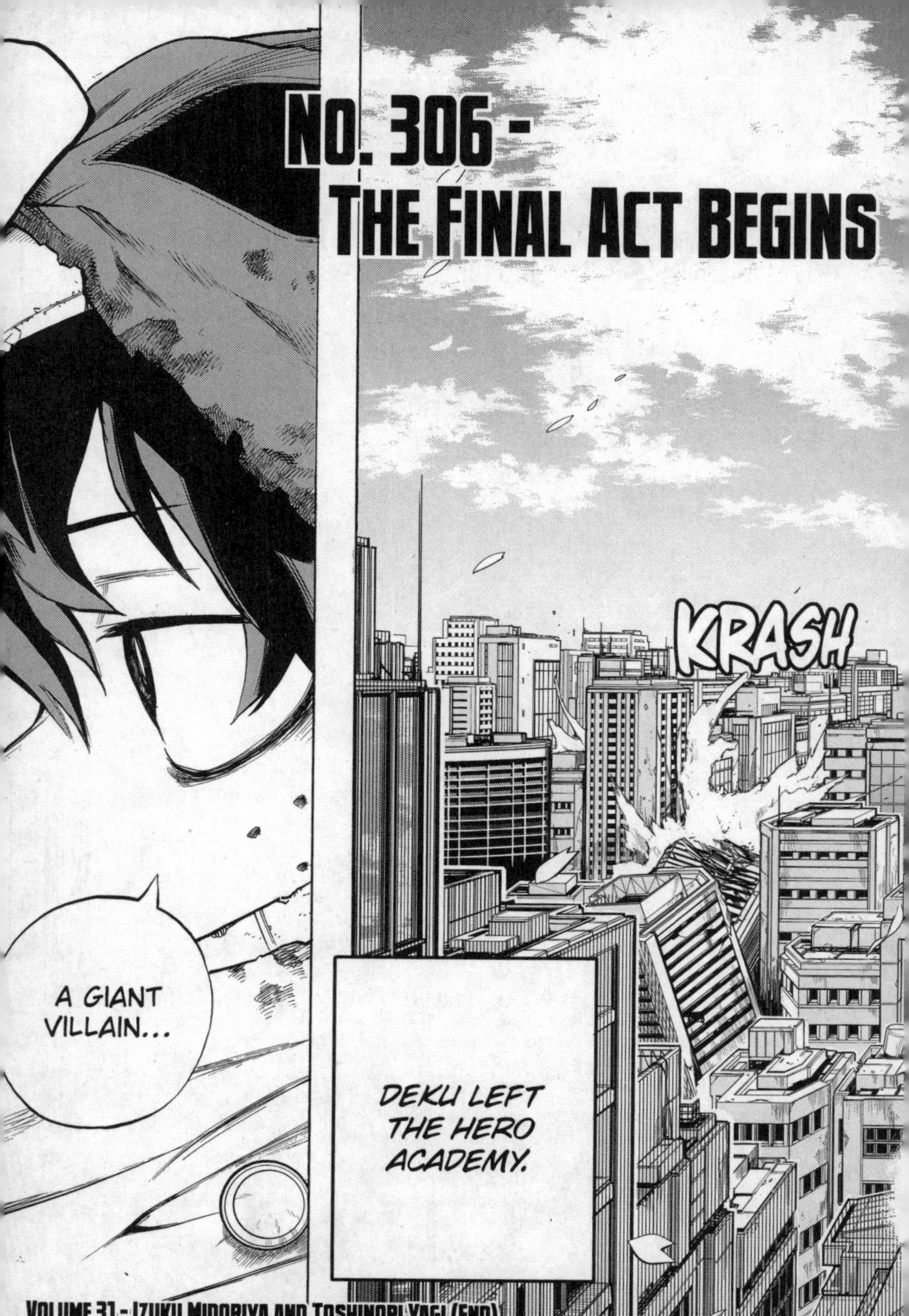
No. 306 - The Final Act Begins
KRASH
DEKU LEFT THE HERO ACADEMY.
A GIANT VILLAIN...

Volume 31 - Izuku Midoriya and Toshinori Yagi (End)

MY HERO ACADEMIA

Ultra Analysis

Every Detail on Your Favorite Characters... and BEYOND!

KOHEI HORIKOSHI

Own the Ultimate Guide to the Smash-Hit Series!

"You're probably thinking, 'Dangit, Horikoshi—there are way too many characters to remember now!' If so, it's your lucky day, since this book was made just for you! Enjoy!"

—Kohei Horikoshi
Creator of *My Hero Academia*